THE BEST
AMERICAN
MAGAZINE
WRITING
2000

THE BEST
AMERICAN
MAGAZINE
WRITING
2000

Edited by

Clay Felker

PublicAffairs NEW YORK

Book design by Jenny Dossin.

LIBRARY OF CONGRESS CATALOGING-IN-PUBLICATION DATA
The best American magazine writing 2000 / edited by Clay Felker.—1st ed.
p. cm.
ISBN 1-58648-009-X
1. American prose literature—20th century. I. Felker, Clay.
PS659.B43 2000
814'.508—dc21
00-057583

First Edition

10 9 8 7 6 5 4 3 2 1

DEDICATED TO THE

MEMBERS OF THE

AMERICAN SOCIETY

OF MAGAZINE EDITORS

HALL OF FAME

Contents

Preface

As Henry Luce, creator of The Time-Life Empire, used to say, the idea is to get the words on the page and into the reader's mind. One of the best ways is a well-written magazine story.

Unlike newspaper articles, which dump the surface details in the first paragraph or two, a skillfully-written magazine article weds factual reporting with traditional literary techniques. The result leaves the reader with a penetrating emotional reality and a deeper understanding of the meaning of the story.

Magazines are essentially interpretive vehicles for an area of special interest, as opposed to newspapers, whose function is to provide a geographical focus of the day's events. A magazine's mandate is to provide a richer level of perspective that can be communicated through the art of writing.

Given the inexorable thrust of ever-faster technology, which is overwhelming us with a tsunami of information from a multiplying number of platforms, it is increasingly important to have a context to help make sense of this flood of headlines and factoids.

Magazines that fulfill this function are needed now more than ever. They can give us a necessary anecdote to the 24-hour news cycle with its sound-byte headlines, bumper-sticker slogans, the in-your-face-presentation, and the cynically sensational tabloid sensibility. They help us make sense of a world that is spinning with increasing speed. At their best they make reading rewarding and enjoyable.

They can do this because they have the luxury of space and time: space to explore the crucial nuances, which illuminate the meaning and importance of a subject, and time for writers and editors to do the reporting, shaping, and polishing that so often make magazines so pleasurable to read. Talent for this is paramount. As the saying goes, there are no bad subjects, only bad writers. American magazines have a plenitude of talented writers who provide a dazzling smorgasbord of different styles and techniques. Selected from many hundreds of stories in a broad spectrum of categories, this book contains what we think are the finest magazine stories of the past year—examples of what a magazine does best.

Clay Felker
Director, Felker Magazine Center
Graduate School of Journalism
University of California,
Berkeley

Acknowledgments

Board members of the American Society of Editors (ASME) have been talking for years about publishing a book showcasing the nation's best magazine writing taken from the winners and finalists of the National Magazine Awards. With this project, that talk has finally become a reality, thanks largely to the enthusiasm of our literary agent, David McCormick of IMG Literary Agency, and the publishing efforts of Peter Osnos and Lisa Kaufman of PublicAffairs. We are especially indebted to Clay Felker for editing this collection. It is never easy to select the best of the best, but Felker did just that. This project would not have been a success without the determination of Marlene Kahan, ASME's executive director, who did everything from obtaining permissions to proofing and editing to keeping the project on schedule. And we are most grateful for the cooperation we received from the writers and their respective magazines. Now an even larger audience will be able to enjoy their gifted writing.

Introduction

The American Society of Magazine Editors (ASME) has been presenting its annual National Magazine Awards, the industry's equivalent of the Pulitzer Prizes, for the past thirty-five years. Until now, the award-winning articles have never been published in one place. But that's about to change. The volume you are now reading represents the first of what we hope will become an annual compilation of the best magazine writing in the United States.

This collection features the best stories written in 1999 by some of our best writers: Janine di Giovanni takes us on a very personal tour of the war in Kosovo; the incomparable Frank Deford engages Bill Russell, the greatest of the great Boston Celtics; Tom Wolfe strays from "convergent thinking"; and Richard Preston shows us how biowarfare can be ignited by terrorists with little more than a rudimentary knowledge of high-school chemistry.

All articles in this book were taken from the group of eighty-two finalists that emerged from an original field of 1,483 entries. The finalists and winners were chosen by distinguished panels of journalists and educators. Because of space constraints, it was impractical to reproduce all of the winning entries. In some cases, such as the general excellence category, there was no way to reproduce an entire issue of a magazine on these pages. Other categories, such as design, were eliminated because they fall outside the scope of a text-oriented book about writing. And still others were excluded because they were similar to other stories selected. Though we were not able to reproduce the work of all finalists, we remain as proud of their accomplishments as we are of the words that appear throughout this book.

As you will see as you turn the pages, we have introduced each story with only a brief paragraph. The stories were not re-edited or shortened; they appear here in their entirety. We deliberately stayed away from a critique of each story, confident that this is a job best left to the reader. And we hope that the readers of this collection will range from editors, journalism students, and professors to people simply interested in good writing and reporting. We trust that it will be as much of a joy to read as it was for us as we collected these articles.

With the dramatic explosion of technology, from the Internet to hand-held portable devices, consumers can read almost anytime, almost anywhere about almost anything. But there is still something special about magazines; they have a special feel, a special mission, and special writing. There are more than 6,000 consumer magazines in the United States, with hundreds of new ones launched each year. There are plenty of old ones, too. Three of these, *Harper's Magazine*, *McCall's*, and *National Geographic*, have been published in three different centuries. Both the old and the new attest to the vitality of the magazine industry.

Finally, a word from our sponsor. The American Society of Magazine Editors is the professional organization for senior editors of consumer magazines and business publications edited, published and sold in the United States. ASME sponsors the National Magazine Awards, which are administered by the Graduate School of Journalism at Columbia University, to honor editorial excellence and encourage editorial vitality. Each spring, ASME awards an "Ellie" (named for the Alexander Calder stabile "Elephant") to each winner at ceremonies held at the Waldorf-Astoria Hotel in New York City.

In addition to sponsoring the National Magazine Awards, ASME works to defend the First Amendment and assist editors in resisting external pressure that might compromise the integrity of the editorial process. It sponsors a summer magazine internship program for college students, hosts member lunches, conducts seminars for senior, as well as junior editors, and issues editorial/advertising guidelines for editors and publishers.

We recognize that magazine writing has never been better. That's why we're confident that we'll have plenty of exceptional stories to publish in the future.

George E. Curry, President
American Society of Magazine Editors

Contributors

Kenneth L. Cain has served as a human rights officer on UN peace-keeping operations in Somalia, Rwanda, Haiti, and Liberia, and as a monitor for the International Human Rights Law Group in Cambodia. Cain was an International Affairs Fellow at the Council on Foreign Relations in New York.

Tom Carson's film criticism appears in *Esquire,* where he is a contributing editor. He also writes for the *Village Voice, Rolling Stone,* and other publications. He is the author of the novel, *Twisted Kicks.*

Frank Deford is a senior contributing writer at *Sports Illustrated.* He is a correspondent on HBO's "RealSports with Bryant Gumbel," and a commentator on National Public Radio's "Morning Edition." Deford is the author of a dozen books, ranging in genre from psychological thriller to memoir. He has received the National Magazine Award, the Christopher Award for service to journalism, an Emmy for his work on NBC, and has twice been voted the Magazine Writer of the Year by the *Washington Journalism Review.*

Janine di Giovanni is currently a special correspondent for *The Times* of London, covering the Balkans, Asia, Africa, and the Middle East. One of three western journalists to witness the fall of Grozny, Chechnya, and cover the Sierra Leone crisis and the struggle in East Timor, di Giovanni has been following wars and armed conflicts since 1987, when she covered the Palestinian Intifada. Di Giovanni is the recipient of the 2000 Amnesty International Award for her coverage of the war in Kosovo and is the author of *Against the Stranger* and *The Quick and the Dead: Under Siege in Sarajevo*. She is working on a third book, *Madness Visible*, based on her award-winning piece for *Vanity Fair*.

BRIAN HAYES is the "Computing Science" columnist for *American Scientist*, and a freelance writer. Over the past twenty years, he has written several science columns for such magazines as *Scientific American*, *Computer Language*, and *The Sciences*. He has served as editor at *Scientific American* and at *American Scientist*. His next book is titled *Infrastructures: A Field Guide to the Industrial Landscape*.

SKIP HOLLANDSWORTH is a Senior Editor at *Texas Monthly*. He has received several awards for journalistic excellence including the 1998 Texas Institute of Letters O'Henry Award for Journalism, the 1996 Charles E. Green Journalism Award, and two previous nominations for the National Magazine Awards.

SEBASTIAN JUNGER is a contributing writer to *Vanity Fair* magazine. He has written two books, *Danger!: True Stories of Trouble and Survival*, and *The Perfect Storm*. He has written for *Outside*, *Men's Journal*, and *American Heritage*, and has also worked as a freelance radio correspondent, covering the war in Bosnia in 1993 and 1994.

JHUMPA LAHIRI's fiction has appeared in *The New Yorker*, *Epoch*, *The Louisville Review*, *Harvard Review*, *Story Quarterly*, and elsewhere. In 1999, she was named by *The New Yorker* as one of the 20 Best American Fiction Writers 40 and Under. Her first book, *Interpreter of Maladies*, a collection of short stories was awarded the 2000 Pulitzer Prize for Fiction.

ANTHONY LANE is a staff writer for *The New Yorker*. He has written for several London papers, including the *Spectator*, *The Independent of London*, and the *Sunday Telegraph*. He has been the deputy literary editor of the *Independent*, and the film critic for the new *Independent on Sunday*.

RICHARD PRESTON has been a regular contributor to *The New Yorker* since 1985. He is the author of four books, including *The Hot Zone* and *The Cobra Event*. Preston has won numerous awards for his writing, including the American Institute of Physics Award, the McDermott Award in the Arts from M.I.T., and the Centers for Disease Control's Champion of Prevention Award. Asteroid 3686 is named "Preston" in honor of the author and his book about astronomy, *First Light*.

GEORGE SAUNDERS's fiction appears regularly in *The New Yorker*. In 1999, he was named by *The New Yorker* as one of the 20 Best American Fiction Writers 40 and Under. He is the author of *The Very Persistent Gappers of Frip*, and two short-story collections, *Pastoralia* and *CivilWarLand in Bad Decline*. He has received two previous National Magazine Awards, was a finalist for the 1996 PEN/Hemingway Award, and has appeared three times in the O. Henry Awards collection. Saunders teaches creative writing at Syracuse University.

GARY SMITH is a Senior Writer at *Sports Illustrated*. His work has been regularly included in *The Best American Sports Writing* anthologies. In 1995, Smith was named Sportswriter of the Year by the National Sportscasters and Sportswriters Association. He has been a staff writer at *Inside Sports*, the *New York Daily News*, the *Philadelphia Daily News*, and the *Wilmington News-Journal*. He has also written for *Rolling Stone*, *Esquire*, and *Life*.

ROBERT STONE is a frequent contributor to *The New Yorker*. He is the author of *A Flag for Sunrise*, *Children of Light*, *Outerbridge Reach*, and *Damascus Gate*. He received the National Book Award for *Dog Soldiers* in 1975.

DANIEL VOLL has reported from South Africa and Bosnia for *Esquire*, and his investigative stories have been adapted into screenplays for Oliver Stone among others. Voll has fought fires with the National Forest Service in New Mexico and for two years led drama and film workshops on a locked psychiatric unit outside Chicago.

TOM WOLFE is the author of twelve books, including *The Electric Kool-Aid Acid Test*, *The Right Stuff*, *The Bonfire of the Vanities*, and most recently, *A Man in Full*. His writing has appeared in *Rolling Stone*, *Harper's*, *The Washington Post*, *New York*, the *New York Herald Tribune*, *Esquire*, and *Forbes ASAP*. Tom Wolfe's books have consistently appeared on the *New York Times* bestseller list since the 1960s. His latest book is a collection of his fiction and nonfiction stories, titled *Hooking Up*.

THE BEST
AMERICAN
MAGAZINE
WRITING
2000

ESQUIRE

Nick Nolte is Racing the Clock to Repair the Damage

In one of the strangest glimpses of a celebrity ever published, readers are taken inside the mind of actor Nick Nolte, as well as into his home—a veritable mad-scientist's laboratory, decorated with CAT scans of Nolte's brain and other souvenirs of the star's strange journeys. The author employs a reporter's eye for detail and a novelist's narrative skill to present a portrait so vivid and revealing that a reader may at times feel the urge to avert his or her gaze. It is hard to imagine getting any closer to a subject.

Daniel Voll

Nick Nolte is Racing the Clock to Repair the Damage

In the laboratory with the mad scientist of Malibu

There's a strip mall in Malibu. The surf crashes right across the highway. At the RadioShack, Eric the audio geek helps me select a new microcassette recorder. He asks what I'm up to. I tell him I'm interviewing a guy.

"Who?" he asks. "I don't want to be pushy."

"It's okay," I shrug. "It's Nick Nolte."

"Cool—why didn't you say so? He comes in here all the time hunting parts for his microscope. Science is his thing. He's got a *big* microscope."

Nolte's rural six-acre compound is a few miles north of RadioShack, back in the hills, away from the ocean. I push a buzzer, the gate opens, and I drive in. Lush grounds, a canopy of trees. A couple houses on the property. Gardeners everywhere. A big yellow Lab with a plastic megaphone around its neck bounds out of the main house. The doors to the house are open. I follow the dog inside.

Nolte is standing in the center of a large room, wearing a black long-sleeved T-shirt and wide-striped Calvin Klein pajama bottoms. He's barefoot. Face tanned and lined, eyes sunk in. Strong neck. Lean as a bull rider. His hair is the same tawny color as the Labrador's and flies back over his ears and floats above his fore-head and down into his eyes. He peers through his hair at me, and there is an energy to those eyes, a crazy vitality. He is mixing a lit-tle something in a small cup, a brown potion, looks earthy. There's a dropper and a spoon and he's stirring and then he drinks it down. I wait for him to say something. But he just looks at me. Finally, I shake his hand and say, "Congratulations on the Nobel prize. Can we talk about your latest science project?"

"Great!" Nolte says, sort of rubbing his hands together. "I've evolved deep into dark-field blood work. Let's go upstairs."

Up the stairs we tramp, through a construction zone of plastic walls with zippers, sawhorses, and power saws, into a massive, high-ceilinged upper room that looks over a garden. This is his bedroom and laboratory. A schoolboy's dream of a room. A Bud-dha watches over the large, book-strewn bed. Naked women with trumpets adorn lamps. Another dog comes in and sniffs us out. And then there it is, in an alcove where he does his work: a vintage, professional-grade Ortholux microscope.

Nolte stands in front of the microscope, eyes wide, a sideways look, mouth cocked open. "My blood?" he asks. "Or yours?"

I tell him I'm squeamish about needles.

He looks at me and growls, voice deep as a lion's. "You'll have to get over that if you want to do blood work."

He pricks his finger, squeezes a drop of his blood. "We don't want the first drop. We want to get down a little deeper." He squeezes again, a second perfect drop onto a glass slide, which he slips under the microscope. "Our blood tells us everything. By watching your blood, you become connected to yourself in a way that you have never before been connected." He's flipping switches. Light passes through the iris, illuminating the blood cells. The picture is projected on a nearby monitor.

"Yes, *yes*, that's it!" He's pointing to cells moving on the screen. "Here's a real good cell structure, perfectly round. When you're young, the red cells are plump and shimmering—that's what you want." He points out a dying cell. "I've watched my blood degenerate over twenty-four hours. You'll actually see long strings of bacteria coming out of them as they decay." He lingers on the word *decay*, giving it a couple more syllables.

The blood cells are quite beautiful, but all of a sudden the microscope is smoking. It's like a magnifying glass that has been left in the sun and now there's fire inside. "Whoa," he says, surprised, blowing at the smoke. "*Whoa!* Who's been messing with this?"

He tries to close the iris, but it's too hot. "We're screwed," he says. "Oh, shit!" He might have burned himself a little. "Oh, Aidan, *Aidan*, what have you *done?*" he moans. The smoke starts up again. Small puffs of it, like smoke signals.

"Brawley!" Nolte bellows, calling his twelve-year-old son.

Brawley is in a room across the hall, and I'm sent to hunt him down. I unzip the plastic sheeting and walk into the space that Brawley calls his cave. He and his best friend, Aidan, are hunched over separate computers playing EverQuest. The game takes nine hours to cross a virtual landscape. The room is pitch-black except for the glowing monitors, and it's throbbing, incredibly loud. I have to shout to get their attention.

The microscope is still smoldering as the boys shuffle into the lab, wanting to know what happened. They crowd around Nolte's shoulders, looking at it.

"Somebody's been on this while I was out of the house," Nolte says. "*That* is my paranoid conclusion." He looks at Aidan, a chubby kid with acne, a real whiz kid, who says, "I get blamed for everything around here. I could be fifty miles away and you'd still blame me."

Aidan is the son of Brawley's shrink. They met when Aidan's

dad was trying to help Brawley cope with Nick's divorce from Brawley's mom six years ago. Then the shrink himself got divorced, and now the two boys are best friends. Sometimes Aidan sleeps on the floor next to Brawley's bed.

The boys want to check out the iris of the microscope, and Nolte cuts a flashlight on. "Maybe it's an aging problem," Aidan says. They all peer through the smoke at the inner workings. Even though Nolte is fifty-eight, and Brawley and Aidan are twelve and thirteen, the three confer like colleagues, and that is, in truth, the relationship. They hang out here, for weeks sometimes, without visitors, plotting new science projects, along with Nolte's girl-friend, the comedic actress Vicki Lewis. The compound is tricked out with ten computers, each with a large color monitor, and Nolte has his own Internet server. To Brawley and Aidan, he's just Nick. No big deal. He's a grown-up kid with a credit card and the best toys.

But his blood work has been interrupted, and his frustration is beginning to show. He doesn't want to scold, doesn't want to accuse, because Brawley's a good kid, and he's still working out this postdivorce relationship. Anyway, you can't yell at them, because if you yell, they'll just sneak around and do bad-boy things. Aw, hell. "Maybe I shouldn't let the two of you in here for a while," Nolte says. "Let's shut it down for now, let it cool down."

"We should test his blood type!" Brawley suggests.

Yes! Let's test his blood type! Nolte is immediately back in motion. Suddenly, all three of them are looking at me hungrily.

Aidan swabs my fingertip with alcohol. "This will hardly hurt at all," he says. "Wanna hear a joke? Something to get your mind off it? Okay, how many blonds can you fit into a van? I mean—oh, shit, that's not it. I mean, four blonds die in a minivan—what's the tragedy?"

He pricks my finger, and Nick squeezes a drop of blood onto the test strip.

"The van could've held eight!" Aidan cries.

Nolte says, "Brawley, Aidan, read this to me. What's the protocol?"

"Um, protocol," Aidan says. "Step one, okay, mix in for thirty seconds, rub it across the thing for thirty seconds."

Brawley studies how the blood instantly starts breaking up, like red paint left in the rain. "I betcha it's A negative," he says. "Me and Aidan are the same type. A negative."

As he waits for the results, Nolte looks over at the wreckage of the microscope, flipping switches again, and says, "It's absolutely *broken. Now* I'm frustrated." He breathes. *Maintain.* He's not going to yell. He knows it can get fixed, damage can be repaired— that's one of the things he's learned. You just have to go to the expert. He knows a guy who can fix it, but still, he's feeling a little jangled. Meanwhile, Brawley was right. I'm A negative.

Nolte pushes away from the microscope. "Who wants a shot of B–12?" he asks.

No, thank you, I say. My needle problem. Maybe coffee? Or a drink?

"*No, no!*" he says. "This is better."

There is a small, gray medical cabinet on his desk. One drawer labeled SYRINGES. Another drawer TOURNIQUETS. He takes out a narrow-gauge needle.

"Don't worry," Brawley says. "He does this all the time."

Every night, for instance, before he goes to bed, Nolte fills a syringe with .5cc of human growth hormone, which is generally illegal unless you are a dwarf, and shoots it into his stomach. Someday, he figures, we'll all just take a pill, encoded with all the testosterone and hormones our body needs, guided toward specific tissues, to retard aging. Until then, he'll keep buying on the underground market. "All the old hippies are doing it now," he says. A lot of corporate executives. "If Charlie Rose and Larry King aren't on human growth hormones," he says, laughing, "they're thinking about it. I guarantee you, they all want to keep a step ahead of the competition.

"And if I'm feeling a little stressed," Nolte says, "I'll come in and shoot a little B with a little pull of folic acid, which is good for the heart, and a little B–12."

In *North Dallas Forty,* he played an over-the-hill football player who shoots painkillers into his knee. "I like needles," the brokendown ballplayer declared. "Anything to keep me in the game."

"Nothing to it," Nolte says. When he's *really* stressed or feeling depleted, he fills an IV bag with thirteen different vitamins and minerals, puts a tourniquet around his arm, and drips them through a needle into his bloodstream. The procedure takes more than an hour, and he figures he does it several times a week, often while in bed.

Well, I guess a little B–12 never hurt anyone. I offer my right arm, but he waves it off. "Need your right butt cheek, just off the hip." He swabs me with alcohol. The needle doesn't go in readily, and he's got to jab it in a second time. Right into muscle. The boys are watching me, and I try not to wince, but the damn needle stings, and immediately I feel the stuff hit my bloodstream. My forehead warms. My feet tingle. An incredible humming rush for about a minute. I'm feeling a little light-headed, I tell Nolte.

"Man, he doesn't look good," Brawley says.

You sure you only put B–12 in there? I ask.

The room has begun to spin, and the boys ease me down onto the floor, where I rest on a round Feldenkrais mat, which feels like a soft, white buoy. I am quite woozy and sweating, and I hear something strange emanating from somewhere—I'm not sure where—a singsongy, possibly computer-generated voice. A very pleasant, clipped voice. Sad Man, a life-sized papier-mâché figure, is seated near the bed, his head bowed in a posture of sadness. Nolte pats Sad Man on the head as he passes. Books are strewn about—scientific journals, Philip Roth's *American Pastoral, Better*

Sex Through Chemistry. From this angle I also see Nolte is filling up another syringe for himself, mixing a vitamin cocktail, holding it above his head, thumping it, squinting. Nolte pulls down his pajamas a bit on one side, exposing a few inches of skin, from his waist to his right cheek, a lean flank for a guy almost sixty.

After shooting up, he's feeling a bit strange himself. He's looking a little worried now, too. You sure you didn't mix the wrong thing? I ask. "No," he says, "I think I'm picking up your vibe. A kind of placebo effect."

When the room stops spinning, the boys help me up, each taking an arm.

"I could give you some ozone," Nolte says. "It will make you feel better."

Ozone? Like the hole?

"This works. I can prove it to you. Bad things can't live in it. Viruses can't live in it, bacteria can't. Cancer can't. Gets more oxygen into your plasma. It's all about getting oxygen into your brain. Everything I do is about getting more oxygen. Need oxygen."

He sits me down. There's a cylinder the size of a standard fire extinguisher bolted to the wall, next to the microscope. He hands me a tube with a nosepiece at the end. "Here, take this." I stick the two soft tubes up my nostrils and breathe deeply, holding this stuff in and, man, is it a buzz. Buzz.

"Have a cigarette," he says, handing me a Marlboro. "The ozone'll scrub the nicotine before it gets into your system."

It's illegal, he tells me, to claim that ozone has medical benefits, but he's convinced it's changed his life, and he's got tanks of it bolted to walls in rooms all over the property. Next to the toilet, in the gym, in his office, in the greenhouse. "If you write 'Nolte uses ozone for medical use,' they may come asking," he says. "They may not. But I'm telling you it works."

He turns to Brawley. "Anybody else need some B–12?"

"Nah, I'll have some raspberries," says Brawley.

"Raspberries! Strawberries! *Great idea!*" Nick yelps. "C! We need vitamin C!" Sometimes he'll just stand out there in his berry patch and eat until he's full, a whole meal. It is late in the afternoon, the golden hour, and this will be Nolte's first meal of the day. And so there he goes, enraptured, the energy of a child, all action, pushing down the hall and out the door and into the garden to pick some plump, juicy organic fruit.

To kill a neuron, Nolte says, you really have to go at it. A night out with amphetamines just won't do it. "You've gotta do amphetamines and maybe some heroin and then a couple of gallons of vodka and then Drāno."

And then you pay a doctor to take a nuclear brain scan so you can see what you have done. Before us is Nolte's brain. Flowing in the glowing yellows and reds are islands of neurons that are dead or misfiring. This is the brain of an actor.

When Nolte's doctor first saw this scan, he wanted to know if he'd ever been knocked out. "Well, doc," Nolte said, "I was an alcoholic; there was drug use." The doctor said, "Well, you've experienced the equivalent of blunt trauma."

There has been quite a lot of damage, he says. Nolte honors the damage, and he considers it a gift, a special knowledge. There's a black binder on the table. It's a three-ring binder labeled CONFIDENTIAL, and it contains the story of Nick Nolte's life. It's a rather clinical story, in black and white and X ray and MRI and brain scan and full-body nuclear PET scan in living color. It is sort of the scrapbook of this whole Nolte reclamation project, which is what his life in the last decade or so has become. This black binder is one of many such binders in Nolte's house. He analyzes and thinks and collects the effects of every character that he plays. To build a real character, it pays to understand his damage. This particular binder, the confidential one, is really just the dossier on another character. Most people don't have such a detailed accounting of their own dysfunctions, their failures, their fuckups, their rate of decay, and their halting human efforts in the face of such. Most people would just rather not know how they stack up against the inevitable. But of course, most people have not had as much of a god's hand in willfully accelerating their own demise as Nick Nolte has, and if a man has the power to find the violence inside to harm himself and bring on the end, then he must surely, Nolte feels, be able to find the grace to reverse the process.

It is, at the very least, an interesting hobby.

"Here's the blunt trauma," he says, pointing to dark areas on the brain scan, which is otherwise a gorgeous swirl of color. His fingers are stained from the strawberries.

To increase Nolte's brain function, his doctor prescribed the same treatment that Edward Teller, the father of the H-bomb, used to jump-start his own brain after he had a stroke: sessions in a hyperbaric chamber, the kind they stick divers into when they have the bends. Nolte spent ten hours in one. The goal was to push oxygen into his plasma so that it would be picked up by the brain and metabolized, and where once had been darkness and stupor and death would be bright colors and vitality and life. A new brain.

Like a schoolboy who's just won the prize, he hands me another brain scan taken after these sessions. "See how these yellow streaks don't shoot clear out to the sides anymore? That means the surface is metabolizing." The dark areas are now blue and yellow. Neurons, he says. Neurons that are *firing*.

"I've had some success." He flips to a chart. "It means my body is almost daily repairing everything that's damaged. And you never can get to zero, because life itself means a certain amount of destruction. You have to use things up in order to live."

Flipping through the black binder, we stop on a recent psychiatric workup, and I read the following aloud:

Results suggest that the patient possesses traits associated with histrionic, narcissistic, and antisocial qualities, which indicate that the patient may seek reassurance or approval from others or may be uncomfortable in situations where he or she is not the center of attention. He may react to criticism with feelings of humiliation. His personality requires attention from others, and he may have a sense of self-importance. His personality type also tends to be a rule-breaker.

The patient's attention as assessed was found to be abnormal. Results indicate anxiety-induced attention deficit, which he committed several times, in the second, third, and fourth quarters of the test. This is also indicative of anxiety or impulsivity.

Notable: He has very rapid brain speed. Approximately at age forty, with a voltage of 5.03, which may cause him to be prone to addiction. His memory is in the very superior range—no doubt this aids him as an actor.

"All true," he says.

Nick Nolte is indeed an actor. And he says that in those years when he was working away at destroying himself with the drugs and the alcohol, he was taking some roles that in their way were destroying him, too.

You see, big movies are toxic. Of course, just because movies are small doesn't make them good. But Nolte is a constant; he is ever present. Whatever role he undertakes, there he'll be, digging, digging, going deep, trying to find something, trying to talk to ghosts. These movies, he says—whether last year's *Affliction,* for which he was nominated for an Oscar, or *Mother Night,* or a pair of new ones, *Simpatico,* from the Sam Shepard play, and *Breakfast of Champions*—they are having the same effect as the ozone. If he chooses them, breathes them in, lives them, they will restore him, cleanse him, clear out the bad stuff, all those movies he shot for $7 million apiece—*I Love Trouble, Mulholland Falls, Blue Chips*—that led him to a heart murmur in the early nineties. And so he's sucking them in, these little movies, because they are like a drug, and if he had to make *Yet Another 48 Hours,* it just might take him around the bend. Eddie Murphy told him that he wanted to do what Nolte was doing, those artistically satisfying, small, gritty movies. Nolte told him he'd have to cut his salary. "Oh, man, I can't do that," Murphy said. "I have my needs."

Now Nolte beckons me into the bathroom. "You want some tea?" he says, waving me in. "This is the best tea. Made in China." We troop into the bathroom, Brawley and Aidan following. The computers have crashed, the server's down, and the boys are at loose ends. Nolte brews the tea on a bureau across from the shower. A tank of ozone is bolted to the wall next to the toilet. He hands me a framed mug shot of himself. Nabbed by the feds at twenty for selling draft cards. Got a forty-five-year sentence, suspended. A felon, he's never voted.

It's a large bathroom, with a huge tub in one corner, a deep, splendid tub with a Jacuzzi. Laminated script pages from his upcoming film are stacked next to the tub. Every morning, he comes in here, turns on the Jacuzzi, and reads his pages. When he was preparing for *The Thin Red Line,* he'd soak in here and yell, *Move those damn troops! Take that goddamn hill!* Pajamas are scattered on the floor. All over the room—in fact, all over this house—are quotes that serve as affirmations, trying to buck Nolte up. One on the bathroom wall reads: "Why are you frightened of being alone? Because you are faced with yourself as you are, and you find that you are empty, dull, stupid, ugly, guilty, and anxious." Nolte thinks it's from Krishnamurti, but he's not sure. The twelve steps of AA are taped to the wall, at his left elbow when he's in the tub. The page is mottled and water-stained. He used to go to meetings regularly, but it wasn't quite enough. Then he discovered science. Now Scotch-taped floor to ceiling on the shower door are pages and pages of large-type definitions from a book on brain chemistry—*addiction* and *craving brain* and *inescapable stress* and so on.

It's dark outside now. The room is illuminated only by a small penlight that Nolte is holding. There is a window above the tub. A large gray-and-white cat with white-socked feet is on the roof, staring into the window. "Coyotes have been trying to ambush him for years," Brawley says. "So he lives on the roof." Nolte opens the window and calls out, "Kitty, kitty, kitty, come in, man, come in." The cat rubs up against Nolte's hand. It's very big. Nolte steps into the empty bathtub, picks the cat up off the roof, and hands it to me. "He's real affectionate," Nolte says.

Brawley and Aidan vanish into their cave, hoping to get back on-line. I follow Nick down the wide, wooden stairs, carrying the cat, its claws sinking deep into my arm. I am hearing water trickling. I look to the ceiling. The Labrador, its tail banging the wall, comes around the corner. The cat is holding on to my forearm for dear life. Now the floor is wet all around our feet, and we're slipping our way down the stairs. I feel wetness running down my pants. The cat has been pissing straight out into the air. Nolte now looks down for the first time and sees the puddle he's standing in.

"Oh, *Jesus*, who pissed all over the place?"

"It wasn't me," says Aidan, sticking his head out of the cave. "I need your credit-card number. Brawley and I found plans for an ultralight on the Internet."

"You know where the card is," Nolte says.

The cat leaps from my arms and runs. Nolte crouches down with a towel and is sopping up the mess. He looks up at my pee-stained khakis. "Looks like you're going to need some pajamas," he says.

He bounds up the stairs and tosses some down. They are like his, soft, with white piping. I put them on and wait for him to come back. A few minutes later, he slowly descends the stairs, rubbing his butt and screwing up his face a little.

"Had to give myself another hit of B–12."

.   .   .

Eating slips his mind sometimes. It is midnight and, save for a handful of berries, he hasn't eaten. I am faint from hunger.

"You hungry?" he asks.

He pulls on a flimsy pair of canvas shoes, gets us each a small flashlight, picks up a basket. "To the garden!" he says. "I'll cook you some dinner."

The garden is ringed with garlic plants to keep rabbits and gophers out. Only one gopher has gotten past the garlic, but it's driving Nolte crazy. The holes he and the gardeners have dug on their hunt for the gopher are wide and deep enough to fit a body in, tunneling in one direction and another. "We throw poison in," he says, "and the gopher throws it back out."

Tall corn is in our faces as we hunt for tomatoes, which are flourishing between the cornstalks. Vines all around our feet. And we're looking for squash. And we keep coming upon watermelon. Nolte is on his knees, rooting around in his pajamas. "*Oooooo,* squash, squash, squash," he mutters to himself. "Oh, these are nice. I'll have some of these. I'll take some of those. These are butternuts. I'm gonna slice 'em and steam 'em a little bit in olive oil with some of the Vidalias."

As he's scooting down the rows, sizing up the butternuts, he's talking about this year's Academy Awards. "Everybody gets devastated," Nolte says, "or everybody gets elated, a little bit. But usually everybody gets devastated. It's horrible, it's rejection. No matter that you're one of only a few actors that have been nominated, or you're one of just a few directors—in the final analysis you're a loser. How can you be happy in that situation?

"Listen, I was glad for Roberto Benigni, you know?" Nick says. "But it's not fun. It's never fun to lose." During the commercial break, after the best-actor award was presented, Nolte saw that Edward Norton and Ian McKellen, his fellow nominees, were no longer in their seats.

"I knew those fuckin' guys were at the bar. So I excuse myself and I find 'em, and I say, 'Motherfuckers!' And Ian says to me right off the bat, deadpan, 'You know, Nick, I don't really see why you expected to get the award. You do nothing but play yourself.' I look at Ian, who played a homosexual artist in *Gods and Monsters*, and I say, 'Look who's calling the kettle fuckin' black,' and then we both turn to Ed, who played a skinhead in *American History X*, and say, 'What'd you think? Bald head and tattoos were gonna win?' And we all just started laughing."

Nolte sat on his hands when they honored Elia Kazan. Sean Penn is Nick's friend. Penn's dad was blacklisted. Kazan, of course, named names. "He was a great director," he says. "No question. So we would have had to do without *On the Waterfront*. So what?"

In another decade of his life, he'd be having this conversation on a barstool. But we're inside now, back in the kitchen, and he's slicing up squash and Kentucky wonder beans and sautéing onions in olive oil, mixing it all with brown rice.

Not that he's an AA purist. He drank on Oscar night. "My soul needed that one," he says. "If I have that occasional drink, I can, you know, end up drinking for a day or so, but I no longer have that illusion that drinking is the only way to deal with life. And invariably, after a coupla days, the body is just aching and hurting, and the soul is in pain 'cause you're destroying it."

The food is all gone and it's 1:00 a.m. and Aidan is worrying about his pimples. "I have the next experiment!" Nolte yells, charging in from another room. He has a jar in his hands. Brawley and Aidan watch him as if he were a magician and a white rabbit might pop out of his hat at any moment. He opens the jar and begins to goop an organic mud mask on Aidan's face. Aidan recoils. "Hey, what's that?" he hollers.

Nick answers, almost tenderly. "Here, you put it on like this." He shows him by applying it to his own face. "It's good for you."

The phone rings. It's Vicki, calling from her office thirty feet away. She's been in there scissoring apart the dresses she wore on her recently canceled TV show, *NewsRadio*—miniskirts, pink taffeta bridesmaid's gowns. Making them into a quilt. "Come on out, baby," Nolte says. "Yeah, he's still here. It's an interview, but it evolved. You gotta come out; it's my big hurrah."

Brawley asks if it's true that there are benefits to playing video games. "Dad, since I play so many video games, I have more of those little roots. . . . What are they?"

"Dendrites," Nolte says. "The more challenged the brain is, the more dendrites it builds. They help make more connections."

Aidan pipes up. "How many do you think I have? 'Cause I do, like, problem solving every day in school. And complicated math." The mask is drying on Aidan's face, pulling his eyes apart. With the paste smeared high into his hairline, Nick looks like the fool from *King Lear.*

Brawley has clear skin, looks very much like his father, and has actually played Nolte as a boy in two films. He was also the kid in *Ransom.* "After doing *Ransom,*" he says, "it was confusing. All of a sudden I understood who all those people were who kept stopping my dad on the street. I thought he had a lot of friends. Now I understood—you get in the movies, you get a lot of friends you don't know." He pulls me aside. "Is it true my dad won the Nobel prize?" he asks quietly.

Nolte is at the computer, a cigarette in his mouth, typing with one finger. It's the middle of the night. Aidan is right next to him at another terminal, his complexion much improved, and a panel of blinking red lights means that Brawley is in the next room, playing EverQuest. Aidan has found a medical-surplus store on-line. He's clicking through the screens, yelling out prices of used electron microscopes.

Nolte says, "We don't want to get too complicated. There are setup protocols that would take us all day."

"The way an electron microscope works," Aidan says, "is they incinerate the stuff you're sampling, and it searches for higher electrons it might give off."

"Wow, would that be fun!" Nolte says, his voice pitched high with excitement.

Nolte is working on his lines for his next movie, *Trixie,* with Emily Watson, in which he plays a senator falsely accused of murder. On the screen, he highlights a speech from the script, then he leans back and waits for the computer to recite it to him.

"I-could-even-have-you-arrested," says the clipped, high-pitched computer voice. "I-am-guilty-of-absolutely-no-wrong-doing-anywhere."

"See how she sounds?" he says. He's rubbing his forehead with a fist, eyes closed, just listening as his right hand, fingers spread wide, tilts outward, dipping and rising in concert with the voice. The voice is amplified throughout the upper room.

He used to ask friends to speak random passages from scripts into tape recorders, just to learn the words in a new way. "I'll have him punched," he repeats along with the computer, which answers, "May-I-say-I-find-you-attractive? You're-so-fresh-and-unspoiled. Is-it-okay-that-I-say-that? Does-that-scare-you-hon?"

The phone rings. It's Alan Rudolph calling from Canada, where he'll be directing *Trixie,* starting in a few weeks. There's the matter of a little S&M to discuss. Nolte sits and listens, pushing his hair off his forehead. He'll be shorn as the senator, hair white. "Do I literally beat her up?" he asks Rudolph. He listens for a few moments, nodding his head. "Well, that's something she and I can figure out."

The computer murmurs in the background. "I'm-single. Are-you-married? A-woman's-sexual-temperature-is-never-lost-on-me. Even-nice-guys-have-nasty-ideas. What-color-underpants-are-you-wearing-right-now?"

Nolte is pacing in his pajamas, intense on the phone. "I think

I'll have prepared well enough to be—like we did with Julie in *After-Glow* with that restaurant scene—I want to be able to be that free with it so we can go anywhere we want to go. I've got the second scene, the big, long one, pretty much that free . . . and that's the one I've been really concentrating on. The other one, it's me and her, you know. It's tricky." He hangs up the phone.

He finds that as time goes by, the roles stay with him more and more. They become sort of encoded. He figures it's the way he prepares in the first place, but he can't help continuing to sort of live them after they're done. After *Jefferson in Paris,* he had to have his windows redone and a gazebo built to match Monticello's. After *U Turn,* the raven that had perched atop the shoulder of his sadistic, incestuous character stayed on here with Nick. The bird died not long ago and is buried in the yard.

In the new adaptation of Kurt Vonnegut's *Breakfast of Champions,* Nolte steals the movie as a cross-dressing car-lot manager.

"I designed my own dress," he says. "I told the costumer, 'It has to feel sensual. It has to be what the men don't get to wear, you know, the silk and this kind of thing.' So I took this one little dress, a sheer red dress, and I had it on and said, 'This would be good, but he'd probably like the silk to flow down here.' And then I took the dress and I spun it around backward, so the top was cut down here and the straps crossed here. Now I was bare-breasted—a Phoenician woman. That was key to the character."

He wants the dress this second. "I loved shaving my chest!" he says. He gets up off his chair to leave the lab. The computer voice croons to him, "A-woman's-sexual-temperature-is-never-lost-on-me." Dark-field photos of his sperm are on the table near the scans of his brain. He is pulling open drawers. One is filled with bottles, another with Scotch tape. He throws open the doors of a large armoire. He's saying he thinks he's found the undergarments, sheer and red. "I know it's here somewhere. I swear it! I'll find the dress!"

The Ring Leader

Of all our great athletes, Bill Russell has been one of the most complex and misunderstood. In this compelling profile, Frank Deford brings to bear his sensitive talents as a writer, earning an amazing trust and candor from Russell. On a 14-hour drive from Seattle to the Bay area to visit Russell's father, a deeper journey emerges: One of an African-American family, the Russells of Louisiana, who have gone from illiteracy to Harvard Law in four fascinating generations. Deford's analysis of Russell as the sport's most generous team player gives even greater meaning to this athlete's majesty.

Frank Deford

The Ring Leader

I t was 30 years ago, and the car containing the old retired basketball player and the young sportswriter stopped at a traffic light on the way to the airport in Los Angeles. (Of course, in the nature of things, old players aren't that much older than young writers.) The old player said, "I'm sorry, I'd like to be your friend."

The young writer said, "But I thought we *were* friends."

"No, I'd like to be your friend, and we can be friendly, but friendship takes a lot of effort if it's going to work, and we're going off in different directions in our lives, so, no, we really can't be friends."

And that was as close as I ever got to being on Bill Russell's team.

In the years after that exchange I often reflected on what Russell had said to me, and I marveled that he would have thought so deeply about what constituted friendship. It was, obviously, the same sort of philosophical contemplation about the concept of Team that had made him the most divine teammate there ever was.

Look, you can stand at a bar and scream all you want about who was the greatest athlete and which was the greatest sports dynasty, and you can shout out your precious statistics, and maybe you're right, and maybe the red-faced guy down the bar—the one with the foam on his beer and the fancy computer rankings—is right, but nobody really knows. The only thing we know for sure about superiority in sports in the United States of America in the 20th century is that Bill Russell and the Boston Celtics teams he led stand alone as the ultimate winners. Fourteen times in Russell's career it came down to one game, win you must, or lose and go home. Fourteen times the team with Bill Russell on it won.

But the fires always smoldered in William Felton Russell, and he simply wouldn't suffer fools—most famously the ones who intruded upon his sovereign privacy to petition him for an autograph. He was that rare star athlete who was also a social presence, a voice to go with the body. Unafraid, he spoke out against all things, great and small, that bothered him. He wouldn't even show up at the Hall of Fame when he was inducted, because he had concluded it was a racist institution. Now, despite the importunings of his friends, he is the only living selection among ESPN's 50 top athletes of the century who hasn't agreed to talk to the network. That is partly because one night he heard an ESPN announcer praise the '64 Celtics as "Bob Cousy's last team." Cousy was retired by then.

Russell says, "They go on television, they're supposed to know."

Cousy says, "What the Celtics did with Russ will never be duplicated in a team sport. Never."

Of course, genuine achievement is everywhere devalued these days. On the 200th anniversary of his death, George Washington has been so forgotten that they're toting his false teeth around the republic, trying to restore interest in the Father of Our Country with a celebrity-style gimmick. So should we be surprised that one spectacular show-off dunk on yesterday's highlight reel counts for more than some ancient decade's worth of championships back-before-Larry&Magic-really-invented-the-sport-of-basketball?

Tommy Heinsohn, who played with Russell for nine years and won 10 NBA titles himself, as player and coach, sums it up best:

"Look, all I know is, the guy won two NCAA championships, 50-some college games in a row, the ['56] Olympics, then he came to Boston and won 11 championships in 13 years, and they named a f——— tunnel after Ted Williams." By that standard, only a cathedral on a hill deserves to have Bill Russell's name attached to it.

But then, too often when I try to explain the passion of Russell himself and his devotion to his team and to victory, I'm inarticulate. It's like trying to describe a color to a blind person. All I can say, in tongue-tied exasperation, is, You had to be there. And I'm sorry for you if you weren't.

Russell was right, too. The two of us did go our separate ways after he dropped me at the airport. He left the playing life exactly 30 years ago this week, on May 5, 1969, with his last championship, and my first child was born on May 7. So there were new things we both had to do, and in the years that followed we were together only a couple of times, briefly.

Then a few weeks ago we met at his house in Seattle, and for the first time in 30 years I climbed into his car. The license plate on the Lexus reads KELTIC 6, and on the driver's hands were two NBA championship rings: his first, from '57, and his last, from 12 years later. We took off together for the San Francisco Bay Area, there to visit Bill's father, Charlie, who is 86 and lives in a nursing home. It was 13 hours on the road. We stopped along the way at McDonald's and for gas and for coffee and for a box of Good 'n' Plenty and to pee and to buy lottery tickets once we got over the California line, because there was a big jackpot that week in the Golden State. In Oakland we found a Holiday Inn and ate a fish dinner at Jack London Square, where a bunch of elderly black ladies sat at the next table. "I was thinking they were old," Bill said, nodding his gray head toward them. "Then I remembered, I'm probably their age." I laughed. "Hey, what are you laughing at?" he roared. So, like that, wherever we happened to be going in the car, our destination was really back in time.

Back to the Russell Era. Back to the Celtics and the University of San Francisco Dons, to the Jones Boys and Cooz. Yes, and back to Wilt. To Satch and Heinie and the sixth men. Red, of course. Elgin and Jerry. But more than just the baskets, more than just the '60s. Russell's family experience describes the arc of a century. Why, when Charlie Russell was growing up in Louisiana, he actually knew men and women who had been slaves. He told me about "making marks in the ground" to help his illiterate father calculate. I was baffled by that expression. "It's from the old country," Bill explained. That is, from Africa, centuries before, passed along orally. And as we were talking, and the old man—wearing a jaunty red sweat suit and a green hat—reminisced about more recent times, he suddenly smiled and said something I couldn't quite make out. I leaned closer. "What's that, Mr. Russell? How *what?*"

"No, *Hal*," he said. "All on account of Hal DeJulio." Charlie remembered so well, after all this time. You see, if young William hadn't, by chance, been there on the one day that DeJulio showed up at Oakland High in the winter of '51, none of this would have happened. None of it at all. But life often hangs by such serendipitous threads, and sometimes, like this time, we are able to take them and weave them into a scarf for history's neck.

The long trip to Oakland was not unusual for Russell. He enjoys driving great distances. After all, he is most comfortable with himself and next most comfortable with close friends, cackling that thunderous laugh of his that Cousy fears he'll hear resonating in the afterlife. *Playful* is the surprising word that former Georgetown coach John Thompson thinks of first for Russell, and old number 6 himself always refers to his Celtics as "the guys" in a way that sounds curiously adolescent. Hey, guys, we can put the game on right here!

Cynosure on the court though he was, Russell never enjoyed being the celebrity alone. "I still think he's a shy, mother's son," says Karen Kenyatta Russell, his daughter, "and even now he's uncomfortable being in the spotlight by himself." Maybe that's one reason the team mattered so to him; it hugged him back. "I got along with all the guys," Russell says, "and nobody had to kiss anybody's ass. We were just a bunch of men—and, oh, what marvelous gifts my teammates gave to me."

"He was just so nice to be with on the team," says Frank Ramsey, who played with Russell from 1956 to '64, Russell's first eight years in the NBA. "It was only when others came around that he set up that wall."

Russell loves nothing better than to talk. "Oh, the philosophizing," recalls Satch Sanders, who played with Russell from '60 to '69. "If he started off and said, 'You see,' we just rolled our eyes, because we knew he was going off on something." Yet in more recent times Russell went for years without permitting himself to be interviewed. "If I'm going to answer the questions, I want them to be my questions, the right questions," he says—a most unlikely prerogative, given the way journalism works. O.K., so no interviews. Privacy edged into reclusiveness.

On the other hand, as upside-down as this may sound, Russell believes he can share more by not giving autographs, because instead of an impersonal scribbled signature, a civil two-way conversation may ensue. Gently: "I'm sorry, I don't give autographs."

"You won't?"

"No, *won't* is personal. I don't. But thank you for asking." And then, if he senses a polite reaction, he might say, "Would you like to shake hands with me?" And maybe chat.

Utterly dogmatic, Russell wouldn't bend even to give his Celtics teammates autographs. One time this precipitated an ugly quarrel with Sanders, who wanted a simple keepsake: the signature of every Celtic he'd played with. "You, Satch, of all people, know how I feel," Russell snapped.

"Dammit, I'm your teammate, Russ."

Nevertheless, when the shouting was over, Russell still wouldn't sign. Thompson, who was Russell's backup on the Celtics for two years, is sure that Russell never took pleasure from these sorts of incidents. "No, it bothered him," Thompson says. "But doing it his way, on his own terms, was more important to him. And that's Bill. Even if it hurt him, he was going to remain consistent."

Russell speaks, often, in aphorisms that reflect his attitudes. "It is better to understand than to be understood," he told his daughter. "A groove can become a rut," he advised his teammates. And perhaps the one that goes most to his own heart: "You should live a life with as few negatives as possible—without acquiescing."

So, alone, unbothered, one of the happiest times Russell ever had was driving around the West on a motorcycle in the '70s. When he takes a long automobile trip by himself these days, he listens to National Public Radio, CDs and tapes he has recorded to suit his own eclectic taste. On one tape, for example, are Stevie Wonder and Burl Ives. On another: Willie Nelson and Aretha Franklin. But also, always, Russell sets aside two hours to drive in complete silence, meditating. He has never forgotten what Huey Newton, the Black Panther, once told him: that the five years he spent in solitary confinement were, in fact, liberating.

Russell returned twice to the NBA after he retired as the Celtics' player-coach following the 1968–69 season. As coach and general manager of the Seattle SuperSonics from 1973 to '77, he built the team that would win the championship two years after he left. A brief tenure with the Sacramento Kings during the '87–88 season was, however, disastrous and unhappy. On the night he was fired, Russell cleaned out his office; returned to his Sacramento house, which was contiguous to a golf course; and stayed there, peacefully by himself, for weeks, venturing out only for provisions and golf. He didn't read the newspapers or watch television news. "To this day, I don't know what they said about me," he says. He put his house on the market immediately, and only when it sold, three weeks later, did he return to Seattle, where for 26 years he has lived in the same house on Mercer Island, one tucked away into a sylvan hillside, peeking down at Lake Washington.

Divorced in 1973, Russell lived as a single parent with Karen for several years, until she left for Georgetown in 1980 and then Harvard Law. Alone after that, Russell says, there were times when he would hole up and practice his household "migratory habits." That is, he would stock the kitchen, turn on the burglar alarm, turn off the phone and, for the next week, migrate about the house, going from one couch to another, reading voraciously and watching TV, ideally *Jeopardy!* or *Star Trek*—just bivouacked there, the tallest of all the Trekkies, sleeping on various sofas. He was quite content. The finest team player ever is by nature a loner who, by his own lights, achieved such group success because of his abject selfishness. You will never begin to understand Bill Russell until you appreciate that he is, at once, consistent and contradictory.

Russell began to emerge from his most pronounced period of solitude about three years ago. Shortly after arriving in Seattle in 1973, he had gone into a jewelry store, where he hit it off with the saleswoman. Her name is Marilyn Nault. "Let me tell you," she sighs, "working in a jewelry store is the worst place to meet a man, because if one comes in, it's to buy something for another woman." But over the years—skipping through Russell's next, brief marriage, to a former Miss USA—Marilyn and Bill remained friends. Also, she impressed him as a very competitive dominoes player. When Bill's secretary died in 1995, Marilyn volunteered to give him a hand, and all of a sudden, after more than two decades, they realized they were in love. So it was that one day, when Marilyn came over to help Bill with his accounts, she just stayed on with him in the house on the hill under the tall firs.

There is a big grandfather clock in the house that chimes every hour. Like Bill, Marilyn doesn't hear it anymore. She has also learned how to sleep with the TV on, because Bill, a terrible night owl, usually falls asleep with the clicker clasped tightly in his hand. Usually the Golf Channel is on. Imagine waking up to the Golf Channel. Marilyn has also learned to appreciate long car trips. Twice she and Bill have driven across the continent and back. Their lives are quite blissful; he has never seemed to be so at peace. "They're the ultimate '50s couple," Karen reports. "They have nothing but kind things to say about each other, and it's part of their arrangement that at least once a day, he has to make her laugh."

Yet for all the insular contentment Russell has always sought in his life, his play was marked by the most extraordinary intensity. If he threw up before a big game, the Celtics were sure everything would be all right. If he didn't, then Boston's coach, Red Auerbach, would tell Russell to go back to the toilet—order him to throw up. Rookies who saw Russell for the first time in training camp invariably thought he had lost it over the summer, because he would pace himself, even play possum in some exhibitions, to deceive pretenders to his throne. Then, in the first game of the real season, the rookies would be bug-eyed as the genuine article suddenly appeared, aflame with competition. It was as if the full moon had brought out a werewolf.

Cousy says, "The level of intensity among the big guys is different. You put a bunch of huge guys, seminaked, out there before thousands of people, and you expect them to become killers. But it just isn't in their nature. Kareem [Abdul-Jabbar] probably had the best skills of all big men, and he played till he was 42. If he'd had Russ's instincts, it's hard to imagine how much better he'd have been. But he'd have burned out long before 42."

Sanders: "There's no reason why some centers today couldn't block shots like Russ did. Only no one has the intestinal fortitude. A center blocks one shot now, the other team grabs the ball and scores, and the center stands there pouting, with that I-can't-do-everything look. Russell would block three, four shots in a row— I mean from different players—and then just glower at us."

Russell: "Once I blocked seven shots in a row. When we finally got the ball, I called timeout and said, 'This s– has got to stop.'" Some years Russell would be so exhausted after the playoffs that, as he describes it, "I'd literally be tired to my bones. I mean, for four, five weeks, my bones would hurt."

Russell believes that Wilt Chamberlain suffered the worst case of big-man syndrome; he was too nice, scared that he might hurt somebody. The year after Russell retired, in the famous seventh game of the NBA Finals at Madison Square Garden, Willis Reed, the New York Knicks center, limped onto the court against the Los Angeles Lakers, inspiring his team and freezing Chamberlain into a benign perplexity. Russell scowls just thinking about it. "If I'm the one playing Willis when he comes out limping," he snarls, "it only would have emphasized my goal to beat them that much worse." Russell would have called Six—his play—again and again, going mercilessly at the cripple, exploiting Reed without remorse. The Celtics would have won. Which was the point. Always.

"To be the best in the world," Russell says, all but licking his lips. "Not last week. Not next year. But right now. You are the best. And it's even more satisfying as a team, because that's more difficult. If I play well, that's one thing. But to make others play better. . . ." He grins, savoring the memory. "You understand what I mean?" Bill often says that, invariably when there is no doubt. It has to do with emphasis more than clarity. In fact, I can sort of visualize him saying that after he blocked a shot. *You understand what I mean?*

Yes.

It is difficult to comprehend whence came Russell's extraordinary will on the court. Karen recalls only once in her life that her father so much as raised his voice to anyone. "I just never saw the warrior in him," she says. "As a matter of fact, as I got to understand men better, I appreciated all the more how much of a feminine side my father has." Ironically it was Russell's mother, Katie, who appears to have given him his fire, while his father, Charlie, instilled the more reflective component.

What do you remember your father telling you, Bill?

"Accept responsibility for your actions. . . . Honor thy father and mother. . . . If they give you $10 for a day's work, you give them $12 worth in return."

Even more clearly, Russell recalls the gritty creed his mother gave him when he was a little boy growing up in segregation and the Depression in West Monroe, La. Katie said, "William, you are going to meet people who just don't like you. On sight. And there's nothing you can do about it, so don't worry. Just be yourself. You're no better than anyone else, but no one's better than you."

One time, when he was nine, William—for that is what he was called till basketball made him just plain Bill—came home to the family's little shotgun shack after being slapped by a boy in a gang. Katie dragged him out to find the gang. She made her son fight every boy, one by one. "The fact is, I had to fight back," Bill says. "It wasn't important whether I won or lost."

When he and I visited his father, Charlie said this about Katie: "She was handsome and sweet, and she loved me, and she showed it by giving me children." Bill was very touched by that, subdued. Then Charlie smiled and added, "She played some basketball too—the bloomer girls."

Bill shot to his feet, screaming, "Daddy, I never knew that!" Then there was such vintage Russellian cackling that the old fellow in the next bed woke up, a little discombobulated by all the fuss.

If Katie Russell had any athletic instincts, though, they paled before her passion for education. It was an article of faith with her, a high school dropout, that her two sons—Charlie Jr., the elder by two years, and William—would go to college. Bill has a vivid memory of his mother taking him to get a library card. That was not mundane; that was a signal event. And this is what he remembers of West Monroe, altogether: "I remember that my mother and father loved me, and we had a good time, but the white people were mean. But I was safe. I was always safe. In all my life, every day, not for one second have I ever thought I could have had better parents."

Then, in 1946, when William was 12, his mother died of kidney failure, with very little warning. Katie Russell was only 32. The last thing she told her husband was, "Make sure to send the boys to college." The last thing she told William was, "Don't be difficult for your father, because he's doing the best he can."

The Russells had moved to Oakland not long before, after Charlie was denied a raise at the mill in West Monroe because he was black. Now the father and his two sons boarded the train with Katie's casket to return to Louisiana to bury her. It was after the funeral that young William heard Katie's sisters arguing about which one of them would take the two motherless boys to raise. That was the custom in these matters. Charlie interrupted. "No," he said, "I won't let you. I'm taking the two boys back with me." Though there was still much protesting from the aunts, that was that.

"I told my two boys they'd lost their best friend," Charlie says, "but we could make it if we tried." The goal remained to get them through college. Charlie Jr. was developing into a pretty good athlete, but his father couldn't spend much time thinking about games. After all, he'd had to quit school to work; unlike Katie, he'd never even been able to play basketball. It certainly never occurred to him that now, for the first time, there were people like Hal DeJulio around, scouting black teenagers, eager to give the best ones a free college education just for playing some ball.

The radar detector on the Lexus beeped. Russell slowed down. A bit. We had driven through Washington and most of Oregon, too. A billboard advertised the Seven Feathers Casino. Ah, fin de siècle America: casinos, cable, cosmetic surgery and scores from around the leagues. Russell, who just turned 65, is fairly pragmatic about the new ways of the world. He never put on any airs—witness that amazing laugh of his, which is the loud leitmotif of his life. "I try not to stifle anything," he says. "It isn't just my laugh. If I have to sneeze, I just let it go. You understand what I mean?"

He is also helped by the fact that even as a young man, he looked venerable. Other players would dart onto the court, all snappy and coltish. Number 6 would stalk out hunched over, stroking that dagger of a goatee, and stand there dark and grim. We always talk about teams "executing." All right, then: Russell appeared very much an executioner.

Jerry West, who was denied about a half-dozen championships strictly because of Russell, remembers. "When the national anthem was played, I always found my eyes going to Bill. He did that just right, stand there for the anthem. He was a statue, but there was a grace to him. Even just standing still: grace."

Whereas Russell is disappointed by much that he sees on the court today, he does not lambaste the players. He is just as prone to blame the coaches for taking so much of the spontaneity out of basketball. "The coaches dumb players down now," he says, clearly irritated. "They're stifling innovation. They're not letting them play outside the system." Pretty soon, it seems, the Celtics' fast break, which was the most gloriously coordinated rapid action in sport, will be nothing more than athletic nostalgia, like the drop-kick.

And the players? Well, it's not just them. "All the kids in this generation—they really don't have a clue," Russell says. "They don't know, but they really don't care. A lot of my peers are annoyed that the players accepted a salary cap. I'm not. I know there's not supposed to be a limit on what you can make in America, but then, the NBA may also be the only place where there's a high roof for a minimum. When I speak to the players, I just say they have a responsibility to be caretakers. When you leave, there should be no less for those who follow you than there was when you arrived."

We started up Mount Ashland, whose other side goes down into California. Russell said, "Of course, a lot of my peers are also annoyed with all this money these kids are making. Me? I love it when I see a guy get a hundred million, because that says something good about what I did. You understand what I mean?"

This is, however, not to say that some of the guys making a hundred million—or getting by on only 50 or 60—have a clue about what Bill Russell did. It took years of hectoring by some of his friends to persuade Russell to step out of the safe shadows, to display himself again. His legacy was fading. John Thompson fairly bellows, "Nobody cares when some turkey like me won't give interviews. But Bill Russell! I say, Bill: You owe it to the people you love not to take this to your grave. I want my grandchildren to hear you talk about all you were."

So, while sometimes it mortifies Russell that he is, like everybody else, marketing himself—"I can't believe I'm doing all the things I swore I'd never do," he moans—there is the reasonable argument that truth nowadays must be packaged; otherwise, only the hype will survive as history. So Russell is planning a speaking tour and an HBO documentary about his life, and Karen is working on a book about motivation with her father, and a huge charitable evening to honor Russell is scheduled at the FleetCenter in Boston on May 26, when his number 6 jersey will be ceremonially re-retired. Russell is even selling about 500 autographs a year, and when we went to ship some signed basketballs to a sports collectibles store, I felt rather as if I had gone over to Handgun Control and mailed out some Saturday Night Specials.

So, O.K., it's the millennium, it's a different world. But we're not that far removed from the old one. Look at Bill Russell in 1999. His grandfather Jake was of the family's first generation born free on this continent. When this fading century began, Jake Russell was trying to scratch out a living with a mule. The Klan went after him because even though he couldn't read or write a lick, he led a campaign to raise money among the poor blacks around West Monroe to build a schoolhouse and pay a teacher to educate their children at a time when the state wouldn't have any truck with that.

At the other end of Jake's life, in 1969, he went over to Shreveport, La., to see the Celtics play an exhibition. By then his grandson had become the first African-American coach in a major professional sport. Jake sat with his son, Charlie, watching Bill closely during timeouts. He wasn't quite sure what he was seeing; Celtics huddles could be terribly democratic back then. It was before teams had a lot of assistants with clipboards. Skeptically Jake asked his son, "He's the boss?" Charlie nodded.

Jake took that in. "Of the white men too?"

"The white men too."

Jake just shook his head. After the game he went into the decrepit locker room, which had only one shower for the whole team. The Celtics were washing up in pairs, and when Jake arrived, Sam Jones and John Havlicek were in the shower, passing the one bar of soap back and forth—first the naked black man, then the naked white man stepping under the water spray. Jake watched, agape. Finally he said, "I never thought I'd see anything like that."

Of course, it was hardly a straight line upward to brotherhood. Nor was Bill Russell afraid to point that out to America; he could be unforgiving and sometimes angry, which meant he was called arrogant by those who didn't care for his kind. Russell invested in a rubber plantation in Liberia, and at a time when African-Americans were known as Negroes, and the word black was an insult, Russell started calling himself black. In the civil rights movement he became a bold, significant figure far beyond the parquet.

Thompson says, "It took a long time for me to be able to accept him as a person, as another guy, because I admired and respected him so. Russell made me feel safe. It was not that he was going to save me if anybody threatened me. Somehow I knew it was going to be all right so long as I was with him. I was going to be safe."

Often, edgy whites misunderstood him, though. Once a magazine quoted him as saying, "I hate all white people." Russell walked into the cramped old Celtics locker room, where equality reigned: Every player had one stool and two nails. Frank Ramsey glanced up from the magazine. "Hey, Russell, I'm white," he said. "You hate me?"

The two teammates looked into each other's eyes. "I was misquoted, Frank," was all Russell said. That was the end of it; he and Ramsey remained as close as ever. A few years earlier, too, there had been a big brouhaha in Kentucky, Ramsey's home state. Russell and other black Celtics had pulled out of an exhibition game there because the hotels were segregated. There was a lot of talk that Russell should not have embarrassed Ramsey that way. None of the talk came from Ramsey, though. Then, in 1966, when Russell succeeded Auerbach and became the first black coach (while continuing to play), he accepted the job only after trying to persuade Ramsey to return to basketball, from which he had retired in 1964, and coach the Celtics. Russell thought that would be better for the team than for him to make history.

The Celtics really did get along the way teams are supposed to in sports mythology. Russell threw Christmas parties for his teammates and their families. In 1962 he took the astonished rookie Havlicek around town to get a good price on a stereo. "All of us were strangers in a place far from home," Russell says. "But we made it into a unique situation. Cousy started it. He was absolutely sincere about being a good teammate."

Still, it was different away from the warm cocoon of the Celtics. One night in 1971 the team assembled in the Boston suburb of Reading, where Russell lived, to be with him as the town proudly honored their captain. It was the first time Heinsohn ever saw Russell cry, he was so happy. A few months later some people broke into Russell's house, rampaged, smashed his trophies, defecated in his bed and spread the excrement over his walls. They didn't want any black man in their town. But in the locker room Russell never talked about the terrible things that happened to him so close to the Celtics' city. "He was too proud to let people know," Heinsohn says.

Cousy still feels guilty. "I wish I'd done more to support Russ," he says. "We were so close, as teammates, but we all should have been more aware of his anger." Cousy draws a deep sigh. "But you know jocks—all into the macho thing. Always afraid to let the conversation be anything more than superficial. We mature so much later than anybody else."

So they just had to settle for winning.

Russell drove the Lexus into Oakland. When he was a little boy, after rural Dixie, his big new California hometown seemed such a wondrously exciting place. But Oakland wasn't Valhalla. "I couldn't even go downtown," he says. "The cops would chase the black kids away. And you still have those soldiers in blue in the streets. In terms of economics, things are certainly better in America today. But the criminal justice system hasn't improved."

Still, even if the police ran young William out of stylish Oakland, he grew up in contentment. Even after Katie's death, the Russells enjoyed the sort of family embrace that is denied so many black boys today. Charlie Jr. would graduate from college and become a social worker and a playwright. William, for his part, was a bookworm. For someone who ended up 6'10", he grew very late and wasn't much noticed on the basketball court. But then, he also wasn't much good. Frank Robinson, the great baseball player, was on the McClymonds High basketball team with Russell, and he says, "He couldn't even put the ball in the basket when he dunked." Russell was scheduled to graduate in January 1951, whereupon it was his intention to get a job in the shipyards and save up to go to college part time.

This is surely what would have happened, too, except that Hal DeJulio, who had played at the University of San Francisco and occasionally steered young players toward the school, went to an Oakland High-McClymonds game one day to help the Oakland coach. USF was a struggling urban Catholic college that didn't even have a gymnasium; the team had to settle for leftovers and overlooks. As a consequence, DeJulio noticed McClymonds' center, the unknown string bean with the incredibly long arms, who had a rare good game that day. A week later DeJulio showed up unannounced at the Russells' house and offered William a scholarship to San Francisco. Only then did he tell Dons coach Phil Woolpert about his find. Woolpert was skeptical but agreed to take William on.

It was that close to there never being a Bill Russell. "It gives me chills," Karen says.

Even as Russell won his first NCAA title, in 1955, his coach—like most everybody else—couldn't yet fathom that Russell was this genius who had, in effect, created a whole new game of basketball. For instance, Woolpert concurred with the conventional wisdom that to play defense you must not leave your feet, "and here I was airborne most of the time," Russell recalls. Although the Dons' victories piled up, Woolpert kept telling Russell he was "fundamentally unsound." He would say, "You can't do that." Russell would respond, "But I just did."

Nevertheless Russell liked Woolpert—"a fine and decent man," he calls the coach—who was being excoriated for starting three black players: Russell, K.C. Jones and Hal Perry. Woolpert was flooded with hate mail, and rival coaches snidely called him Saperstein, after Abe, the coach of the Harlem Globetrotters.

Although the NCAA championship won by the 1965–66 Texas Western team, with five black starters, has over time been painted as a watershed event, the fact is that Russell was as much pioneer as avatar. The African-American domination of basketball traces to two teams, his teams: USF in college, Boston in the pros. Texas Western was but the end product of what Russell inspired—and what he had suffered through—a decade earlier.

K.C. Jones remembers an occasion in Oklahoma City, where USF was practicing, when local citizens threw coins at the players as if they were clowns in the circus. Inside, Jones raged. But Russell, smiling sardonically, picked up the change and handed it to Woolpert. "Here, Coach, hold this for me," was all he said.

"Then," Jones says, "he took it out on the opposition."

"I decided in college to win," Russell says matter-of-factly. "Then it's a historical fact, and nobody can take it away from me. You understand what I mean?"

Indisputably, his race diminished Russell in the eyes of many biased observers, but, withal, it was the rare fair-minded expert who could comprehend the brilliance of this original force. Indeed, even as Russell won every year in the NBA, the fact that Chamberlain averaged skyrocket numbers was more beguiling to the unsophisticated. Meanwhile, in Boston, the stylish—and Caucasian—Cousy continued to hold the greater affection. Auerbach recalls one time when Cousy was injured but the Celtics swept a five-game road trip, with "Russ blocking a million shots." When the team returned home, it was greeted by a headline that made no reference to the victory streak, asking only, WILL COUSY PLAY TONIGHT? "This coulda killed my team," Auerbach says. He felt obliged to order the exhausted players to go directly from the airport to the Garden, there to air the matter as a team.

Russell was a great admirer of Cousy, though, and the two led together. If they called a team meeting, they'd start off by soliciting opinions on how they—Cousy and Russell—were lacking.

After that, who could bitch about anybody else? Jones cannot recall a single instance, either in college or in the NBA, when Russell "jumped on anyone's butt. But Bill definitely had his Machiavellian side. Anybody who didn't fit in, he'd just dismiss him."

Russell's simple key to a successful team was to encourage each player to do what he did best. "Remember," he says, "each of us has a finite amount of energy, and things you do well don't require as much. Things you don't do well take more concentration. And if you're fatigued by that, then the things you do best are going to be affected." The selfishness of successful team play—"I was very selfish," he declares—sounds paradoxical, but a team profits if each player revels in his strength. Still, Russell points out, there is a fine line between idealistic shared greed and typical self-gratification. "You must let your energy flow to the team," he says.

And sometimes, of course, you simply must sacrifice. For instance, one of the hardest things Russell had to learn to accept was that if he filled one lane on a fast break and Heinsohn was on the other flank, Cousy would give Heinsohn the ball—and the basket. Every time. "He simply had so much confidence in Heinie," Russell says. "So I had to discipline myself to run that break all-out, even if I knew I wasn't going to get the ball."

Above all, though, the key to Russell's success was that his greatest individual talent was the one that most benefited the team. It was not only that he blocked shots; Auerbach estimates that 80% of the time Russell could also direct the blocked ball into Celtics hands, usually fast-break bound. Moreover—and here is why statistical analyses of Russell's play are meaningless—the mere threat of a Russell block made opponents think twice about shooting, while the other Celtics could gamble aggressively on defense, knowing that number 6 would save them. "Other teams, all you hear is 'Switch!' 'Pick!' 'Help!'" Thompson says. "On the Celtics you'd only hear one word: 'Russ!'"

. . .

Although Russell made his *team* nearly invincible, the singular image that survives is of that one extraordinary athlete. That's the trouble with old sportswriters: They remember the beauty they saw far better than people today can visualize it from reading statistics. "It wasn't just that Bill was the whole package—and he was," West says, "but there was such presence he brought to the game."

By himself, in fact, Russell was hugely responsible for changing the way the public thought about big men in basketball. Before Russell, the giants were often dismissed as gawky goons or, like Chamberlain, bully-boy Goliaths. But Russell was as comfortable in his shape as he was in his skin, and it showed. "I am tall," he says. "O.K.? And if that's the only reason I can play, that's all right too. Don't deny your biggest asset. I'm a tall black guy. O.K.? No apologies, no bragging." In a game that was much more choreographed than the one today, no one could fail to see the elegance of Russell—this great winged bird swooping about, long angles that magically curved, rising high before your eyes. In fact, Russell saw himself as an artist, his play as a work of art. "If you can take something to levels that very few other people can reach," he says without vanity, "then what you're doing becomes art."

Unashamed, he sought to play the perfect game. "Certain standards I set for that," he says. "First, of course, we had to win. I had to get at least 25 rebounds, eight assists and eight blocks. I had to make 60% of my shots, and I had to run all my plays perfectly, setting picks and filling the lanes. Also, I had to say all the right things to my teammates—and to my opponents." Ironically, the closest he ever came to achieving that ideal was one night when he lived up to all his standards except the most obvious one: He did not make a single basket in 11 attempts.

Never mind. There were many discrete exquisite moments that made up for never quite attaining that comprehensive dream. "Sometimes," Russell told me in the car, breaking into a smile at the recollection, "sometimes if I could do something exactly the way I wanted, it was such an exhilarating feeling that I wanted to scream."

That memory was so joyous, in fact, that he missed the turn to the airport. Yes, 30 years later, he was driving me to an airport again. We had seen his father that morning, so our mission was accomplished. And now Karen was coming up to visit Charlie, so three generations of Russells would be together, Bill in the middle.

Karen returned, not long ago, from her first visit to West Monroe. "We're like so many other Americans, all scattered to the winds," she says, "and it was, for me, like finding my lost tribe. It also put my father's incredible journey into a context I'd never been able to put it before." She visited Katie's grave, and it made Karen think: "She had the vision for my father, as he had the vision for me."

Charlie was touched when Karen hugged him and told him this. Bill looked at them—the father who had a sixth-grade education and the daughter who'd graduated from Harvard Law. There they were, a whole century's worth of one American family. When Bill was young, in his game, players like him were known as pivotmen. Now, in his family, he is something of that again, the axis on which the Russells, ahead and behind him, turn. But then, it was the same way with basketball. Bill Russell was the pivot on which the whole sport turned. You understand what I mean?

TEXAS MONTHLY

"No One Knows What Could be Happening to Those Kids"

With so many stories published about child abuse, it's hard to imagine a unique way to further the discussion on the subject. Skip Hollandsworth meets and exceeds the challenge with his compelling, year-long, on-the-scene account of the beleaguered, hopelessly undermanned and underfunded Austin, Texas child-abuse investigative unit. Combined with a broader exposé of the state's Child Protective Services agency, Hollandsworth's article caused the kind of public outrage that finally led to legislative action.

Skip Hollandsworth

"No One Knows What Could be Happening to Those Kids"

Here's another one," Randy Shell said, opening a manila folder. It was a Monday morning in July 1998, and four women in their early twenties were gathered around his desk in his spare North Austin office. "A mother is reported to be living in a cheap motel with her children, ages two and four. She's using all her money and food stamps for crack. The kids are left alone all day in the motel room. They're not being fed."

Randy ran a hand through his long salt-and-pepper hair and stared at the women. Their faces were blank; the fluorescent strip lighting had drained the color from their cheeks. Already that morning they had divided eight manila folders among themselves, and another five were still sitting on Randy's desk. "There's just one problem," he said matter of factly. "All we know is that Mom is in some motel along Interstate 35. She keeps moving from one place to another. No one knows what could be happening to those kids."

The women seemed frozen in place, their eyes focused on the folder. Randy didn't need to be told what they were thinking: *Don't give it to me. Don't give it to me.* This was a "door knocker," a case that could require an entire day of knocking on doors of fleabag motels. None of them had time to play detective, though that is exactly what they had been hired to do. They were members of

Unit 25, a child abuse investigative team for the state's Child Protective Services (CPS) office in Travis County, and as they had been told over and over in their training sessions, they were the last line of defense for helpless children. It was their job to keep kids from getting their cheekbones crushed by beatings or their skin stripped away by scalding water. They were supposed to find the sick toddlers turning jaundiced from lack of medical treatment and the helpless grade-schoolers who stifled screams at night while an uncle or a stepfather fondled them.

For several seconds, the 38-year-old Randy, Unit 25's supervisor, studied his caseworkers and wondered who was going to quit first. They were all rookies—they had been with him less than a year—and he had no doubt that they were all thinking about resigning. CPS has the highest employee turnover of any state agency: More than one out of every three caseworkers quit within twelve months. Randy was a rarity, an eight-year veteran who *wanted* to stay in the investigative division. He was something of a legend around CPS, so dedicated to his job that he occasionally spent the night on a bedroll on the floor of his office.

"Anyone interested in the motel case?" he asked. Standing at the far left of his desk was one of his best staffers, Christine Cheshire, a thoughtful 23-year-old who carried a Carson McCullers novel in her car to read during her breaks as a way to keep herself sane. On this day Randy had given her two case folders and both needed immediate work. The first concerned a two-year-old girl and her ten-month-old sister, daughters of teenage parents who lived in a mobile home. The older girl reportedly had little round burns on her ankles, the kind made by lit cigarettes; she was also vomiting blood. The second folder told the story of a three-year-old boy who was seen standing alone in front of his house at two in the morning. The person who called CPS's 800-number to file the report had said the boy's mother regularly left him outside with a bag of potato chips while she went off to prostitute herself to buy drugs.

Christine might have been able to handle the two cases if there were not forty older folders already piled up on her desk. Unlike the ones Randy was passing out, most of those did not require instant attention, but she knew that if she disregarded them for too long, they were liable to blow up in her face. On her desk, for instance, was a report on an eleven-year-old boy who had told a teacher at school that he had seen his father hit his mother over the head with a lamp. His father had then picked up a piece of the lamp and pointed it at him. Because there was no evidence of abuse, Christine was supposed to close the case. But she couldn't do it. In her conversation with the boy, she could sense how scared he was. He kept licking his lips and looking over his shoulder as she talked to him.

"Something's going to happen to that one," she had told another Unit 25 investigator, 24-year-old Reneé Munn, who also had more than forty open cases. Reneé was the staff sentimental- ist: On the walls of her office were photos of kids she'd tried to help, including one of four beautiful young sisters who were sex- ually abused by a relative. She had come to work that morning hoping to find time to talk to five children from a middle-class Austin family who kept showing up at school with bruises and welts on their legs. But Randy had quickly handed her two more folders, one of which told the story of a 17-year-old who had just given birth to a girl. Nurses at an Austin hospital had called CPS to say the mother seemed mentally slow, didn't know how to feed the baby, and was unwilling to change her diaper—and because she had no insurance and was not registered for a government aid program, the hospital had to discharge them. "Reneé, that mother needs some support services," Randy had told her. He didn't have to say what else was on his mind: Without supervision, the baby could easily die of neglect.

Randy thought about giving the motel case to his newest case- worker, 23-year-old Stephanie Fambro. He could tell she was a fighter. Whenever she heard him describe a gruesome case, she would narrow her eyes and angrily purse her lips. But on this day he really needed her to focus on another report that had just come in: An 8-year-old girl with bruises was hiding every afternoon in a drainage tunnel near her apartment complex, and no one knew where her mother was.

Finally, Randy handed the file to the caseworker standing on the far right of his desk. Jackie Rowe, a pretty, blue-eyed 24-year-old who had swum competitively at Ohio University, worked as a social worker in her native Kentucky for a year before moving to Austin because, as she put it, she was ready for a change of pace from her genteel life. Yet after only a few days on the job, she was already talking about how different life in Texas was for children. "How do you get to all the cases?" she had once asked her co-workers when she too found herself with a backlog of forty files. There was a long silence before someone replied, "You don't."

"Do the best you can on this one," Randy said as Jackie took the folder. She twisted her lips in what looked like a smile. But Randy noticed that her shoulders were slumping, a clear sign that she was succumbing to the pressure. Jackie put the folder on top of another one—a case involving a boy in the East Austin projects who wore cotton in his ears to keep out the roaches that crawled on his bed at night—and walked out the door.

When Governor George W. Bush proposed earlier this year to allocate funds to hire 380 more CPS caseworkers, you might have thought that something was finally being done to fight child abuse in Texas. Perhaps because they didn't want to risk alienating Bush and state legislators, CPS officials spoke out publicly in support of the plan. Newspaper editorialists applauded what they saw as a commitment by politicians to address the problems of an underfunded and understaffed agency.

What no one said, however, was that the new caseworkers

would have no noticeable effect whatsoever on the safety of the state's children. The brutal truth about abuse and neglect in Texas is that it's escalating out of control, and recent front-page headlines—child abuse deaths increased from 103 in 1997 to a record 176 in 1998, newspapers reported in January—only tell a small part of the story. There are so many kids now being abused or neglected that the 2,631 CPS workers statewide (fewer than a third of whom work full-time in investigative units) are completely overwhelmed. Out of desperation, they've taken a "triage" approach to their job, much as doctors on battlefields do: Less serious wounds that would have been fully investigated five years ago (such as bruises on an older child as a result of spanking) are now ignored so that more attention can be paid to the worst cases.

In fact, of the 360,000 calls made to CPS last year reporting what was thought to be abuse or neglect, only 151,349—well under half—were considered significant enough to be labeled potential cases. (The other calls were classified as too vague to be investigated or outside the CPS definition of abuse or neglect.) Of those 151,349 calls, caseworkers only looked into 111,147. Even more disturbing, fewer than 30,000 of those 111,000 or so reports—less than 10 percent of the total number of calls—were labeled "confirmed" instances of abuse or neglect, the standard that must be met before CPS can monitor a family or remove a child from the home.

Some might suggest that the reason for this low number of full-scale investigations is that CPS is inundated with false or unfounded reports—the kind of reports, for instance, filed by parents who level child abuse allegations against their ex-spouse to win divorce or custody cases. Not so. In the past thirteen years, the number of children living in Texas has shot up by 16 percent, to 5.5 million. Of those, 1.5 million—more than 25 percent—live in poverty, which child abuse experts say is where most abuse and neglect occurs. It is no secret that rampant use of drugs like crack cocaine has also led to the greater deterioration of families. CPS reports that nearly 900,000 Texas children were at risk for abuse or neglect in 1998, a 7 percent increase over 1992.

The first warning bells about Texas' child abuse crisis were set off last year by state district judge F. Scott McCown, who oversees many of the child-welfare cases for Austin and the rest of Travis County. While flipping through some old records, he noticed that in 1985, when the state's child population was just under 4.8 million, CPS officially designated 62,233 children as abused or neglected. How, he wondered, could the number of children being abused have dropped from 62,233 children in 1985 to 44,536 in 1998? He then discovered that the number of potential child abuse cases assigned for investigation was also dropping steadily year after year. In 1993, 21.91 cases were investigated for every 1,000 reports made. But in 1997, only 16.93 cases were investigated per 1,000 reports. Upon further examination, McCown realized that CPS caseworkers in Texas were not removing children from abusive or neglectful environments as often as caseworkers in other states did. Texas ranked thirtieth in "removals," taking a mere 7,723 children out of their homes—a far cry from California, which had 26,987 removals. If Texas had just raised its numbers to the national average, an additional 5,897 children would have been removed from their homes. What was going on? How could it be that, while other states were increasing their investigations and confirming a larger percentage of cases of abuse or neglect, Texas' CPS caseworkers were doing fewer investigations, confirming a smaller percentage of those cases, and then not removing enough children from potentially life-threatening circumstances?

The answer, of course, has to do with money. Texas ranks near the bottom of the fifty states in the amount it spends per capita for child welfare, and CPS officials are consistently told to cut their budget. Often that means cutting staff, since salaries and benefits are a particularly juicy budget line; in fact, CPS has fewer staff today than it did in 1995. The agency's increasingly heavy work-load compounds the problem. Not only is CPS charged with investigating cases, but also it is legally required to supervise all of the children it takes out of abusive homes and places in foster homes or with extended family members or close friends. In 1997 CPS was responsible for 23,595 children, nearly 15,000 more than in 1985. As a result, most of its money is spent on taking care of them, leaving less available every year to investigate the predicaments of children in need of help but outside the system. CPS is now little more than a leaky rescue boat, according to Judge McCown, "so heavily loaded with children . . . that it moves slowly to the scene of the next crisis and once there has little space for new passengers."

What's more, the department's triage policy simply isn't working, for as any CPS staffer can tell you, it's often the smaller cases that quickly escalate into disaster. Some of the kids who are dying or showing up in emergency rooms with their bones broken have been the subjects of previous CPS investigations that were closed too early. Others are not saved because overly stressed caseworkers are starting to make mistakes. In Kingsville last June, a twelve-year-old boy was beaten to death with a belt, a hose, a board, and a rock by his father and stepmother. His body was found on the bathroom floor, covered with fire ants. The local CPS office had been informed about the allegedly abusive relationship, but as one CPS official admitted, the young caseworker who went to the house "didn't see the bruises on the boy or have time to double-check answers or talk to other people about what they knew. He didn't do any follow-up."

Sadly, critics say, this is the rule rather than the exception. The policy of the state of Texas is, in effect, to put the safety of our at-risk children in the hands of young, typically inexperienced case-workers who earn an average of $23,000 a year. And they do the most mind-numbingly difficult job imaginable, as I learned when

I spent eight months following around Randy Shell's Unit 25, one of three investigative units that cover Travis County. I wanted not only to see the kinds of challenges the unit faced but also to assess its ability—or lack thereof—to make a difference in the lives of children at risk. "There's hardly a day that goes by that I don't ask myself if this is the day a kid dies from my unit," Randy told me not long after I met him. "It's happened to me before, and I know how quickly it could happen again."

The baby girl was lying on a white table, her bruises shining like freshly washed plums under the hospital lights. Unit 25 investigator Christine Cheshire sucked in her breath as she listened to a nurse read from a chart. The girl, fourteen months old, had a large lesion on her chin, a burn on her shoulder, three bruises on her back, one bruise on her chest between her nipples, and more bruises on her arms, thighs, and buttocks. There were lesions in the area of her vagina that could not be explained. Her left leg was fractured in two places; one of the fractures was several months old. She had sustained retinal damage in her eyes that was consistent with shaken baby syndrome. A CAT scan revealed a bleeding bruise to the brain.

"It's amazing she's alive," Christine said when she called Randy Shell. She tried to keep her composure. "The mother says she thinks the baby-sitter did it, and the baby-sitter says she thinks the mother did it."

"Anybody else saying anything?"

"Nothing."

It was late August, one month after Randy had assigned the cases involving the crack-addicted mother in the motel, the child left outside at night with the potato chips, and the little girl hiding in the drainage ditch. When I asked him what had come of those investigations, he paused. "Sorry," he said. "We've had so many cases come through here since then that I have trouble remembering all of them."

As it turned out, they'd been lucky in July. After two full days of searching, caseworker Jackie Rowe had finally found the motel where the mother was staying and persuaded her to let CPS move her two children to their grandmother's home. "But to tell you the truth," Jackie told me, "it's probably going to be a matter of days before the mother realizes that CPS has filed away her case and goes back and gets her kids. And then, eventually, one of us will get another report about her."

To help the teenage mother who was about to be released from the hospital with no clear idea how to care for her newborn, Randy had called his longtime contacts at other county agencies and arranged for social workers to be brought in to watch over the child. Still, on her off days, caseworker Reneé Munn was dropping by the house, just to say hello. "In a few weeks the social workers are going to leave that mother with the baby," Reneé said, "and she is going be alone with that child."

"And then what?" I asked.

"We have to cross our fingers and hope for the best."

As for the girl in the drainage ditch, Stephanie Fambro tracked down the girl's mother—she was in a tattoo parlor—then pointed her finger at her and told her to find relatives who would keep the child after school.

And Christine's case of the two young sisters, one of whom had cigarette burns? She was able to get the courts to temporarily remove them from their home until the parents had gone through CPS-sponsored counseling (a three-hour session with a psychologist) and a series of parenting-skills classes. She had found the girls space in the usually packed Austin Children's Shelter, which provides living quarters for abused kids who have no other place to go, and for a few minutes, before heading off to another case, she had sat with them in the kitchen of the shelter, watching them eat sliced peaches. They kept putting down their spoons and smiling at her. "Sometimes you try to tell yourself it's all worth it, you know?" Christine said that week. "You think that, just maybe, you did something to make their lives a little better."

But now, a month later, standing at the hospital alongside a child who was nearly dead, Christine was in a daze. No matter how many hours a day she spent at her job, she still could not comprehend why an adult would deliberately hurt a child. Even if the mother wasn't abusing her daughter, she surely had to have known for months that someone else was. "This is one of those cases where you ought to be able to go to a judge, tell him the facts, and get that child to a family who will love her," Christine said.

Yet she couldn't. Instead, she had to go back to work and prepare an affidavit asking a judge to remove the child from her mother's home. Pulling together the twenty pages of paperwork would take the rest of the day and much of the night, putting her farther behind on her other cases. Even then, she knew that there was a good chance the mother would get the child back. Since Christine had found no hard evidence suggesting the mother was the abuser—the child was, of course, too young to give a statement—the mother could easily challenge the affidavit. It was a scene that played out over and over at the child welfare courtroom in downtown Austin: a parent tearfully proclaiming his or her innocence before a judge, then lambasting CPS caseworkers as storm troopers with a license to rip apart families.

Back at the office, other caseworkers were immersed in new cases of their own. A toddler with gums that were bleeding from forced feedings. A three-year-old boy seen holding a marijuana cigarette. A thirteen-year-old girl, mentally unbalanced since her stepfather shot her in the head when she was four, living on the streets because her mother said she could no longer care for her. When I told Christine that the Child Welfare League of America recommends that a caseworker handle just twelve cases at any one time, she laughed. "Where did that number come from?" she asked. "Fantasyland?" In the investigative units in Texas' urban areas, caseworkers rarely have fewer than forty cases going at once. "Unless you are willing to be here all day and all night and on weekends," Randy said, "you will never have time to build a relationship with these families, some of whom really would like some help. You don't get the chance to prevent fires. You're lucky if you're able to put a few out before they burn out of control."

As opposed to the typical CPS staffer who receives a college degree in social work and comes straight to the agency, Randy began his career as a Chinese linguist with the Air Force. When he left the service in 1990, he could have made a nice living as a national security consultant, but instead he joined CPS's Austin office as a caseworker. "Nothing sounded more heroic than rescuing abused children," he told me. He quickly learned, however, that there were few chances to be a hero. In one of his first cases, he went to the hospital to look at a baby who had been shaken so badly by the father that his brain was disconnected from his spine. Randy held the baby's hand as a nurse turned off the life-support machine.

A few years after arriving at the agency, he realized that all 24 people who had been in his training classes had resigned. Many quit out of exhaustion or because of the extraordinarily low pay. Some quit because they kept waking up in the middle of the night, terrified that a kid in one of the cases they didn't have time to investigate would turn up dead. "They didn't want blood on their hands," Randy said. "Who could blame them?"

But Randy stayed. He bought a rusty school bus, towed it to a piece of land he owned outside of Austin, and converted it into a home for himself. He purchased a beat-up Mercedes that often broke down but had a back seat that was big enough to accommodate several kids at once. Although many abused children hid under beds or ran from their homes when they saw him tooling through their neighborhoods—their parents had told them CPS wanted to put them in prison—Randy kept coming back around. After he removed his first three kids—he got a court order to take them from their mother, an aging prostitute who was reportedly trying to sell them to her johns—he became so attached to them that he looked them up each Christmas thereafter and gave them presents.

In July 1996, after working in a CPS conservatorship unit (a group that watches over kids who have been removed from their homes), Randy was named the supervisor of Unit 25. Waves of new caseworkers were put in his charge, and he tried to teach each one everything he knew: how to stay calm when listening to threats from parents, how to avoid gasping when a child began reciting the litany of ways he'd been kicked or punched, how to let a child know quietly that nothing he'd done was deserving of such punishment. He made a point of going on calls with the new caseworkers, making sure they looked in refrigerators to see if there was food and ran their fingers through the ashtrays to see if there was any marijuana or crack. He insisted that his caseworkers have cute stuffed animals in their offices so that visiting children could have something to play with, and he provided them with anatomically correct dolls that could be handed to a child to learn whether someone had touched him in a "good place" or a "bad place." He stopped taking vacations. He worked on Christmas Eve and Christmas Day. He started spending nights at the office.

And yet the cases kept coming. By 1998 Travis County was leading all other Texas counties with 9.5 cases of reported child abuse and neglect for every one thousand children—second-place Bexar County had 8.1 cases—and more kids were slipping through the cracks. In the fall of 1997 Randy received a phone call from a caseworker at a dilapidated house less than a mile from the state capitol. Inside was a nine-year-old girl named Victoria. She apparently had been living in a single room and had never once ventured outside. Her clothes were stained with feces. She urinated on the floor and, as a cat does, attempted to cover it up. She had no language skills; she only made squeaking sounds, imitating the rats that climbed around the windows of her room and rustled underneath the piles of trash on the floor.

Randy did some checking and learned that CPS had received its first phone call about Victoria in December 1994. Yet the report was never assigned to a caseworker because the information was too "vague." After two more referrals about the girl in 1995, it was turned over to another unit. An investigator made quick visits to the home but did no follow-up after the mother assured him the girl was mentally retarded and was being home-schooled. Not long afterward, that caseworker quit the agency for another job, and the manila folder containing details of Victoria's life of squalor went untouched for more than two years. Only when another complaint came in did the case get the attention it deserved.

Around the same time, a two-month-old baby boy named Nakia was found dead in his crib in another ramshackle, trash-filled Austin house overrun with rats and roaches. The baby had died from a respiratory infection that was possibly caused by rat feces. His mother was just seventeen years old, and she was living with her own mother and her seven younger brothers and sisters. Randy was devastated when he found out. The family had been the subject of ten CPS investigations between June 1994—more than three years before Nakia was born—and February 1997. The last time, a just-hired caseworker had gone to the house to look into reports of physical and medical neglect of the children, but he had closed the case after the adult mother promised to fix the broken stove, clean the refrigerator, where roaches were nesting, and get rid of the rats. It never happened. "The hardest thing for a new caseworker is to decide whether children should be removed from a home where there is no abuse," said Randy. "No matter how impoverished the home life is, it's still home for those kids, and you know that moving them out and putting them in foster care will scar them forever. On the other hand, if you give a neglectful parent too many chances, those kids will be scarred in another way altogether. In this job, you can feel damned if you do and damned if you don't."

Predictably, it didn't take too long for most of Randy's caseworkers from that period to resign or transfer to other CPS jobs. The woman who had handled Victoria's case was so shocked by what she had seen that she quit working with children and moved to Chicago. Replacements arrived, though not much changed: One lasted only a day.

But when Christine, Reneé, Jackie, Stephanie, and others arrived in late 1997 and early 1998, Randy thought he had finally turned a corner. They were willing to do whatever it took to protect kids. On her own, Stephanie marched up to a crack dealer's house and demanded to see a mother who supposedly was living there with three unfed, unclothed children. "Get off my f—ing property or I'll kick your ass," the crack dealer told her. The mother quickly moved to another crack house, but Stephanie found her, showed up with the police, and got the children removed.

By last November, however, Randy could sense the dynamic shifting. His staff had grown tired of writing up the notes from all their investigations, especially those that turned out to be false reports. They resented having to spend all day standing outside a courtroom waiting for a hearing, only to have lawyers postpone it for another week. They hated having to work holidays, when parents were more likely to be home drinking and losing patience with their kids. And they were sickened by seeing so many child abusers getting off scot-free. Randy himself knew the feeling all too well. Once, he had worked on a case in which a father had beaten his child to a bloody pulp, then drop-kicked him into a wall and stuffed him between pillows. But because there was no corroborating evidence—as in many cases, the wife and children were too scared to testify against him—the father was never prosecuted. A few years later, the father was riding his bicycle when he was accidentally hit by a truck and killed. Randy and his CPS colleagues could barely keep from hugging one another when they heard the news.

In January, after a difficult month in which more than 550 cases were assigned to just three investigative units in Travis County, Jackie Rowe quit. She had not been able to sleep at night, she said. When she closed her eyes, she would see the faces of children. She would lie in bed wondering about kids she'd not been able to visit that day. When Randy asked her what she would do next, she said, "I don't know. I'm just leaving."

Jackie's co-workers openly admitted that they were jealous. While sitting in Reneé's office one afternoon, Christine said, "Every morning when I open the newspaper, I look for the stories about dead children to see if one of them was mine. I want to know what it feels like to get up in the mornings and not have to worry." In the last six months of 1998 Christine had gained 25 pounds. Instead of Carson McCullers, she had taken to reading Sylvia Plath. She had begun scouring online classified ads for another job. "Sometimes when I'm alone in my office around all my files," she told me, "I shut the door and put my head down on my desk, and I try not to cry."

But Christine was not the next to go. In early February Randy gathered his staff around his desk and told them he had been chosen to manage a statewide program that would set up contracts with organizations to provide more services to children, such as runaway shelters and outreach programs. The money was a little better—after eight years at CPS, he was making only $34,000 a year—but the real reason he was leaving, he said, was because he too was overwhelmed. His caseworkers stared at him open-mouthed. Soon, other workers from around the building were coming over to Randy's office to ask if the news was true. They told him that he couldn't leave: He was the only investigative supervisor with more than a few months of supervisory experience. "I just need to take a break," he told me that day. "Whenever I've tried to take a vacation, I spend all day on the phone talking to caseworkers who need help."

He paused for several seconds. "Maybe I'll come back. Maybe I will. But, God, I've never felt so weary. I'm having a hard time giving my old pep talks to the caseworkers about how they are making a difference. I just gave Christine a case about a father carving 666 in his chest, bleeding on his own six-year-old daughter, and then taking her to a funeral home to dance in a fountain. And here's another one about a three-year-old girl from Honduras who's been abandoned here. She's dying of AIDS. She'll die alone somewhere, wondering where her mommy is."

As it happened, Randy barely had time to say his good-byes. In his last days on the job, he had new cases to assign and a new caseworker to train: Ambrose "A.J." Jones, a bright 33-year-old who was hired to take Jackie's place. Like Randy, A.J. had been in the military—in his case, the U.S. Navy. After his time in the service, he returned to college to get a degree in social work. He joined CPS, he told me, "because I wanted other children to know they felt protected, the same way my own seven-year-old son feels."

On February 11 A.J. left the office to look into a report that a young boy was being neglected at a shabby home in South Austin. Randy decided to go with him, and as he read over the initial report, he recognized the name of the nineteen-year-old father. When the father had been a boy himself, Randy had removed him from his home after discovering that his parents were neglecting him. "It's amazing the way this cycle works," Randy said. "The kids I once tried to help are now the parents I'm having to investigate. Maybe I *have* been in this business too long."

The house smelled like sewage and dogs and rotting food. The floor was covered with tops from old vegetable cans, soiled magazines, old clothes, beer bottles, and cigarette butts. The broken toilet was full of feces, the bathtub half full of brown water and garbage. The stove had been ripped from the kitchen wall. The father was gone—he had moved out days before—but sleeping in the house were two young men in punk outfits who, Randy guessed, spent their days begging for money along the University of Texas Drag. A.J. and Randy went into a front bedroom and saw a two-year-old boy with dirt on his feet and hands lying on a bare mattress. The boy's mother, wearing overalls and a tank top, was sitting beside him. She had clearly not bathed in a long time: There was a ring of dirt around her neck. Both she and the boy sounded congested.

A.J. did the initial questioning. The mother told him that she was doing her best with her son. She said she had taken him to the doctor—and, indeed, she showed A.J. the medicine she had been given for the boy's cough. "I love my child," she said. "I do everything I can for him. Do you want to punish me just because I'm poor?" As filthy as the house was, A.J. had to admit that he'd seen worse. He also had met parents who were far more neglectful and who never would have gone to the trouble to get medicine for their sick children. He decided to give the mother a stern warning about the condition of the house. He was going to leave the boy in her care, but he would return in a few days to see how things looked.

But after studying the medicine bottle himself, Randy took A.J.

outside and said, "We're removing the child. The mom's not giving the child the proper dosage of medicine. She should have finished this bottle by now. There's no telling how sick this kid is." A.J. stared at Randy. He had not even thought of checking the medicine. "It's all right," Randy said. "You only learn this stuff from experience."

When Randy told the mother they were taking the boy with them and getting a court order to keep him until the house was no longer a health hazard, the mother began screaming, "No! No!"

"What gives you the right to play God, you motherf—er?" one of the young punks shouted at Randy. "I bet your place looks like shit too!"

For several minutes, the mother wouldn't let go of the boy. Neighbors surrounded Randy and A.J. and insisted that the woman didn't mistreat her child. "Get your ass out of here," someone shouted. "Why do you like ruining other people's lives?"

When Randy finally got the boy out of his mother's arms, she collapsed and began sobbing uncontrollably. Randy and A.J. then drove him to the emergency room, where doctors discovered that he had severe bronchitis, infections in both ears, and a temperature of 103.7.

"If I had left him at the house, he could have died that day," a visibly shaken A.J. told Randy that night. At first Randy said nothing; then he told A.J. to go home and get some sleep. But A.J. didn't sleep a wink. He lay awake in bed, wondering if he would be able to last a year on the job.

A few days later, Randy's colleagues gathered at a nearby restaurant for his good-bye party. Everyone was determined not to talk about work, but within fifteen minutes the air was thick with stories about the latest CPS investigations. Christine came with her new boyfriend, an Austin police officer she'd met while working on a case. "Where else does a CPS worker meet someone?" she asked me. A.J. sat quietly at another table and left early. Reneé sipped cocktails with a couple of CPS staffers who used to work for Randy. ("I'm staying," she was overheard murmuring. Although she and Christine had quietly put in for transfers soon after learning of Randy's resignation, they had made a pact to remain with Unit 25 until the fall of 1999 so that they could say they had lasted two years.) Most of the group didn't go home until around midnight. Randy, one of the last to leave, said he was going to take a long-deserved three-day vacation before starting his new job.

But the next morning, he slipped back into his old office. It was a Saturday. No one else was there. He began to pack his things, but then he saw some manila folders on his desk. He stopped what he was doing, flipped open the top one, and started reading. "I just want to make sure no one is slipping through the cracks," he said.

THE NEW YORKER

The Demon in the Freezer

This exhaustive, unsparing, and riveting account brings into the public consciousness what may prove to be the single most frightening threat of the twenty-first century—the reemergence of smallpox. In his masterful account, Richard Preston shows the potential for terrorists to reintroduce this devastating plague, which the world's scientists brilliantly removed from nature, inadvertently making it yet more attractive as a weapon in a world without vaccinated individuals. Because of public outcries as a result of this article, the U.S. government has funded a major effort to prepare the nation for this global threat.

Richard Preston

The Demon in the Freezer

T he smallpox virus first became entangled with the human species somewhere between three thousand and twelve thousand years ago—possibly in Egypt at the time of the Pharaohs. Somewhere on earth at roughly that time, the virus jumped out of an unknown animal into its first human victim, and began to spread. Viruses are parasites that multiply inside the cells of their hosts, and they are the smallest life forms. Smallpox developed a deep affinity for human beings. It is thought to have killed more people than any other infectious disease, including the Black Death of the Middle Ages. It was declared eradicated from the human species in 1979, after a twelve-year effort by a team of doctors and health workers from the World Health Organization. Smallpox now exists only in laboratories.

Smallpox is explosively contagious, and it travels through the air. Virus particles in the mouth become airborne when the host talks. If you inhale a single particle of smallpox, you can come down with the disease. After you've been infected, there is a typical incubation period of ten days. During that time, you feel normal. Then the illness hits with a spike of fever, a backache, and vomiting, and a bit later tiny red spots appear all over the body. The spots turn into blisters, called pustules, and the pustules enlarge, filling with pressurized opalescent pus. The eruption of pustules is sometimes called the splitting of the dermis. The skin doesn't break, but splits horizontally, tearing away from its under-layers. The pustules become hard, bloated sacs the size of peas, encasing the body with pus, and the skin resembles a cobblestone street.

The pain of the splitting is extraordinary. People lose the ability to speak, and their eyes can squeeze shut with pustules, but they remain alert. Death comes with a breathing arrest or a heart attack or shock or an immune-system storm, though exactly how small-pox kills a person is not known. There are many mysteries about the smallpox virus. Since the seventeenth century, doctors have understood that if the pustules merge into sheets across the body the victim will usually die: the virus has split the whole skin. If the victim survives, the pustules turn into scabs and fall off, leaving scars. This is known as ordinary smallpox.

Some people develop extreme smallpox, which is loosely called black pox. Doctors separate black pox into two forms—flat small-pox and hemorrhagic smallpox. In a case of flat smallpox, the skin remains smooth and doesn't pustulate, but it darkens until it looks charred, and it can slip off the body in sheets. In hemorrhagic smallpox, black, unclotted blood oozes or runs from the mouth and other body orifices. Black pox is close to a hundred per cent fatal. If any sign of it appears in the body, the victim will almost certainly die. In the bloody cases, the virus destroys the linings of the throat, the stomach, the intestines, the rectum, and the vagina, and these membranes disintegrate. Fatal smallpox can destroy the body's entire skin—both the exterior skin and the interior skin that lines the passages of the body.

Smallpox virus's scientific name is variola. It means "spotted" in Latin, and it was given to the disease by a medieval bishop. The virus, as a life form, comes in two subspecies: *Variola minor* and *Variola major*. Minor is a weak mutant, and was first described in 1863 by doctors in Jamaica. People usually survive it. Classic major kills one out of three people if they haven't been vaccinated or if they've lost their immunity. The death rate with major can go higher—how much higher no one knows. *Variola major* killed half of its victims in an outbreak in Canada in 1924, and presumably many of them developed black pox. Smallpox is less contagious than measles but more contagious than mumps. It tends to go around until it has infected nearly everyone.

Most people today have no immunity to smallpox. The vaccine begins to wear off in many people after ten years. Mass vaccination for smallpox came to a worldwide halt around twenty-five years ago. There is now very little smallpox vaccine on hand in the United States or anywhere else in the world. The World Health Organization once had ten million doses of the vaccine in storage in Geneva, Switzerland, but in 1990 an advisory committee recommended that most of it be destroyed, feeling that smallpox was no longer a threat. Nine and a half million doses are assumed to have been cooked in an oven, leaving the W.H.O. with a total supply of half a million doses—one dose of smallpox vaccine for every twelve thousand people on earth. A recent survey by the W.H.O. revealed that there is only one factory in the world that has recently made even a small quantity of the vaccine, and there may be no factory capable of making sizable amounts. The vaccine was discovered in the age of Thomas Jefferson, and making a lot of it would seem simple, but so far the United States government has been unable to get any made at all. Variola virus is now classified as a Biosafety Level 4 hot agent—the most dangerous kind of virus—because it is lethal, airborne, and highly contagious, and is now exotic to the human species, and there is not enough vaccine to stop an outbreak. Experts feel that the appearance of a single case of smallpox anywhere on earth would be a global medical emergency.

At the present time, smallpox lives officially in only two repositories on the planet. One repository is in the United States, in a freezer at the headquarters of the federal Centers for Disease Control and Prevention, in Atlanta—the C.D.C. The other official smallpox repository is in a freezer at a Russian virology institute called Vector, also known as the State Research Institute of Virology and Biotechnology, which is situated outside the city of Novosibirsk, in Siberia. Vector is a huge, financially troubled former virus-weapons-development facility—a kind of decayed Los Alamos of viruses—which is trying to convert to peaceful enterprises.

There is a growing suspicion among experts that the smallpox virus may also live unofficially in clandestine biowarfare laboratories in a number of countries around the world, including labs on military bases in Russia that are closed to outside observers. The Central Intelligence Agency has become deeply alarmed about smallpox. Since 1995, a number of leading American biologists and public-health doctors have been given classified national-security briefings on smallpox. They have been shown classified evidence that as recently as 1992 Russia had the apparent capability of launching strategic-weapons-grade smallpox in special biological warheads on giant SS–18 intercontinental missiles that were targeted on the major cities of the United States. In the summer of last year, North Korea fired a ballistic missile over Japan in a test, and the missile fell into the sea. Some knowledgeable observers thought that the missile could have been designed to carry a biologic warhead. If it had carried smallpox and landed in Japan, it could have devastated Japan's population: Japan has almost no smallpox vaccine on hand and its government seems to have no ability to deal with a biological attack. The United States government keeps a list of nations and groups that it suspects either have clandestine stocks of smallpox or seem to be trying to buy or steal the virus. The list is classified, but it is said to include Russia, China, India, Pakistan, Israel, North Korea, Iraq, Iran, Cuba, and Serbia. The list may also include the terrorist organization of Osama bin Laden and, possibly, the Aum Shinrikyo sect of Japan—a quasi-religious group that had Ph.D. biologists as members and a belief that an apocalyptic war will bring them worldwide power. Aum members released nerve gas in the Tokyo subway in 1995, and, as the year 2000 approaches, the group is still active in Japan and in Russia. In any case, the idea that smallpox lives in only two freezers was never anything more than a comfortable fiction. No one knows exactly who has smallpox today, or where they keep the virus, or what they intend to do with it.

The man who is most widely credited with the eradication of smallpox from the human species is a doctor named Donald Ainslie Henderson. Everyone calls him D.A. Henderson. He was the director of the World Health Organization's Smallpox Eradication Unit from its inception, in 1966, to 1977, just before the last case occurred. "I'm one of many in the eradication," Henderson said to me once. "There's Frank Fenner, there's Isao Arita, Bill Foege, Nicole Grasset, Zdenek Jezek, Jock Copland, John Wickett—I could come up with fifty names. Let alone the tens of thousands who worked in the infected countries." Nevertheless, Henderson ran it. Smallpox killed at least three hundred million people in the twentieth century. During that time, humanity was largely immune to smallpox, which is not the case today. When D. A. Henderson arrived on the scene in 1966, two million people a year were dying of smallpox. In the years since the eradication effort began, Henderson and his team have effectively saved more than fifty million lives. This could be the most impressive achievement in the history of medicine. Henderson and his colleagues, however, have never received the Nobel Prize for their work.

D. A. Henderson is now a professor at the Johns Hopkins School of Public Health. He is the founder and the director of the Johns Hopkins Center for Civilian Biodefense Studies, a think tank that considers what might be done to protect the American population during a biological event. The term "biological event" hardly existed two years ago, but it is now used by emergency planners and by the F.B.I. to mean a terrorist attack with a bioweapon—an unnatural event, caused by human intent.

Henderson lives with his wife in a large brick house in Baltimore. I arrived there on a cold, drizzly Saturday, and he ambled to the door. Henderson is an imposing man, six feet two inches tall. He is seventy years old. He has broad shoulders and a broad, seamed, angular face, pointed ears that stick out at angles from his head, a brush of gray hair, metal-framed eyeglasses, sharp blue eyes, and an easygoing voice that can flash with calculation. He was wearing a red checked shirt, with suspenders that held up Saturday slacks.

"In the last ten days, we've had fourteen different anthrax scares," he remarked in an offhand way as we stood in the front hallway of his house and he loomed over me. He has a top-secret-level national-security clearance, and he hears about little bioterror events that don't get noticed by the media. He went on to say, "Everybody and his brother is threatening to use anthrax. This week, it happened in Atlanta, in Washington, D.C., in Michigan, and in California. It's largely hoaxes. Of course, a real bioterror event is going to happen one of these days."

We settled into easy chairs in the family room. The walls and shelves of the room were crowded with African and Asian sculptures and wooden Ethiopian crosses, which he had picked up in his global hunt for smallpox. A Japanese garden was visible through sliding-glass doors.

We ate ham and roast-beef sandwiches, and drank Molson Ice beers. Henderson bit into a sandwich and chewed thoughtfully. Then he said, "Often, you get a worried look on your face, with the first signs of rash. We speak of the 'worried face' of smallpox. That face is a diagnostic sign. The rash comes up all at once. It's more dense on the face and the extremities. That's how you can tell smallpox from chicken pox. With chicken pox, the rash crops up over a period of days, and it's more dense on the chest and trunk of the body. Smallpox pustules have a dimple, a dent in the center. Doctors say that the pustules have a 'shotty' feel, like shotgun pellets. You can roll them between your fingertips under the skin."

"How many doctors could recognize smallpox today?" I asked.

"Virtually none. Smallpox takes forms that even I can't diagnose. And I wrote the textbook." He is a co-author of "Smallpox and Its Eradication," a large book in red covers, which experts call the Big Red Book of Smallpox. It was supposed to be the final word on smallpox—the tombstone of the virus.

On February 15, 1972, a thirty-eight-year-old Muslim clergyman returned to his home town of Damnjane, in Kosovo, Yugoslavia, after he'd been on a pilgrimage to Mecca, stopping at holy sites in Iraq. I will call him the Pilgrim. A photograph of the Pilgrim shows a man who looks well educated, has an intelligent face, and is wearing a clipped mustache and a beret. He had travelled by bus for his entire journey. The morning after his return home, he woke up feeling achy. At first, he thought he was tired from the long bus ride, but then he realized that he had caught a bug. He shivered for a day or two, and developed a red rash brought on by his fever, but quickly recovered. He had been vaccinated for smallpox two months earlier. Indeed, the Yugoslav medical authorities had been vaccinating the population of Yugoslavia relentlessly for more than fifty years, and the country was considered to be thoroughly immunized. The last case of smallpox in Yugoslavia had occurred in 1930.

The Pilgrim's family members and friends came to visit him. They wanted to hear about his trip, and he enjoyed telling them about it. Meanwhile, variola particles were leaking out of raw spots in the back of his throat and mixing with his saliva. When he spoke, tiny droplets of saliva, too small to be seen, drifted around him in a droplet cloud. If the person is throwing off a lethal virus, the cloud becomes a hot zone that can extend ten feet in all directions. Although the raw spots in the Pilgrim's throat amounted to a tiny surface of virus emission, smaller than a postage stamp, in a biological sense it was as hot as the surface of the sun, and it put enough smallpox into the air to paralyze Yugoslavia.

Variola particles are built to survive in the air. They are rounded-off rectangles that have a knobby, patterned surface—a gnarly hand-grenade look. Some experts call the particles bricks. The whole brick is made of a hundred different proteins, assembled and interlocked in a three-dimensional puzzle, which nobody has ever figured out. Virus experts feel that the structure of a smallpox particle is almost breathtakingly beautiful and deeply mathematical—one of the unexplored wonders of the viral universe. The structure protects the virus's genetic material: a long strand of DNA coiled in the center of the brick.

Pox bricks are the largest viruses. If a smallpox brick were the size of a real brick, then a cold-virus particle would be a blueberry sitting on the brick. But smallpox particles are still extremely small; about three million smallpox bricks laid down in rows would pave the period at the end of this sentence. A smallpox victim emits several bricks in each invisible droplet of saliva that spews into the air when the person speaks or coughs. When an airborne smallpox particle lands on a mucus membrane in someone's throat or lung, it sticks. It enters a cell and begins to make copies of itself. For one to three weeks, the virus spreads from cell to cell, amplifying silently in the body. No one has discovered exactly where the virus hides during its incubation phase. Probably it gets into the lymph cells, confusing the immune system, and victims are said to experience terrible dreams.

On February 21st, when the Pilgrim had been feeling achy for almost a week, a thirty-year-old man, a schoolteacher, who is known to experts as Ljatif M., arrived in Djakovica, a few miles from the Pilgrim's town, to enroll in the Higher Institute of Education. Doctors who later investigated the schoolteacher's case never found out how he had come in contact with the Pilgrim. One of them must have ended up in the other's town. Possibly they stood next to each other in a shop—something like that.

On March 3rd, Ljatif developed a fever. Two days later, he went to a local medical center, where doctors gave him penicillin for his fever. Antibiotics have no effect on a virus. Then his skin broke with dark spots, and he may have developed a worried face. He felt worse, and a few days later his brother took him by bus to a hospital in the town of Cacak, about a hundred miles away. The dark spots were by this time merging into blackened, mottled splashes, which the doctors in Cacak didn't recognize. Ljatif became sicker. Finally, he was transferred by ambulance to Belgrade, where he was admitted to the Dermatology and Venereal Diseases Department of the city's main hospital. By then, his skin may have turned almost black in patches. We don't have access to his clinical reports, so I am describing a generalized extreme smallpox of the kind Ljatif had.

Inside the cells of the host, smallpox bricks pile up as if they were coming off a production line. Some of the particles develop tails. The tails are pieces of the cell's protein, which the virus steals from the cell for its own use. The tailed smallpox particles look like comets or spermatozoa. They begin to twist and wriggle, and they corkscrew through the cell, propelled by their tails toward the cell's outer membrane. You can see them with a microscope, thrashing with the same furious drive as sperm. They bump up against the inside of the cell membrane, and their heads make lumps, and the cell horripilates. Then something wonderful happens. Finger tubes begin to extend from the cell. The tubes grow longer. The cell turns into a Koosh ball. Inside each finger tube is a smallpox comet. The fingers lengthen until they touch and join nearby cells, and the smallpox comets squirm through the finger tubes into the next cell. The comets are protected from attack by the immune system, because they stay inside the finger tubes, where antibodies and killer white blood cells can't reach them. Then the Koosh ball explodes. Out pour heaps of bricks that don't have tails. These smallpox particles are wrapped in a special armor, like hand grenades. They float away, still protected by their armor, and they stick to other cells and go inside them, and those cells turn into Koosh balls. Each infected cell releases up to a hundred thousand virus particles, and they are added to the quadrillions of particles replicating in the universe of the ruined host.

Ljatif's skin had become blackened, mottled, and silky to the touch, and sheets of small blood blisters may have peppered his face. In a case of black pox, variola shocks the immune system so that it can't produce pus. Small blood vessels were leaking and breaking in his skin, and blood was seeping under the surface. His skin had developed large areas of continuous bruises.

On March 9th, the Belgrade doctors showed Ljatif to students and staff as a case that demonstrated an unusual reaction to penicillin. (In fact, a very bad reaction to penicillin can look like this.) Ljatif's eyes may have turned dark red. In hemorrhagic smallpox, one or two large hemorrhages appear in each eye, in the white encircling the iris, making the eyes look as if they could sag or leak blood. The eyes never do leak, but the blood in the eyes darkens, until the whites can sometimes seem almost black.

During the day of March 10th, Ljatif suffered catastrophic hemorrhages into the intestines. His intestines filled up with blood, and he expelled quarts of it, staining the sheets black, and he developed grave anemia from blood loss. For some unknown reason, black-pox patients remain conscious, in a kind of paralyzed shock, and they seem acutely aware of what is happening nearly up to the point of death—"a peculiar state of apprehension and mental alertness that were said to be unlike the manifestations of any other infectious disease," in the words of the Big Red Book of Smallpox. We can imagine that Ljatif was extremely frightened and witnessed his hemorrhages with a sense that his insides were coming apart. During the final phase of a smallpox intestinal bleedout, the lining of the intestines or the rectum can slip off. The lining is expelled through the anus, coming out in pieces or in lengths of tube. This bloody tissue is known as a tubular cast. When a smallpox patient throws a tubular cast, death is imminent. All we know about Ljatif is that his bleeds were unstoppable, that he was rushed to the Surgical Clinic of the Belgrade hospital, and that he died in the evening. The duty physician listed the cause of death as a bad reaction to penicillin.

"These hemorrhagic smallpox cases put an incredible amount of virus into the air," D. A. Henderson said. Some of the doctors and nurses who treated Ljatif were doomed. Indeed, Ljatif had seeded smallpox across Yugoslavia. Investigators later found that while he was in the hospital in Cacak he infected eight other patients and a nurse. The nurse died. One of the patients was a schoolboy, and he was sent home, where he broke with smallpox and infected his mother, and she died. In the Belgrade hospital, Ljatif infected twenty-seven more people, including seven nurses and doctors. Those victims infected five more people. Ljatif directly infected a total of thirty-eight people. They caught the virus by breathing the air near him. Eight of them died.

Meanwhile, the Pilgrim's smallpox travelled in waves through Yugoslavia. A rising tide of smallpox typically comes in fourteen-day waves—a wave of cases, a lull down to zero, and then a much bigger wave, another lull down to zero, then a huge and terrifying wave. The waves reflect the incubation periods, or generations, of the virus. Each wave or generation is anywhere from ten to twenty times as large as the last, so the virus grows exponentially and explosively, gathering strength like some kind of biological tsunami. This is because each infected person infects an average of ten to twenty more people. By the end of March, 1972, more than a hundred and fifty cases had occurred.

The Pilgrim had long since recovered. He didn't even know that he had started the outbreak. By then, however, Yugoslav doctors knew that they were dealing with smallpox, and they sent an urgent cable to the World Health Organization, asking for help.

Luckily, Yugoslavia had an authoritarian Communist government, under Josip Broz Tito, and he exercised full emergency powers. His government mobilized the Army and imposed strong measures to stop people from travelling and spreading the virus. Villages were closed by the Army, roadblocks were thrown up, public meetings were prohibited, and hotels and apartment buildings were made into quarantine wards to hold people who had had contact with smallpox cases. Ten thousand people were locked up in these buildings by the Yugoslav military. The daily life of the country came to a shocked halt. At the same time, all the countries surrounding Yugoslavia closed their borders with it, to prevent any travellers from coming out. Yugoslavia was cut off from the world. There were twenty-five foci of smallpox in the country. The virus had leapfrogged from town to town, even though the population had been heavily vaccinated. The Yugoslav authorities, helped by the W.H.O., began a massive campaign to revaccinate every person in Yugoslavia against smallpox; the population was twenty-one million. "They gave eighteen million doses in ten days," D. A. Henderson said. A person's immunity begins to grow immediately after the vaccination; it takes full effect within a week.

At the beginning of April, Henderson flew to Belgrade, where he found government officials in a state of deep alarm. The officials expected to see thousands of blistered, dying, contagious people streaming into hospitals any day. Henderson sat down with the Minister of Health and examined the statistics. He plotted the cases on a time line, and now he could see the generations of smallpox—one, two, three waves, each far larger than the previous one. Henderson had seen such waves appear many times before as smallpox rippled and amplified through human populations. Reading the viral surf with a practiced eye, he could see the start of the fourth wave. It was not climbing as steeply as he had expected. This meant that the waves had peaked. The outbreak was declining. Because of the military roadblocks, people weren't travelling, and the government was vaccinating everyone as fast as possible. "The outbreak is near an end," he declared to the Minister of Health. "I don't think you'll have more than ten additional cases." There were about a dozen: Henderson was right—the fourth wave never really materialized. The outbreak had been started by one man with the shivers. It was ended by a military crackdown and vaccination for every citizen.

At the present time, the United States' national stockpile of smallpox vaccine is a collection of four cardboard boxes that sit on a single pallet behind a chain-link fence inside a walk-in freezer in a warehouse in Lancaster County, Pennsylvania, near the Susquehanna River, at a facility owned by Wyeth-Ayerst Laboratories. The vaccine is slowly deteriorating. The Food and Drug Administration has put a hold on the smallpox vaccine, and right now no one can use it—not even emergency personnel or key government leaders.

The vaccine is owned by the federal government and is managed by Wyeth-Ayerst, which is the company that made it, twenty-five to thirty years ago. It is stored in glass vials. The vials contain freeze-dried nuggets of live vaccinia virus. Vaccinia is a mild virus. When you are infected with it by vaccination, it causes a pustule to appear, and afterward you are immune to smallpox for some years. People who have been vaccinated have a circular scar the

size of a nickel on their upper arm, left by the vaccinia-virus pustule they had in childhood after vaccination. Some adults can
remember how much the pustule hurt.

People from Wyeth periodically open the boxes and send some
of the vials out for testing, to see how the vaccine is doing. The
vials once held fifteen million good doses, but now moisture has
invaded some of them. The nuggets are normally dry and white in
color, but when moisture invades they turn brown and look sticky,
and the vaccine may be weakened. The vaccine was made by a traditional method: the manufacturer had a farm where calves were
raised. The calves' bellies were scratched with vaccinia virus, and
their bellies developed pustules. Then the calves were killed and
hung up on hooks, the blood was drained out of them, and the
pustules were scraped with a knife. The resulting pus was freeze-
dried. The vaccine is dried calf pus. According to one virologist
who examined it under a microscope, "It looks like nose snot. It's
all hair and wads of crap." It was a good vaccine for its time, but
the F.D.A. would never clear it for general use today except in a
national emergency. Furthermore, some people have bad or fatal
reactions to the vaccine. There is an antidote, but the supplies of it
have turned strangely pink, and the F.D.A. has put a hold on the
use of these supplies, too.

D. A. Henderson believes that in practice doctors could obtain
about seven million doses of vaccine from the vials. Unaccountably, most of the vaccine has not recently been tested for potency,
so it has not been absolutely proved to work. The experts believe
that it would work, but there still isn't enough.

Henderson explained the problem this way: "If there's a bioterror event, and someone releases enough smallpox to create a hundred cases—let's say in the Baltimore area—it would be a national
emergency. The demand for vaccine would be beyond all belief."
In Yugoslavia in 1972, the outbreak was started by one man, and
eighteen million doses of vaccine were needed—one for almost
every person in the country.

"That first wave after the bioterror event could be a hundred people with smallpox," Henderson said. "It takes two weeks after exposure before doctors can diagnose smallpox. Meanwhile, those hundred people will give smallpox to a thousand or two thousand people. That's the second wave. Some of those first hundred people will go to other cities—to Washington, to New York, all over. So the second wave will include cases in other American cities, and probably in foreign countries. By then, it'll be too late to treat them, and we'll lose the second wave. We'll be well into the third wave—ten to twenty thousand people with smallpox—before we can really start vaccinating people. By then, we'll begin to pick up so many cases in the Baltimore area that we won't be able to track cases, and we'll just have to vaccinate everybody around Baltimore. A lot of people in Baltimore work in Washington. And so you're going to have a whole lot of people in Washington with smallpox. You can see the deal. Immediately, you would have to vaccinate Washington." Henderson thinks that a hundred million doses of vaccine would be needed in the United States alone to stop a surging outbreak triggered by a hundred initial cases of smallpox from a bioterror event. That much vaccine could be stored in the space occupied by a one-car garage.

Raindrops splattered on a wooden deck in Henderson's garden, and the room grew dark, until it was a pool of shadows full of African masks. Henderson's voice came out of the gloom. He didn't bother to get up and turn on the lights. He said, "The way air travel is now, about six weeks would be enough time to seed cases around the world. Dropping an atomic bomb could cause casualties in a specific area, but dropping smallpox could engulf the world."

Henderson passionately wants to get rid of the virus. "What we need to do is create a general moral climate where smallpox is considered too morally reprehensible to be used as a weapon. That would make the possession of smallpox in a laboratory, anywhere, effectively a crime against humanity. The likelihood that it would be used as a weapon is diminished by a global commitment to destroy it. How much it is diminished I don't know. But it adds a level of safety."

In the late seventeen-hundreds, the English country doctor Edward Jenner noticed that dairymaids who had contracted cowpox from cows seemed to be protected from catching smallpox, and he thought he would do an experiment. Cowpox (it probably lives in rodents, and only occasionally infects cows) produced a mild disease. On May 14, 1796, Jenner scratched the arm of a boy named James Phipps, introducing into the boy's arm a droplet of cowpox pus that he'd taken from a blister on the hand of a dairy worker named Sarah Nelmes. A few months later, he scratched the boy's arm with deadly pus he had taken from a smallpox patient, and the boy didn't come down with smallpox. The boy had become immune. Jenner had discovered what he called vaccination, after the Latin word for cow. He saw the road to eradication clearly. In 1801, he wrote, "It now becomes too manifest to admit of controversy, that the annihilation of the Small Pox, the most dreadful scourge of the human species, must be the final result of this practice."

A Soviet epidemiologist, Viktor Zhdanov, deserves credit for kick-starting the modern effort. At the 1958 annual meeting of the World Health Assembly, in Minneapolis, he called for the global eradication of smallpox. He spoke passionately and logically, but the scientific community was skeptical. Many biologists held a common view that it was impossible to separate a wild microorganism from the ecological web it lived in. In 1965, President Lyndon Johnson endorsed the idea of smallpox eradication. It was a political move to help improve American-Soviet relations. D. A. Henderson was then the head of disease surveillance at the C.D.C. He was given an order to report to Geneva to head the W.H.O.'s new Smallpox Eradication Unit. He didn't want the job, but he was told that if he didn't take it he would have to resign from government service. He went to Geneva, where he formed a hand-picked team. "The World Health Assembly proposed a ten-year program, because Kennedy had said we could land a man on the moon in ten years," he recalled.

The team set a goal of vaccinating eighty per cent of the population of countries that harbored smallpox. Henderson says that from the beginning they had another idea as well, and it proved to be the key. The idea was to track smallpox outbreaks and vaccinate people in a ring around any outbreak. This is known as surveillance and ring vaccination. In order to throw a ring around smallpox, they had to know where the demon was moving at all times, and they started showing villagers photographs of a baby with smallpox, so that the villagers could recognize and report cases to the authorities.

Henderson's team needed a way of vaccinating people fast. They tried a machine called the Ped-o-Jet, which was operated by foot pedal. It could shoot jets of vaccine into the arms of thousands of people in a day, but it broke down. Then they tried a needle with two points. It was known as the bifurcated needle, and it looked like a tiny two-pronged fork. The points of the fork held a droplet of vaccine, and the needle was to be jabbed repeatedly into a person's arm. It could be used by a volunteer who had no medical training.

They discovered that the virus rose and fell in seasonal waves, like flu. This led to an idea to attack the virus with a ring assault when it was at its ebb. The virus was a wild organism that lived only in humans. It needed to find and invade a susceptible human every fourteen days or it would die. If each outbreak of the virus could be surrounded by a ring of immune people during the virus's low season, the virus would not be able to complete its fourteen-day life cycle. It would be cut off, unable to move to the next human host, and its chain of infection would be broken.

The ring had to be tight. If it developed a leak, smallpox would blow out. In January, 1975, smallpox blew out in Bangladesh, after the eradicators thought they were on the verge of stopping it everywhere in Asia. *Variola major* swept through more than five hundred towns and villages. Henderson began shuttling between Geneva and Bangladesh, and in April of that year, when things were still not under control, he visited the Infectious Disease Hospital in Dacca, the nation's capital. He wanted to do rounds in a smallpox ward. "I went down the rows of beds," he told me. There were seventy or eighty people, and half of them were dying. "There is nothing you can do for any of these patients. They were afraid to move. There were a lot of flies crawling all over the place. My God, they talk about the odor of smallpox. It *is* an odd smell, not like anything else."

The skin gives off gases. "It's a sickly odor, like rotting flesh, but it's not decay, because the skin remains sealed and the pus isn't leaking out," Henderson said. "That smell is one of the mysteries of smallpox. No one knows what it is. I was with this British guy, Nick Ward, M.D. He had worked in Africa—he was a tough guy. At the end, he stood by a fence looking at the ground. Finally, he said to me, 'I don't know that I could go through another situation like that again.'"

Nicholas Ward, who now lives in France, remembered that moment. "I've spent a fair amount of my life working with tropical diseases, and I can truly say there is nothing so awful as a case of smallpox, particularly the type where a person becomes a bloody mess," he said. He knew the odor. "I would have a shrewd idea of a diagnosis after walking into a home. I could smell it."

Henderson and his team mounted ring vaccinations across Bangladesh, and they traced cases and contacts, trying to surround the life form. Finally, in the fall of 1975, they cornered variola on an island off the coast of Bangladesh. It was a marshy, poor place called Bhola Island, and there, on October 16th, a three-year-old girl named Rahima Banu broke with the last case of naturally occurring *Variola major* anywhere on earth. She survived. Rahima Banu would be twenty-seven years old today; researchers have lost track of her. Doctors from the Smallpox Eradication Unit collected six of the girl's pustules after they had dried into scabs, peeling them off her skin gently, with tweezers. Two years later, on October 26, 1977, the last natural case of the mild type of smallpox, *Variola minor,* popped up in a cook in Somalia named Ali Maow Maalin. He survived, and the last ring tightened around variola, and its life cycle stopped.

The headquarters of the Centers for Disease Control, in Atlanta, is a jumble of old and new buildings, joined by elevated walkways, which give the place the feel of a maze. The buildings sit along Clifton Road, an artery that winds through green neighborhoods in the northeastern part of Atlanta. I arrived at the C.D.C. on a perfect day in spring. Changeable clouds marched across a deep sky, and oak trees were shedding green flowers. Across the street from the entrance, a blue jay screamed in a pine tree, and the branches glittered in the sun, throwing off a scent of pitch.

Joseph J. Esposito, Ph.D., who is the chief of the C.D.C.'s Poxvirus Section, led me along an outdoor walkway toward his laboratory and office. Esposito is a stocky man of moderate height, in his mid-fifties, who runs to keep his weight down, and he has a dark beard and wears eyeglasses over brown eyes that are perceptive and serious. I asked him if we could get closer to smallpox. We passed along an aerial walkway covered with a chain-link fence, and we turned onto another walkway. We stopped and leaned on a railing. We were facing the C.D.C.'s Level 4 biocontainment building. It contains the Level 4 hot suites—labs where researchers work with lethal viruses while wearing pressurized spacesuits. The building has a line of windows tinted blue-green, like fish tanks.

"The variola is in there somewhere," Joe Esposito said, offering me a grave smile and nodding at the Level 4 building. "There is a kind of electricity in the air when we're working with smallpox. Everybody around here always seems to know—'Joe's got the smallpox out of the freezer.'"

The smallpox freezer may be encircled by alarms and motion detectors. It may or may not be wrapped in chains. It may be a stainless-steel cylinder. Or it may be a white box intended to look like any other freezer. Officials at the C.D.C. won't comment.

Inside the freezer, the entire collection of smallpox occupies a volume slightly larger than that of a basketball. It consists of approximately four hundred little plastic vials the size of pencil stubs, the residue of D. A. Henderson's war with variola. They're an inch long and they have plastic screw caps. They sit in seven little white cardboard boxes, in a rack inside the freezer, which keeps the virus not strictly alive, not exactly dead, but potent. Most of the vials contain milky ice or bloody ice. The virus has been cultured in flasks of live cells (milky ice) or in live chicken eggs (live eggs have a blood system). Around twenty-five of the vials contain human scabs—dried smallpox pustules. The scabs look like pencil erasers.

The six scabs that were collected from the girl in Bangladesh named Rahima Banu used to sit in a vial, but recently Esposito's group used the last of her scabs for research. The strain that came out of her scabs is known as Bangladesh 1975—or, informally, as the Rahima. Now that the scabs are gone, the Rahima exists in vials of milky ice.

Esposito sat hunched in his chair in front of his computer. His office is a windowless room with cinder-block walls. A troll with Shocking-pink hair stood on top of the computer, staring at him wide-eyed. "I like to think like a virus," Esposito said. "If you can think like a virus, then you can begin to understand why a virus does what it does. A smallpox particle gets into a person's body and, in a way, it's thinking, I'm this one particle sitting here sur-rounded by an angry immune system. I have to multiply fast. Then I have to get out of this host fast. It escapes into the air before the pustules develop." By the time the host feels sick, the virus has already moved on to its next host. The previous host has become a cast-off husk (and is now becoming saturated with virus), but whether the person lives or dies no longer matters to the virus. However, the dried scabs, when they fall off, contain live virus. The scabs are the virus's seeds. They preserve it for a long time, just in case it hasn't managed to reach a host in the air. The scabs give the virus a second chance.

Poxviruses move easily through the animal kingdom. Along with herds of animals or swarms of insects come poxviruses cir-culating among them like pickpockets at a fair. Esposito once classified what he and other virologists have glimpsed of the poxviruses in nature. He noted monkeypox, swinepox, buffalo-pox, skunkpox, raccoonpox, gerbilpox, a few deerpoxes, a sealpox, turkeypox, canarypox, pigeonpox, starlingpox, peacockpox, dol-phinpox, Nile crocodilepox, penguinpox, two kangaroopoxes, and a quokkapox. (The quokka is an Australian wallaby.) Any attempt to get to the bottom of the butterflypoxes, mothpoxes, and beetle-poxes would be something like enumerating the nine billion names of God.

A caterpillar that has caught an insectpox dissolves into a liq-uefaction of insect guts mixed with pure crystals of poxvirus. This is known as a virus melt. The melt pours out of the dead caterpil-lar, and other caterpillars come along and accidentally eat the crystals lying on a leaf, and *they* melt, and so it goes for millions of years in the happy life of an insectpox. "It is a good thing no per-son has been known to catch an insectpox," Esposito remarked. (You might avoid eating melted caterpillars.) The yellow-fever mosquito, *Aedes aegypti*, suffers from a fatal mosquitopox. At least two midgepoxes torment midges. Grasshoppers are known to get at least six poxes. If a grasshopperpox breaks out in a swarm of African locusts, it can wipe them out with a plague.

Viruses have an ability to move from one type of host to another in what is known as a trans-species jump. The virus changes during the course of a jump, adapting to its new host. The trans-species jump is the virus's most important means of long-term survival. Species go extinct; viruses move on. There is something impressive in the trans-species jump of a virus, like an unfurling of wings or a flash of stripes when a predator makes a rush. Some fifty years ago, in central Africa, the AIDS virus apparently moved out of chimpanzees into people. Chimpanzees are now endangered, while the AIDS virus is booming.

For most of human prehistory, people lived in small groups of hunter-gatherers. The poxviruses did not deign to notice *Homo sapiens* as long as the species consisted of scattered groups; there was no percentage in it for a pox. With the growth of agriculture, the human population of the earth swelled and became more tightly packed. Villages became towns and cities, and people were crowded together in river valleys.

Epidemiologists have done some mathematics on the spread of smallpox, and they find that the virus needs a population of about two hundred thousand people living within a fourteen-day travel time from one another or the virus can't keep its life cycle going, and it dies out. Those conditions didn't occur in history until the appearance of settled agricultural areas and cities. At that point— roughly seven thousand years ago—the human species became an accident with a poxvirus waiting to happen.

Smallpox could be described as the first urban virus. It is thought to have made a trans-species jump into humans in one of the early agricultural river valleys—perhaps in the Nile Valley, or in Mesopotamia, or in the Indus River Valley. In the Cairo

Museum, the mummy of the Pharoah Ramses V, who died as a young man in 1157 B.C., is speckled with yellow blisters from face to scrotum.

In 1991, Joe Esposito and the molecular biologist Craig Venter, who was at the National Institutes of Health, sequenced the entire genome of the Rahima strain of smallpox; that is, they mapped all its DNA. They found that the virus contains a hundred and eighty-six thousand base pairs of DNA (each base pair being a step on the ladder of the molecule), and that the DNA contains about a hundred and eighty-seven genes—making smallpox one of the most complicated viruses known. (The AIDS virus has only ten genes.) A gene is a piece of DNA, which contains the recipe for making one protein. Esposito's team noticed that smallpox has a gene that is also found in the placenta of a mouse. Smallpox knows how to make a mouse protein. How did small-pox learn that? "The poxviruses are promiscuous at capturing genes from their hosts," Esposito said. "It tells you that smallpox was once inside a mouse or some other small rodent." D. A. Henderson speculates that the original host of smallpox may have been an African rodent that lived in a crescent of green forests along the southern Nile River. The forests disappeared, cut down by people, and possibly the rodent has gone extinct. This is only a guess. Smallpox moved on.

The principal American biodefense laboratory is the United States Army Medical Research Institute of Infectious Diseases, or USAMRIID, in Fort Detrick, Maryland—an Army base that nestles against the eastern front of the Appalachian Mountains in the city of Frederick, an hour's drive northwest of Washington. There is no smallpox at USAMRIID, for only the two W.H.O. repositories are allowed to have it. The principal scientific adviser at USAMRIID is Peter Jahrling, a civilian in his fifties with gray-blond hair, PhotoGray glasses, and a craggy face. Jahrling was the primary scientist during the 1989 outbreak of Ebola virus in Reston, Virginia: he discovered and named the Ebola-Reston virus.

"I don't think there is any higher biological threat to this nation than smallpox," Jahrling said to me, in his office, a windowless retreat jammed with paper. His voice was croaking. "I was over in Geneva for a meeting on smallpox, and I came back with some flu strain," he said hoarsely. The flu strain had swept through the world's smallpox experts. "Shows how fast a virus can move. If we have some kind of bioterror emergency with smallpox, there will be no time to start stroking our beards. We'd better have vaccine pre-positioned on pallets and ready to go."

Jahrling opposes the destruction of the official stocks of small-pox. "If you really believe there's a bioterrorist threat out there, then you can't get rid of smallpox," he said. "If smallpox is out-lawed, only outlaws will have smallpox." His group has been test-ing antiviral drugs that might work on smallpox, and he feels that in order to verify the effectiveness of a new drug it would be nec-essary to test it on live smallpox virus.

One of Jahrling's researchers, John Huggins, led me into the central areas of USAMRIID. Huggins is a chunky man with round Fiorucci eyeglasses. He turned into a corridor leading to the Level 4 spacesuit hot suites, or hot zones. The walls were cinder block, and the light turned bile green. A smoky reek drifted in the corri-dors, coming from huge autoclaves—pressure cookers—where contaminated equipment and waste were being heated and steril-ized after being brought out of a hot zone. We stopped at a door that had a window of thick glass, looking into hot suite AA5, the Ebola hot zone.

I pressed my nose against the glass. It was cool, and there was a faint rumble of blowers, keeping the zone at negative pressure, so that no contaminated air would flow out through cracks. The suite was dark and drowned in shadows, illuminated only by light coming from lab equipment. I could see no one in there but white mice in racks of plastic boxes. They were scribble-scrabbling in pine shavings.

"These mice are all infected with Ebola," Huggins said. "They bleed when they die. Like humans."

The mice looked fine. I couldn't see any blood in the shavings.

"We're giving them an antiviral drug that saves their lives," Huggins explained. "They're kind of perky. It's called an S.A.H. drug. It's not ready for human testing. It could work in humans, but we don't know."

In 1995, Huggins spent time in a spacesuit at the C.D.C. Level 4 lab in Atlanta, testing drugs on live smallpox. He found that a drug called cidofovir can block smallpox replication. Cidofovir, which is normally used against a virus that infects AIDS patients, has drawbacks. It must be given to people by I.V. drip, and there is some concern that it might damage the kidneys. Huggins and Jahrling believe that within five years better smallpox drugs are likely to be discovered. They say they will need to test the drugs directly on the virus. They add that the drug must be tested on the live virus in order to receive F.D.A. approval.

In March, a committee of the highly respected Institute of Medicine, in Washington, D.C., concluded that one of the main reasons for retaining live smallpox virus would be to help develop drugs against it. D. A. Henderson, who was not a member of the Institute of Medicine committee and thoroughly disagrees with its conclusions, thought that Jahrling was being too optimistic. "To get a new antiviral drug against smallpox is going to cost three hundred million dollars," he said. "The money simply isn't there."

Jahrling stood his ground. "Ceremonial destruction of small-pox is the crown jewel in D. A. Henderson's career," he said. "He would like to throw the lever on smallpox himself. If I had spent my life tramping the planet to eradicate the virus, I would want to throw the lever, too. What he did was a great accomplishment, but he has become blinded by the last glittering crown jewel of total eradication."

Ken Alibek, who was once Kanatjan Alibekov, a leading Soviet bioweaponeer and the inventor of the world's most powerful anthrax, shocked the American intelligence community when he defected, in 1992, and revealed how far the Soviet Union had gone with bioweapons. In a new book of his, entitled "Biohazard," Alibek says that there were twenty tons of liquid smallpox kept on hand at Soviet military bases; it was kept ready for loading on biowarheads on missiles targeted on American cities. I contacted certain government sources and asked them if there was any evidence to corroborate Alibek's claims.

One person who asked not to be named said, "I really have to be careful what I say. Yeah, Alibek's claims have been corroborated in multiple ways. There's not a lot of evidence. There's some."

Another person who asked not to be named said that the Soviet Union had put the biowarheads on ICBM missiles and test launched them sometime before 1991 over the Pacific Ocean. The United States—probably using spy satellites that orbited near the tests—was able to monitor the missiles as they soared into space and then punched back through the atmosphere and landed in the sea. The warheads were spinning weirdly: they were unusually heavy, and they had a strange shape. The warhead was heavy because it had an active refrigeration system to keep its temperature near or below the boiling temperature of water during reëntry. Nuclear warheads don't need to be actively cooled. Why would a warhead need to be cooled? Presumably, because it was designed to contain something alive. But what? The person said, "The warhead was built to carry a very small quantity of biological weapon. Anthrax wouldn't have worked too well, because you need to put a lot of anthrax in the air to kill people, and anthrax isn't contagious. With smallpox, you don't need much. If you use smallpox, you get around the most difficult technical problem of bioweapons—the problem of dissemination. With smallpox, you use people as disseminators."

In 1989, a Soviet biologist named Vladimir Pasechnik defected to Britain. British intelligence agents spent a year debriefing him in a safe house. By the end, the British agents felt they had confirmed that the U.S.S.R. had biological missiles aimed at the United States. This information reached President George Bush and the British Prime Minister, Margaret Thatcher. Mrs. Thatcher then apparently telephoned the Soviet leader, Mikhail Gorbachev, and sternly confronted him. She was furious, and so was Bush. Gorbachev responded by allowing a small, secret team of American and British biological-weapons inspectors to tour Soviet biowarfare facilities. In January of 1991, the inspectors travelled across the U.S.S.R., getting whirlwind looks at some of the major clandestine bases of the Soviet biowarfare program, which was called Biopreparat. The inspectors were frightened by what they discovered. ("I would describe it as scary, and I feel a responsibility to tell the world medical community about what I saw, because doctors could face these diseases," an inspector, Frank Malinoski, M.D., Ph.D., said to me.) On January 14th, the team arrived at Vector, the main virology complex, in Siberia, and the next day, after being treated to vodka and piles of caviar, they were shown into a laboratory called Building 6, where one of the inspectors, David Kelly, took a technician aside and asked him what virus they had been working with. The technician said that they had been working with smallpox. Kelly repeated the question three times. Three times, he asked the technician, "You mean you were working with *Variola major?*" and he emphasized to the technician that his answer was very important. The technician responded emphatically that it was *Variola major*. Kelly says that his interpreter was the best Russian interpreter the British government has. "There was no ambiguity," Kelly says.

The inspectors were stunned. Vector was not supposed to have any smallpox at all, much less be working with it. All the Russian smallpox stocks were supposed to be kept in one freezer in Moscow, which was supposed to be under the control of the World Health Organization. For Vector to have smallpox would be a supreme violation of rules set down by the W.H.O.

Then they went upstairs into Building 6, and entered a long corridor. On one side was a line of glass windows looking in on a giant airtight steel chamber of a type known as a dynamic aerosol test chamber. The device is for testing bioweapons. Small explosives are detonated inside the chamber, throwing a biological agent into the air of the chamber. The chamber in Building 6 had an octopuslike structure of tubes coming out of it where sensors could be attached or monkeys could be clamped with their faces exposed to the chamber's air. An airborne bioweapon would get into the sensors or into the animals' lungs. On the other side of the corridor was a room that Frank Malinoski said "looked like a NASA control room," and video cameras provided views inside the chamber, so that Vector scientists could watch the release of a bioweapon.

Vector scientists later told the inspectors that the chamber was a Model UKZD–25—a bioweapons explosion-test chamber. It was the largest and most sophisticated modern bioweapons test chamber that has ever been found by inspectors in any country. It was used for testing smallpox.

The inspectors asked to put on spacesuits and to go inside. (They had brought along Q-Tip-like swab kits: they would have liked to swab the inner walls of the chamber, in the hope of collecting a virus.) The Russians refused. "They said our vaccines might not protect us," Malinoski says. "It suggested that they had developed viruses that were resistant to American vaccines." The Russians ordered the inspectors to leave Building 6.

At a large gathering that evening, three inspectors—David Kelly, Frank Malinoski, and Christopher Davis—publicly confronted the head of Vector, a virologist named Lev Sandakhchiev, about Vector's smallpox. (His name is pronounced "Sun-dock-chev.") He backpedalled angrily. Davis, a medical doctor with a Ph.D. who was then with British intelligence, now recalls, "Lev is gnomelike, a short man with a wizened, weather-beaten, lined face, and black hair. He's very bright and capable, a tough individual, full of bonhomie, but he can be very nasty when he is upset." Sandakhchiev heatedly insisted that his technician had misspoken. He called on his deputy, Sergei Netesov, to support him. The two Vector leaders insisted that there had been no work with smallpox at Vector. They had been doing genetic engineering with smallpox genes, they said, but Vector didn't have any live smallpox, only the virus's DNA—and the more they spoke the murkier their statements seemed. David Kelly remembers, "They were both lying, and it was a very, very tense moment. It seemed like an eternity, but it only lasted about fifteen minutes. And then there were so many other aspects of Vector we had to explore."

"The brazenness of these people!" one inspector later fumed. "They had been testing smallpox in their explosion chamber the week before we arrived."

Lev Sandakhchiev is still the head of Vector. He declined to be interviewed for this account but has steadfastly maintained that no offensive bioweapons research occurs now at Vector. In January of this year, at the Geneva meeting of smallpox experts, Sandakhchiev delivered a paper (and may have caught their flu). In his paper he claimed that Vector did not have any smallpox until 1994, when, he said, Vector had obtained it legally from Moscow. D. A. Henderson was also at that meeting. "It was quite elaborate and quite unbelievable," Henderson said. "I rolled my eyes, and saw other people rolling their eyes at me. We're sitting there, he's presenting us with all this horseshit, and he *knows* it's horseshit. Sandakhchiev is lying flagrantly."

Four sources have suggested to me that Lev Sandakhchiev was in charge of a Vector research group that in 1990 devised a more efficient way to grow weapons-grade smallpox in industrial-scale pharmaceutical tanks known as bioreactors. The Vector smallpox bioreactors had a capacity of six hundred and thirty litres—virus tanks big enough for a microbrewery. Once the Vector scientists had worked out the details of variola manufacturing, the results were written up in master production protocols—recipe books—and these protocols ended up at the Russian Ministry of Defense, in Moscow. At the time, weapons-grade smallpox was being manufactured by two older methods at a top-secret virus-munitions production plant near the city of Sergiyev Posad, forty-five miles northeast of Moscow. At another virus-munitions plant, near Pokrov, about two hundred miles southeast of Moscow, military virus-production specialists converted the plant to the new Vector method of making smallpox in the large virus bioreactors, but apparently never started the reaction. When one considers that a single person infected with smallpox would be considered a global medical emergency, this is rather a lot of smallpox activity to have bubbling near Moscow. It means that live smallpox virus and the protocols for how to mass-produce it had spread to various places in Russia by the nineteen-nineties. Indeed, live smallpox could be bubbling in reactors now at Sergiyev Posad—no one in the United States government admits to having a clue, and no Russian journalists have seen the place. Peter Jahrling said, "I really think that Vector is out of the offensive BW [biowarfare] business. But Sergiyev Posad is the black hole. We have no contacts there, and the Russians won't allow us to visit the place."

These days, Lev Sandakhchiev has cordial relationships with Peter Jahrling and Joe Esposito. They are eager to draw their colleague into the circle of open international science. During their visits to Siberia, Sandakhchiev has come across to them as warm and human, and desperate for research money to support his institute.

Sometimes, candid remarks slip out from the Russians. Jahrling put it this way: "There were tons of smallpox virus made in the Soviet Union. We know that. The Russians have admitted that to us. I was in a room with one of the Vector leaders when he said to us, 'Listen, we didn't account for every ampule of the virus. We had large quantities of it on hand. There were plenty of opportunities for staff members to walk away with an ampule. Although we think we know where our formerly employed scientists are, we can't account for all of them—we don't know where all of them are.'" Today, smallpox and its protocols could be anywhere in the world. A master seed strain of smallpox could be carried in a person's pocket. The seed itself could be a freeze-dried lump of virus the size of a jimmy on an ice-cream cone.

While I was sitting with D. A. Henderson in his house, I mentioned what seemed to me the great and tragic paradox of his life's work. The eradication caused the human species to lose its immunity to smallpox, and that was what made it possible for the Soviets to turn smallpox into a weapon rivalling the hydrogen bomb.

Henderson responded with silence, and then he said, thoughtfully, "I feel very sad about this. The eradication never would have succeeded without the Russians. Viktor Zhdanov started it, and they did so much. They were extremely proud of what they had done. I felt the virus was in good hands with the Russians. I never would have suspected. They made twenty tons—twenty tons—of smallpox. For us to have come so far with the disease, and now to have to deal with this human creation, when there are so many other problems in the world . . ." He was quiet again. "It's a great letdown," he said.

For years, the scientific community generally thought that biological weapons weren't effective as weapons, especially because it was thought that they're difficult to disperse in the air. This view persists, and one reason is that biologists know little or nothing about aerosol-particle technology. The silicon-chip industry is full of machines that can spread particles in the air. To learn more,

I called a leading epidemiologist and bioterrorism expert, Michael Osterholm, who has been poking around companies and labs where these devices are invented. "I have a device the size of a credit card sitting on my desk," he said. "It makes an invisible mist of particles in the one-to-five-micron size range—that size hangs in the air for hours, and gets into the lungs. You can run it on a camcorder battery. If you load it with two tablespoons of infectious fluid, it could fill a whole airport terminal with particles." Osterholm speculated that the device could create thousands of smallpox cases in the first wave. He feels that D. A. Henderson's estimate of how fast smallpox could balloon nationally is conservative. "D.A. is looking at Yugoslavia, where the population in 1972 had a lot of protective immunity," he said. "Those immune people are like control rods in a nuclear reactor. The American population has little immunity, so it's a reactor with no control rods. We could have an uncontrolled smallpox chain reaction." This would be something that terrorism experts refer to as a "soft kill" of the United States of America.

The idea that a biological credit card could execute a soft kill of the United States has reached the White House. The chief terrorism expert on the National Security Council, Richard Clarke, has sent word through the federal government that getting national stockpiles of smallpox vaccine is a top priority.

The effort started four years ago. So far, the government has little to show except numerous meetings among agencies, with no hope of vaccine anytime soon. The Department of Defense has put all its vaccine efforts into something called the Joint Vaccine Acquisition Program, which is run by the Joint Program Office for Biological Defense. People inside the military don't want their names used when they talk about the Pentagon's efforts. "It's a fucking disaster," said one knowledgeable military officer who has had direct experience in the matter. Last year, the Pentagon hired a systems contractor called Dynport, headquartered in Reston, Virginia, to develop and make a number of different vaccines for troops. The smallpox-vaccine contract calls for three hundred thousand doses, at a cost of $22.4 million, or seventy-five dollars a dose, with delivery now scheduled for 2006. (The date has been pushed back at least once already.) This amount of vaccine could be made in about fifteen flasks the size of soda bottles. There are 2.3 million people in the armed forces, and they have several million more dependents. "Three hundred thousand doses is not enough vaccine to protect anyone—not even our troops. It totally ignores the fact that smallpox is contagious," one military man said. "These guys ought to be buying tank treads and belt buckles. They know nothing about vaccines."

The Department of Health and Human Services (H.H.S.) has been given the responsibility by the White House for producing a stockpile of smallpox vaccine large enough to protect the American civilian population in case of a bioterror event; originally, the idea was for H.H.S. to consider hiring the military's contractor, Dynport, to make forty million extra doses, in addition to the three hundred thousand that Dynport was making for the Pentagon. (Any such initiative would require competitive bidding.)

At a series of meetings at H.H.S., a top Dynport executive said that forty million doses could be quite expensive. One scientist asked if a group of knowledgeable people could be drawn together to come up with an estimate of costs. The Dynport man answered, "Yes, we can do a study that will list the questions that need to be asked. It will cost two hundred and forty thousand dollars and will take six weeks."

Somebody then asked how much it would cost to *answer* the questions. The Dynport official responded, "That will be a different study. That study will cost two million dollars and will take six months."

With that, one scientist at the meeting burst out, "This is horseshit! We're asking an encyclopedia salesman if we need an encyclopedia!"

The C.E.O. of Dynport, Stephen Prior, said that the situation is more complicated: "The civilian population is very different from the military. There's an age spread from newborns to the elderly; there's more compromised immunity, with AIDS, chemotherapy, and organ transplants. And possibly thirty-five per cent of people have never been vaccinated. So it's not just scaling up the manufacturing."

Another knowledgeable observer is the retired Army General Philip K. Russell, M.D., who gave the order to send biohazard troops into Reston in 1989 to deal with a building full of monkeys infected with Ebola. Russell said to me, "Many of us are afraid that Dynport won't deliver the goods without wasting an inordinate amount of money."

However, H.H.S. has quietly opened talks with other potential contractors, preparing to solicit bids to make a civilian stockpile of smallpox vaccine, though there has been no announcement. "The effort at H.H.S. still isn't organized," D. A. Henderson said. General Russell said, "If smallpox really got going, people should be most concerned about a lack of effective leadership on the part of their government."

I wanted to get closer to smallpox virus. In Joe Esposito's lab, at the Centers for Disease Control, there was a test going of a biosensor device for detecting smallpox. It was a machine in a black suitcase. It could detect a bioweapon using the process called the polymerase chain reaction, or P.C.R.—the same kind of molecular fingerprinting that police use to identify the DNA of a crime suspect. The suitcase thing was called a Cepheid Briefcase Smart Cycler, and it had been co-invented by M. Allen Northrup, a biomedical engineer who founded a company to make and sell biosensors. He was there, along with a cluster of other scientists.

Esposito, the official guardian of one half of the world's official supply of smallpox, handed a box of tubes to a scientist in the room. Two of the tubes contained the whole DNA of smallpox virus but not live smallpox. The DNA drifted in a drop of water; it was the Rahima strain. Two other tubes contained anthrax. The samples were snapped into slots in the machine.

Northrup turned his attention to a laptop computer that nestled in the machine. Northrup is a chunky man with a mustache and reddish-brown hair. He tapped on the keys.

We waited around, chatting. Meanwhile, the Cepheid was working silently. It showed colored lines on its screen. In fifteen minutes, the anthrax lines started going straight up, and someone said, "The anthrax is screaming." Finally, one of the smallpox lines crept upward, slowly. "That's a positive for smallpox, not so bad," a scientist said. Emergency-response teams could carry a Cepheid suitcase to the scene of a bioterror event and begin testing people immediately for anthrax or smallpox. The machine is priced at sixty thousand dollars.

Afterward, Joe Esposito went around collecting the used tubes. The smallpox-sample holder—a plastic thing the size of a thumbnail—had been left on a counter. I picked it up.

Esposito wasn't about to let anyone walk off with smallpox. "Leave me that tube," he said. "You are not allowed to have more than twenty per cent of the DNA."

Before I handed it to him, I glanced at a little window in the tube. When I held it up to the light, the liquid looked like clear water. The water contained the whole molecules of life from variola, a parasite that had colonized us thousands of years ago. We had almost freed ourselves of it, but we found we had developed a strong affinity for smallpox. Some of us had made it into a weapon, and now we couldn't get rid of it. I wondered if we ever would, for the story of our entanglement with smallpox is not yet ended.

Clock of Ages

In a wonderfully original and contrarian look at millennial legacies, Brian Hayes examines a triumphantly ingenious nineteenth-century clock designed to last 10,000 years. More than a description of technical virtuosity, this erudite and stylishly articulated essay casts light on the Y2K non-crisis and our sense of the future.

Brian Hayes

Clock of Ages

When one millennium's bright ideas become inscrutable legacies for the next

As the world spirals on toward 01–01–00, survivalists are hoarding cash, canned goods and shotgun shells. It's not the Rapture or the Revolution they await, but a technological apocalypse. Y2K! The lights are going out, they warn. Banks may fail. Airplanes may crash. Your VCR will go on the blink. Who could have foreseen such turmoil? Decades back, one might have predicted anxiety and unrest at the end of the millennium, but no one could have guessed that the cause would be an obscure shortcut written into computer software by unknown programmers in the 1960s and 1970s.

Whether or not civilization collapses on January 1, those programmers do seem, in hindsight, to have been pretty short on foresight. How could they have failed to look beyond year 99? But I give them the benefit of the doubt. All the evidence suggests they were neither stupid nor malicious. What led to the Y2K bug was not arrogant indifference to the future ("I'll be retired by then. Let the next shift fix it"). On the contrary, it was an excess of modesty ("No way *my* code will still be running thirty years out"). The programmers could not envision that their hurried hacks and kludges would become the next generation's "legacy systems."

Against this background of throwaway products that someone forgot to throw away, it may be instructive to reflect on a computational device built in a much different spirit. This machine was carefully crafted for Y2K compliance, even though it was manufactured when the millennium was still a couple of lifetimes away. As a matter of fact, the computer is equipped to run until the year 9999—and perhaps even beyond, with a simple Y10K patch. This achievement might serve as an object lesson to the software engineers of the present era. But I am not quite sure just what the lesson is.

The machine I speak of is the astronomical clock of Strasbourg Cathedral, built and rebuilt several times in the past 600 years. The present version is a nineteenth-century construction, still ticking along smartly at age 150-something. If all goes as planned, it will navigate the various calendrical cataracts of the coming months without incident, unfazed by January 1, 2000, or the subsequent February 29, or the revels of the latter-day millenarians on New Year's Day, 2001.

The Strasbourg Cathedral clock is not a tower clock, like Big Ben in London, meant to broadcast the hours to the city. It stands inside the cathedral in a case of carved stone and wood fifty feet high and twenty-four feet wide, with three ornamented spires and a gigantic instrument panel of dials and globes, plus a large cast of performing automata. Inside the clock is a glory of gears.

"Clock" is hardly an adequate description. More than a timepiece, it is an astronomical and calendrical computer. A celestial globe in front of the main cabinet tracks the positions of 5,000 stars, while a device much like an orrery models the motions of the six innermost planets. The current phase of the moon is indicated by a rotating globe, half gilt and half black.

If you want to know what time it is, the clock offers a choice of answers. A dial mounted on the celestial globe shows sidereal time, as measured by the earth's rotation with respect to the fixed stars. A larger dial on the front of the clock indicates local solar time, which is essentially what a sundial provides; the prick of noon by that measure always comes when the sun is highest overhead. The pointer for local lunar time is similarly synchronized to the height of the moon. Still another dial, with familiar-looking hour and minute hands, shows mean solar time, which averages out the seasonal variations in the earth's orbital velocity to make all days equal in length, exactly twenty-four hours. A second pair of hands on the same dial show civil time, which in Strasbourg runs thirty minutes ahead of mean solar time.

There's more. A golden wheel nine feet in diameter, marked off into 365 divisions, turns once a year, while Apollo stands at one side to point out today's date. What about leap years? Presto: an extra day magically appears when needed. Each daily slot on the calendar wheel is marked with the name of a saint or some church occasion. Of particular importance is the inclusion of Easter and the other "movable feasts" of the ecclesiastical calendar. Calculating the dates of those holidays requires feats of mechanical trickery.

For the Y2K police, the crucial component of the clock is, of course, the counter of years. It is an inconspicuous four-digit register that anyone from our age of automobiles will instantly recognize as an odometer. On December 31, at midnight mean solar time—and thus half an hour late by French official time—the digits will roll over from one-triple-nine to two-triple-zero.

Wait! There's even more! The clock is inhabited by enough animated figures to open a small theme park. The day of the week is marked by a slow procession of seven Greco-Roman gods in chariots. Each day at noon (that's mean solar noon) the twelve apostles appear, saluting a figure of Christ, who blesses each in turn. Every hour a putto overturns a sandglass. At various other times figures representing the four ages of man and a skeletal Death emerge to strike their chimes.

All of that apparatus is housed in a structure of unembarrassed eclecticism, both stylistic and intellectual. The central tower of the clock is topped with a froth of German-baroque frosting, whereas the smaller turret on the left (which houses the weights that drive the clockwork) has been given a more Frenchified treatment. The third tower, on the right, is a stone spiral staircase that might have been salvaged from an Italian Renaissance belvedere. In the base of the cabinet, two glass panels allowing a view of brass gear trains are a distinctively nineteenth-century element; they look like the store windows of an apothecary's shop. The paintings and statues are mainly on religious themes—death and resurrection, fall and salvation—but they also include portraits of Urania (the muse of astronomy) and Copernicus. Another painting portrays Jean-Baptiste Schwilgué, whose part in this story I shall return to presently.

It's all done with gears. Also pinions, worms, snails, arbors; pawls and ratchets; cams and cam followers; cables, levers, bell cranks and pivots.

The actual timekeeping mechanism—a pendulum and escapement much like the ones present in other clocks—drives the gear train for mean solar time. All the other astronomical and calendrical functions are derived from that basic, steady motion. For example, local solar time is calculated by applying two corrections to mean solar time. The first correction compensates for seasonal changes in the length of the day, the second for variations in the earth's orbital velocity as it follows its slightly elliptical path around the sun. The corrections are computed by a pair of "profile wheels" whose rims are machined to trace out a graph of the appropriate mathematical function. A roller, following the profile as the wheel turns, adjusts the speed of the local-solar-time pointer accordingly. The computation of lunar motion requires five correction terms and five profile wheels. They all have names: anomaly, evection, variation, annual equation, reduction.

The overall accuracy of the clock can be no better than the adjustment of the pendulum, which requires continual intervention, but for the subsidiary timekeeping functions there is another kind of error to be considered as well. Even if the mean solar time is exact, will all the solar, lunar and planetary indicators keep pace correctly? The answer depends on how well celestial motions can be approximated by rational arithmetic—specifically, by gear ratios. The Strasbourg clock comes impressively close. For example, the true sidereal day is twenty-three hours, fifty-six minutes, 4.0905324 seconds, whereas the mean solar day is, by definition, exactly twenty-four hours. The ratio of the two intervals is 78,892,313 to 79,108,313, but grinding gears with nearly 80 million teeth is out of the question. The clock approximates the ratio as the reciprocal of $1 + (450/611 \times 1/269)$, which works out to a sidereal day of twenty-three hours, fifty-six minutes, 4.0905533 seconds. The error is less than a second a century.

The most intricate calculations are the ones for leap years and the movable feasts of the church. The rule for leap years states that a year N has an extra day if N is divisible by 4, unless N is also divisible by 100, in which case the year is a common year, with only the usual 365 days—but if N happens also to be divisible by 400, the year becomes a leap year again. Thus 1700, 1800 and 1900 were all common years, but 2000 will have a February 29. How can you encode such a nest of if-then-else rules in a gear train?

The clock has a wheel with twenty-four teeth and space for an omitted twenty-fifth. That wheel is driven at a rate of one turn per century, and so every four years a tooth comes into position to actuate the leap-year mechanism. The gap where the twenty-fifth tooth would be takes care of the divisible-by-100 exception. For the divisible-by-400 exception, a second wheel turns once every 400 years. It carries the missing twenty-fifth tooth and slides it into place on every fourth revolution of the century wheel, just in time to trigger the quadricentennial leap year.

The display of leap years calls for as much ingenuity as their calculation. On the large calendar ring, an open space between December 31 and January 1 bears the legend *Commencement de l'année commune* ("start of common year"). Shortly before midnight on the December 31 before a leap year, a sliding flange that carries the first sixty days of the year ratchets backward by the space of one day, covering up the word *commune* at one end of the flange and at the same time exposing February 29 at the other end. The flange remains in that position throughout the year, then shifts forward again to cover up the twenty-ninth and reveal *commune* just as the following year begins.

The rules for finding the date of Easter are even more intricate than the leap-year rule. Donald E. Knuth, in his *Art of Computer Programming*, remarks: "There are many indications that the sole important application of arithmetic in Europe during the Middle Ages was the calculation of [the] Easter date." Knuth's version of a sixteenth-century algorithm for the calculation has eight major steps, and some of the steps are fairly complicated. Here (to paraphrase the mathematics slightly) is step five:

Calculate the sum $11G + 20 + Z - X$, where the numbers G, Z and X come from earlier steps in the algorithm. Now reduce that sum modulo 30—that is, divide by 30 and keep only the remainder. Label the result E, for the so-called epact, the "age" of the moon at the start of the year. Finally, if E is equal to 25 and G is greater than 11, or if E is 24, then increase E by 1.

Programming a modern computer to perform the Easter calculation requires some care; programming a box of brass gears to do the arithmetic is truly a tour de force. I have stared at diagrams of the gears and linkages, and tried to trace out their action, but I still don't fully understand how it all fits together.

In the abstract, it's not hard to see how a mechanical linkage could carry out the basic steps of the epact calculation. A wheel with thirty teeth or cogs would ratchet $11G$ notches clockwise, then add twenty steps more in the same direction, then another Z steps; finally, it would turn X steps counterclockwise. The "modulo 30" part of the program would be taken care of automatically if the arithmetic were done on a circle with thirty divisions. So far, so good. The thirty-tooth wheel does exist in the Strasbourg clock, and it is even helpfully labeled "*Epacte.*" Where I get lost is in trying to understand the various lever arms and rack-and-pinion assemblies that drive the epact wheel, and the cam followers that communicate its state to the rest of the system. There appear to be a number of optimizations in the works, which doubtless save a little brass but make the operation more obscure. Perhaps if I had a model of the clock that I could take apart and put back together. . . .

But never mind my failures of spatiotemporal reasoning. The mechanism does work. Each New Year's Eve a metal tag that marks the date of Easter slides along the circumference of the calendar ring and takes up a position over the correct Sunday for the coming year. All the other movable feasts of the church are determined by the date of Easter, so the indicators of their dates are linked to the Easter tag and move along with it.

The present Strasbourg clock is the third in a series. The first was built in the middle of the fourteenth century, just as the cathedral itself was being completed. The original clock had three mechanical Magi that bowed down before the Virgin and child every hour on the hour.

By the middle of the sixteenth century, the Clock of the Three Kings was no longer running and no longer at the leading edge of horological technology. To supervise an upgrade, the Strasbourgeois hired Conrad Dasypodius, the professor of mathematics at Strasbourg, as well as the clock maker Isaac Habrecht and the artist Tobias Stimmer. Those three laid out the basic plan of the instrument still seen today, including the three-turreted case and most of the paintings and sculptures. A curiosity surviving from that era is the portrait of Copernicus—a curiosity because the planetary display on the Dasypodius clock was Ptolemaic. The second clock lasted another 200 years or so.

The story of the third clock starts with an anecdote so charming that I can't bear to look too closely into its authenticity. Early in the 1800s, the story goes, a beadle was giving a tour of the cathedral, and mentioned that the clock had been stopped for twenty years. No one knew how to fix it. A small voice piped up: "*I will make it go!*" The boy who made the declaration was Jean-Baptiste Schwilgué, and forty years later he made good on his promise.

There was mild conflict over the terms of Schwilgué's commission. He wanted to build an entirely new clock; the cathedral administration wanted to repair the old one. They compromised: he gutted the works but kept the case, and built his new indicators and automata to fit the old design. The new mechanism began ticking on October 2, 1842.

Schwilgué was clearly thinking long-term when he undertook the project. As I noted earlier, the leap-year mechanism includes parts that engage only once every 400 years—parts that will soon be tested for the first time, and then lie dormant again until 2400. Such very rare events might have been left for manual correction: it would have been only a small imposition on the clock's maintainers to ask that the hands be reset every four centuries. But Schwilgué evidently took pride and pleasure in getting the details right. He couldn't know whether the clock would still be running in 2000 or 2400, but he could build it in such a way that if it *did* survive, it would not perpetrate error.

.   .   .

The contrast with recent practice in computer hardware and software could hardly be more stark. Some computer programs, even if they survive the Y2K scare, are explicitly limited to dates between 1901 and 2099. The reason for choosing that particular span is that it makes the leap-year rule so simple: it's just a test of divisibility by 4. Under the circumstances, that design choice seems pretty wimpy. If Schwilgué could take the trouble to fabricate wheels that make one revolution every 100 years and every 400 years, surely a programmer could write the extra line of code needed to check for the century exceptions. The line might never be needed, but there's the satisfaction of knowing it's there.

Other parts of Schwilgué's clock look even further into the future. There is a gear deep in the works of the ecclesiastical computer that turns once every 2,500 years. And the celestial sphere out in front of the clock has a still-slower motion. In addition to the sphere's daily rotation, it pirouettes slowly on another axis to reflect the precession of the equinoxes of the earth's orbit through the constellations of the zodiac. In the real solar system, that stately motion is what has lately brought us to the dawning of the age of Aquarius. In the clock, the once-per-sidereal-day spinning of the globe is geared down at a ratio of 9,451,512 to 1, so that the equinoxes will complete one full precessional cycle after the passage of a bit more than 25,806 years. (The actual period is now thought to be 25,784 years.) At that point we'll be back to the cusp of Aquarius again, and no doubt paisley bell-bottoms will be back in fashion.

The odometer of years, as I mentioned earlier, runs to 9999. According to some accounts, Schwilgué suggested that if the clock is still going in 10000, a numeral 1 could be painted to the left of the thousands digit. The simplicity of that proposed solution suggests that the Y10K crisis may turn out to be less severe than the Y2K one. Unfortunately, though, it appears that Schwilgué's clever little patch doesn't actually work for his own clock, at least not without some further tinkering. The pattern of leap years would continue correctly (assuming there is no change to the Gregorian calendar), but the date of Easter does not repeat on a 10,000-year cycle. If the Strasbourg clock treats 11999 as if it were identical to 1999, Easter will fall on April 4. In reality, that holiday 10,000 years from now should be celebrated on April 11.

In reality? Whose reality? From another point of view, worrying about the date of Easter in the 120th century is a sure sign we have left reality far behind. I hear another small child's voice piping up in the crowd gathered around the cathedral clock. The voice calls out: "Get a life!" Surely there must be *something* that needs doing more urgently than planning an Easter egg hunt for the spring of 11999.

Is there any chance the Strasbourg clock will actually run for 10,000 years? No products of human artifice have yet lasted so long, with the exception of cave paintings and some sharpened flints. Stonehenge and the pyramids of Egypt are half that age. The two earlier Strasbourg clocks, built with similar technology, both failed after roughly two centuries. Very few complex machines with moving parts have lasted more than a few hundred years.

Even if the clock keeps ticking, will anyone in 11999 want to know the date of Easter? Will people still be counting the years of the Common Era? No system of timekeeping has lasted anywhere near 10,000 years. The Roman calendar was abandoned after 1,500 years; the Mayan one may have lasted as long as 2,000 years, the Egyptian, possibly 3,000. The Chinese have been recording dates by cycles and reigns for something like 3,500 years. The Hebrew calendar is at the year 5760—but that's not to say the scheme has been in use that long (there was no one around, after all, to turn the page on 1 Tishri 1). The Julian day system was invented only 400 years ago. Meanwhile, other calendars have come and gone. If Schwilgué had rebuilt the Strasbourg clock just a few decades earlier, it would have listed dates in Brumaire, Thermidor, Fructidor and the other months decreed by the French Revolution in September 1792, and the clock's register of years would now be reading just 208.

I want to address another question. Even if a clock can be kept ticking, and even if the calendar it keeps retains some meaning, is the building of such multimillennial machines a good idea? I have my doubts, and they have been redoubled by a recent proposal to build another 10,000-year clock.

The new plan comes from Danny Hillis, the architect of the Connection Machine, an innovative and widely admired supercomputer of the 1980s (Hillis is now at the Walt Disney Corporation in Glendale, California). Together with several friends and colleagues he has proposed building a clock described as "the world's slowest computer." The project is outlined in *The Clock of the Long Now,* a book by Stewart Brand, the instigator of the *Whole Earth Catalog.*

Technical details of the Long Now clock remain to be worked out, but the provisional design that Brand describes has a torsion pendulum (one that twists rather than swings) and a digital counter of pendulum oscillations instead of an analog gear train. Although the counter is digital, it is emphatically not electronic; Hillis's design uses mechanical wheels, pegs and levers to count in binary notation.

The plan is to build several clocks of increasing grandeur. A prototype now under construction will be eight feet high. A twenty-foot model will be placed in a large city for ease of access, then a sixty-footer will be installed somewhere out in the desert for safekeeping. Here is one of Hillis's visions of how the big clock might be experienced:

Imagine the clock is a series of rooms. In the first chamber is a large, slow pendulum. This is your heart beating, but slower. In the next chamber is a simple twenty-four-hour clock that goes around once a day. In the next chamber, just a Moon globe, showing the phase of the lunar month. In the next chamber is an armillary sphere tracking the equinoxes, the solstices, and the inclination of the Sun. . . .

The final chamber is much larger than the rest. This is the calendar room. It contains a ring that rotates once a century and the 10,000-year segment of a much larger ring that rotates once every precession of the equinoxes. These two rings intersect to show the current calendrical date.

The motive for building such a monument to slow motion is not timekeeping per se; Hillis is not worried about losing count of the centuries. The aim is psychological. The clock is meant to encourage long-term thinking, to remind people of the needs and claims of future generations. The preamble to the project summary begins: "Civilization is revving itself into a pathologically short attention span. The trend might be coming from the acceleration of technology, the short-horizon perspective of market-driven economics, the next-election perspective of democracies, or the distractions of personal multitasking." The big, slow clock would offer a counterpoise to those frenetic tendencies; it would "embody deep time."

The wisdom of planning ahead, husbanding resources, saving something for those who will come after, leaving the world a better place—it's hard to quibble with all that. Concern for the welfare of one's children and grandchildren is surely a virtue—or at least a Darwinian imperative—and more general benevolence toward future inhabitants of the planet is also widely esteemed.

But if looking ahead two or three generations is good, does that mean looking ahead twenty or thirty generations is better? What about 200 or 300 generations? Perhaps the answer depends on how far ahead you can actually see.

The Long Now group urges us to act in the best interests of posterity, but beyond a century or two I have no idea what those interests might be. To assume that the values of our own age embody eternal verities and virtues is foolish and arrogant. For all I know, some future generation will thank us for burning up all that noxious petroleum and curse us for exterminating the smallpox virus.

From a reading of Brand's book, I don't sense that the Long Now organizers can see any further ahead than the rest of us; as a matter of fact, they seem to be living in quite a short Now. All those afflictions listed in their preamble—the focus on quarterly earnings, quadrennial elections and so forth—are bugaboos of recent years and decades. They would have been incomprehensible a few centuries ago, and there's not much reason to suppose they will make anybody's list of pressing concerns a few centuries hence.

The emphasis on the superiority of binary digital computing is something else that puts a late-twentieth-century date stamp on the project. A time may come when Hillis's binary counters will look just as quaint as Schwilgué's brass gears.

Long-term thinking is really hard. Of course, that's the point of the Long Now project, but it's also a point of weakness. It's hard to keep in mind that what seems most steadfast over the human life span may be evanescent on a geological or astronomical timescale. Consider the plan to put one clock in a city (New York, say) and another in a desert (Nevada). This makes sense now, but will New York remain urban and Nevada sparsely populated for the next 10,000 years? Many a desolate spot in the desert today was once a city, and vice versa.

Needless to say, the difficulty of predicting the future is no warrant to ignore it. The current Y2K predicament is clear evidence that a time horizon of two digits is too short. But four digits is plenty. If we take up the habit of building machines meant to last past 10000, or if we write our computer programs with room for five-digit years, we are not doing the future a favor. We're merely nourishing our own delusions. In the 1500s, Dasypodius and his colleagues could have chosen to restore the 200-year-old Clock of the Three Kings in Strasbourg Cathedral, but instead they ripped out all traces of it and built a new and better clock. Two hundred years later, Schwilgué was asked to repair the Dasypodius clock, but instead he eviscerated it and installed his own mechanism in the hollowed-out carcass. Today, after another two centuries, the Long Now group is not threatening to destroy the Schwilgué clock, but neither are they working to ensure its longevity. They ignore it. They want to build a newer, better, different clock, good for 10,000 years.

I begin to detect a pattern. The fact is, winding and dusting and fixing somebody else's old clock is boring. Building a brand-new clock of your own is much more fun, particularly if you can pretend that it's going to inspire awe and wonder for ages to come. So why not have the fun now and let the next 300 generations do the boring parts?

If I thought that Hillis and his associates might possibly succeed in this act of chronocolonialism, enslaving future generations to maintain our legacy systems, I would consider it my duty to posterity to oppose the project, even to sabotage it. But in fact I don't worry. I have faith in the future. Sometime in the 2100s a small child touring the ruins of the Clock of the Long Now will proclaim: "*I* will make it go!" And that child will surely scrap the whole mess and build a new and better clock, good for 10,000 years.

Digibabble, Fairy Dust, and the Human Anthill

Of all the concepts and buzzwords that have enthralled the world in the digital age, perhaps none has seemed as revolutionary—or as nebulous—as the notion of "convergence." Tom Wolfe, in his masterful essay, explores the sprawling implications of this latest obsession. Tying together three widely divergent forefathers of "convergent thinking"—priest and anthropologist Pierre Teilhard de Chardin, cultural critic Marshall McLuhan, and biologist E. O. Wilson—Wolfe reveals both the deeper roots and the inherent limitations of this seemingly new way of thinking.

Tom Wolfe

Digibabble, Fairy Dust, and the Human Anthill

T he scene was the Suntory Museum, Osaka, Japan, in an auditorium so postmodern it made your teeth vibrate. In the audience were hundreds of Japanese art students. The occasion was the opening of a show of the work of four of the greatest American illustrators of the 20th century: Seymour Chwast, Paul Davis, Milton Glaser, and James McMullan, the core of New York's fabled Push Pin Studio. The show was titled *Push Pin and Beyond: The Celebrated Studio That Transformed Graphic Design.* Up on the stage, aglow with global fame, the Americans had every reason to feel terrific about themselves.

Seated facing them was an interpreter. The Suntory's director began his introduction in Japanese, then paused for the interpreter's English translation:

"Our guests today are a group of American artists from the Manual Age."

Now the director was speaking again, but his American guests were no longer listening. They were too busy trying to process his opening line. *The Manual Age . . . The Manual Age . . .* The phrase ricocheted about inside their skulls . . . bounced off their pyramids of Betz, whistled through their corpora callosa, and lodged in the Broca's and Wernicke's areas of their brains.

All at once they got it. The hundreds of young Japanese staring at them from the auditorium seats saw them not as visionaries on the cutting edge . . . but as woolly old mammoths who had somehow wandered into the Suntory Museum from out of the mists of a Pliocene past . . . a lineup of relics unaccountably still living, still breathing, left over from . . . *the Manual Age!*

Marvelous. I wish I had known Japanese and could have talked to all those students as they scrutinized the primeval spectacle before them. They were children of the dawn of—need one spell it out?—the Digital Age. Manual, "freehand" illustrations? How brave of those old men to have persevered, having so little to work with. Here and now in the Digital Age illustrators used—what else?—the digital computer. Creating images from scratch? What a quaint old term, "from scratch," and what a quaint old notion . . . In the Digital Age, illustrators "morphed" existing pictures into altered forms on the digital screen. The very concept of postmodernity was based on the universal use of the digital computer . . . whether one was morphing illustrations or synthesizing music or sending rocket probes into space or achieving, on the Internet, instantaneous communication and information retrieval among people all over the globe. The world had shrunk, shrink-wrapped in an electronic membrane. No person on earth was more than six mouse clicks away from any other. The Digital Age was fast rendering national boundaries and city limits and other old geographical notions obsolete. Likewise, regional markets, labor pools, and industries. The world was now unified . . . online. There remained only one "region," and its name was the Digital Universe.

Out of that fond belief has come the concept of convergence.

Or perhaps I should say out of that *faith*, since the origin of the concept is religious; Roman Catholic, to be specific. The term itself, *convergence*, as we are using it in these pages, was coined by a Jesuit priest, Pierre Teilhard de Chardin. Another ardent Roman Catholic, Marshall McLuhan, broadcast the message throughout the intellectual world and gave the Digital Universe its first and most memorable name: "the global village." Thousands of dot.com dreamers are now busy amplifying the message without the faintest idea where it came from.

Teilhard de Chardin—usually referred to by the first part of his last name, Teilhard, pronounced TAY-yar—was one of those geniuses who, in Nietzsche's phrase (and as in Nietzsche's case), was doomed to be understood only after his death. Teilhard died in 1955. It has taken the current Web mania, nearly half a century later, for this romantic figure's theories to catch fire. Born in 1881, he was the second son among 11 children in the family of one of the richest landowners in France's Auvergne region. As a young man he experienced three passionate callings: the priesthood, science, and Paris. He was the sort of worldly priest European hostesses at the turn of the century died for: tall, dark, and handsome, and aristocratic on top of that, with beautifully tailored black clerical suits and masculinity to burn. His athletic body and ruddy complexion he came by honestly, from the outdoor life he led as a paleontologist in archeological digs all over the world. And the way that hard, lean, weathered face of his would break into a confidential smile when he met a pretty woman—by all accounts, every other woman in *le monde* swore she would be the one to separate this glamorous Jesuit from his vows.

For Teilhard also had glamour to burn, three kinds of it. At the age of 32 he had been the French star of the most sensational archeological find of all time, the Piltdown man, the so-called missing link in the evolution of ape to man, in a dig near Lewes, England, led by the Englishman Charles Dawson. One year later, when the First World War broke out, Teilhard refused the chance to serve as a chaplain in favor of going to the front as a stretcher bearer rescuing the wounded in the midst of combat. He was decorated for bravery in that worst-of-all-infantry-wars' bloodiest battles: Ypres, Artois, Verdun, Villers-Cotterêts, and the Marne.

Meantime, in the lulls between battles he had begun writing the treatise with which he hoped to unify all of science and all of religion, all of matter and all of spirit, heralding God's plan to turn all the world, from inert rock to humankind, into a single sublime Holy Spirit.

"With the evolution of Man," he wrote, "a new law of Nature has come into force—that of convergence." Biological evolution had created step one, "expansive convergence." Now, in the 20th century, by means of technology, God was creating "compressive convergence." Thanks to technology, "the hitherto scattered" species *Homo sapiens* was being united by a single "nervous system for humanity," a "living membrane," a single "stupendous thinking machine," a unified consciousness that would cover the earth like "a thinking skin," a "noösphere," to use Teilhard's favorite neologism. And just what technology was going to bring about this convergence, this noösphere? On this point, in later years, Teilhard was quite specific: radio, television, the telephone, and "those astonishing electronic computers, pulsating with signals at the rate of hundreds of thousands a second."

One can think whatever one wants about Teilhard's theology, but no one can deny his stunning prescience. When he died in 1955, television was in its infancy and there was no such thing as a computer you could buy ready-made. Computers were huge, hellishly expensive, made-to-order machines as big as a suburban living room and bristling with vacuum tubes that gave off an unbearable heat. Since the microchip and the microprocessor had not yet been invented, no one was even speculating about a personal computer in every home, much less about combining the personal computer with the telephone to create an entirely new medium of communication. Half a century ago, only Teilhard foresaw what is now known as the Internet.

What Teilhard's superiors in the Society of Jesus and the church hierarchy thought about it all in the 1920s, however, was not much. The plain fact was that Teilhard accepted the Darwinian theory of evolution. He argued that biological evolution had been nothing more than God's first step in an infinitely grander design. Nevertheless, he accepted it. When Teilhard had first felt his call to the priesthood, it had been during the intellectually liberal papacy of Leo XIII. But by the 1920s the pendulum had swung back within the church, and evolutionism was not acceptable in any guise. At this point began the central dilemma, the great sorrow—the tragedy, I am tempted to say—of this remarkable man's life. A priest was not allowed to put anything into public print without his superiors' approval. Teilhard's dilemma was precisely the fact that science and religion were not unified. As a scientist, he could not bear to disregard scientific truth; and in his opinion, as a man who had devoted decades to paleontology, the theory of evolution was indisputably correct. At the same time he could not envision a life lived outside of the church.

God knew there were plenty of women who were busy envisioning it for him. Teilhard's longest, closest, tenderest relationship was with an American sculptress named Lucile Swan. Lovely little Mrs. Swan was in her late 30s and had arrived in Peking in 1929 on the China leg of a world tour aimed at diluting the bitterness of her recent breakup with her husband. Teilhard was in town officially to engage in some major archeological digs in China and had only recently played a part in discovering the second great "missing link," the Peking man. In fact, the church had exiled him from Europe for fear he would ply his evolutionism among priests and other intellectuals. Lucile Swan couldn't get over him. He was the right age, 48, a celebrated scientist, a war hero, and the most gorgeous white man in Peking. The crowning touch of glamour was his brave, doomed relationship with his own church. She had him over to her house daily "for tea." In addition to her charms, which were many, she seems also to have offered an argument aimed at teasing him out of the shell of celibacy. In effect, the church was forsaking him because he had founded his own new religion. Correct? Since it was his religion, couldn't he have his priests do anything he wanted them to do? When she was away, he wrote her letters of great tenderness and longing. "For the very reason that you are such a treasure to me, dear Lucile," he wrote at one point, "I ask you not to build too much of your life on me. . . . Remember, whatever sweetness I force myself not to give you, I do in order to be worthy of you."

The final three decades of his life played out with the same unvarying frustration. He completed half a dozen books, including his great work, *The Phenomenon of Man.* The church allowed him to publish none of it and kept him in perpetual exile from Europe and his beloved Paris. His only pleasure and ease came from the generosity of women, who remained attracted to him even in his old age. In 1953, two years before his death, he suffered one especially cruel blow. It was discovered that the Piltdown man had been, in fact, a colossal hoax pulled off by Charles Dawson, who had hidden various doctored ape and human bones like Easter eggs for Teilhard and others to find. He was in an acute state of depression when he died of a cerebral hemorrhage at the age of 74, still in exile. His final abode was a dim little room in the Hotel Fourteen on East 60th Street in Manhattan, with a single window looking out on a filthy air shaft comprised, in part, of a blank exterior wall of the Copacabana nightclub.

The All-In-One Global Village

Not a word of his great masterwork had ever been published, and yet Teilhard had enjoyed a certain shady eminence for years. Some of his manuscripts had circulated among his fellow Jesuits, *sub rosa, sotto voce,* in a Jesuit *samizdat.* In Canada he was a frequent topic of conversation at St. Michael's, the Roman Catholic college of the University of Toronto. Immediately following his death, his Paris secretary, Jeanne Mortier, to whom he had left his papers, began publishing his writings in a steady stream, including *The Phenomenon of Man.* No one paid closer attention to this gusher of Teilhardiana than a 44-year-old St. Michael's teaching fellow named Marshall McLuhan, who taught English literature. McLuhan was already something of a campus star at the University of Toronto when Teilhard died. He had dreamed up an extracurricular seminar on popular culture and was drawing packed houses as he held forth on topics such as the use of sex in advertising, a discourse that had led to his first book, *The Mechanical Bride,* in 1951. He was a tall, slender man, handsome in a lairdly Scottish way, who played the droll don to a "T," popping off deadpan three-liners— not one-liners but three-liners—people couldn't forget.

One time I asked him how it was that Pierre Trudeau managed to stay in power as prime minister through all the twists and turns of Canadian politics. Without even the twitch of a smile, McLuhan responded, "It's simple. He has a French name, he thinks like an Englishman, and he looks like an Indian. We all feel very guilty about the Indians here in Canada."

Another time I was in San Francisco doing stories on both McLuhan and topless restaurants, each of which was a new phenomenon. So I got the bright idea of taking the great communications theorist to a topless restaurant called the Off Broadway. Neither of us had ever seen such a thing. Here were scores of businessmen in drab suits skulking at tables in the dark as spotlights followed the waitresses, each of whom had astounding silicone-enlarged breasts and wore nothing but high heels, a G-string, and rouge on her nipples. Frankly, I was shocked and speechless. Not McLuhan.

"Very interesting," he said.

"What is, Marshall?"

He nodded at the waitresses. "They're wearing . . . us."

"What do you mean, Marshall?"

He said it very slowly, to make sure I got it:

"They're . . . putting . . . us . . . on."

But the three-liners and the pop culture seminar were nothing compared to what came next, in the wake of Teilhard's death: namely, McLuhanism.

McLuhanism was Marshall's synthesis of the ideas of two men. One was his fellow Canadian, the economic historian Harold Innis, who had written two books arguing that new technologies were primal, fundamental forces steering human history. The other was Teilhard. McLuhan was scrupulous about crediting scholars who had influenced him, so much so that he described his first book of communications theory, *The Gutenberg Galaxy,* as "a footnote to the work of Harold Innis." In the case of Teilhard, however, he was caught in a bind. McLuhan's "global village" was nothing other than Teilhard's "noösphere," but the church had declared Teilhard's work heterodox, and McLuhan was not merely a Roman Catholic, he was a convert. He had been raised as a Baptist but had converted to Catholicism while in England studying at Cambridge during the 1930s, the palmy days of England's great Catholic literary intellectuals, G. K. Chesterton and Hilaire Belloc. Like most converts, he was highly devout. So in his own writings he mentioned neither Teilhard nor the two-step theory of evolution that was the foundation of Teilhard's worldview. Only a single reference, a mere *obiter dictum,* attached any religious significance whatsoever to the global village: "The Christian concept of the mystical body—all men as members of the body of Christ—this becomes technologically a fact under electronic conditions."

I don't have the slightest doubt that what fascinated him about television was the possibility it might help make real Teilhard's dream of the Christian unity of all souls on earth. At the same time, he was well aware that he was publishing his major works, *The Gutenberg Galaxy* (1962) and *Understanding Media* (1964), at a moment when even the slightest whiff of religiosity was taboo, if he cared to command the stage in the intellectual community. And that, I assure you, he did care to do. His father had been an obscure insurance and real estate salesman, but his mother, Elsie, had been an actress who toured Canada giving dramatic readings, and he had inherited her love of the limelight. So he presented his theory in entirely secular terms, arguing that a new, dominant medium such as television altered human consciousness by literally changing what he called the central nervous system's "sensory balance." For reasons that were never clear to me—although I did question him on the subject—McLuhan regarded television as not a visual but an "aural and tactile" medium that was thrusting the new television generation back into what he termed a "tribal" frame of mind. These are matters that today fall under the purview of neuroscience, the study of the brain and the central nervous system. Neuroscience has made spectacular progress over the past 25 years and is now the hottest field in science and, for that matter, in all of academia. But neuroscientists are not even remotely close to being able to determine something such as the effect of television upon one individual, much less an entire generation.

That didn't hold back McLuhan, or the spread of McLuhanism, for a second. He successfully established the concept that new media such as television have the power to alter the human mind and thereby history itself. He died in 1980 at the age of 69 after a series of strokes, more than a decade before the creation of the Internet. Dear God—if only he were alive today! What heaven the present moment would have been for him! How he would have loved the Web! What a shimmering Oz he would have turned his global village into!

But by 1980 he had spawned swarms of believers who were

ready to take over where he left off. It is they, entirely secular souls, who dream up our *fin de siècle* notions of convergence for the Digital Age, never realizing for a moment that their ideas are founded upon Teilhard's and McLuhan's faith in the power of electronic technology to alter the human mind and unite all souls in a seamless Christian web, the All-in-One. Today you can pick up any organ of the digital press, those magazines for dot.com lizards that have been spawned thick as shad since 1993, and close your eyes and riffle through the pages and stab your forefinger and come across evangelical prose that sounds like a hallelujah! for the ideas of Teilhard or McLuhan or both.

I did just that, and in *Wired* magazine my finger landed on the name Danny Hillis, the man credited with pioneering the concept of massively parallel computers, who writes, "Telephony, computers, and CD-ROMs are all specialized mechanisms we've built to bind us together. Now evolution takes place in microseconds. . . . We're taking off. We're at that point analogous to when single-celled organisms were turning into multicelled organisms. We are amoebas and we can't figure out what the hell this thing is that we're creating. . . . We are not evolution's ultimate product. There's something coming after us, and I imagine it is something wonderful. But we may never be able to comprehend it, any more than a caterpillar can comprehend turning into a butterfly."

Teilhard seemed to think the phase-two technological evolution of man might take a century or more. But you will note that Hillis has it reduced to microseconds. Compared to Hillis, Bill Gates of Microsoft seems positively tentative and cautious as he rhapsodizes in *The Road Ahead:* "We are watching something historic happen, and it will affect the world seismically." He's "thrilled" by "squinting into the future and catching that first revealing hint of revolutionary possibilities." He feels "incredibly lucky" to be playing a part "in the beginning of an epochal change . . . "

We can only appreciate Gates' self-restraint when we take a stab at the pages of the September 1998 issue of *Upside* magazine and come across its editor in chief, Richard L. Brandt, revealing just how epochally revolutionary Gates' Microsoft really is: "I expect to see the overthrow of the U.S. government in my lifetime. But it won't come from revolutionaries or armed conflict. It won't be a quick-and-bloody coup; it will be a gradual takeover. . . . Microsoft is gradually taking over everything. But I'm not suggesting that Microsoft will be the upstart that will gradually make the U.S. government obsolete. The culprit is more obvious. It's the Internet, damn it. The Internet is a global phenomenon on a scale we've never witnessed."

In less able hands such speculations quickly degenerate into what all who follow the digital press have become accustomed to: Digibabble. All of our digifuturists, even the best, suffer from what the philosopher Joseph Levine calls "the explanatory gap." There is never an explanation of just why or how such vast changes, such evolutionary and revolutionary great leaps forward, are going to take place. McLuhan at least recognized the problem and went to the trouble of offering a neuroscientific hypothesis, his theory of how various media alter the human nervous system by changing the "sensory balance." Everyone after him has succumbed to what is known as the "Web-mind fallacy," the purely magical assumption that as the Web, the Internet, spreads over the globe, the human mind expands with it. Magical beliefs are leaps of logic based on proximity or resemblance. Many primitive tribes have associated the waving of the crops or tall grass in the wind with the rain that follows. During a drought the tribesmen get together and create harmonic waves with their bodies in the belief that it is the waving that brings on the rain. Anthropologists have posited these tribal hulas as the origin of dance. Similarly, we have the current magical Web euphoria. A computer is a computer, and the human brain is a computer. Therefore, a computer is a brain, too, and if we get a sufficient number of them, millions, billions, operating all over the world, in a single seamless Web, we will have a superbrain that converges on a plane far above such old-fashioned concerns as nationalism and racial and ethnic competition.

I hate to be the one who brings this news to the tribe, to the magic Digikingdom, but the simple truth is that the Web, the Internet, does one thing. It speeds up the retrieval and dissemination of information, messages, and images, partially eliminating such chores as going outdoors to the mailbox or the adult bookstore, or having to pick up the phone to get ahold of your stockbroker or some buddies to shoot the breeze with. That one thing the Internet does, and only that. All the rest is Digibabble.

May I log on to the past for a moment? Ever since the 1830s, people in the Western Hemisphere have been told that technology was making the world smaller, the assumption being that only good could come of the shrinkage. When the railroad locomotive first came into use, in the 1830s, people marveled and said it made the world smaller by bringing widely separated populations closer together. When the telephone was invented, and the transoceanic cable and the telegraph and the radio and the automobile and the airplane and the television and the fax, people marveled and said it all over again, many times. But if these inventions, remarkable as they surely are, have improved the human mind or reduced the human beast's zeal for banding together with his blood brethren against other human beasts, it has escaped my notice. One hundred and seventy years after the introduction of the locomotive, the Balkans today are a cluster of virulent spores more bloody-minded than ever. The former Soviet Union is now 15 nations split up along ethnic bloodlines. The very zeitgeist of the end of the 20th century is summed up in the cry, "Back to blood!" The thin crust of nationhoods the British established in Asia and Africa at the zenith of their imperial might has vanished, and it is the tribes of old that rule. What has made national boundaries obsolete in so much of eastern Europe, Africa, and Asia? Not the Internet but the tribes. What have the breathtaking advances in communications technology done for the human mind? Beats me. SAT scores among the top tenth of high school students in the United States, that fraction who are prime candidates for higher education in any period, are lower today than they were in the early 1960s. Believe, if you wish, that computers and the Internet in the classroom will change all that, but I assure you it is sheer Digibabble.

The Little People

Since so many theories of convergence were magical assumptions about the human mind in the Digital Age, notions that had no neuroscientific foundation whatsoever, I wondered what was going on in neuroscience that might bear upon the subject. This quickly led me back to neuroscience's most extraordinary figure, Edward O. Wilson. Three years ago the first Big Issue of *Forbes ASAP* asked the question, "What will be the most important development in technology over the next 10 years?" My nomination was brain imaging, the recording of brain activity on-screen in real time. And why? Specifically because I saw brain imaging as a means, eventually, of testing Edward O. Wilson's arresting theories of the brain and human behavior. I dubbed him "Darwin II," for two reasons. He is a painfully devout Darwinist—more about that in a moment—and his influence as a scientist and an interpreter of the human condition is as great as Charles Darwin's was a century ago.

Wilson's own life is a good argument for his thesis, which is that among humans, no less than among racehorses, inbred traits will trump upbringing and environment every time. In its bare outlines his childhood biography reads like a case history for the sort of boy who today winds up as the subject of a tabloid headline: DISSED DORK SNIPERS JOCKS. He was born in Alabama to a farmer's daughter and a railroad engineer's son who became an accountant and an alcoholic. His parents separated when Wilson was 7 years old and he was sent off to the Gulf Coast Military Academy. A chaotic childhood was to follow. His father worked for the federal Rural Electrification Administration, which kept reassigning him to different locations, from the Deep South to Washington, D.C., and back again, so that in 11 years Wilson attended 14 different public schools. He grew up shy and introverted and liked the company only of other loners, preferably those who shared his enthusiasm for collecting insects. For years he was a skinny runt, and then for years after that he was a beanpole. But no matter what ectomorphic shape he took and no matter what school he went to, his life had one great center of gravity: He could be stuck anywhere on God's green earth and he would always be the smartest person in his class. That remained true after he graduated with a bachelor's degree and a master's in biology from the University of Alabama and became a doctoral candidate and then a teacher of biology at Harvard for the next half century. He remained the best in his class every inch of the way. Seething Harvard savant after seething Harvard savant, including one Nobel laureate, has seen his reputation eclipsed by this terribly reserved, terribly polite Alabamian, Edward O. Wilson.

Wilson's field within the discipline of biology was zoology; and within zoology, entomology, the study of insects; and within entomology, myrmecology, the study of ants. Year after year he studied his ants, from Massachusetts to the wilds of Suriname. He made major discoveries about ants, concerning, for example, their system of communicating via the scent of sticky chemical substances known as pheromones—all this to great applause in the world of myrmecology, considerable applause in the world of entomology, fair-to-middling applause in the world of zoology, and polite applause in the vast world of biology generally. The consensus was that quiet Ed Wilson was doing precisely what quiet Ed Wilson had been born to do, namely, study ants, and God bless him. Apparently none of them realized that Wilson had experienced that moment of blazing revelation all scientists dream of having. It is known as the "Aha!" phenomenon.

In 1971 Wilson began publishing his now-famous sociobiology trilogy. Volume one, *The Insect Societies,* was a grand picture of the complex social structure of insect colonies in general, starring the ants, of course. The applause was well nigh universal, even among Harvard faculty members who kept their envy and resentment on a hair trigger. So far Ed Wilson had not tipped his hand.

The Insect Societies spelled out in great detail just how extraordinarily diverse and finely calibrated the career paths and social rankings of insects were. A single ant queen gave birth to a million offspring in an astonishing variety of sizes, with each ant fated for a particular career. Forager ants went out to find and bring back food. Big army ants went forth as marauders, "the Huns and Tartars of the insect world," slaughtering other ant colonies, eating their dead victims, and even bringing back captured ant larvae to feed the colony. Still other ants went forth as herdsmen, going up tree trunks and capturing mealybugs and caterpillars, milking them for the viscous ooze they egested (more food), and driving them down into the underground colony for the night, i.e., to the stables. Livestock!

But what steered the bugs into their various, highly specialized callings? Nobody trained them, and they did not learn by observation. They were born, and they went to work. The answer, as every entomologist knew, was genetics, the codes imprinted (or hardwired, to use another metaphor) at birth. So what, if anything, did this have to do with humans, who in advanced societies typically spent 12 or 13 years, and often much longer, going to school, taking aptitude tests, talking to job counselors, before deciding upon a career?

The answer, Wilson knew, was to be found in the jungles of a Caribbean island. Fifteen years earlier, in 1956, he had been a freshly minted Harvard biology instructor accompanying his first graduate student, Stuart Altmann, to Cayo Santiago, known among zoologists as "monkey island," off the coast of Puerto Rico. Altmann was studying rhesus macaque monkeys in their own habitat. This was four years before Jane Goodall began studying chimpanzees in the wild in East Africa. Wilson, as he put it later in his autobiography, was bowled over by the monkeys' "sophisticated and often brutal world of dominance orders, alliances, kinship bonds, territorial disputes, threats and displays, and unnerving intrigues." In the evenings, teacher and student, both in their 20s, talked about the possibility of finding common characteristics among social animals, even among those as outwardly different as ants and rhesus macaques. They decided they would have to ignore glib surface comparisons and find deep principles, statistically demonstrable principles. Altmann already had a name for such a discipline, "sociobiology," which would cover all animals that lived within social orders, from insects to primates. Wilson thought about that—

Aha!

—human beings were primates, too. It took him 19 years and excursions into such esoteric and highly statistical disciplines as population biology and allometry ("relative growth of a part in relation to an entire organism") to work it out to the point of a compelling synthesis grounded in detailed observation, in the wild and in the laboratory, and set forth in terms of precise measurements. *The Insect Societies* had been merely the groundwork. In 1975 he published the central thesis itself: *Sociobiology: The New Synthesis*. Not, as everyone in the world of biology noticed, *A* new synthesis but *The* new synthesis. *The* with a capital *T*.

In the book's final chapter, the now famous Chapter 27, he announced that man and all of man's works were the products of deep patterns running throughout the story of evolution, from ants one tenth of an inch long to the species *Homo sapiens*. Among *Homo sapiens*, the division of roles and work assignments between men and women, the division of labor between the rulers and the ruled, between the great pioneers and the lifelong drudges, could not be explained by such superficial, external approaches as history, economics, sociology, or anthropology. Only sociobiology, firmly grounded in genetics and the Darwinian theory of evolution, could do the job.

During the furor that followed, Wilson compressed his theory into one sentence during an interview. Every human brain, he said, is born not as a blank slate waiting to be filled in by experience but as "an exposed negative waiting to be slipped into developer fluid." The negative might be developed well or it might be developed poorly, but all you were going to get was what was already on the negative at birth.

In one of the most remarkable displays of wounded Marxist chauvinism in American academic history (and there have been many), two of Wilson's well-known colleagues at Harvard's Museum of Comparative Zoology, paleontologist Stephen Jay Gould and geneticist Richard Lewontin, joined a group of radical activists called Science for the People to form what can only be called an "antiseptic squad." The goal, judging by their public statements, was to demonize Wilson as a reactionary eugenicist, a Nazi in embryo, and exterminate sociobiology as an approach to the study of human behavior. After three months of organizing, the cadre opened its campaign with a letter, signed by 15 faculty members and students in the Boston area, to the leading American organ of intellectual etiquette and deviation sniffing, the *New York Review of Books*. Theories like Wilson's, they charged, "tend to provide a genetic justification of the *status quo* and of existing privileges for certain groups according to class, race, or sex." In the past, vile Wilson-like intellectual poisons had "provided an important basis for the enactment of sterilization laws . . . and also for the eugenics policies which led to the establishment of gas chambers in Nazi Germany." The campaign went on for years. Protesters picketed Wilson's sociobiology class at Harvard (and the university and the faculty kept mum and did nothing). Members of INCAR, the International Committee Against Racism, a group known for its violent confrontations, stormed the annual meeting of the American Association for the Advancement of Science in Washington and commandeered the podium just before Wilson was supposed to speak. One goony seized the microphone and delivered a diatribe against Wilson while the others jeered and held up signs with swastikas—whereupon a woman positioned behind Wilson poured a carafe of ice water, cubes and all, over his head, and the entire antiseptic squad joined in the chorus: "You're all wet! You're all wet! You're all wet!"

The long smear campaign against Edward O. Wilson was one of the most sickening episodes in American academic history—and it could not have backfired more completely. As Freud once said, "Many enemies, much honor." Overnight, Ed Wilson became the most famous biologist in the United States. He was soon adorned with the usual ribbons of celebrity: appearances on the *Today Show,* the *Dick Cavett Show, Good Morning America,* and the covers of *Time* and the *New York Times Magazine . . .* while Gould and Lewontin seethed . . . and seethed . . . and contemplated their likely place in the history of science in the 20th century: a footnote or two down in the ibid. thickets of the biographies of Edward Osborne Wilson.

In 1977 Wilson won the National Medal for Science. In 1979 he won the Pulitzer Prize for nonfiction for the third volume of his sociobiology trilogy, *On Human Nature.* Eleven years later he and his fellow myrmecologist, Bert Hölldobler, published a massive (7½ pounds), highly technical work, *The Ants,* meant as the last word on these industrious creatures who had played such a big part in Wilson's career. The book won the two men Pulitzer Prizes. It was Wilson's second.

His smashing success revived Darwinism in a big way. Sociobiology had presented evolution as the ultimate theory, the convergence of all knowledge. Darwinists had been with us always, of course, ever since the days of the great man himself. But in the 20th century the Darwinist story of human life—natural selection, sexual selection, survival of the fittest, and the rest of it—had been overshadowed by the Freudian and Marxist stories. Marx said social class determined a human being's destiny; Freud said it was the Oedipal drama within the family. Both were forces external to the newborn infant. Darwinists, Wilson foremost among them, turned all that upside down and proclaimed that the genes the infant was born with determined his destiny.

A field called evolutionary psychology became all the rage, attracting many young biologists and philosophers who enjoyed the naughty and delicious thrill of being Darwinian fundamentalists. The influence of genes was absolute. Free will among humans, no less than among ants, was an illusion. The "soul" and the "mind" were illusions, too, and so was the very notion of a "self." The quotation marks began spreading like dermatitis over all the commonsense beliefs about human nature. The new breed, the fundamentalists, hesitated to use Wilson's term, sociobiology, because there was always the danger that the antiseptic squads, the Goulds and the Lewontins and the INCAR goonies and goonettes, might come gitchoo. But all the bright new fundamentalists were Ed Wilson's offspring, nevertheless.

They soon ran into a problem that Wilson had largely finessed by offering only the broadest strokes. Darwin's theory provided a wonderfully elegant story of how the human beast evolved from a single cell in the primordial ooze and became the fittest beast on earth—but offered precious little to account for what man had created once he reached the level of the wheel, the shoe, and the toothbrush. Somehow the story of man's evolution from the apes had not set the stage for what came next. Religions, ideologies, scholarly disciplines, aesthetic experiences such as art, music, literature, and the movies, technological wonders such as the Brooklyn Bridge and breaking the bonds of Earth's gravity with spaceships, not to mention the ability to create words and grammars and record such extraordinary accomplishments—there was nothing even remotely homologous to be found among gorillas, chimpanzees, or any other beasts. So was it really just Darwinian evolution? Anthropologists had always chalked such things up to culture. But it had to be Darwinian evolution! Genetics had to be the answer! Otherwise, fundamentalism did not mean much.

In 1976, a year after Wilson had lit up the sky with *Sociobiology: The New Synthesis,* a British zoologist and Darwinian fundamentalist, Richard Dawkins, published a book called *The Selfish Gene* in which he announced the discovery of memes. Memes were viruses in the form of ideas, slogans, tunes, styles, images, doctrines, anything with sufficient attractiveness or catchiness to infect the brain—infect, like virus, became part of the subject's earnest, wannabe-scientific terminology—after which they operated like genes, passing along what had been naively thought of as the creations of culture.

Dawkins' memes definitely infected the fundamentalists, in any event. The literature of Memeland began pouring out: Daniel C. Dennett's *Darwin's Dangerous Idea,* William H. Calvin's *How Brains Think,* Steven Pinker's *How the Mind Works,* Robert Wright's *The Moral Animal,* and, recently, *The Meme Machine* by Susan Blackmore (with a foreword by Richard Dawkins), and on and on. Dawkins has many devout followers precisely because his memes are seen as the missing link in Darwinism as a theory, a theoretical discovery every bit as important as the skull of the Peking man. One of Bill Gates' epigones at Microsoft, Charles Simonyi, was so impressed with Dawkins and his memes and their historic place on the scientific frontier, he endowed a chair at Oxford University titled the Charles Simonyi Professor of the Public Understanding of Science and installed Dawkins in it. This makes Dawkins the postmodern equivalent of the Archbishop of Canterbury. Dawkins is now Archbishop of Darwinian Fundamentalism and Hierophant of the Memes.

There turns out to be one serious problem with memes, however. They don't exist. A neurophysiologist can use the most powerful and sophisticated brain imaging now available—three-dimensional electroencephalography, the functional MRI, the PET scan, the PET reporter gene/PET reporter probe, which can cause genes in the brain to light up on a screen when they are being used—a neurophysiologist can try all these instruments and still not find a meme. The Darwinian fundamentalists, like fundamentalists in any area, are ready for such an obvious objection. They will explain that memes operate in a way analogous to genes, i.e., through natural selection and survival of the fittest memes. But in science, unfortunately, "analogous to" just won't do. The tribal hula is analogous to the waving of a wheat field in the wind before the rain, too. Here the explanatory gap becomes enormous. Even though some of the fundamentalists have scientific credentials, not one even hazards a guess as to how, in physiological, neural terms, the meme "infection" is supposed to take place. Although no scientist, McLuhan at least offered a neuroscientific hypothesis for McLuhanism.

So our fundamentalists find themselves in the awkward position of being like those Englishmen in the year 1000 who believed quite literally in the little people, the fairies, trolls, and elves. To them, Jack Frost was not merely a twee personification of winter weather. Jack Frost was one of the little people, an elf who made your fingers cold, froze the tip of your nose like an icicle, and left the ground too hard to plow. You couldn't see him, but he was there. Thus also with memes. Memes are little people who sprinkle fairy dust on genes to enable them to pass along so-called cultural information to succeeding generations in a proper Darwinian way.

Wilson, who has a lot to answer for, transmitted more than fairy dust to his progeny, however. He gave them the urge to be popular. After all, he was a serious scientist who had become a celebrity. Not only that, he had made the best-seller lists. As they say in scholarly circles, much of his work has been really quite accessible. But there is accessible . . . and there is cute. The fundamentalists have developed the habit of cozying up to the reader or, as they are likely to put it, "cozying up." When they are courting the book-buying public, they use quotation marks as friendly winks. They are quick to use the second person singular in order to make you ("you") feel right at home ("right at home") and italicized words to make sure you *get it* and lots of conversational contractions so you *won't* feel intimidated by a lot of big words such as "algorithms," which *you're* not likely to tolerate unless *there's* some way to bring you closer to your wise friend, the author, by a just-between-us-pals approach. Simple, *I'd* say! One fundamentalist book begins with the statement that "intelligence is what you use when you don't know what to do (an apt description of my present predicament as I attempt to write about intelligence). If you're good at finding the one right answer to life's multiple-choice questions, you're *smart*. But there's more to being *intelligent*—a creative aspect, whereby you invent something new 'on the fly'" (*How Brains Think* by William H. Calvin, who also came up with a marvelously loopy synonym for fairy dust: "Darwinian soft-wiring").

The Match Game

Meantime, as far as Darwin II himself is concerned, he has nice things to say about Dawkins and his Neuro Pop brood, and he wishes them well in their study of the little people, the memes, but he is far too savvy to buy the idea himself. He theorizes about something called "culturgens," which sound suspiciously like memes, but then goes on to speak of the possibility of a "gene-culture coevolution." I am convinced that in his heart Edward O. Wilson believes just as strongly as Dawkins in Darwinian fundamentalism. I am sure he believes just as absolutely in the idea that human beings, for all of their extraordinary works, consist solely of matter and water, of strings of molecules containing DNA that are connected to a chemical analog computer known as the brain, a mechanism that creates such illusions as "free will" and . . . "me." But Darwin II is patient, and he is a scientist. He is not going to engage in any such sci-fi as meme theory. To test meme theory it would be necessary first to fill in two vast Saharas in the field of brain research: memory and consciousness itself. Memory has largely defied detailed neural analysis, and consciousness has proven totally baffling. No one can even define it. Anesthesiologists who administer drugs and gases to turn their patients' consciousness off before surgery have no idea why they work. Until memory and consciousness are understood, meme theory will remain what it is today: amateur night.

But Wilson is convinced that in time the entire physics and chemistry, the entire neurobiology of the brain and the central nervous system will be known, just as the 100,000-or-so genes are now being identified and located one by one in the Human Genome Project. When the process is completed, he believes, then all knowledge of living things will converge . . . under the umbrella of biology. All mental activity, from using allometry to enjoying music, will be understood in biological terms.

He actually said as much a quarter of a century ago in the opening paragraph of *Sociobiology*'s incendiary Chapter 27. The humanities and social sciences, he said, would "shrink to specialized branches of biology." Such venerable genres as history, biography, and the novel would become "the research protocols," i.e., preliminary reports of the study of human evolution. Anthropology and sociology would disappear as separate disciplines and be subsumed by "the sociobiology of a single primate species," *Homo sapiens.* There was so much else in Chapter 27 to outrage the conventional wisdom of the Goulds and the Lewontins of the academic world that they didn't pay much attention to this convergence of all human disciplines and literary pursuits.

But in 1998 Wilson spelled it out at length and so clearly that no one inside or outside of academia could fail to get the point. He published an entire book on the subject, *Consilience,* which immediately became a best-seller, despite the theoretical nature of the material. The term "consilience" was an obsolete word referring to the coming together, the confluence, of different branches of knowledge.

The ruckus *Consilience* kicked up spread far beyond the fields of biology and evolutionism. *Consilience* was a stick in the eye of every novelist, every historian, every biographer, every social scientist—every intellectual of any stripe, come to think of it. They were all about to be downsized, if not terminated, in a vast intellectual merger. The counterattack began. Jeremy Bernstein, writing in *Commentary,* drew first blood with a review titled "E. O. Wilson's Theory of Everything." It began, "It is not uncommon for people approaching the outer shores of middle age to go slightly dotty." Oh, Lord, another theory of everything from the dotty professor. This became an intellectual drumbeat—"just another theory of everything"—and Wilson saw himself tried and hanged on a charge of *hubris.*

As for me, despite the prospect of becoming a mere research protocol drudge for evolutionism, I am willing to wait for the evidence. I am skeptical, but like Wilson, I am willing to wait. If Wilson is right, what interests me is not so much what happens when all knowledge flows together as what people will do with it once every nanometer and every action and reaction of the human brain has been calibrated and made manifest in predictable statistical formulas. I can't help thinking of our children of the dawn, the art students we last saw in the Suntory Museum, Osaka, Japan. Not only will they be able to morph illustrations on the digital computer, they will also be able to predict, with breathtaking accuracy, the effect that certain types of illustrations will have on certain types of brains. But, of course, the illustrators' targets will be able to dial up the same formulas and information and diagnose the effect that any illustration, any commercial, any speech, any flirtation, any bill, any coo has been crafted to produce. Life will become one incessant, colossal round of the match game or liar's poker or one-finger-two-finger or rock-paper-scissors.

Something tells me, mere research protocol drudge though I may be, that I will love it all, cherish it, press it to my bosom. For I already have a working title, *The Human Comedy,* and I promise you, you will laugh your head off . . . your head and that damnable, unfathomable chemical analog computer inside of it, too.

THE NEW YORKER

The Barber's Unhappiness

This funny, weird, cranky, startling, moving and tender tale reveals that its author has an uncanny knack for different voices. Bluntly described, it is a love story of an unlikely pair who find happiness. But no description could do justice to the pure, unrestrained glee of its telling. This story, the first of three fiction pieces in this book, is an exhilarating read—one that you won't want to end.

George Saunders

The Barber's Unhappiness

Mornings the barber left his stylists inside and sat out front of his shop, drinking coffee and ogling every woman in sight. He ogled old women and pregnant women and women whose photographs were passing on the sides of buses and, this morning, a woman with close-cropped black hair and tear-stained cheeks, who wouldn't be half bad if she'd just make an effort, clean up her face a little and invest in some decent clothes, some white tights and a short skirt maybe, knee boots and a cowboy hat and a cigarillo, say, and he pictured her kneeling on a crude Mexican sofa in a little mud hut, daring him to take her, and soon they'd screwed their way into some sort of bean field while gaucho guys played soft guitars, although actually he'd better put the gaucho guys behind some trees or a rock wall so they wouldn't get all hot and bothered from watching the screwing and swoop down and stab him and have their way with Miss Hacienda as he bled to death, and, come to think of it, forget the gauchos altogether, he'd just put some soft guitars on the stereo in the hut and leave the door open, although actually what was a stereo doing in a Mexican hut? Were there outlets? Plus how could he meet her? He could compliment her hair, then ask her out for coffee. He could say that, as a hair-care professional, he knew a little about hair, and boy did she ever have great hair, and by the way did she like coffee? Except they always said no. Lately no no no was all he got. Plus he had zero access to a bean field or mud hut. They could do it in his yard, but it wouldn't be the same, because Jeepers had basically made of it a museum of poop, plus Ma would call 911 at the first hint of a sexy moan.

Miss Hacienda passed through a gap in a hedge and disappeared into the Episcopal church.

Why was she going into church on a weekday? Maybe she had a problem. Maybe she was knocked up. Maybe if he followed her into the church and told her he knew a little about problems, having been born with no toes, she'd have coffee with him. He was tired of going home to just Ma. Lately she'd been falling asleep with her head on his shoulder while they watched TV. Sometimes he worried that somebody would look in the window and wonder why he'd married such an old lady. Plus sometimes he worried that Ma would wake up and catch him watching the black girl in the silver bikini riding her horse through that tidal pool in slow motion on 1–900-DREMGAL. He wondered how Miss Hacienda would look in a silver bikini in slow motion. Although if she was knocked up she shouldn't be riding a horse. She should be sitting down, taking it easy. Somebody should be bringing her a cup of tea. She should move in with him and Ma. He wouldn't rub it in that she was knocked up. He'd be loving about it. He'd be a good friend to her and wouldn't even try to screw her, and pretty soon she'd start wondering why not and start really wanting him. He'd be her labor coach and cheerfully change diapers in the wee hours and finally when she'd lost all the pregnancy weight she'd come to his bed and screw his brains out in gratitude, after which he'd have a meditative smoke by the window and decide to marry her. He nearly got tears in his eyes thinking of how she'd get tears in her eyes as he went down on one knee to pop the question, a nice touch the dolt who'd knocked her up wouldn't have thought of in a million years, the nimrod, and that S.O.B. could drive by as often as he wanted, deeply regretting his foolishness as the baby frolicked in the yard, it was too late, they were a family, and nothing would ever break them up.

But he'd have to remember to stick a towel under the door while meditatively smoking or Ma would have a cow, because after he smoked she always claimed everything smelled like smoke, and made him wash every piece of clothing in the house. And they'd better screw quietly if they weren't married, because Ma was old-fashioned. It was sort of a pain living with Ma. But Miss Hacienda had better be prepared to tolerate Ma, who was actually pretty good company when she stayed on her meds, and so what if she was nearly eighty and went around the house flossing in her bra? It was her damn house. He'd better never hear Miss Hacienda say a word against Ma, who'd paid his way through barber college, like for example asking why Ma had thick sprays of gray hair growing out of her ears, because that would kill Ma, who was always reminding the gas man she'd been a dish in high school. How would Miss Hacienda like it if after a lifetime of hard work she got wrinkled and forgetful and some knocked-up slut dressed like a Mexican cowgirl moved in and started complaining about her ear hair? Who did Miss Hacienda think she was, the Queen of Sheba? She could go into labor in the damn Episcopal church for all he cared, he'd keep wanking it in the pantry on the little milking stool for the rest of his life before he'd let Ma be hurt, and that was final.

As Miss Hacienda came out of the church she saw a thick-waisted, beak-nosed, middle-aged man rise angrily from a wooden bench and stomp into Mickey's Hairport, slamming the door behind him.

Next morning Ma wanted an omelette. When he said he was running late, she said never mind in a tone that made it clear she was going to accidentally on purpose burn herself again while ostensibly making her own omelette. So he made the omelette.

When he asked was it good, she said it was fine, which meant it was bad and he had to make pancakes. So he made pancakes. Then he kissed her cheek and flew out the door, very, very late for Remedial Driving School.

Remedial Driving School was being held in what had been a trendy office park in the Carter years and was now a flat white overgrown stucco bunker with tinted windows and a towable signboard that said "Driving School." Inside was a conference table that smelled like a conference table sitting in direct sunlight with some spilled burned coffee on it.

"Latecomers will be beaten," said the Driving School instructor.

"Sorry," said the barber.

"Joking!" said the instructor, thrusting a wad of handouts at the barber, who was trying to get his clip-ons off. "What I was just saying was that, our aim is, we're going to be looking at some things or aspects, in terms of driving? Meaning safety, meaning, is speeding something we do in a vacuum, or could it involve a pedestrian or fatality or a family out for a fun drive, and then here you come, speeding, with the safety or destiny of that family not held firmly in your mind, and what happens next? Who knows?"

"A crash?" said someone.

"An accident?" said someone else.

"I didn't hit nobody," said a girl in a T-shirt that said "Buggin'." "Cop just stopped me."

"But I'm talking the possibility aspect?" the instructor said kindly.

"Oh," said the Buggin' girl, who now seemed chastened and convinced.

Outside the tinted window were a little forest and a stream and an insurance agency and a FedEx drop-off tilted by some pipeline digging. There were six students. One was the barber. One was a country boy with a briefcase, who took laborious notes and kept asking questions with a furrowed brow, as if, having been caught speeding, he was now considering a career in law enforcement. Did radar work via sonar beams? How snotty did someone have to get before you could stun them with your stun gun? Next to the country boy was the Buggin' girl. Next to the Buggin' girl was a very, very happy crew-cut older man in a cowboy shirt and bolo tie who laughed at everything and seemed to consider it a great privilege to be here at the driving school on this particular day with this particular bunch of excellent people, and who by the end of the session had proposed holding a monthly barbecue at his place so they wouldn't lose touch. Across the table from the Happy Man was a white-haired woman who kept making sly references to films and books the barber had never heard of and rolling her eyes at things the instructor said, while writing "Help Me!" and "Beam Me Up!" on her notepad and shoving it across the table for the Happy Man to read, which seemed to make the Happy Man uncomfortable.

Next to the white-haired woman was a pretty girl. A very pretty girl. Wow. One of the prettiest girls the barber had ever seen. Boy was she pretty. Her hair was crimped and waist-length and her eyes were doelike and Egyptian and about her there was a sincerity and intelligence that made it hard for him to look away. She certainly looked out of place here at the conference table, with one hand before her in a strip of sunlight which shone on a very pretty turquoise ring that seemed to confirm her as someone exotic and darkish and schooled in things Eastern, someone you could easily imagine making love to on a barge on the Nile, say, surrounded by thousands of candles that smelled weird, or come to think of it maybe she was American Indian, and he saw her standing at the door of a tepee wearing that same sincere and intelligent expression as he came home from the hunt with a long string of dead rabbits, having been accepted into the tribe at her request after killing a cute rabbit publicly to prove he was a man of the woods, or actually they had let him skip the rabbit part because he had spoken to them so frankly about the white man's deviousness and given them secret information about an important fort after first making them promise not to kill any women or children. He pictured one of the braves saying to her, as she rubbed two corncobs together in the dying sunlight near a spectacular mesa, that she was lucky to have the barber, and silently she smiled, rubbing the corncobs together perhaps a little faster, remembering the barber naked in their tepee, although on closer inspection it appeared she was actually probably Italian.

The girl looked up and caught him staring at her. He dropped his eyes and began leafing through his course materials.

The instructor asked did anyone know how many Gs a person pulled when he or she went through a windshield at eighty miles per after hitting a cow.

No one knew.

The instructor said quite a few.

The Happy Man said he'd had a feeling it was quite a few, which was why, wasn't it, that people died?

"So what's my point?" the instructor said, pointing with his pointer to an overhead of a cartoon man driving a little car toward a tombstone while talking gaily on a car phone. "Say we're feeling good, very good, or bad, which is the opposite, say we've just had a death or a promotion or the birth of a child or a fight with our wife or spouse. Because what we then maybe forget is that two tons of car is what you are inside of, driving, and I hope not speeding, although for the sake of this pretend example I'm afraid we have to assume yes, you are, which is how this next bad graphic occurs."

Now on the overhead the cartoon man's body parts were scattered and his car phone was flying up to Heaven on little angel wings. The barber looked at the pretty girl again. She smiled at him. His heart began to race. This never happened. They never smiled back. Well, she was young. Maybe she didn't know better than to smile back at an older guy she didn't want. Or maybe she wanted him. Maybe she'd had it with young horny guys just out for quick rolls in the hay, and wanted someone old enough to really appreciate her, who didn't come too quickly and owned his own business and knew how to pick up after himself. He hoped she was a strict religious virgin who'd never had a roll in the hay. Not that he hoped she was frigid. He hoped she was the kind of strict religious virgin who, once married, would let it all hang out, and when not letting it all hang out would move with quiet dignity in conservative clothes so that no one would suspect how completely and totally she could let it all hang out when she chose to, and that she came from a poor family and could therefore really appreciate the hard work that went into running a small business, and maybe even had some accounting experience and could help with the books. Although truthfully, even if she'd had hundreds of rolls in the hay and couldn't add a stinking row of figures, he didn't care, she was so pretty, they'd work it out, assuming of course she'd have him, and with a sinking heart he thought of his missing toes. He remembered that day at the lake with Mary Ellen Kovski, when it had been over a hundred degrees and he'd sat on a beach chair fully dressed, claiming to be chilly. A crowd of Mary Ellen's friends had gathered to help her undress him and throw him in, and in desperation he'd whispered to her about his toes, and she'd gone white and called off her friends and two months later married Phil Anpesto, that idiotic beanpole. Oh, he was tired of hiding his toes. Maybe this girl had a wisdom beyond her years. Maybe her father had a deformity, a glass eye or a facial scar, maybe through long years of loving this kindly but deformed man she had come to almost need the man she loved to be somewhat deformed. Not that he liked the idea of her trotting after a bunch of deformed guys, and also not that he considered himself deformed, exactly, although, admittedly, ten barely discernible bright-pink nubs were no picnic. He pictured her lying nude in front of a fireplace, so comfortable with his feet that she'd given each nub a pet name, and sometimes during lovemaking she got a little carried away and tried to lick his nubs, although certainly he didn't expect that, and in fact found it sort of disgusting, and for a split second he thought somewhat less of her, then pictured himself gently pulling her up, away from his feet, and the slightly shamed look on her face made him forgive her completely for the disgusting thing she'd been about to do out of her deep deep love for him.

The instructor held up a small bloodied baby doll, which he then tossed across the room into a trunk.

"Blammo," he said. "Let's let that trunk represent a tomb, and it's your fault, from speeding. How then do you feel?"

"Bad," said the Buggin' girl.

The pretty girl passed the barber the Attendance Log, which had to be signed to obtain Course Credit and Associated Conviction Waivers/Point Reductions.

They looked frankly at each other for what felt like a very long time.

"Hokay!" the instructor said brightly. "I suppose I don't have to grind you into absolute putty, so now it's a break, so you don't view me as some sort of Marquis de Sade requiring you to watch gross visuals and graphics until your mind rots out."

The barber took a deep breath. He would speak to her. Maybe buy her a soda. The girl stood up. The barber got a shock. Her face was the same lovely exotic intelligent slim Cleopatran face, but her body seemed scaled to a head twice the size of the one she had. She was a big girl. Her arms were round and thick. Her mannerisms were a big girl's mannerisms. She hunched her shoulders and tugged at her smock. He felt a little miffed at her for having misled him and a little miffed at himself for having ogled such a fatty. Well, not a fatty, exactly, her body was O.K., it seemed solid enough, it was just too big for her head. If you could somehow reduce the body to put it in scale with the head, or enlarge the head and shrink down the entire package, then you'd have a body that would do justice to that beautiful, beautiful face that he, even now, tidying up his handouts, was regretting having lost.

"Hi," she said.

"Hello," he said, and went outside and sat in his car, and when she came out with two Cokes he pretended to be cleaning his ashtray until she went away.

A month or so later the barber sat stiffly at a wedding reception at the edge of a kind of mock Japanese tearoom at the Hilton while some goofball inside a full-body PuppetPlayers groom costume, complete with top hat and tails and a huge yellow felt head and three-fingered yellow felt hands, was making vulgar thrusting motions with his hips in the barber's direction, as if to say: Do you like to do this? Have you done this? Can you show me how to do this, because soon I'm going to have to do this with that Puppet-Players bride over there!

Everyone was laughing and giving the barber inexplicable thumbs-ups as the PuppetPlayers groom then dragged the PuppetPlayers bride across the dance floor and introduced her to the barber, and she appeared to be very taken with him, and sat on his lap and forced his head into her yellow felt cleavage, which was stained with wine and had a big cigarette burn at the neckline. Then the PuppetPlayers newlyweds sprinted across the room and bowed low before the real newlyweds, Arnie and Evelyn, who were sitting sullenly on the bandstand, apparently in the middle of a snit.

"Mickey!" Uncle Edgar shouted to the barber. "Mickey, you should've boffed that puppet broad! So what if she's a puppet! You're no prize! You're going to be choosy? Think of it! Think of it! Arnie's half your age!"

"Edgar, for Christ's sake, you're embarrassing him!" shouted

Aunt Jean. "It's like you're saying he's old! Like he's an old maid, only he's a guy! See what I mean? You think that's nice?"

"I am!" shouted Uncle Edgar. "I am saying that! He's a damned old lady! I don't mean no offense! I'm just saying, Get out and live! I love him! That's why I'm saying! The sun's setting! Pork some young babe, and if you like it, if you like the way she porks, what the hell, put down roots! What do you care? Love you can learn! But you gotta start somewhere! I mean, my God, even these little so-and-sos here are trying to get some of it!"

And Uncle Edgar threw a dinner roll at a group of four adolescent boys whom the barber vaguely remembered having once pulled around the block in a little red wagon. The boys gave Uncle Edgar the finger and said that not only were they trying to get some of it, they were actually getting some of it, and not always from the same chick, and sometimes more than once a day, and sometimes right after football practice, and quite possibly in the near future from a very hot shop teacher they had reason to believe would probably give it to all of them at once if only they approached it the right way.

"Holy Cow!" shouted Uncle Edgar. "Let me go to that school!"

"Edgar, you pig, be logical!" shouted Aunt Jean. "Just because Mickey's not married don't mean he ain't getting any! He could be getting some from a lady friend, or several lady friends, lady friends his own age, who already know the score, whose kids are full grown! You don't know what goes on in his bed at night!" Now the PuppetPlayers groom was trying to remove the real bride's garter, and some little suited boys were walking a ledge along a goldfish stream that separated the Wedding Area from Okinawa Memories, where several clearly non-Japanese women in kimonos were hustling drinks. The little suited boys began prying up the screen that kept the goldfish from going over a tiny waterfall, to see if they would die in a shallow pond near the Vending Area.

"For example, those kids torturing those fish," shouted Uncle

Edgar. "You know who those kids are? Them are Brendan's kids. You know who Brendan is? He's Dick's kid. You remember Dick? Your second cousin the same age as you, man! Remember I took you guys to the ballgame and he threw up in my Rambler? So them kids are Dick's grandkids, and here Dick's the same age as you, which means you're old enough to be a grandpa, Grandpa, but you ain't even a pa yet, which I don't know how you feel about it but I think is sort of sad or weird!"

"You do, but maybe he don't!" shouted Aunt Jean. "Why do you think everything you think is everything everybody else thinks? Plus Dick's no saint and neither are those kids! Dick was a teen dad and Brendan was a teen dad and probably those kids on that ledge are going to be teen dads as soon as they finish killing those poor fish!"

"Agreed!" shouted Uncle Edgar. "Hey, I got no abiding love for Dick! You want to have a fight with me at a wedding over my feelings for Dick, whose throwing up in my Rambler was just the start of the crap he's pulled on me? All's I'm saying is, there's no danger of Mickey here being a teen dad, and he better think about what I'm saying and get on the stick before his shooter ain't a viable shooter no more!"

"I'm sure you start talking about the poor guy's shooter at a wedding!" shouted Aunt Jean. "You're drunk!"

"Who ain't?" shouted Uncle Edgar, and the table exploded in laughter and one of the adolescents fell mock-drunk off his chair and when this got a laugh all the other adolescents fell mock-drunk off their chairs.

The barber excused himself and walked quickly out of the Wedding Area past three stunning girls in low-cut white gowns, who stood in what would have been shade from the fake overhanging Japanese cherry trees had the trees been outside and had it been daytime.

In the bathroom the Oriental theme receded and all was shiny chrome. The barber peed, mentally defending himself against

Uncle Edgar. First off, he'd had plenty of women. Five. Five wasn't bad. Five was more than most guys, and for sure it was more than Uncle Edgar, who'd married Jean right out of high school and had a lower lip like a fish. Who would Uncle Edgar have had him marry? Sara DelBianco, with her little red face? Ellen Wiest, that tall drink of water? Ann DeMann, who was swaybacked and had claimed he was a bad screw? Why in the world was he, a successful small businessman, expected to take advice from someone who'd spent the best years of his life transferring partial flanges from one conveyor belt to another while spraying them with a protective solvent mist?

The barber wet his comb the way he'd been wetting his comb since high school and prepared to slick back his hair. A big vital man with a sweaty face came in and whacked the barber on the back as if they were old pals. In the mirror was a skeletal mask that the barber knew was his face but couldn't quite believe was his face, because in the past his face could always be counted on to amount to more than the sum of its parts when he smiled winningly, but now when he smiled winningly he looked like a corpse trying to appear cheerful in a wind tunnel. His eyes bulged, his lips were thin, his forehead wrinkles were deep as stick lines in mud. It had to be the lighting. He was ugly. He was old. How had this happened? Who would want him now?

"You look like hell," thundered the big man from a stall, and the barber fled the mirror without slicking back his hair.

As he rushed past the stunning girls, a boy in a fraternity sweatshirt came over. Seeing the barber, he made a comic geriatric coughing noise in his throat, and one of the girls giggled and adjusted her shoulder strap as if to keep the barber from seeing down her dress.

A few weeks before the wedding, the barber had received in the mail a greeting card showing a cowboy roping a steer. The barber's name was scrawled across the steer's torso and "Me (Mr. Jenks)" across the cowboy.

"Here's hoping you will remember me from our driving school," said a note inside, "and attend a small barbecue at my home. My hope being to renew those acquaintances we started back then, which I found enjoyable and which since the loss of my wife I've had far too few of. Please come and bring nothing. As you can see from the cover, I am roping you in, not to brand you but only to show you my hospitality, I hope. Your friend, Larry Jenks."

Who was Jenks? Was Jenks the Happy Man? The barber threw the card in the bathroom trash, imagining the Driving School kooks seated glumly on folding chairs in a trailer house. For a week or so the card sat there, cowboy side up, vaguely reproaching him. Then he took out the trash.

A few days after the wedding, he received a second card from Jenks, with a black flower on the front.

"A good time was had by all," it said. "Sorry you were unable to attend. Even the younger folks, I think, enjoyed. Many folks took home quite a few sodas, because, as I am alone now, I never could have drank that many sodas in my life. This note, on a sadder note, and that is why the black flower, is to inform you that Eldora Ronsen is moving to Seattle. You may remember her as the older woman to your immediate right. She is high up in her company and just got higher, which is good for her but bad for us, as she is such a super gal. Please join us Tuesday next, Corrigan's Pub, for farewell drinks, map enclosed, your friend, Larry Jenks."

Tuesday next was tomorrow.

"Well, you can't go," Ma said. "The girls are coming over."

The girls were the Rosary and Altar Society. When they came over he had to wait on them hand and foot while they talked about which priest they would marry if only the priests weren't priests. When one lifted her blouse to show her recent scar, he had to say it was the worst scar ever. When one asked if her eye looked rheumy, he had to get very close to her rheumy eye and say it looked non-rheumy to him.

"Well, I think I might want to go," he said.

"I just said you can't," she said. "The girls are coming."

She was trying to guilt him. Once she'd faked a seizure when he tried to go to Detroit for a hair show.

"Ma," he said. "I'm going."

"Mr. Big Shot," she said. "Bullying an old lady."

"I'm not bullying you," he said. "And you're not old."

"Oh, I'm young, I'm a tiny baby," she said, tapping her dentures.

That night he dreamed of the pretty but heavy girl. In his dream she was all slimmed down. Her body looked like the body of Daisy Mae in the "Li'l Abner" cartoon. She came into the shop in cut-off jeans, chewing a blade of grass, and said she found his accomplishments amazing, especially considering the hardships he'd had to overcome, like his dad dying young and his mother being so nervous, and then she took the blade of grass out of her mouth and put it on the magazine table and stretched out across the Waiting Area couch while he undressed, and seeing his unit she said it was the biggest unit she'd ever seen, and arched her back in a sexy way, and then she called him over and gave him a deep warm kiss on the mouth that was so much like the kiss he'd been waiting for all his life that it abruptly woke him.

Sitting up in bed, he missed her. He missed how much she loved and understood him. She knew everything about him and yet still liked him. His gut sort of ached with wanting.

In his boyhood mirror he caught sight of himself and flexed his chest the way he used to flex his chest in the weight-lifting days, and looked so much like a little old man trying to take a dump in his bed that he hopped up and stood panting on the round green rug.

Ma was blundering around in the hallway. Because of the

dream, he had a partial bone. To hide his partial bone, he kept his groin behind the door as he thrust his head into the hall.

"I was walking in my sleep," Ma said. "I'm so worried I was walking in my sleep."

"What are you worried about?" he said.

"I'm worried about when the girls come," she said.

"Well, don't worry," he said. "It'll be fine."

"Thanks a million," she said, going back into her room. "Very reassuring."

Well, it would be fine. If they ran out of coffee, one of the old ladies could make coffee, if they ran out of snacks they could go a little hungry, if something really disastrous happened they could call him at Corrigan's, he'd leave Ma the number.

Because he was going.

In the morning he called Jenks and accepted the invitation, while Ma winced and clutched her stomach and pulled over a heavy wooden chair and collapsed into it.

Corrigan's was meant to feel like a pub at the edge of a Scottish golf course, there was a roaring fire, and many ancient-looking golf clubs hanging above tremendous tables of a hard plastic material meant to appear gnarled and scarred, and kilted waitresses with names like Heather and Zoe were sloshing chicken wings and fried cheese and lobster chunks into metal vats near an aerial photo of the Old Course at St. Andrews, Scotland.

The barber was early. He felt it was polite to be early, except when he was late, at which time he felt being early was anal. Where the heck was everybody? They weren't very polite. He looked down at his special shoes. They were blocky and black and had big removable metal stays in the sides and squeaked when he walked.

"Sorry we're late!" Mr. Jenks shouted, and the Driving School group settled in around the long gnarled table.

The pretty but heavy girl hung her purse across the back of her chair. Her hair looked like her hair in the dream and her eyes looked like her eyes in the dream, and as for her body he couldn't tell, she was wearing a muumuu. But certainly facially she was pretty. Facially she was very possibly the prettiest girl here. Was she? If aliens came down and forced each man to pick one woman to reproduce with in a chain-link enclosure while they took notes, would he choose her, based solely on face? Here was a woman with a good rear but a doglike face, and there was a woman with a nice perm but a blop at the end of her nose, and there was the Buggin' girl, who looked like a chicken, and the white-haired woman, whose face was all wrinkled, and here was the pretty but heavy girl. Was she the prettiest? Facially? He thought she very possibly was.

He regarded her fondly from across the table, waiting for her to catch him regarding her fondly, so he could quickly avert his eyes, so she'd know he was still possibly interested, and then she dropped her menu and bent to retrieve it and the barber had a chance to look briefly down her dress.

Well, she definitely had something going on in the chest category. So facially she was the prettiest in the room, plus she had decent boobs. Attractive breasts. The thing was, would she want him? He was old. Oldish. When he stood up too fast, his knee joints popped. Lately his gums had started to bleed. Plus he had no toes. Although why sell himself short? Who was perfect? He wasn't perfect and she wasn't perfect but they obviously had some sort of special chemistry, based on what had happened at the Driving School, and, anyway, what the heck, he wasn't proposing, he was just considering possibly trying to get to know her somewhat better.

In this way, he decided to ask the pretty but heavy girl out.

How to do it, that was the thing. How to ask her. He could get her alone and say her hair looked super. While saying it looked super, he could run a curl through his fingers in a professional way, as if looking for split ends. He could say he'd love a chance to cut such excellent hair, then slip her a card for One Free Cut and Coffee. That had worked with Sylvia Reynolds, a bank teller with crow's-feet and a weird laugh who turned out to be an excellent kisser. When she'd come in for her Free Cut and Coffee, he'd claimed they were out of coffee and taken her to Bean Men Roasters. A few dates later they'd got carried away, because of her excellent kissing, and done more than he ever would've imagined doing with someone with crow's-feet and a weird laugh and strangely wide hips, and when he'd got home that night and had a good hard look inside the locket she'd given him after they'd done it, he'd instantly felt bad, because wow could you ever see the crow's-feet in that picture. As he looked at Sylvia standing in that bright sunlit meadow in the picture, her head thrown back, joyfully laughing, her crow's-feet so very pronounced, an image had sprung into his mind of her coming wide-hipped toward him while holding a baby, and suddenly he'd been deeply disappointed in himself for doing it with someone so unusual-looking, and to insure that he didn't make matters worse by inadvertently doing it with her a second time he'd sort of never called her again, and had even switched banks.

He glanced at the pretty but heavy girl and found her making her way toward the ladies'.

Now was as good a time as any.

He waited a few minutes, then excused himself and stood outside the ladies', reading ads posted on a corkboard, until the pretty but heavy girl came out.

He cleared his throat and asked was she having fun?

She said yes.

Then he said wow did her hair look great. And in terms of great hair, he knew what he was talking about, he was a professional. Where did she have it cut? He ran one of her curls through his fingers, as if looking for split ends, and said he'd love the chance to work with such dynamite hair, and took from his shirt pocket the card for One Free Cut and Coffee.

"Maybe you could stop by sometime," he said.

"That's nice of you," she said, and blushed.

So she was a shy girl. Sort of cutely nerdy. Not exactly confident. That was too bad. He liked confidence. He found it sexy. On the other hand, who could blame her, he could sometimes be very intimidating. Also her lack of confidence indicated he could perhaps afford to be a little bit bold.

"Like, say, tomorrow?" he said. "Like, say, tomorrow at noon?"

"Ha," she said. "You move quick."

"Not too quick, I hope," he said.

"No," she said. "Not too quick."

So he had her. By saying he wasn't moving too quick, wasn't she implicitly implying that he was moving at exactly the right speed? All he had to do now was close the deal.

"I'll be honest," he said. "I've been thinking about you since Driving School."

"You have?" she said.

"I have," he said.

"So you're saying tomorrow?" she said, blushing again.

"If that's O.K. for you," he said.

"It's O.K. for me," she said.

Then she started uncertainly back to the table, and the barber raced into the men's. Yes! Yes yes yes. It was a date. He had her. He couldn't believe it. He'd really played that smart. What had he been worried about? He was cute, women had always considered him cute, never mind the thin hair and minor gut, there was just something about him women liked.

Wow she was pretty, he had done very very well for himself.

Back at the table, Mr. Jenks was taking Polaroids. He announced his intention of taking six shots of the Driving School group, one for each member to keep, and the barber stood behind the pretty but heavy girl, with his hands on her shoulders, and she reached up and gave his wrist a little squeeze.

At home old-lady cars were in the driveway, and old-lady coats were piled on the couch, and the house smelled like old lady, and the members of the Rosary and Altar Society were gathered around the dining-room table looking frail. The barber could never keep them straight. There was a crone in a lime pants suit, and another crone in a pink pants suit, and two crones in blue pants suits. As he came in they began asking Ma why was he out so late, why hadn't he been here to help, wasn't he normally a fairly good son? And Ma said yes, he was normally a fairly good son, except he hadn't given her any grandkids yet and often wasted water by bathing twice a day.

"My son had that problem," said one of the blue crones. "His wife once pulled me aside."

"Has his wife ever pulled you aside?" the pink crone said to Ma.

"He's not married," said Ma.

"Maybe the not married is related to the bathing too often," said the lime crone.

"Maybe he holds himself aloof from others," said the blue crone. "My son held himself aloof from others."

"My daughter holds herself aloof from others," said the pink crone.

"Does she bathe too often?" said Ma.

"She doesn't bathe too often," said the pink crone. "She just thinks she's smarter than everyone."

"Do you think you're smarter than everyone?" asked the lime crone severely, and thank God at that moment Ma reached up and pulled him down by the shirt and roughly kissed his cheek.

"Have a good time?" she said, and the group photo fell out of his pocket and into the dip.

"Very nice," he said.

"Who are these people?" Ma said, wiping a bit of dip off the photo with her finger. "Are these the people you went to meet? Who is this you're embracing? This big one."

"I'm not embracing her, Ma," he said. "I'm just standing behind her. She's a friend."

"She's big," Ma said. "You smell like beer."

"Actually I don't consider her big," said the barber, in a tone of disinterested interest.

"Whatever you say," said the lime crone.

"He's been drinking," said Ma.

Oh he didn't care what they thought, he was happy. He jokingly snatched the photo away and dashed up to his room, taking two stairs at a time.

Gabby Gabby Gabby, her name was Gabby, short for Gabrielle. Tomorrow they had a date for lunch. Breakfast, rather. They'd moved it up to breakfast. While they'd been kissing against her car, she'd said she wasn't sure she could wait until lunch to see him again. He felt the same way. Even breakfast seemed a long time to wait. He wished she was sitting next to him on the bed right now, holding his hand, listening to the sounds of the crones cackling as they left. In his mind, he stroked her hair and said he was glad he'd finally found her, and she said she was glad to have been found, she'd never dreamed that someone so distinguished, with such a broad chest and wide shoulders, could love a girl like her. Was she happy? he tenderly asked. Oh, she was so happy, she said, so happy to be sitting next to this accomplished, distinguished man in this amazing house, which in his mind was not the current house, a pea-green ranch with a tilted cracked sidewalk, but a mansion, on a lake, with a smaller house nearby for Ma, down a very very long wooded path, and he'd paid cash for the mansion with money he'd made from his international chain of barbershops, each of which was an exact copy of his current barbershop, and when he and

Gabby visited his London, England, shop, leaving Ma behind in the little house, his English barbers would always burst into applause and say, "Jolly good, jolly good," as the happy couple walked in the door.

"I'm leaving you the dishes, Romeo," Ma shouted from the bottom of the stairs.

Early next morning, he sat in the bath, getting ready for his date. Here was his floating weenie, like some kind of sea creature. He danced his nubs nervously against the tiles, like Fred Astaire dancing on a wall, and swirled the washrag through the water, holding it by one corner, so that it, too, was like a sea creature, a blue ray, a blue monogrammed ray that now crossed the land that was his belly and attacked the sea creature that was his weenie, and remembering what Uncle Edgar had said at the wedding about his shooter not being viable, he gave his shooter a good, hard, reassuring shake, as if congratulating it for being so very viable. It was a great shooter, perfectly fine, in spite of what Ann DeMann had once said about him being a bad screw, it had got hard quick last night and stayed hard throughout the kissing, and wow he wished Uncle Edgar could have seen that big boner.

Oh, he felt good, in spite of a slight hangover he was very happy.

Flipping his unit carelessly from side to side with thumb and forefinger, he looked at the group photo, which he'd placed near the sink. God, she was pretty. He was so lucky. He had a date with a pretty young girl. Ma was nuts, Gabby wasn't big, no bigger than any other girl. Not much bigger, anyway. How wide were her shoulders compared to, say, the shoulders of the Buggin' girl? Well, he wasn't going to dignify that with a response. She was perfect just the way she was. He leaned out of the tub to look closer at the photo. Well, Gabby's shoulders were maybe a little wider than the Buggin' girl's shoulders. Definitely wider. Were they wider than the shoulders of the white-haired woman? Actually, in the photo they were even wider than the shoulders of the country boy.

Oh, he didn't care, he just really liked her. He liked her laugh and the way she had of raising one eyebrow when skeptical, he liked the way that, when he moved his hand to her boob as they leaned against her car, she let out a happy little sigh. He liked how, after a few minutes of kissing her while feeling her boobs, which were super, very firm, when he dropped his hand down between her legs she said she thought that was probably enough for one night, which was good, it showed good morals, it showed she knew when to call it quits.

Ma was in her room, banging things around.

Because for a while there last night he'd been worried. Worried she wasn't going to stop him. Which would have been disappointing. Because she barely knew him. He could've been anybody. For a few minutes there against the car, he'd wondered if she wasn't a little on the easy side. He wondered this now. Did he want to wonder this now? Wasn't that sort of doubting her? No, no, it was fine, there was no sin in looking at things honestly. So was she? Too easy? Why had she so quickly agreed to go out with him? Why so willing to give it away so easily to some old guy she barely knew? Some old balding guy she barely knew? Well, he thought he might know why. Possibly it was due to her size. Possibly the guys her own age had passed her by, due to the big bod, and, nearing thirty, she'd heard her biologic clock ticking and decided it was time to lower her standards, which, possibly, was where he came in. Possibly, seeing him at the Driving School, she'd thought, since all old guys like young girls, big bods notwithstanding, this old pear-shaped balding guy can ergo be had no problem.

Was that it? Was that how it was?

"Some girl just called," Ma said, leaning heavily against the bathroom door. "Some girl, Gabby or Tabby or something? Said you had a date. Wanted you to know she's running late. Is that the same girl? The same fat girl you were embracing?"

Sitting in the tub, he noticed that his penis was gripped nervously in his fist, and let it go, and it fell to one side, as if it had just passed out.

"Do the girl a favor, Mickey," Ma said. "Call it off. She's too big for you. You'll never stick with her. You never stick with anyone. You couldn't even stick with Ellen Wiest, for crying out loud, who was so wonderful, you honestly think you're going to stick with this Tabby or Zippy or whatever?"

Of course Ma had to bring up Ellen Wiest. Ma had loved Ellen, who had a regal face and great manners and was always kissing up to Ma by saying what a great mother Ma was. He remembered the time he and Ellen had hiked up to Butternut Falls and stood getting wet in the mist, holding hands, smiling sweetly at each other, which had really been fun, and she'd said she thought she loved him, which was nice, except wow she was tall. You could hold hands with her for only so long before your back started to hurt. Plus they'd had that fight on the way down. Well, there were a lot of things about Ellen that Ma wasn't aware of, such as her nasty temper, and he remembered Ellen storming ahead of him on the trail, glaring back now and then, just because he'd made a funny remark about her blocking out the sun, and hadn't he also said something about her being able to eat leaves from the tallest of the trees they were passing under? Well, that had been funny, it had all been in fun, why did she have to get so mad about it? Where was Ellen now? Hadn't she married Ed Trott? Well, Trott could have her. Trott was probably suffering the consequences of being married to Miss Thin Skin even now, and he remembered having recently seen Ed and Ellen at the ValueWay, Ellen pregnant and looking so odd, with her big belly pressing against the cart as she craned that giraffelike neck down to nuzzle Ed, who had a big stupid happy grin on his face like he was the luckiest guy in the world.

The barber stood up angrily from the tub. Here in the mirror were his age-spotted deltoids and his age-spotted roundish pecs and his strange pale love handles.

Ma resettled against the door with a big whump.

"So what's the conclusion, lover boy?" she said. "Are you cancelling? Are you calling up and cancelling?"

"No, I'm not," he said.

"Well, poor her," Ma said.

South Street was an old wagon road. Cars took the bend too fast. Often he scowled at the speeding cars on his way to work, imagining the drivers laughing to themselves about the way he walked. Because on days when his special shoes hurt he sort of minced. They hurt today. He shouldn't have worn the thin gray socks. He was mincing a bit but trying not to, because what if Gabby drove up South on her way to meet him at the shop and saw him mincing?

He turned up Lincoln Avenue and passed the Liquor Mart, and La Belle Époque, the antique store with the joyful dog inside, and as always the joyful dog sprang over the white settee and threw itself against the glass, and then there was Gabby, down the block, peering into his locked shop, and he corrected his mincing and began walking normally, though it killed.

Did she like the shop? He took big bold steps with his head thrown back so he'd look happy. Happy and strong, with all his toes. With all his toes, in the prime of his life. Did she notice how neat the shop was? How professional? Or did she notice that four of the chairs were of one type and the fifth was totally different? Did it seem to her that the shop was geared to old blue-hairs, which was something he'd once heard a young woman say as he took out the trash?

How did she look? Did she look good?

It was still too far to tell.

Now she saw him. Her face brightened, she waved like a little girl. Oh, she was pretty. It was as if he'd known her forever. She looked so hopeful. But, oops. Oh my God, she was big. She'd dressed all wrong, tight jeans and a tight shirt. As if testing him. Jesus, this was the biggest he'd ever seen her look. What was she doing, testing him, trying to look her worst? Here was an alley, should he swerve into the alley and call her later? Or not. Not call her later? Forget the whole thing? Pretend last night had never happened? Although now she'd seen him. And he didn't want to forget the whole thing. Last night for the first time in a long time he'd felt like someone other than a guy who wanks it on the milking stool in his mother's pantry. Last night he'd bought a pitcher for the Driving School group and Jenks had called him a sport. Last night she'd said he was a sexy kisser.

Thinking about forgetting last night gave him a pit in his stomach. Forgetting last night was not an option. What were the options? Well, she could trim down. That was an option. Maybe all she needed was someone to tell her the simple truth, someone to sit her down and say, Look, you have an incredibly beautiful intelligent face, but from the neck down, sweetie, wow, we've got some serious work to do. And after their frank talk she'd send him flowers with a card that said, Thanks for your honesty, let's get this thing done. And every night as she stood at the mirror in her panties and bra he'd point out places that needed improvement, and the next day she'd energetically address those areas in the gym, and soon the head-bod discrepancy would be eliminated, and he imagined her in a fancy dress at a little table on a veranda, a veranda by the sea, thanking him for the honeymoon trip, she came from a poor family and had never even been on a vacation, much less a six-week tour of Europe, and then she'd say, Honey, why not put down that boring report on how much your international chain of barbershops earned us this month and join me in the bedroom so I can show you how grateful I am, and in the bedroom she'd start stripping, and was good at it, not that she'd ever done it before, no, she hadn't, she was just naturally good at it, and when she was done there she was, with her perfect face and the Daisy Mae body, smiling at him with unconditional love.

It wouldn't be easy. It would take hard work. He knew a little about hard work, having made a barbershop out of a former pet store. Tearing out a counter, he'd found a dead mouse. From a sump pump he'd pulled three hardened snakes. But he'd never quit. Because he was a worker. He wasn't afraid of hard work. Was she a worker? He didn't know. He'd have to find out.

They'd find out together.

She stood beside his wooden bench, under his shop awning, and the shadow of her wild mane fell at his feet.

What a wild ride this had been, how much he had learned about himself already!

"Here I am," she said, with a shy, pretty smile.

"I'm so glad you are," he said, and bent to unlock the door of the shop.

THE NEW YORKER

Dominion

This great work of literature is not the achievement of a young writer; it is an intricate, highly developed piece of fiction that arises out of preoccupations that its author has been developing and nurturing for years. Ostensibly a hunting story, it is a tale about reflection—about faith, the need for it, and the ambivalence toward it.

Robert Stone

Dominion

By gad, sir," Michael Ahearn said to his son, Paul, "you present a distressing spectacle."

A few nights earlier they had watched "The Maltese Falcon" together. Paul, who had never seen it before, appeared to be delighted by his father's rendition of Sydney Greenstreet. Sometimes he would even try doing Greenstreet himself.

"By gad, sir!"

Paul's attempts at movie voices were not subtle but commanded inflections normally beyond the comic repertory of a twelve-year-old boy from a small town on the northern plains. His voice and manner were coming to resemble his father's.

The boy was lying in bed with a copy of "The Hobbit" open across his counterpane. This time he was not amused at his father's old-movie impressions. He looked up with resentment. His beautiful long-lashed eyes—his mother's—were angry. But Michael easily met the reproach there. He took any opportunity to look at his son. There was something new every day, a different ray, an unexpected facet reflected in the aspects of this creature enduring his twelvedness.

"I want to go, Dad," Paul said evenly, attempting to exercise his powers of persuasion to best effect.

He had been literally praying to go. Michael knew that because he had been spying on Paul while the boy knelt beside the bed to say his evening prayers. He had lurked in the hallway outside the boy's room, watching and listening to his careful recitation of the Our Father and the Hail Mary and the Gloria—rote prayers, courtesy of the Catholic school to which the Ahearns, with misgivings, regularly dispatched him. Michael and his wife had been raised in religion and they were warily trying it on again as parents. Sending Paul to St. Emmerich's meant laughing away the horror stories they liked to tell about their own religious education in the hope of winning a few wholesome apparent certainties for the next generation.

"I was fourteen before my father took me hunting," Michael said. "I think that's the right age."

"You said kids do everything sooner."

"I didn't say I thought kids doing everything sooner was a good idea."

"You don't even like to hunt," Paul said. "You don't believe in it."

"Really? And what makes us think that?"

"Well, I've heard you with Mom. You, like, agree with her it's cruel and stuff."

"I don't agree with her. I understand her position. Anyway, if I didn't believe in it why should I take a tender runt like you?"

Paul was immune to his father's goading. He went for the substance.

"Because I really believe in it."

"Oh yes? You believe in whacking innocent creatures?"

"You know what?" Paul asked. "This was a Christian Ethics topic. Hunting was. And I was like pro—in favor. Because Genesis says 'dominion over beasts.' If you eat the meat, it's O.K. And we do."

"You don't."

"Yes, I do," Paul said. "I eat venison kielbasa."

Michael loomed over him and with his left hand put out the lamp on the bed table.

"'Tis blasphemy to vent thy rage against a dumb brute," he informed his son. He had been teaching "Moby Dick" with his favorite assistant, a very pretty South Dakota girl named Phyllis Strom. "Now, good night. I don't want you to read too late."

"Why? I'm not going anywhere."

"Maybe next year," Michael said.

"Sure, Dad," said Paul.

He left the bedroom door its customary inch ajar and went downstairs to the study, where his wife was grading Chaucer papers.

"Did he beg and plead?" she asked, looking up.

"I don't think he's absolutely sure if he wants to go or not. But he takes a pro-hunting position."

She laughed. Her son's eyes. "A what?"

"In Christian Ethics," Michael pronounced solemnly. "Dominion over the beasts. He argues from Genesis. Christian Ethics," he repeated when she looked at him blankly. "At school."

"Oh, that," she said. "Well, it doesn't say kill the poor beasts. Or does it? Maybe one of those teachers is a gun nut."

Kristin had been raised in a Lutheran family. Although religiously inclined, she was a practical person who worked at maintaining her critical distance from dogmatic instruction, especially of the Roman variety. She concurred in Paul's attendance at the Catholic school because, to her own rather conservative but independent thinking, the position of the Catholics of their college town had incorporated Luther's reforms. Many Sundays she went to Mass with them. At Christmas, they went to both churches and every Good Friday to the Lutheran Tenebrae.

"It's him," Michael said. "It's his funny little mind."

Kristin frowned and put her finger to her lips.

"His funny little mind," Michael whispered, chastened. "He thought it up."

"He always sees you going. Not that you ever get much."

"I get birds. But deer season . . . "

"Right," she said.

The circle of unspoken thought she closed was that Michael used the pheasant season as an excuse to walk the autumn fields around their house. With the dog and a twenty-gauge shotgun borrowed from a colleague, he would set out over the frosted brown prairie, scrambling under wire where the land was not posted, past thinly frozen ponds and rutted pasture, making his way from one wooded hill to another. It was a pleasure to walk the short autumn days, each knoll bright with yellowed alder, red-brown ash, and flaming maple. And if the dog startled a pheasant into a headlong, clucking sacrificial dash he might have a shot. Or not. Then, if he brought a bird down, he would have to pluck it, trying to soften the skin by heating it on the stove without quite letting it cook, picking out the shot with tweezers. Kristin refused to do it. Michael disliked the job and did not much care for pheasant. But you had to eat them.

And in deer season, certain years, Michael would go out with a couple of friends from the university who were good shots and the kind of avid hunters he was not. He went for the canoe trip into the half-frozen swamp and the November woods under their first covering of snow. The silence there, in the deep woods they prowled, was broken by nothing but crows, and stay-behind chanting sparrows and the occasional distant echo of firing. If they got lucky, there might be the call of an errant Canadian wolf at night. And there were the winter birds, grosbeaks, juncos, eagles gliding silent above the tree line. And the savor of good whiskey around the potbellied stove of the cabin they used as field headquarters. Killing deer was not the object for him.

Kristin, though she had grown up on her family's farm, forever borrowing her male relatives' jackets with pockets full of jerky, tobacco plugs, and bright-red shotgun shells, mildly disapproved of hunting. At first, she had objected to Michael's going. He was nearsighted, a daydreamer.

"You shouldn't carry a weapon if you don't intend to take a deer."

"I don't shoot seriously."

"But you shouldn't shoot at all. It's worse if you wound one."

"I hardly ever discharge the piece, Kristin."

But a man had to carry one, in the deep woods, in winter. It was sinister, suspicious to encounter someone in the forest without a gun. Farmers who welcomed hunters on their land in season looked fearfully on unarmed strollers, trespassing. And sometimes, if he was standing with the others and a band of deer came in view and everyone let go, he would take his shot with the rest of them. He had never claimed one.

From the living room next to Kristin's study, their black Labrador gave up his place beside the fire and trotted over for attention. Olaf had been Paul's Christmas puppy six years before and served as Michael's shooting companion every fall. Michael bent to scratch his neck.

Kristin put her papers aside.

"Christian ethics," she said, as though she were weighing their general usefulness. "I don't think Genesis likes hunter-gatherers much. I think it favors the shepherds."

"I must look it up. You always learn something, right? Reading Genesis."

Early the next morning, two of Michael's colleagues from State came by in a Jeep Cherokee. Kristin served them coffee and handed out bagged sandwiches to take along.

Alvin Mahoney, a tall, balding historian with a rosy drinker's face, presented Michael with his hunting piece.

"Remember this? Remington twelve-gauge?"

Michael jammed three deer slugs into the magazine and pumped them forward to get the feel of the gun.

"You can put six in there," Mahoney reminded him. "Only if you do—remember they're there."

"Yep." Michael lowered the shotgun, unloaded it, and stuffed the shells in his jacket pocket.

The third hunter was a sociologist named Norman Cevic, whom students liked to think of as coming from New York, though he was actually from Iron Falls, a tough little smelter town on the lake not far away. Norman did his best to affect a streetwise quality for the small-town adolescents at the university. He was about the same age as Mahoney, twenty years older than Michael, though he seemed younger.

"Norm went out opening day," Mahoney said. "Straight out of the shotgun. So to speak."

"Wasn't it a zoo out there?" Kristin asked. "I mean human-wise?"

"Not if you know the territory," Norman said. "I didn't see a soul."

"You took the canoe?" Michael asked.

"Sure." Norman had a gravelly voice that amused the students. "Had to use it to get in there. Didn't see a soul," he told them again.

No one said anything. Paul was lurking in the kitchen doorway in his bathrobe. Norman took a sip of coffee.

"Except," he said, "Hmongs. I saw some Hmongs in the distance. Probably walked all the way in there. No snow yet."

"They need the meat," Kristin said. "They live on it."

"Roots," Norman said. "Winter greens. Squirrel. Raccoon."

"How did you know they were Hmongs?" Paul asked from his half-concealment.

"Good question," Norman said. "Smart kid. We should take him hunting next year. Want to know how?"

Paul looked to his father, then nodded.

"How I knew they were Hmongs," Norman declared, as though it were the title of a lecture. He had been cradling a Mossberg thirty-thirty in one arm while he drank his coffee. Now he put the cup down and let the rifle slip through his fingers until he was holding it by the tip of the barrel just short of the end-sight. "Because," he told Paul, "they carried their weapons by the end of the barrel. Sort of trailing the stock."

"Huh," said Alvin Mahoney.

"Which is how they carried them in Vietnam. And Hmongs are very numerous in Iron Falls. So," he said, addressing himself to young Paul, "when I see a man in deep woods carrying a rifle that way I presume he's a Hmong. Does that answer your question, my friend?"

"Yes, sir," Paul said.

"Hmongs are a tribal people in Vietnam and Laos," Norman told Paul. "Do you know where Vietnam is? Do you know what happened there?"

Paul was silent for a moment and then said, "Yes. I think so. A little."

"Good," said Norman. "Then you know more than three-quarters of our student body."

"Mr. Cevic was in Vietnam during the war," Kristin told her son. She turned to Norman, whom she rather admired. "How long was it that you spent there?"

"A year. All day, every day. And all night, too."

Just before they left, the telephone rang. From his wife's tone, Michael knew it was his teaching assistant Phyllis Strom. Descended from prairie sodbusters, Kristin did not always trouble to enliven her voice when addressing strangers and people she disliked. She had a way of sounding very bleak indeed, and that was how she sounded then, impatiently accumulating Phyllis's information.

"Phyllis," she sternly announced. "Says she may not be able to monitor midterms on Thursday. Wonders if you'll be back?" There was an edge of unsympathetic mimicry.

Michael made a face. "Phyllis," he said. "Phyllis, fair and use-less." In fact, he felt sorry for the kid. She was engagingly shy and frightened of Kristin.

"I told her you'd left," his wife told him. "She'll call back." The new and rigorously enforced regulations required chastity in stu-dent-faculty collaborations, but Kristin was not reassured. She imagined that her anxieties about Phyllis were a dark, close secret.

"Do I really have to come back for this?" Michael said as they went out to the car. "I'll call you from Ehrlich's tomorrow night after six."

They drove past dun farm fields, toward the huge wooded marshes that lined the Three Rivers where their narrow valleys conjoined. In about four and a half hours they passed Ehrlich's, a sprawling pseudo-Alpine *bierstube* and restaurant.

"I want to go on to the Hunter's," Michael said.

"The food's not as good," Mahoney said mildly.

"True," said Michael. "But Hunter's sells an Irish single malt called Willoughby's on their retail side. Only place they sell the stuff west of Minneapolis. And I want to buy a bottle for us to drink tonight."

"Ah," Mahoney said. "Sheer bliss."

On his tongue, the phrase could only be ironic, Michael thought. Bliss was unavailable to Mahoney. It was simply not there for him, though Michael was sure he'd like the Willoughby's well enough. But for me, Michael thought, bliss is still a possibility. He imagined himself as still capable of experiencing it, a few meas-ures, a few seconds at a time. No need of fancy whiskey, the real thing. He felt certain of it.

"How's Kristin?" Norman asked Michael.

"How do you mean, Norm? You just talked to her."

"Has she seen Phyllis Strom this term?"

"Oh, come on," Michael said. "Think she's jealous of little Phyl-lis? Kris could swallow Phyllis Strom with a glass of water."

Norman laughed. "Let me level with you, buddy. I'm scared to death of Kristin. Fire and ice, man."

Mind your business, he thought. Cevic had appointed himself sociologist to the north country. In fact, Michael thought, at home the ice might be almost imperceptibly thickening. Kristin had taken to rhapsodizing more and more about her father, upon whose forge her elegantly shaped, unbending angles had been hammered. The god in the iron mask, mediator of manhood and its measure. Still alive under the granite. A man might well dread his own shortcomings in that shadow.

"Smartest move I ever made," said Michael, "marrying that girl. Definitely sleep nights."

Perhaps, he thought, that had not been the best way to phrase it, for Cevic the curious and curiously minded.

The landscape grew more wooded as they approached Mahoney's cabin, where they planned to spend the night. Farm fields gave way to sunken meadows lined with bare oak and pine forest. Thirty miles along, they came to the Hunter's Supper Club, a diner in blue aluminum and silver chrome. Incongruously attached to the diner, extending from it, was a building of treated pine logs with a varnished door of its own. At eye level on the door was the building's single window, a diamond-shaped spy hole, double-glazed and tinted green. A hand-painted sign the length of the roof read "Souvenirs Tagging Station."

They parked beside the half-dozen battered cars in the lot, and walked across the sandy, resin-scalded ground and into the metal diner. There were banquettes and a counter and a heavy young waitress in a checkered dress and blue apron. The restaurant itself was empty except for two old farmers at the counter, who shifted themselves arthritically to see who had come in. From the bar, which sounded more crowded, came jukebox music. Waylon Jennings' "Lowdown Freedom."

Their table looked out on the empty two-lane highway. Michael ordered coffee with his ham and eggs and got up to buy the whiskey at the adjoining bar.

The bar had eight or nine customers, half of them middle-aged men, burnt-up drunk, unhealthy-looking and ill-disposed. There were also two Indian youths with ponytails and druggy, glittery eyes. One had a round, apparently placid face. The other was lean and edgy, his features set in what at first appeared to be a smile but wasn't. Michael stood at the take-away counter, resolutely minding his own business. Then the barmaid, whom he had not seen at first, came out from some storage space behind the mirror and the stacked bottles and the pigs'-feet jars.

The barmaid looked only just old enough to serve liquor. She had jet-black hair and brilliant blue eyes evenly set, a thin perfect nose and long pale lips without a trace of lipstick. She was tall, wearing black cowgirl clothes, a rodeo shirt with little waves of white frosting and mother-of-pearl buttons. Her hair was thick and swept to one side at the back.

"Say," she said.

"Do you have Willoughby's today?"

"Could be we do," she said. "Like, what is it?"

Michael pondered other, different, questions. Could he drive out every Friday and Saturday and have a Friday and Saturday kind of cowboy life with her? But not really. But could he? Would she like poetry with a joint, after sex? Not seriously. Idle speculation.

"It's whiskey," he told her. He thought he must sound impatient. "It's unblended Irish whiskey. You used to carry it."

"Unblended is good, right? Sounds good. What you want."

"Yes," Michael said. "It is. It's what I'm after."

"If it's good, we mostly don't have it," she said.

And he was, as it were, stumped. No comeback. No zingers.

"Really?" he asked.

Someone behind, one of the young Indians it might have been, did him in falsetto imitation. "Really?" As though it were an outrageously affected, silly-ass question.

"But I can surely find out," she said.

When she turned away he saw that her black pants were as tight as they could be and cut to stirrup length like a real cowgirl's, and her boot heels scuffed but not worn down from walking. He also saw that where her hair was swept to the side at the back of her collar what appeared to be the forked tongue of a tattooed snake rose from either side of the bone at the nape of her neck. A serpent, ascending her spine. Her skin was alabaster.

He heard voices from the back. An old man's voice raised in proprietary anger. When she came back she was carrying a bottle, inspecting it.

"What do you know?" she said. "Specialty of the house, huh? You Irish?"

Michael shrugged. "Back somewhere. How about you?"

"Me? I'm like everybody else around here."

"Is that right?"

"Megan," one of the smoldering drunks at the bar muttered, "get your butt over this way."

"George," Megan called sweetly, still addressing Michael, "would you not be a knee-walking piece of pig shit?"

She took her time selling him the Willoughby's. Worn menace rumbled down the bar. She put her hand to her ear. Hark, like a tragedienne in a Victorian melodrama.

"What did he say?" she asked Michael, displaying active, intelligent concern.

Michael shook his head. "Didn't hear him."

As he walked back to the diner section, he heard her boots on the wooden flooring behind the bar.

"Yes, Georgie, baby pie. How may I serve you today?"

Back in the restaurant, their table had been cleared.

"He ate your eggs," Norman said, indicating Alvin Mahoney.

"Naw, I didn't," Alvin said. "Norm did."

"Anyway," Norman said, "they were getting cold. You want something to take along?"

Michael showed them the sack with the whiskey.

"I'll just take this. I'm not hungry." When he tasted his untouched coffee, it was cold as well.

Beyond the Hunter's Supper Club, the big swamp took shape, and snow was falling before they reached the cabin. They followed the dirt road to it, facing icy, wind-driven volleys that rattled against the windshield and fouled the wipers. As they were getting their bags out of the trunk, the snow's quality changed and softened, the flakes enlarged. A heavier silence settled on the woods.

As soon as it grew dark, Michael opened the Willoughby's. It was wonderfully smooth. Its texture seemed, at first, to impose on the blessedly warm room a familiar quietude. People said things they had said before, on other nights sheltering from other storms in past seasons. Norman Cevic groused about Vietnam. Alvin Mahoney talked about the single time he had brought his wife to the cabin.

"My then wife," he said. "She didn't much like it out here. Naw, not at all."

Michael turned to look at Alvin's worn, flushed country face with its faint mottled web of boozy angiomas. Then wife? Alvin was a widower. Where had he picked up this phrase to signal the louche sophistication of *la ronde?* Late wife, Alvin. Dead wife. Because Alma or Mildred or whatever her obviated name was had simply died on him. In what Michael had conceived of as his own sweet silent thought, he was surprised by his bitterness, his sudden, pointless, contemptuous anger.

He finished his glass. At Alvin's age, given their common vocabulary of features, their common weakness, he might come to look very much the same. But the anger kept swelling in his throat, beating time with his pulse, a vital sign.

"Well," Norman said, "all is forgiven now."

Michael, distracted by his own thoughts, had no idea what Cevic was talking about. What was forgiven? All? Forgiven whom?

In the morning they helped Alvin secure the cabin. His twelve-foot aluminum canoe was in a padlocked shed down the hill. Getting the canoe out, they found the padlock broken, but the burglars, in their laziness and inefficiency, had not managed to make off with the boat. One year they had found the bow full of hammered dents. Still working in darkness, they placed the canoe in its fittings atop the Jeep.

A blurred dawn was unveiling itself when they reached the stream that would take them into the islands of the swamp. There was still very little light. Black streaks crisscrossed the little patch of morning, the day's inklings. They loaded the canoe by flashlight. Glassy ice crackled under their boots at the shore's edge.

Michael took the after paddle, steering, digging deep into the slow, black stream. He kept the flashlight between the seat and his thigh so that its shaft beams would sweep the bank. Paddling up front, Norman also had a light.

"Nice easy stream," Alvin said. "I keep forgetting."

"It speeds up a lot toward the big river," Michael said. "There's a gorge."

"A minor gorge," Norman said.

"Yes," said Michael. "Definitely minor."

"But it gets 'em," said Cevic. "Every spring they go. Half a dozen some years." He meant drowned fishermen.

Yards short of the landing, Michael picked up the flashlight, lost his gloved grip, and sent it tumbling over the side. He swore.

They circled back, and riding the slight current got a look at the flashlight resting on the bottom, lighting the weedy marbled rocks seven, maybe eight feet below.

They circled again.

"How deep is it?" Alvin asked, and answered his own question. "Too deep."

"Too deep," Michael said. "My fault. Sorry."

"No problem," Norman said. "I've got one. And it's getting light."

By the time they had off-loaded, the day had composed itself around the skeletal woods, each branch bearing a coat of snow. They fanned out from the river, within sight of the glacial rock face that would be their rendezvous point. Each man carried a pack of provisions, a gun, a compass, and a portable stand. Michael made for high ground, following a slope north of the rock. The snow was around four inches deep. He saw quite a few deer tracks, the little handprints of raccoons, the hip-hop brush patterns of rabbits. There were others, too, suggesting more exciting creatures, what might be fox, marten, or wolverine.

He fixed his stand in the tallest tree among a cluster of oaks on sloping, rocky ground. The view was good, commanding a deer trail out of the pines above him which led toward the river. Now the animals would be prowling down from the high ground where they had passed the night, struggling only slightly in the new-fallen layer, browsing for edibles. He waited. Invisible crows warned of his presence.

Then there commenced the curious passage into long silence, empty of event. Confronted by stillness without motion, a landscape of line and shadow which seemed outside time, he took in every feature of the shooting ground, every tree and snowy hummock. It was always a strange, suspended state. Notions thrived.

He watched, alert for the glimpse of streaked ivory horn, the muddy camouflage coat incredibly hard to define against the mix of white, the shades of brown tree trunks and waving dark evergreen. Braced for that flash of the flag. Every sound became the focus of his concentration. He got to know each tree, from the adjoining oak to the stand of tall pines at the top of the rise.

Michael had come armed into the woods for the customary reason, to simplify life, to assume an ancient, uncomplicated identity. But the thoughts that surfaced in his silence were not comforting. The image of himself, for instance, as an agent of providence. The fact that for every creature things waited.

He regretted coming out. Somehow he could not make the day turn out to be the one he had imagined and looked forward to. The decision about whether to shoot led straight back to the life he had left in town. To other questions: who he was, what he wanted. To the wintry shadows across his bond with Kristin. He sat with the safety off, tense, vigilant, unhappy, waiting for the deer. He considered the wind, although there was hardly any.

The empty time passed quickly, as such time, strangely, often did. It was late in the darkening afternoon when he heard a voice. As soon as he heard it, he applied the safety on his shotgun.

The voice was a man's. At first, Michael thought the man was singing. But as the voice grew closer, he realized that the slight musical quality there reflected pain. He came completely out of the long day's trance and prepared to get down and help. Then, the vocalist still approaching, he caught the anger, the quality in the voice that dominated all others, the rage of someone utterly beside himself. Presently the words came—obscenities, strung together without a breath, alternately bellowed and shrieked as though they were coming from someone walking with difficulty. It still seemed possible to Michael that someone was hurt.

He scanned the woods in front of him, then adjusted his position to take in the ground just over his shoulder. At that point, he saw the fool.

A man about fifty came out of the pine cover forty yards away, slightly up the slope. If Michael's stand had not been placed so high, he realized, the man might easily have seen him. But the man's attention was altogether focussed on the buck he had brought down, a fine ten-pointer with a wide rack.

"Oh shit," he cried piteously, "oh goddam fucking shit cock-sucker."

He was struggling with the odd wheelbarrow across which he had slung his prize deer. It was a thing full of seams and joins and springs. Though it appeared large enough to contain the kill, it could not, and its inutility was the source of his sobs and curses and rage and despair. As the unfortunate man shoved and hauled, pushed and pulled his burden, covering the ground by inches, the extent of his rage became apparent. To Michael, observing from the tree, it was terrifying.

And justified. Because against every snow-covered rock and log the wheels of the weird contraption locked. Its useless container spilled forth the corpse of the deer and its antlers caught on the brush. Each time, the hunter manhandled it back aboard, where-upon it fell out again the other way, and the crazy wheelbarrow tipped on its side, and the handle slid from his grasp and he screeched in impotent but blood-chilling fury. Some men were poets when they swore. But the hunter below was not a poet; he was humorless and venomous and mean.

On and on, tripping on boulders, slipping on the ice and falling on his ass, endlessly locked in a death grip with his victim as though he had singlehandedly strangled the poor thing.

"Oh shit, oh goddam shit the fuck cocksucker."

And when he stopped to stand to one side and kick the con-traption—and followed that by kicking the deer—Michael, hardly daring to stir lest he be seen, buried his face in his sleeve against the trunk to repress the laughter welling up in him.

But now the fool, following the deer trail in his one-man danse macabre, was coming under the sparse bare branches of Michael's very tree. Michael could see his eyes and they were terrible and his red face and the freezing spittle on his graying beard. The man was covered with blood. He was humiliated and armed. Michael prayed that he would not look up.

He held his breath and watched fascinated as the man and the deer and the wheelbarrow passed beneath him in fits and starts and howlings. If the hunter below was possessed of the violent paranoid's tortured intuition, of the faintest sense of being spied on in his ghastly mortification—if he tilted back his head far enough to wail at the sky—he would see the witness to his folly. High above him lurked a Day-Glo-painted watcher in a tree, his masked, delighted face warped in a fiendish grin. If he sees me, Michael thought suddenly, he will kill me. Michael slipped his shotgun's safety off and put his gloved finger at the trigger.

Iced by fear, Michael's hilarity was transformed into a rage of his own. Oh priceless, he thought. Bozo sits up late drinking Old Bohemian in his trailer. In between commercials for schools that will teach him to drive an eighteen-wheeler and make big money, or be a forest ranger and give people orders and live in the open air instead of cleaning shovels down at the guano mill, he sees an ad for this idiotic conveyance to haul killed deer out of the forest. No more jacklighting them off the Interstate ramp or chainsawing road kill, hell no, he'll go into the forest like a macho male man with his nifty collapsible wheelbarrow. Folds up into twenty-five tiny parts so you can stick it in your back pocket like a roll-up measuring tape or wear it on your belt. It was shocking, he thought, the satisfaction you took in contemplating another man's disgrace. Another man's atoned for your own.

Finally, cursing and howling, the hunter bore his burden on. When he was gone, Michael realized he had been tracking the man down the barrel of his shotgun, every stumbling inch of the way. He shivered. It had got colder, no question. A wind had come up, whistling through the branches, rattling the icy leaves that still clung to them. When he looked at his watch, it was nearly four and time for the rendezvous. He tossed his pack, climbed from his tree, and set out for the base of the granite rock where he had left the others.

.   .   .

Alvin Mahoney was already waiting, hunkering down out of the wind. He stood up when Michael approached.

"See anything?"

"No deer. I did have something to watch though."

Norman Cevic came trudging up from the direction of the creek, his red-banded felt hat low over his eyes.

"So, I didn't hear any firing, fellas. Nothing to report?"

With all the suppressed energy of his long solitary day, Michael spun out the story of the sorry, angry man and his wonderful device.

"Didn't you hear the guy?" he asked his friends.

Norman said he had heard nothing but crows and wind in the trees.

"Poor bastard," Alvin said.

"You're lucky," Norman said. "Lucky he didn't look up and shoot you. A local. Probably needs the meat."

Michael wiped his lenses with a Kleenex. "You're breaking my heart."

"Revenge on the underclass," Norman said. "Nothing like it."

"Oh, come on," said Michael. "Don't be so fucking high-minded."

"We all enjoy it," Norman said. Then he said, "You know more game wardens get killed in the line of duty than any other law-enforcement officer?"

For a while they talked about populism and guns and militia-men. They had fallen silent in the dimming light when Alvin silently put a delaying hand on Michael's arm. Everyone stopped where they stood. There were deer, four of them, an eight-point buck and three females. One of the females looked little older than a yearling. The deer were drinking from the icy river, upstream, upwind. The three men began to ease closer to the stream, where a bend would provide them a clear line of fire. The deer were something more than thirty-five yards away. Michael tried shuffling through the snow, which was topped with a thin frozen layer, just thick enough ice to sound underfoot. He stepped on a frozen stick. It cracked. One of the does looked up and in their direction, then returned to her drinking. Finally, they came to a point beyond the tree line and looked at one another.

The target of choice would be the big buck. If they were after meat, the does, even the youngest, were legal game. The buck was splashing his way to the edge of deep water. In a moment all four of the deer tensed in place, ears up. A doe bent her foreleg, ready to spring. There was no more time. Everyone raised his weapon. Michael, without a scope, found himself sighting the shoulder of the buck. It was a beautiful animal. Magical in the fading light. Things change, he thought. Everything changes. His finger was on the trigger. When the other men fired, he did not. He had no clear idea why. Maybe the experience of having a man in his sights that day.

The buck raised his head and took a step forward. His forelegs buckled, and he shifted his hindquarters so that somehow his hind legs might take up the weight being surrendered by his weakening body. Michael watched the creature's dying. It was always hard to watch their legs give way. You could feel it in your own. The pain and vertigo.

"If he falls in that stream," Norman said, "he'll float halfway to Sioux City."

But the animal staggered briefly toward the bank and toppled sidewise into the shallows. The does vanished without a sound.

"Did you take a shot?" Norman asked Michael. Michael shook his head.

Examining the kill, they found two shotgun wounds close to the animal's heart.

"Guess we both got him," Norman said.

"He's yours," said Alvin. "You shot first."

Norman laughed. "No, man. We'll have the butcher divide him. Three ways."

Michael helped drag the dead deer by its antlers out of the water.

"Anybody want to mount that rack?" Norman asked.

"I don't think my wife would live with it," Michael told him.

"Mine either," Norman said. "Anyway it's not trophy size."

They were only a short distance from the canoe, but it was dark by the time they had hauled the deer aboard. Paddling upriver, they came to the place where Michael had dropped his flashlight overboard. The beam was still soldiering on, illuminating the bottom of the stream.

They secured the buck to the hood of their Jeep and set out for the state highway. This time they did not stop at the Hunter's Supper Club but drove all the way to Ehrlich's to get the deer tagged. When they had finished the forms for Fish & Game, they went into the restaurant and sat down to dinner. Mahoney was the designated driver and abstained from drink. He would, Michael thought, make up for it at home. He and Norman had Scotch, but it was not nearly as good as the Willoughby's. Then they ordered a pitcher of beer.

The menu featured wurst, schnitzel, potato pancakes, noodles, and dumplings. There were deer heads and antlers with brass plaques on the dark wood walls and scrolled mottos in Gothic script. A polka was on the jukebox and the place was filled with hunters. At Ehrlich's many of the hunters had family members along. There were women and children, even babies. Happy couples danced. The entire place rejoiced in an atmosphere of good-hearted revelry.

"Boy, is this place ever different from the Hunter's," Michael said. "It's not just the food."

"Know why?" Norman asked.

"Different people," said Michael.

"Different folks," Norman said. "This is Prevost County. They're Germans here. They're peace-loving. Orderly. You gotta love 'em."

"Do you?"

"Sure. Whereas the Hunter's is in the fucking swamp. Harrison County. Irish, Scotch-Irish. French Canadian. They're poor and surly. They're over at the Hunter's getting nasty drunk and selling one another wolf tickets. While here, *hier ist frölich.*"

He spread his arms, and with a cold, false smile enacted a parody of gemütlichkeit.

"Maybe we belong over there," Alvin Mahoney said.

Michael and Norman looked at each other and laughed.

Norman raised his beer glass. "Here's looking at you, Alvin," he said.

Alvin laughed. He was nervous, drinkless. It might be safer driving, Michael thought, to let him have a belt.

Michael was aware of Norman's watching him. "You didn't shoot today," Norman said.

Michael shrugged.

As they were waiting for the check, Norman said, "I have to ask you something. Over at St. Emmerich's, what are they teaching my friend Paulie about abortion? Me, I don't think there's much wrong with the world that doesn't come from there being too many people."

Michael poured out the last of the beer.

"I'm sorry," Norman said. "You're the only person I know to ask."

For the second time Michael was annoyed with Norman. Of course, sociologizing was the man's job. And he had never been subtle or discreet. He had been to Vietnam. He owned the big questions.

"They don't talk about it," Michael said. "Not at that level." He put a paper napkin to a tiny puddle of foam on the table before him. "They talked about hunting the other day." What he said was not exactly true. Paul was being taught that life began at conception. The rest, of course, would follow. But Michael was not in the mood to defend the theses of St. Emmerich's Christian instruction. Embarrassed, he flushed and hid behind his beer. He felt besieged. As though they were trying to take something away from him. Something he was not even sure he possessed.

Because I believe, he thought. They know I believe. If I believe. But faith is not what you believe, he thought. Faith was something else.

A blond waitress with a pretty, wholesome smile came over to them but she did not have the check.

"Is one of you guys Michael Ahearn?" she asked.

"Me," Michael said.

"Sir, you got a phone call. Want to take it in the kitchen?"

He followed her across the room, resounding with polkas, laughter, the rattle of plates and foaming schooners. In the kitchen three generations of women, the oldest in her late sixties, the youngest a little older than his son, worked purposefully. The warm room smelled of vinegary marinades. His wife was on the phone.

"Michael," she said. Her voice was distant and, he thought, chill. It made him think of the woods. Or of the light shining at the bottom of the freezing stream. "Paul is not accounted for. He was at the gym and then I thought he was going to Jimmy Collings'. But he's not there. And his schoolbooks are here. And Olaf is missing." She paused. "It's snowing here."

He remembered the deer at the edge of the stream. Its life ebbing, legs giving way.

"I suppose I called for moral support," she said. "I'm afraid."

"Hang in," he told her.

He walked unseeing back through the noisy room. Alvin and Norman were paying the check. Michael went into his wallet, took out two twenties, and threw them on the table.

"That's too much," Norman said.

"Kristin is worried about Paul. He's out late."

"I think he eloped with June," Norman said. "She's hot for him." June was Norman's wife. Then he looked at Michael and saw how things stood.

It was snowing on Ehrlich's parking lot when they got to the Jeep. Alvin checked the lines securing the carcass of the deer. Michael took a back seat.

"You know," Alvin said, "kids are always getting up to some caper and you get all hot and bothered and it's nothing."

It was the last thing anyone said on the ride home.

The snow came harder as they drove, slowing them down. Michael watched it fall. He thought of the man with the deer in his wheelbarrow. By gad, sir, you present a distressing spectacle. If he could make it up somehow. His thoughts had all been mean and low. What he did not want in his mind's eye now was his son's face. But it was there after all and the boy under snow. Hang in.

"Did I pass out?" he asked them.

"You were sleeping," Norman said.

How could he sleep? He had slept but forgotten nothing. His boy had been there the whole time. Prayer. No. You did not pray for things. Prayers, like Franklin's key on a kite, attracted lightning, burned out your mind and soul.

When, hours later, they drove into town there were dead deer hanging from the trees on everyone's lawn. The lawns were wide in that prairie town. They supported many trees and almost every bare tree on almost every lawn in front of almost every house had a dead deer, or even two, slung over the low boughs. There were bucks and does and fawns. All fair game, legal. There were too many deer.

A police car was blocking Michael's driveway. Norman parked the Jeep on the street, across the lawn from his front door. Everyone got out and when they did the young town policeman, whom Michael knew, whose name was Vandervliet, climbed out of his cruiser.

"Sir," Vandervliet said, "they're not here. They're at MacIvor."

MacIvor was the tri-county hospital on the north edge of town. Norman put a hand on his shoulder. Michael climbed into Vandervliet's Plymouth cruiser.

"What?" Michael asked the young cop. "Is my son alive?"

"Yes, sir. But he's suffering from exposure."

And it did not sound so good because as they both knew the cold, at a certain point, was irreversible, and all the heat, the fire, the cocoa, hot-water bottles, sleeping bags, down jackets, quilts, whiskey, medicine, nothing could make a child stop trembling and his temperature rise.

"Your wife is injured, Professor. I mean she ain't injured bad but she fell down trying to carry the boy I guess and so she's admitted also over there at MacIvor."

"I see," Michael said.

"See, the boy was looking for the dog 'cause the dog was out in the snow."

On the way to the hospital, Michael said, "I think I'm going to shoot that dog."

"I would," said Vandervliet.

At MacIvor, they were waiting for him. There was a nurse whose husband ran the Seattle-inspired coffee shop in town and a young doctor from back East. They looked so agitated, he went numb with fear. The doctor introduced himself but Michael heard none of it.

"Paul's vital signs are low," the doctor said. "We're hoping he'll respond. Unfortunately he's not conscious and we're concerned. We don't know how long he was outside in the storm."

Michael managed to speak. "His body temperature . . . ?"

"That's a cause of concern," the doctor said. "That will have to show improvement."

Michael did not look at him.

"We can treat this," the doctor said. "We see it here. There's hope."

"Thank you," Michael said. Above all, he did not want to see the boy. That fair vision and he kept repelling it. He was afraid to watch Paul die, though surely even in death he would be beautiful.

"We'd like you to talk to . . . to your wife," the doctor said. "We're sure she has a fracture and she won't go to X-ray." He hesitated for a moment and went off down the corridor.

At MacIvor the passageways had the form of an "X." As the doctor walked off down one bar of the pattern, Michael saw what appeared to be his wife at the end of the other. She was in a wheelchair. The nurse followed him as he walked toward her.

"She won't go to X-ray," the nurse complained. "Her leg's been splinted and she's had pain medication and we have a bed ready for her but she won't rest. She won't let the medication do its thing."

Kristin, huge-eyed and white as chalk, wheeled herself in their direction. But when Michael came up, the nurse in tow, she looked through him. There was an open Bible on her lap.

The nurse went to take the handles of Kristin's wheelchair. Michael stepped in and took them himself. Do its thing? He had trouble turning the wheelchair around. The rear wheels refused to straighten out. Do their thing. He pushed his wife toward the wall. Her splinted right leg extended straight out and when her foot touched the wall she uttered a soft cry. Tears ran down her face.

"There's a little trick to it," said the nurse. She made a sound that was not quite a laugh. "Let me."

Michael ignored her. The wheelchair resisted his trembling pressure. Oh goddam shit.

"Take me in to him," Kristin said.

"Better not," the nurse said, to Michael's relief.

If he could see himself, futilely trying to ambulate his wife on wheels, Michael thought, it would be funny. But hospitals never had mirrors. There was a discovery. In the place of undoings, where things came apart, your children changed to cadavers, you spun your wife in wheelies, no mirrors. The joke was on you but you did not have to watch yourself.

When they were in the room she said, "I fell carrying him. He was by the garden fence—I fell in the snow." He could picture her carrying Paul up from the garden, tripping, slipping, stumbling. He took her icy hand but she withdrew it. "He was so cold."

"Lie down," he said. "Can you?"

"No, it hurts."

He stood and rang for the nurse.

Kristin took up the Bible as though she were entranced and began to read aloud.

"'Be merciful unto me, O God, be merciful unto me: for my soul trusteth in thee: yea, in the shadow of thy wings will I make my refuge.'"

Closing his eyes, he tried to hold on to the words. Listening to her read in her mother's strange featureless tone he could imagine Luther's Bible the way her mother out on the plains must have heard it from her own parents. A psalm for fools in the snow. Really expecting nothing but cold and death in the shadow of those wings. Odin's raven.

"'Until these calamities be overpast. I will cry unto God most high.'"

Michael sat listening, despising the leaden resignation of his wife's prayer, its acceptance, surrender. His impulse was flight.

"'My soul is among lions,'" she read, "'and I lie even among them that are set on fire.'"

His impulse was flight. He sat there burning until the nurse came in. For some reason, she looked merry, confidential.

"I think we turned a corner," she said. "Michael! Kristin! I think we turned a corner."

Then the doctor entered quietly and they got Kristin into bed and she went under the medication. Even unconscious her eyes were half open.

The doctor said you responded or you didn't and Paul had responded. His temperature was going up. He was coming up. He would even get his fingers and toes back and his ethical little Christian brain going, it appeared. The doctor looked so relieved.

"You can have a minute while we get the gurney. We've gotta get her X-rayed pronto because she's got a broken leg there."

"You can see Paul," the nurse said. "He's sleeping. Real sleep now."

The doctor laughed. "It's very exhausting to half freeze to death."

"It would be," Michael said.

While they got the gurney, he looked into Kristin's half-open, tortured, long-lashed blue eyes and brushed the slightly graying black hair from them. With her long face and buck teeth she looked like the Christus on a Viking crucifix. Given her, he thought, given me, why didn't he die? Maybe he still will, Michael thought. The notion terrified him. He had stood up to make his escape when the orderlies came in to take Kristin away. Michael rubbed her cold hand.

The chapel was down at the end of the corridor. It had a kind of altar, stained-glass windows that opened on nothing, that were inlaid with clouds and doves and other fine inspirational things.

Michael had been afraid, for a while, that there was something out there, at the beginning and end of consciousness. An alpha and an omega to things. He had believed it for years on and off. And that night, he had felt certain, the fire would be visited on him. His boy would be taken away and he would know, know absolutely the power of the most high. Its horrible providence. Its mysteries, its hide-and-seek, and lessons, and redefined top-secret mercies to be understood through prayer and meditation. But only at really special moments of rhapsody and ecstasy and, O, wondrous clarity. Behold now behemoth. Who can draw Leviathan? Et cetera.

But now his son's life was saved. And the great thing had come of nothing, of absolutely nothing, out of a kaleidoscope, out of a Cracker Jack box. Every day its own flower, to every day its own stink and savor. Good old random singularity and you could exercise a proper revulsion for life's rank overabundance and everybody could have their rights and be happy.

And he could be a serious person, a grownup at last and not worry over things that educated people had not troubled themselves with practically for centuries. Free at last and it didn't mean a thing and it would all be over, some things sooner than later. His marriage, for one, sealed in faith like the Sepulchral stone. Vain now. No one watched over us. Or rather we watched over each other. That was providence, what a relief. He turned his back on the inspirations of the chapel and went out to watch his lovely son survive another day.

THE NEW YORKER

**The Third and
Final Continent**

*Jhumpa Lahiri is a young writer
with an original voice and an
extraordinary feel for grace and dignity and silence. The daughter of
Indian immigrants, she works out,
through her stories, the struggles
that people like her parents, or
members of her parents' family,
underwent in becoming American.*

Jhumpa Lahiri

The Third and Final Continent

I left India in 1964 with a certificate in commerce and the equivalent, in those days, of ten dollars to my name. For three weeks I sailed on the S.S. Roma, an Italian cargo vessel, in a cabin next to the ship's engine, across the Arabian Sea, the Red Sea, the Mediterranean, and finally to England. I lived in London, in Finsbury Park, in a house occupied entirely by penniless Bengali bachelors like myself, at least a dozen and sometimes more, all struggling to educate and establish ourselves abroad.

I attended lectures at L.S.E. and worked at the university library to get by. We lived three or four to a room, shared a single, icy toilet, and took turns cooking pots of egg curry, which we ate with our hands on a table covered with newspapers. Apart from our jobs we had few responsibilities. On weekends we lounged barefoot in drawstring pajamas, drinking tea and smoking Rothmans, or set out to watch cricket at Lord's. Some weekends the house was crammed with still more Bengalis, to whom we had introduced ourselves at the greengrocer, or on the Tube, and we made yet more egg curry, and played Mukesh on a Grundig reel-to-reel, and soaked our dirty dishes in the bathtub. Every now and then someone in the house moved out, to live with a woman whom his family back in Calcutta had determined he was to wed. In 1969, when I was thirty-six years old, my own marriage was arranged. Around the same time, I was offered a full-time job in

America, in the processing department of a library at M.I.T. The salary was generous enough to support a wife, and I was honored to be hired by a world-famous university, and so I obtained a green card, and prepared to travel farther still.

By then I had enough money to go by plane. I flew first to Calcutta, to attend my wedding, and a week later to Boston, to begin my new job. During the flight I read "The Student Guide to North America," for although I was no longer a student, I was on a budget all the same. I learned that Americans drove on the right side of the road, not the left, and that they called a lift an elevator and an engaged phone busy. "The pace of life in North America is different from Britain, as you will soon discover," the guidebook informed me. "Everybody feels he must get to the top. Don't expect an English cup of tea." As the plane began its descent over Boston Harbor, the pilot announced the weather and the time, and that President Nixon had declared a national holiday: two American men had landed on the moon. Several passengers cheered. "God bless America!" one of them hollered. Across the aisle, I saw a woman praying.

I spent my first night at the Y.M.C.A. in Central Square, Cambridge, an inexpensive accommodation recommended by my guidebook which was within walking distance of M.I.T. The room contained a cot, a desk, and a small wooden cross on one wall. A sign on the door said that cooking was strictly forbidden. A bare window overlooked Massachusetts Avenue. Car horns, shrill and prolonged, blared one after another. Sirens and flashing lights heralded endless emergencies, and a succession of buses rumbled past, their doors opening and closing with a powerful hiss, throughout the night. The noise was constantly distracting, at times suffocating. I felt it deep in my ribs, just as I had felt the furious drone of the engine on the S.S. Roma. But there was no ship's deck to escape to, no glittering ocean to thrill my soul, no breeze to cool my face, no one to talk to. I was too tired to pace the gloomy corridors of the Y.M.C.A. in my pajamas. Instead I sat at the desk and stared out the window. In the morning I reported to my job at the Dewey Library, a beige fortlike building by Memorial Drive. I also opened a bank account, rented a post-office box, and bought a plastic bowl and a spoon. I went to a supermarket called Purity Supreme, wandering up and down the aisles, comparing prices with those in England. In the end I bought a carton of milk and a box of cornflakes. This was my first meal in America. Even the simple chore of buying milk was new to me; in London we'd had bottles delivered each morning to our door.

In a week I had adjusted, more or less. I ate cornflakes and milk morning and night, and bought some bananas for variety, slicing them into the bowl with the edge of my spoon. I left my carton of milk on the shaded part of the windowsill, as I had seen other residents at the Y.M.C.A. do. To pass the time in the evenings I read the Boston *Globe* downstairs, in a spacious room with stained-glass windows. I read every article and advertisement, so that I would grow familiar with things, and when my eyes grew tired I slept. Only I did not sleep well. Each night I had to keep the window wide open; it was the only source of air in the stifling room, and the noise was intolerable. I would lie on the cot with my fingers pressed into my ears, but when I drifted off to sleep my hands fell away, and the noise of the traffic would wake me up again. Pigeon feathers drifted onto the windowsill, and one evening, when I poured milk over my cornflakes, I saw that it had soured. Nevertheless I resolved to stay at the Y.M.C.A. for six weeks, until my wife's passport and green card were ready. Once she arrived I would have to rent a proper apartment, and from time to time I studied the classified section of the newspaper, or stopped in at the housing office at M.I.T. during my lunch break to see what was available. It was in this manner that I discovered a room for immediate occupancy, in a house on a quiet street, the listing said, for eight dollars per week. I dialled the number from a pay telephone, sorting through the coins, with which I was still unfamiliar, smaller and lighter than shillings, heavier and brighter than paisas.

"Who is speaking?" a woman demanded. Her voice was bold and clamorous.

"Yes, good afternoon, Madam. I am calling about the room for rent."

"Harvard or Tech?"

"I beg your pardon?"

"Are you from Harvard or Tech?"

Gathering that Tech referred to the Massachusetts Institute of Technology, I replied, "I work at Dewey Library," adding tentatively, "at Tech."

"I only rent rooms to boys from Harvard or Tech!"

"Yes, Madam."

I was given an address and an appointment for seven o'clock that evening. Thirty minutes before the hour I set out, my guidebook in my pocket, my breath fresh with Listerine. I turned down a street shaded with trees, perpendicular to Massachusetts Avenue. In spite of the heat I wore a coat and tie, regarding the event as I would any other interview; I had never lived in the home of a person who was not Indian. The house, surrounded by a chain-link fence, was off-white with dark-brown trim, with a tangle of forsythia bushes plastered against its front and sides. When I pressed the bell, the woman with whom I had spoken on the phone hollered from what seemed to be just the other side of the door, "One minute, please!"

Several minutes later the door was opened by a tiny, extremely old woman. A mass of snowy hair was arranged like a small sack on top of her head. As I stepped into the house she sat down on a wooden bench positioned at the bottom of a narrow carpeted staircase. Once she was settled on the bench, in a small pool of light, she peered up at me, giving me her undivided attention. She wore a long black skirt that spread like a stiff tent to the floor, and a starched white shirt edged with ruffles at the throat and cuffs. Her hands, folded together in her lap, had long pallid fingers, with swollen knuckles and tough yellow nails. Age had battered her features so that she almost resembled a man, with sharp, shrunken eyes and prominent creases on either side of her nose. Her lips, chapped and faded, had nearly disappeared, and her eyebrows were missing altogether. Nevertheless she looked fierce.

"Lock up!" she commanded. She shouted even though I stood only a few feet away. "Fasten the chain and firmly press that button on the knob! This is the first thing you shall do when you enter, is that clear?"

I locked the door as directed and examined the house. Next to the bench was a small round table, its legs fully concealed, much like the woman's, by a skirt of lace. The table held a lamp, a transistor radio, a leather change purse with a silver clasp, and a telephone. A thick wooden cane was propped against one side. There was a parlor to my right, lined with bookcases and filled with shabby claw-footed furniture. In the corner of the parlor I saw a grand piano with its top down, piled with papers. The piano's bench was missing; it seemed to be the one on which the woman was sitting. Somewhere in the house a clock chimed seven times.

"You're punctual!" the woman proclaimed. "I expect you shall be so with the rent!"

"I have a letter, Madam." In my jacket pocket was a letter from M.I.T. confirming my employment, which I had brought along to prove that I was indeed from Tech.

She stared at the letter, then handed it back to me carefully, gripping it with her fingers as if it were a plate heaped with food. She did not wear glasses, and I wondered if she'd read a word of it. "The last boy was always late! Still owes me eight dollars! Harvard boys aren't what they used to be! Only Harvard and Tech in this house! How's Tech, boy?"

"It is very well."

"You checked the lock?"

"Yes, Madam."

She unclasped her fingers, slapped the space beside her on the bench with one hand, and told me to sit down. For a moment she was silent. Then she intoned, as if she alone possessed this knowledge:

"There is an American flag on the moon!"

"Yes, Madam." Until then I had not thought very much about the moon shot. It was in the newspaper, of course, article upon article. The astronauts had landed on the shores of the Sea of Tranquillity, I had read, travelling farther than anyone in the history of civilization. For a few hours they explored the moon's surface. They gathered rocks in their pockets, described their surroundings (a magnificent desolation, according to one astronaut), spoke by phone to the President, and planted a flag in lunar soil. The voyage was hailed as man's most awesome achievement.

The woman bellowed, "A flag on the moon, boy! I heard it on the radio! Isn't that splendid?"

"Yes, Madam."

But she was not satisfied with my reply. Instead she commanded, "Say 'Splendid!'"

I was both baffled and somewhat insulted by the request. It reminded me of the way I was taught multiplication tables as a child, repeating after the master, sitting cross-legged on the floor of my one-room Tollygunge school. It also reminded me of my wedding, when I had repeated endless Sanskrit verses after the priest, verses I barely understood, which joined me to my wife. I said nothing.

"Say 'Splendid!'" the woman bellowed once again.

"Splendid," I murmured. I had to repeat the word a second time at the top of my lungs, so she could hear. I was reluctant to raise my voice to an elderly woman, but she did not appear to be offended. If anything the reply pleased her, because her next command was:

"Go see the room!"

I rose from the bench and mounted the narrow staircase. There were five doors, two on either side of an equally narrow hallway, and one at the opposite end. Only one door was open. The room contained a twin bed under a sloping ceiling, a brown oval rug, a basin with an exposed pipe, and a chest of drawers. One door led to a closet, another to a toilet and a tub. The window was open; net curtains stirred in the breeze. I lifted them away and inspected the view: a small back yard, with a few fruit trees and an empty clothesline. I was satisfied.

When I returned to the foyer the woman picked up the leather change purse on the table, opened the clasp, fished about with her fingers, and produced a key on a thin wire hoop. She informed me that there was a kitchen at the back of the house, accessible through the parlor. I was welcome to use the stove as long as I left it as I found it. Sheets and towels were provided, but keeping them clean was my own responsibility. The rent was due Friday mornings on the ledge above the piano keys. "And no lady visitors!"

"I am a married man, Madam." It was the first time I had announced this fact to anyone.

But she had not heard. "No lady visitors!" she insisted. She introduced herself as Mrs. Croft.

My wife's name was Mala. The marriage had been arranged by my older brother and his wife. I regarded the proposition with neither objection nor enthusiasm. It was a duty expected of me, as it was expected of every man. She was the daughter of a school-teacher in Beleghata. I was told that she could cook, knit, embroi-der, sketch landscapes, and recite poems by Tagore, but these talents could not make up for the fact that she did not possess a fair complexion, and so a string of men had rejected her to her face. She was twenty-seven, an age when her parents had begun to fear that she would never marry, and so they were willing to ship their only child halfway across the world in order to save her from spinsterhood.

For five nights we shared a bed. Each of those nights, after applying cold cream and braiding her hair, she turned from me and wept; she missed her parents. Although I would be leaving the country in a few days, custom dictated that she was now a part of my household, and for the next six weeks she was to live with my brother and his wife, cooking, cleaning, serving tea and sweets to guests. I did nothing to console her. I lay on my own side of the bed, reading my guidebook by flashlight. At times I thought of the tiny room on the other side of the wall which had belonged to my mother. Now the room was practically empty; the wooden pallet on which she'd once slept was piled with trunks and old bedding. Nearly six years ago, before leaving for London, I had watched her die on that bed, had found her playing with her excrement in her final days. Before we cremated her I had cleaned each of her fingernails with a hairpin, and then, because my brother could not bear it, I had assumed the role of eldest son, and had touched the flame to her temple, to release her tormented soul to heaven.

The next morning I moved into Mrs. Croft's house. When I unlocked the door I saw that she was sitting on the piano bench, on the same side as the previous evening. She wore the same black skirt, the same starched white blouse, and had her hands folded together the same way in her lap. She looked so much the same that I wondered if she'd spent the whole night on the bench. I put my suitcase upstairs and then headed off to work. That evening when I came home from the university, she was still there.

"Sit down, boy!" She slapped the space beside her.

I perched on the bench. I had a bag of groceries with me—more milk, more cornflakes, and more bananas, for my inspection of the kitchen earlier in the day had revealed no spare pots or pans. There were only two saucepans in the refrigerator, both containing some orange broth, and a copper kettle on the stove.

"Good evening, Madam."

She asked me if I had checked the lock. I told her I had.

For a moment she was silent. Then suddenly she declared, with the equal measures of disbelief and delight as the night before, "There's an American flag on the moon, boy!"

"Yes, Madam."

"A flag on the moon! Isn't that splendid?"

I nodded, dreading what I knew was coming. "Yes, Madam."

"Say 'Splendid!'"

This time I paused, looking to either side in case anyone was there to overhear me, though I knew perfectly well that the house was empty. I felt like an idiot. But it was a small enough thing to ask. "Splendid!" I cried out.

Within days it became our routine. In the mornings when I left for the library Mrs. Croft was either hidden away in her bedroom, on the other side of the staircase, or sitting on the bench, oblivious of my presence, listening to the news or classical music on the radio. But each evening when I returned the same thing happened: she slapped the bench, ordered me to sit down, declared that there was a flag on the moon, and declared that it was splendid. I said it was splendid, too, and then we sat in silence. As awkward as it was, and as endless as it felt to me then, the nightly encounter lasted only about ten minutes; inevitably she would drift off to sleep, her head falling abruptly toward her chest, leaving me free to retire to my room. By then, of course, there was no flag standing on the moon. The astronauts, I read in the paper, had seen it fall before they flew back to Earth. But I did not have the heart to tell her.

.   .   .

Friday morning, when my first week's rent was due, I went to the piano in the parlor to place my money on the ledge. The piano keys were dull and discolored. When I pressed one, it made no sound at all. I had put eight dollar bills in an envelope and written Mrs. Croft's name on the front of it. I was not in the habit of leaving money unmarked and unattended. From where I stood I could see the profile of her tent-shaped skirt in the hall. It seemed unnecessary to make her get up and walk all the way to the piano. I never saw her walking about, and assumed, from the cane propped against the round table, that she did so with difficulty. When I approached the bench she peered up at me and demanded:

"What is your business?"

"The rent, Madam."

"On the ledge above the piano keys!"

"I have it here." I extended the envelope toward her, but her fingers, folded together in her lap, did not budge. I bowed slightly and lowered the envelope, so that it hovered just above her hands. After a moment she accepted it, and nodded her head.

That night when I came home, she did not slap the bench, but out of habit I sat beside her as usual. She asked me if I had checked the lock, but she mentioned nothing about the flag on the moon. Instead she said:

"It was very kind of you!"

"I beg your pardon, Madam?"

"Very kind of you!"

She was still holding the envelope in her hands.

On Sunday there was a knock on my door. An elderly woman introduced herself: she was Mrs. Croft's daughter, Helen. She walked into the room and looked at each of the walls as if for signs of change, glancing at the shirts that hung in the closet, the neckties draped over the doorknob, the box of cornflakes on the chest of drawers, the dirty bowl and spoon in the basin. She was short and thick-waisted, with cropped silver hair and bright pink lip-stick. She wore a sleeveless summer dress, a necklace of white plastic beads, and spectacles on a chain that hung like a swing against her chest. The backs of her legs were mapped with dark-blue veins, and her upper arms sagged like the flesh of a roasted egg-plant. She told me she lived in Arlington, a town farther up Massachusetts Avenue. "I come once a week to bring Mother groceries. Has she sent you packing yet?"

"It is very well, Madam."

"Some of the boys run screaming. But I think she likes you. You're the first boarder she's ever referred to as a gentleman."

She looked at me, noticing my bare feet. (I still felt strange wearing shoes indoors, and always removed them before entering my room.) "Are you new to Boston?"

"New to America, Madam."

"From?" She raised her eyebrows.

"I am from Calcutta, India."

"Is that right? We had a Brazilian fellow, about a year ago. You'll find Cambridge a very international city."

I nodded, and began to wonder how long our conversation would last. But at that moment we heard Mrs. Croft's electrifying voice rising up the stairs.

"You are to come downstairs immediately!"

"What is it?" Helen cried back.

"Immediately!"

I put on my shoes. Helen sighed.

I followed Helen down the staircase. She seemed to be in no hurry, and complained at one point that she had a bad knee. "Have you been walking without your cane?" Helen called out. "You know you're not supposed to walk without that cane." She paused, resting her hand on the bannister, and looked back at me. "She slips sometimes."

For the first time Mrs. Croft seemed vulnerable. I pictured her on the floor in front of the bench, flat on her back, staring at the ceiling, her feet pointing in opposite directions. But when we reached the bottom of the staircase she was sitting there as usual, her hands folded together in her lap. Two grocery bags were at her feet. She did not slap the bench, or ask us to sit down. She glared.

"What is it, Mother?"

"It's improper!"

"What's improper?"

"It is improper for a lady and gentleman who are not married to one another to hold a private conversation without a chaperone!"

Helen said she was sixty-eight years old, old enough to be my mother, but Mrs. Croft insisted that Helen and I speak to each other downstairs, in the parlor. She added that it was also improper for a lady of Helen's station to reveal her age, and to wear a dress so high above the ankle.

"For your information, Mother, it's 1969. What would you do if you actually left the house one day and saw a girl in a miniskirt?"

Mrs. Croft sniffed. "I'd have her arrested."

Helen shook her head and picked up one of the grocery bags. I picked up the other one, and followed her through the parlor and into the kitchen. The bags were filled with cans of soup, which Helen opened up one by one with a few cranks of a can opener. She tossed the old soup into the sink, rinsed the saucepans under the tap, filled them with soup from the newly opened cans, and put them back in the refrigerator. "A few years ago she could still open the cans herself," Helen said. "She hates that I do it for her now. But the piano killed her hands." She put on her spectacles, glanced at the cupboards, and spotted my tea bags. "Shall we have a cup?"

I filled the kettle on the stove. "I beg your pardon, Madam. The piano?"

"She used to give lessons. For forty years. It was how she raised us after my father died." Helen put her hands on her hips, staring at the open refrigerator. She reached into the back, pulled out a wrapped stick of butter, frowned, and tossed it into the garbage. "That ought to do it," she said, and put the unopened cans of soup in the cupboard. I sat at the table and watched as Helen washed the dirty dishes, tied up the garbage bag, and poured boiling water into two cups. She handed one to me without milk, and sat down at the table.

"Excuse me, Madam, but is it enough?"

Helen took a sip of her tea. Her lipstick left a smiling pink stain on the rim of the cup. "Is what enough?"

"The soup in the pans. Is it enough food for Mrs. Croft?"

"She won't eat anything else. She stopped eating solids after she turned one hundred. That was, let's see, three years ago."

I was mortified. I had assumed Mrs. Croft was in her eighties, perhaps as old as ninety. I had never known a person who had lived for over a century. That this person was a widow who lived alone mortified me further still. Widowhood had driven my own mother insane. My father, who worked as a clerk at the General Post Office of Calcutta, died of encephalitis when I was sixteen. My mother refused to adjust to life without him; instead she sank deeper into a world of darkness from which neither I, nor my brother, nor concerned relatives, nor psychiatric clinics on Rash Behari Avenue could save her. What pained me most was to see her so unguarded, to hear her burp after meals or expel gas in front of company without the slightest embarrassment. After my father's death my brother abandoned his schooling and began to work in the jute mill he would eventually manage, in order to keep the household running. And so it was my job to sit by my mother's feet and study for my exams as she counted and recounted the bracelets on her arm as if they were the beads of an abacus. We tried to keep an eye on her. Once she had wandered half naked to the tram depot before we were able to bring her inside again.

"I am happy to warm Mrs. Croft's soup in the evenings," I suggested. "It is no trouble."

Helen looked at her watch, stood up, and poured the rest of her tea into the sink. "I wouldn't if I were you. That's the sort of thing that would kill her altogether."

That evening, when Helen had gone and Mrs. Croft and I were alone again, I began to worry. Now that I knew how very old she was, I worried that something would happen to her in the middle of the night, or when I was out during the day. As vigorous as her voice was, and imperious as she seemed, I knew that even a scratch or a cough could kill a person that old; each day she lived, I knew, was something of a miracle. Helen didn't seem concerned. She came and went, bringing soup for Mrs. Croft, one Sunday after the next.

In this manner the six weeks of that summer passed. I came home each evening, after my hours at the library, and spent a few minutes on the piano bench with Mrs. Croft. Some evenings I sat beside her long after she had drifted off to sleep, still in awe of how many years she had spent on this earth. At times I tried to picture the world she had been born into, in 1866—a world, I imagined, filled with women in long black skirts, and chaste conversations in the parlor. Now, when I looked at her hands with their swollen knuckles folded together in her lap, I imagined them smooth and slim, striking the piano keys. At times I came downstairs before going to sleep, to make sure she was sitting upright on the bench, or was safe in her bedroom. On Fridays I put the rent in her hands. There was nothing I could do for her beyond these simple gestures. I was not her son, and, apart from those eight dollars, I owed her nothing.

At the end of August, Mala's passport and green card were ready. I received a telegram with her flight information; my brother's house in Calcutta had no telephone. Around that time I also received a letter from her, written only a few days after we had parted. There was no salutation; addressing me by name would have assumed an intimacy we had not yet discovered. It contained only a few lines. "I write in English in preparation for the journey. Here I am very much lonely. Is it very cold there. Is there snow. Yours, Mala."

I was not touched by her words. We had spent only a handful of days in each other's company. And yet we were bound together; for six weeks she had worn an iron bangle on her wrist, and applied vermillion powder to the part in her hair, to signify to the world that she was a bride. In those six weeks I regarded her arrival as I would the arrival of a coming month, or season—something inevitable, but meaningless at the time. So little did I know her that, while details of her face sometimes rose to my memory, I could not conjure up the whole of it.

A few days after receiving the letter, as I was walking to work in the morning, I saw an Indian woman on Massachusetts Avenue, wearing a sari with its free end nearly dragging on the footpath, and pushing a child in a stroller. An American woman with a small black dog on a leash was walking to one side of her. Suddenly the dog began barking. I watched as the Indian woman, startled, stopped in her path, at which point the dog leaped up and seized the end of the sari between its teeth. The American woman scolded the dog, appeared to apologize, and walked quickly away, leaving the Indian woman to fix her sari, and quiet her crying child. She did not see me standing there, and eventually she continued on her way. Such a mishap, I realized that morning, would soon be my concern. It was my duty to take care of Mala, to welcome her and protect her. I would have to buy her her first pair of snow boots, her first winter coat. I would have to tell her which streets to avoid, which way the traffic came, tell her to wear her sari so that the free end did not drag on the footpath. A five-mile separation from her parents, I recalled with some irritation, had caused her to weep.

Unlike Mala, I was used to it all by then: used to cornflakes and milk, used to Helen's visits, used to sitting on the bench with Mrs. Croft. The only thing I was not used to was Mala. Nevertheless I did what I had to do. I went to the housing office at M.I.T. and found a furnished apartment a few blocks away, with a double bed and a private kitchen and bath, for forty dollars a week. One last Friday I handed Mrs. Croft eight dollar bills in an envelope, brought my suitcase downstairs, and informed her that I was moving. She put my key into her change purse. The last thing she asked me to do was hand her the cane propped against the table, so that she could walk to the door and lock it behind me. "Good-bye, then," she said, and retreated back into the house. I did not expect any display of emotion, but I was disappointed all the same. I was only a boarder, a man who paid her a bit of money and passed in and out of her home for six weeks. Compared with a century, it was no time at all.

At the airport I recognized Mala immediately. The free end of her sari did not drag on the floor, but was draped in a sign of bridal modesty over her head, just as it had draped my mother until the day my father died. Her thin brown arms were stacked with gold bracelets, a small red circle was painted on her forehead, and the edges of her feet were tinted with a decorative red dye. I did not embrace her, or kiss her, or take her hand. Instead I asked her, speaking Bengali for the first time in America, if she was hungry.

She hesitated, then nodded yes.

I told her I had prepared some egg curry at home. "What did they give you to eat on the plane?"

"I didn't eat."

"All the way from Calcutta?"

"The menu said oxtail soup."

"But surely there were other items."

"The thought of eating an ox's tail made me lose my appetite."

When we arrived home, Mala opened up one of her suitcases, and presented me with two pullover sweaters, both made with bright-blue wool, which she had knitted in the course of our separation, one with a V neck, the other covered with cables. I tried them on; both were tight under the arms. She had also brought me two new pairs of drawstring pajamas, a letter from my brother, and a packet of loose Darjeeling tea. I had no present for her apart from the egg curry. We sat at a bare table, staring at our plates. We ate with our hands, another thing I had not yet done in America.

"The house is nice," she said. "Also the egg curry." With her left hand she held the end of her sari to her chest, so it would not slip off her head.

"I don't know many recipes."

She nodded, peeling the skin off each of her potatoes before eating them. At one point the sari slipped to her shoulders. She readjusted it at once.

"There is no need to cover your head," I said. "I don't mind. It doesn't matter here."

She kept it covered anyway.

I waited to get used to her, to her presence at my side, at my table and in my bed, but a week later we were still strangers. I still was not used to coming home to an apartment that smelled of steamed rice, and finding that the basin in the bathroom was always wiped clean, our two toothbrushes lying side by side, a cake of Pears soap residing in the soap dish. I was not used to the fragrance of the coconut oil she rubbed every other night into her scalp, or the delicate sound her bracelets made as she moved about the apartment. In the mornings she was always awake before I was. The first morning when I came into the kitchen she had heated up the leftovers and set a plate with a spoonful of salt on its edge, assuming I would eat rice for breakfast, as most Bengali husbands did. I told her cereal would do, and the next morning when I came into the kitchen she had already poured the cornflakes into my bowl. One morning she walked with me to M.I.T., where I gave her a short tour of the campus. The next morning before I left for work she asked me for a few dollars. I parted with them reluctantly, but I knew that this, too, was now normal. When I came home from work there was a potato peeler in the kitchen drawer, and a tablecloth on the table, and chicken curry made with fresh garlic and ginger on the stove. After dinner I read the newspaper, while Mala sat at the kitchen table, working on a cardigan for herself with more of the blue wool, or writing letters home.

On Friday, I suggested going out. Mala sat down her knitting and disappeared into the bathroom. When she emerged I regretted the suggestion; she had put on a silk sari and extra bracelets, and coiled her hair with a flattering side part on top of her head. She was prepared as if for a party, or at the very least for the cinema, but I had no such destination in mind. The evening was balmy. We walked several blocks down Massachusetts Avenue, looking into the windows of restaurants and shops. Then, without thinking, I led her down the quiet street where for so many nights I had walked alone.

"This is where I lived before you came," I said, stopping at Mrs. Croft's chain-link fence.

"In such a big house?"

"I had a small room upstairs. At the back."

"Who else lives there?"

"A very old woman."

"With her family?"

"Alone."

"But who takes care of her?"

I opened the gate. "For the most part she takes care of herself."

I wondered if Mrs. Croft would remember me; I wondered if she had a new boarder to sit with her each evening. When I pressed the bell I expected the same long wait as that day of our first meeting, when I did not have a key. But this time the door was opened almost immediately, by Helen. Mrs. Croft was not sitting on the bench. The bench was gone.

"Hello there," Helen said, smiling with her bright pink lips at Mala. "Mother's in the parlor. Will you be visiting awhile?"

"As you wish, Madam."

"Then I think I'll run to the store, if you don't mind. She had a little accident. We can't leave her alone these days, not even for a minute."

I locked the door after Helen and walked into the parlor. Mrs. Croft was lying flat on her back, her head on a peach-colored cushion, a thin white quilt spread over her body. Her hands were folded together on her chest. When she saw me she pointed at the sofa, and told me to sit down. I took my place as directed, but Mala wandered over to the piano and sat on the bench, which was now positioned where it belonged.

"I broke my hip!" Mrs. Croft announced, as if no time had passed.

"Oh dear, Madam."

"I fell off the bench!"

"I am so sorry, Madam."

"It was the middle of the night! Do you know what I did, boy?"

I shook my head.

"I called the police!"

She stared up at the ceiling and grinned sedately, exposing a crowded row of long gray teeth. "What do you say to that, boy?"

As stunned as I was, I knew what I had to say. With no hesitation at all, I cried out, "Splendid!"

Mala laughed then. Her voice was full of kindness, her eyes bright with amusement. I had never heard her laugh before, and it was loud enough so that Mrs. Croft heard, too. She turned to Mala and glared.

"Who is she, boy?"

"She is my wife, Madam."

Mrs. Croft pressed her head at an angle against the cushion to get a better look. "Can you play the piano?"

"No, Madam," Mala replied.

"Then stand up!"

Mala rose to her feet, adjusting the end of her sari over her head and holding it to her chest, and, for the first time since her arrival, I felt sympathy. I remembered my first days in London, learning how to take the Tube to Russell Square, riding an escalator for the first time, unable to understand that when the man cried "piper" it meant "paper," unable to decipher, for a whole year, that the conductor said "Mind the gap" as the train pulled away from each station. Like me, Mala had travelled far from home, not knowing where she was going, or what she would find, for no reason other than to be my wife. As strange as it seemed, I knew in my heart that one day her death would affect me, and stranger still, that mine would affect her. I wanted somehow to explain this to Mrs. Croft, who was still scrutinizing Mala from top to toe with what seemed to be placid disdain. I wondered if Mrs. Croft had ever seen a woman in a sari, with a dot painted on her forehead and bracelets stacked on her wrists. I wondered what she would object to. I wondered if she could see the red dye still vivid on Mala's feet, all but obscured by the bottom edge of her sari. At last Mrs. Croft declared, with the equal measures of disbelief and delight I knew well:

"She is a perfect lady!"

Now it was I who laughed. I did so quietly, and Mrs. Croft did not hear me. But Mala had heard, and, for the first time, we looked at each other and smiled.

I like to think of that moment in Mrs. Croft's parlor as the moment when the distance between Mala and me began to lessen. Although we were not yet fully in love, I like to think of the months that followed as a honeymoon of sorts. Together we explored the city and met other Bengalis, some of whom are still friends today. We discovered that a man named Bill sold fresh fish on Prospect Street, and that a shop in Harvard Square called Cardullo's sold bay leaves and cloves. In the evenings we walked to the Charles River to watch sailboats drift across the water, or had ice-cream cones in Harvard Yard. We bought a camera with which to document our life together, and I took pictures of her posing in front of the Prudential Building, so that she could send them to her parents. At night we kissed, shy at first but quickly bold, and discovered pleasure and solace in each other's arms. I told her about my voyage on the S.S. Roma, and about Finsbury Park and the Y.M.C.A., and my evenings on the bench with Mrs. Croft. When I told her stories about my mother, she wept. It was Mala who consoled me when, reading the *Globe* one evening, I came across Mrs. Croft's obituary. I had not thought of her in several months—by then those six weeks of the summer were already a remote interlude in my past—but when I learned of her death I was stricken, so much so that when Mala looked up from her knitting she found me staring at the wall, unable to speak. Mrs. Croft's was the first death I mourned in America, for hers was the first life I had admired; she had left this world at last, ancient and alone, never to return.

As for me, I have not strayed much farther. Mala and I live in a town about twenty miles from Boston, on a tree-lined street much like Mrs. Croft's, in a house we own, with room for guests, and a garden that saves us from buying tomatoes in summer. We are American citizens now, so that we can collect Social Security when it is time. Though we visit Calcutta every few years, we have decided to grow old here. I work in a small college library. We have a son who attends Harvard University. Mala no longer drapes the end of her sari over her head, or weeps at night for her parents, but occasionally she weeps for our son. So we drive to Cambridge to visit him, or bring him home for a weekend, so that he can eat rice with us with his hands, and speak in Bengali, things we sometimes worry he will no longer do after we die.

Whenever we make that drive, I always take Massachusetts Avenue, in spite of the traffic. I barely recognize the buildings now, but each time I am there I return instantly to those six weeks as if they were only the other day, and I slow down and point to Mrs. Croft's street, saying to my son, Here was my first home in America, where I lived with a woman who was a hundred and three. "Remember?" Mala says, and smiles, amazed, as I am, that there was ever a time that we were strangers. My son always expresses his astonishment, not at Mrs. Croft's age but at how little I paid in rent, a fact nearly as inconceivable to him as a flag on the moon was to a woman born in 1866. In my son's eyes I see the ambition that had first hurled me across the world. In a few years he will graduate and pave his own way, alone and unprotected. But I remind myself that he has a father who is still living, a mother who is happy and strong. Whenever he is discouraged, I tell him that if I can survive on three continents, then there is no obstacle he cannot conquer. While the astronauts, heroes forever, spent mere hours on the moon, I have remained in this new world for nearly thirty years. I know that my achievement is quite ordinary. I am not the only man to seek his fortune far from home, and certainly I am not the first. Still, there are times I am bewildered by each mile I have travelled, each meal I have eaten, each person I have known, each room in which I have slept. As ordinary as it all appears, there are times when it is beyond my imagination.

SPORTS ILLUSTRATED

Moment of Truth

This story deftly captures a long-ago era, and artfully anticipates profound changes not only for the individuals involved but for sports and society as well. Using as inspiration a contemplative photograph of the Texas Christian University locker room just before the January 1957 Cotton Bowl versus Syracuse (and its seemingly indomitable star, Jim Brown), writer Gary Smith persuades readers that what's most important and meaningful actually occurs before the game, privately—as each player questions his will and willingness to accept the challenges just outside the door. This is a beautiful story, lyrical and transporting, a tale of dramatic moments thought irretrievable, but gloriously preserved, in words that won't fade.

Gary Smith

Moment of Truth

You heard me right: Come in. No, you won't disturb a soul in this locker room. They're all lost in that place most folks go maybe once or twice in a lifetime, when their mamas or daddies die or their children are born, a place they don't go nearly as often as they should. Trust me, these boys will never know you're here. All right, maybe that fellow in white will notice, the one looking your way, but Willard McClung would be the last to make a peep.

See, that's one reason we picked this, out of all the crackerjack sports pictures we might've chosen, as our favorite of the century. Not claiming it's better than that famous one of Muhammad Ali standing and snarling over Sonny Liston laid out like a cockroach the morning after the bug man comes. Or that picture of Willie Mays catching the ball over his shoulder in the '54 World Series, or any number of others. But you can walk around inside this picture in a way you can't in those others, peer right inside the tunnel these boys have entered. Their boxer shorts are hanging right there, on the hooks behind their heads, but their faces are showing something even more personal than that. Almost reminds you of a painting by Norman Rockwell.

Can you smell it? No, not the jockstrap sweat, or the cigar reek wafting off the coach, Orthol Martin—better known as Abe, or Honest Abe—in the brown hat. It's the smell of men about to go to war. What I'm inviting you into is 12:50 p.m. at the Cotton Bowl on Jan. 1, 1957, just a few minutes after the boys have returned from pregame warmups, just a quarter of an hour before a legend is born. A roomful of young men from Texas Christian University are about to try and stop the best football player in history, a fellow from Syracuse by the name of Jim Brown, in his last college game—but only his second in front of the entire nation, thanks to the NBC cameras waiting outside.

No denying it, a lot of folks might whip right past this in a collection of sports pictures, rushing to get to those slam-bang plays at home plate or those high-flying Michael Jordan circus shots. But it's funny. The older you get, the more you realize that *this* is what sports are most about: the moments *before,* the times when a person takes a flashlight to his soul and inspects himself for will and courage and spirit, the stuff that separates men such as Jordan and Ali from the rest more than anything in their forearms or their fingers or their feet. *Who am I?* And, *Is that going to be enough?* That's what you're peeking at through the door, and believe me, those are two big and scary questions, the two best reasons for all of god's children to play sports, so they can start chewing on them early. Because once the whistle blows and a game begins, everything's just a blur, a crazy ricochet of ball and bodies that springs—inevitably, you might say—from whatever it is that these boys are discovering right here, right now.

But you're still hesitating, a little intimidated by all those cleats and helmets and knees. Come on, there are things I want to show you. See? Told you nobody would bat an eye. You're *in.*

Maybe it was like this for you, too, back when you played. All the posturing and bluffing and the silly airs that human beings put on get demolished in a moment like this. A team is never more a *team* than it is now, yet look at the looks on the Horned Frogs! Ever see so many guys look so alone?

Look at Buddy Dike, number 38, just behind old Abe. He's the Frogs' starting fullback and inside linebacker, and he's just gotten a good look at Jim Brown's 46-inch chest and 32-inch waist in warmups. Doctors advised Buddy never to play football again after he ruptured a kidney tackling another phenom of the era, Penn State's Lenny Moore, two years earlier. The kidney healed and hemorrhaged four more times, doubling Buddy over with pain, making blood gush out his urethra, bringing him within a whisker of bleeding to death, yet here he is, with a look on his face that might not be seen again until the day he loses his 18-year-old son in a car wreck.

There are 32 more young men suited up in this room, besides the 17 you're looking at. Almost every one's a kid from a small town or ranch or farm in west or south Texas, where all his life he's watched everyone drop everything, climb into automobiles and form caravans for only two occasions: funerals and football games. Nine of the 11 TCU starters—remember, they have to play both ways—are seniors, most of them staring into the biggest and last football game of their lives. Eleven wars are about to burst out on every play, because that's what football is, and what those wars hinge on, more than most folks realize, is the question lurking in the shadows of this room: Who has the most tolerance for pain?

That's a loaded question about manhood, and a matter of geography too. Jim Brown be damned, the Southwest Conference team that loses to an Eastern school in the Cotton Bowl in the 1950s might as well run right past the locker room door at the end of the game, exit the stadium and just keep going, till it's lost in the prairie.

Let's take a good look at old Abe. Country boy from Jacksboro, Texas, who played end at TCU in the late 1920s and kept to the grass on campus, claiming the sidewalk was too hard for his feet.

Some folks take him for a hick, but be careful, every shut eye isn't asleep. Notice, Abe's not working the boys into one of those tent-preacher lathers. Not his style. The season after this one, just before the Horned Frogs take the field at Ohio State with 80,000-plus fans licking their fangs, all Abe will tell his boys is "Laddies, you're playin' the best team in *the* United States of America"—then walk away. Another game, what he'll say is, "These are big guys. Hope you don't get hurt." He's a master of the subtle psychological ploy, a man who lacks both the strategic genius and the double-knotted sphincter of your other big football honchos, but who maneuvers a college of 4,700 students, most of them female, into three Cotton Bowls in four seasons between '55 and '58 and humbles elephants such as Southern Cal and Penn State and Texas along the way. "You just believe in human beings, that they're all pretty good folks, and you just try to keep 'em that way"—that's how Abe sums up his coaching philosophy in the Cotton Bowl program they're hawking outside that locker room right now.

In practice he'll drop to his hands and knees and crawl into the huddle, gaze up at his gang like a gopher and declare, "Boys, run a 34." Late in a game, when the Froggies are driving for a score they need desperately, old Abe will come down off the chair he always sits on—fanny on the seat back, feet on the seat—take another chomp of the unlit cigar he alternately sucks and rolls between his palms until it disintegrates, and walk down the sideline murmuring to his troops, "Hold your left nut, laddies—we need this one."

Oh, sure, Abe can get riled. But the vilest oath he ever musters—with his fist clenched and his thumb in an odd place, on top of his index finger instead of around his knuckles—is "Shistol pot!" which is a spoonerism for *pistol shot,* in case you need a translation. Usually Abe just walks a player away from the group with an arm around the boy's shoulders and quietly says, "Now, you know better 'n that." You know what troubles the fellows most at a moment like this, 15 minutes before kickoff? The thought that they might let Abe down.

All right, let's be honest, not everyone's dying to please the boss, not in any locker room in the world. See number 67, Norman Ashley, sitting third from the left against the back wall? He's in Abe's doghouse for late hits in practice and for tackling quarterback Chuck Curtis so hard one day that Curtis peed blood. Ashley will never play a lick, and he knows it. He'll end up spending four decades in Alaska flying a Piper Super Cub just big enough for him, his rifle, his rod and his hunting dog, searching for places where there are no whistles and no quarterbacks to flatten. And over on the other side, second from your right, that's center Jim Ozee, who started all season, till today. Damn near half a century later, when he's a grandpa tossing raisins to the mockingbird that visits him in his backyard in Fort Worth each day, he'll still remember, "That's despair on my face. I'm offended by Abe at this moment. I couldn't figure why I wasn't starting. I didn't hear anything he said. . . ."

". . . *wanna thank you fellas. Seniors in this room . . . no need to tell you how I feel 'bout you. You were my first recruitin' class, came in green just like me, and accomplished some great things. Now you're 'bout to split up, go your separate ways, and this'll be the game you remember the rest of your days. Life's about to change, laddies. You're never gonna capture this moment again. . . ."*

Two in this room will end up in early coffins when their hearts quit: Dick Finney, on your far right, and John Mitchell, second from your left, the lad inspecting the fingernails he's just chewed. Two other players will lose sons in car accidents, which is worse than a heart attack. Another, Jack Webb, seated in the deep corner just to the left of the youngster holding his chin in his hand, will relish the tension of moments like this so much that he'll become a fighter pilot, only to lose his life when his jet crashes in the Philippines. Two will get rich, then go bankrupt. Allen Garrard, number 84, the guy seated on the floor near the corner, will get multiple sclerosis and draw on moments like this 40 years from now, when his car blows a tire in a rainstorm in the dead of night and he has to hobble painfully on his cane far beyond the 200 feet he's usually able to walk. Of course, Abe himself, when he's in his 70s, will be found draped across his bed by his wife one morning when his ticker quits.

See that fellow on the floor behind Abe, number 53, Joe Williams? Can you tell? A year ago he lost his mom, who attended every game he ever played, in a car accident, and he's worried sick about his dad, sleepwalking awake ever since she died, who's somewhere in the stands high above this room. Here's what Joe will say 42 years from now, when his hair's as white as snow and arthritis has racked his joints with pain and stolen his right hand: "I should've expressed my gratitude to Abe. I'm still living by the principles he taught us. I'm not gonna give in. I'm still coming out of bed swinging even though I might not hit a thing. He guided us through those years. He looked out for us the way our parents presumed he would.

"You know something? Nothing ever again will match the intensity, the passion of moments like this. What it takes to overcome yourself—because if you listen to your body, you'll always be a coward. Don't get me wrong, I love my wife and kids, but I'd give anything to go back. More than who you're looking at now, that guy in the picture, *that's* me. *That's* who I really am."

"... *Hasn't been an easy road for us this season, laddies. Stubbed our toe real bad, and a lot of folks started calling us a second-rate team. But we didn't roll up in a ball, and by going through what we did and coming together, we're more a team now 'n we've ever been....*"

This is how the boys will recollect Abe's speech four decades later. The coach doesn't dwell on details, but here are the facts:

You're listening to a coach who was hung in effigy and made it to the Cotton Bowl in the same season. Right now, as Possum Elenburg, the fellow gnawing his knuckles on your far left, puts it, "Abe's done a rare thing—got all his coons up the same tree." He's got them all ruminating on a season that began with the Horned Frogs as heavy favorites in the Southwest Conference, returning a slew of starters from the nation's sixth-ranked team the year before, busting out to a 3–0 start with a 32–0 blitzing of Kansas, a 41–6 crushing of Arkansas and a 23–6 spanking of Alabama. Next came TCU's blood enemy, Texas A&M, with Bear Bryant at the wheel, the team that had handed the Frogs their only regular-season defeat the year before.

So now it was payback time, a gorgeous Saturday in College Station, the Aggies' stadium jammed and the 3–0 Frogs cross-eyed crazy in their locker room. And what happened? Sometime during the first quarter, all the friction between the two squads was more than the sky could hold, and the ugliest wall of black clouds you ever saw came rolling in from the north. The wind began to howl so hard that flagpoles bent into upside-down L's, and the ref had to put a foot on the ball between plays to keep it from sailing to Mexico. The rain came in sheets so thick that the subs on the sideline couldn't see the starters on the field, and then the rain turned to hail so helmet-drumming heavy that the linemen couldn't hear the signals from the quarterback screeching at their butts. Postpone the game? This is Texas, y'all! This is football!

The Frogs knifed through winds that gusted up to 90 mph, penetrated the A&M two-yard line on three drives behind their All-America running back, Jim Swink—and couldn't get it in! On one series Swink crossed the goal line twice—the Frogs had the film to prove it—but either the refs couldn't see or it was too slippery to get a good grip on your left nut in a monsoon. TCU finally scored in the third quarter but missed the extra point, and the Aggies stole the game with a fourth-quarter touchdown, 7–6.

Ever drive a car into the exit of a drive-in theater when you were 16, not knowing about those metal teeth? That's the sound that leaked out of the Froggies after that. Miami rocked them 14–0 the next week, Baylor scared the daylights out of them before succumbing 7–6, and then Texas Tech, a team that didn't belong in the same county with the Frogs, pasted them 21–7. Another ferocious storm fell on the team bus on the way home from Lubbock, and the Frogs crawled through it, wondering if their senior-laden squad had lost focus, become more concerned with the honeys they were fixing to marry and the careers they were fixing to start than with the mission at hand.

Back on campus, there dangled poor Abe from a rope lashed to a tree not far from the athletic dorm, brown hat and sport coat over a pillow head and sheet body. It was a startling sight at a university that many players had chosen because it had the homey feel of a big high school, a cow-town college where guys felt at home wearing cowboy hats and boots, or jeans rolled up at the cuffs and penny loafers. Just like that, the dispirited Frogs had a cause. Their starting quarterback, Chuck Curtis—that's him, number 46, sitting two to the left of Abe—along with end O'Day Williams and backup end Neil Hoskins, the youngster two to the left of Curtis, with his chin in his hand, went out to do a little rectifyin'. Curtis slashed down the effigy with a pocket knife, then led his mates, rumor by rumor, to the perpetrator, who turned tail after a little shouting and shoving. Two days later the Frogs called a players-only meeting at the dining hall, where the subs vented their frustration over lack of playing time, and Cotton Eye Joe Williams, the captain, promised to take their beef to Abe. The players all agreed that an attack on Abe was like an attack on their daddies, and they closed ranks.

To Cotton Eye's suggestion that the second fiddlers fiddle more, Abe said, Great idea. To the notion that the boys were steamed about the hanging effigy, Abe said, Couldn't've been me—I'm a lot better lookin' than that. To the proposition that the Froggies might still make it to the Cotton Bowl (A&M had been hit with NCAA sanctions for recruiting violations and wouldn't be eligible), Abe said, Let's go make hay. That's what the Frogs did, slapping Texas in the face 46–0, elbowing a ripsnorting Rice squad by three and thumping SMU 21–6 to finish 7–3, second to A&M, and scoop up the Aggies' fumbled Cotton Bowl bid. Then came a month to heal and prepare, a half-hour Greyhound bus ride to Dallas a few days before the big one, the formal dance and then the downtown parade on the fire engine, eyeing that big load on the other fire truck, the one that scored a record-breaking 43 points against Colgate: Jim Brown.

Finally all the buildup is over. The Southwest Conference princesses in convertibles and the high-stepping high school bands are drumming up one last buzz among the 68,000 waiting outside the locker room. But here inside there's only quiet, broken by a soft sob just outside the frame, from the Frogs' All-America lineman Norman Hamilton—who'll swear decades later that no matter what his teammates recollect, he didn't cry before games.

Quiet, broken by the calm drawl of Honest Abe. Whose calm is a lie, so keep your eye on him, because any minute he might just sneak off to the john and throw up. That's what Virgil Miller—he's number 18, the little guy in the dark corner with his head down—will find Abe doing before a game a few years later, when Virgil returns to visit the coach. "Ever get nervous like that?" Abe will ask Virgil. It's safe, since Virgil has graduated and gone.

It's almost like going to church, being here, isn't it? Nope, it's more religious than church, because half of the people here aren't faking it. Maybe folks who never played can't understand how you can be 15 minutes from tearing somebody's head off, 15 seconds from vomiting and a half inch from God, all at the same time. But

Chuck Curtis knows. Forty-two years from now, when this picture is placed under his eyes, he'll say, "Look at us. Compared to players today? We weren't great athletes. But we were a team from top to bottom, all giving entire respect to our leader and wanting the same thing wholeheartedly. A *sin*-cere group of young men. It'd take a miracle to get the feeling we had in that moment again. With that attitude, there's not a sin that's not erased." When he looks up, there will be tears in his eyes.

Henry B. (Doc) Hardt, he'd understand. He's the old-timer wearing his brown Sunday best and that purple-and-white ribbon on his left arm, so lost in his meditation that he doesn't know that his pants leg is climbing up his calf and that three decades have vanished since he last suited up for a football game—he'd snatch a helmet and storm through that door if Abe would just say the word. That's reverence, the look of a man with four Methodist minister brothers and a missionary sister. Doc's the head of the TCU chemistry department and the Frogs' NCAA faculty representative, the man who makes sure the flunkers aren't playing and the boosters aren't paying, and he's so good at it that he'll become president of the NCAA a few years after this game. Huge hands, grip like a vise and a kind word for everyone, even when he hobbles on a cane to Frogs games a quarter century later. Nice to know he'll make it to 90.

But you need to meet the rest of the boys. Just behind Doc's left shoulder is Mr. Clean: Willard McClung, the quiet assistant to renowned trainer Elmer Brown. Brown's busy right now shooting up guard Vernon Uecker's ankle with novocaine, but Willard would be glad to go fetch a glass of Elmer's concoction for those whose steak and eggs are about to come up, a cocktail the boys call "the green s———." Trouble is, Elmer's green s——— usually comes up along with everything else.

Willard's the only man here who never played, the only one not crawled inside himself—no coincidence there. His ankles were too weak for him to play ball, but he was determined to jimmy his way into moments like this, so he climbed aboard a train his senior year of high school, a fuzzy-cheeked kid from Minden, La., and rode all day to reach the National Trainers' Convention, in Kansas City. Trainers were so thrilled to see a kid show up that Elmer Brown finagled him a scholarship at TCU.

That's Frankie Hyde just behind Doc Hardt's right shoulder, the blond studying the hairs on his left calf. He's the Frogs' scout-team quarterback and an all-around good guy. Doesn't know that he'll hurt his shoulder a few months from now in spring training, that he'll never suit up for a football game again. Doesn't know that Abe's steering his rudder, that he'll end up coaching football just like six of the 17 players in the picture. That he'll end up guiding wave after wave of teenage boys through this moment, some who'll start chattering like monkeys, some who'll go quieter than the dead, some who'll slam their shoulder pads into lockers and poles, some who'll pray like a priest on his third cup of coffee, some who'll get too sick to play. Take it from Frankie: "People who don't experience this don't know themselves like they should."

Or take it from Hunter Enis, the handsome raven-haired boy leaning forward in the dark corner, the one who'll make a bundle in oil: "Sure, there's times in business when you'll work together with a group of men to meet a goal. But that's not about anything as important as this. It's just about money."

Or Possum Elenburg, the sub on the far left, sitting there thinking, Heck, yes, it'd be nice to get in and quarterback a few plays on national TV, but heck, no, I don't want to have to play defense and risk getting burned deep like I did against Texas Tech. Forty-two years later, here's Possum: "This is reality stripped to its nakedness. There's no place to hide. Time is standing still. It's funny, but all your life people tell you that football's just a game, that so many things more important will happen to you in life that'll make sports seem insignificant." Listen to Possum. He's a man who came within a quarter inch of losing his life in '60 when an oil rig crashed into his skull and paralyzed his right side for a year, a man who lost a fortune overnight when oil prices crashed on his head two decades later. "But it's not true, what people tell ya," he says. "I'm fixing to be tested in this moment, and I'm gonna be tested again and again in my life, and I'm gonna get nervous and wonder about myself every single time. Your priorities as a kid are just as important to you as your priorities as a 60-year-old man, because all your aspirations and goals are on the line. At any age, each thing that's important to you . . . is *important* to you, and each fight needs to be fought with every effort."

We're looking at a roomful of bladders fixing to bust, but it's just a hoax—any doctor could explain the phenomenon. It's just anxiety sending a surge of adrenaline to the nerve endings in the bladder, causing it to tighten and creating the feeling that you gotta go. These boys are like a pack of hunting dogs spraying all over the place just before the hunt, only dogs are lucky enough not to have all those laces and hip pads and jockstraps to fumble with.

"*. . . don't need to remind you, laddies, what happened to us in the Cotton Bowl last year, and what that felt like. Not many folks in life get a second chance, but we've got it right here, today . . . the chance to redeem ourselves. . . .*"

Redemption. That's all that thumps through the hearts and heads of two players who happen to be sitting elbow to elbow: Chuck Curtis and, on his right, Harold (Toad) Pollard, number 16, with the dirty-blond crew cut and the eye black. See, Toad's missed extra point was the margin of defeat in TCU's 14–13 Cotton Bowl loss to Mississippi last year. And Toad's missed extra point in the monsoon at A&M cost the Frogs that 7–6 heartache. Before you get the idea that Toad's a lost cause, you need to know that he led the nation's kickers in scoring last season and that his nickname is Abe's bungled version of Toad's true moniker, the Golden Toe. But ever since that wide-right boot in the Cotton Bowl, Toad has walked around imagining that the entire campus is thinking or saying, "There goes the guy who missed the extra point." Every morning last summer, before his 3–to–11 shift as a roughneck in the oil fields, he toted a tee to a high school field and kicked 40 through the pipes, alone, to prepare for his redemption. "It's a lot more hurt," he'll admit years later, "than a person would realize." Especially since Toad always seems to be clowning, doing that dead-on Donald Duck imitation. But right now he's more nervous than he's ever been, trying to swallow back the notion that he could bungle another critical extra point and be stuck with seeing himself in the mirror every time his hair needs combing the rest of his life.

It's a double-wide hot seat over there, cooking Chuck Curtis's fanny too. Because it was in this very room, at this very moment at the Cotton Bowl last year, that Abe concluded his pregame talk by reminding Chuck-a-luck, as he was fond of calling his quarterback, that he was absolutely *not* to run back the kickoff, that he was to pitch it back to Swink. But Chuck-a-luck, who believed fiercely in his ability to perform or charm his way out of any fix, walked out of this room and fielded that kickoff on the run, down near his shins, and decided that all that forward momentum shouldn't be wasted on a backward lateral, and actually traveled a few yards before—*crunch!*—he took a lick that cracked three ribs and partially dislocated his shoulder, and the Frogs' star quarterback was gone on the game's first play.

Of course, Dick Finney, the backup quarterback—that's him on your farthest right, the one who used to call audibles with fruits instead of numbers ("Apples! Oranges! *Bananas!*")—came trotting into the huddle with that bird-eating grin of his and declared, "Have no fear, Finney's here." But fear truly was in order, because although Diamond Dick ran like a jackrabbit, he also passed like one, and Ole Miss stacked everybody but the trombone players on the line to create a terrible constipation.

Imagine what that did to Chuck Curtis, a strapping 6' 4", 200-pound All-Conference signal-caller, a Pentecostal preacher's son who could sell a bikini to an Eskimo. In a few years he'll be buying cattle like crazy, owning a bank, winning three state championships as a high school coach and selling automobiles to boot, joking with a former Frogs teammate who protests that he can't afford to pay for a car, "Hey, ol' buddy, I didn't ask you to *pay* for a car—I just wanna *sell* you a car." In the '70s, when he comes up on charges of making false statements on bank-loan applications, there will be preachers preaching in his favor on the courthouse steps, alongside his Jacksboro High football team, cheerleaders and band, all crooning the school's alma mater, and he'll get off with a $500 fine. But no amount of preaching or singing or selling can hide the fact that Chuck-a-luck's ego, more than Toad's blown extra point, cost his teammates the '56 Cotton Bowl, and that he'll have to wear that around like a stained pair of chaps for the rest of his life . . . unless, in about 10 minutes, he can maneuver the Frogs past Jim Brown.

Now turn around. It's long past time you met Marvin Newman, the well-groomed fellow with the side of his snout pressed against that camera. Nearly forgot about him, he's been so quiet, but none of this would've been possible without him. Funny guy, Marvin: your classic pushy New Yorker when there's something he really wants, but when what he really wants is to disappear into the woodwork—presto, Marvin's a mouse. You can barely hear the click of that Leica he's pointing toward Abe.

He can't use a flash—that would be like taking a hammer to a moment like this. So he has to spread his legs, brace his knees, lock his elbows against his sides and hold his breath to keep that camera stone still. He has to become the tripod, because the quarter second that the shutter needs to be open to drink in enough light is enough to turn Chuck-a-luck and Toad and Buddy and Joe into a purple smear if Marvin's paws move even a hair. Doesn't hurt that he's only 29, because the hands won't let you do that at, say, 59. Doesn't hurt that he rarely drinks, either, because more than a few magazine shooters would still have the shakes at 10 minutes to one in the afternoon on New Year's Day.

He's a Bronx kid, a baker's only son who knew at 19 that he wasn't going to keep burying his arms to the elbows in a wooden vat of rye dough, wasn't going to do what his father and grandfather and great-grandfather had done, even if his old man nearly blew a fuse when that first $90 camera was delivered to the door. Marvin was too brainy, having jumped two grades before he finished high school, and too hungry for something he couldn't even give a name to, so he surprised his old man again, telling him he'd go to Chicago and study art at the Illinois Institute of Technology on his own dime, not that he owned one. Crawled right out on the limb and then had to prove to his dad that he could dance on it.

Who knows, maybe that's why he lies in hotel beds for hours, boiling with plans A, B, C and Z on the night before an assignment, brainstorming about how to come home with an image nobody else would have thought of. Maybe that's why his gut's already working on that ulcer. Could be why he hangs around the photo department at SPORTS ILLUSTRATED, promoting ideas that might snag him a color spread worth $600, till finally the photo editor nods, or maybe his head just sags in exhausted surrender. See, Marvin was one of the first to figure this out: If you're technically sound and willing to invest in the best equipment on the shelf—all those long lenses and motor drives just coming out—and if you played some ball and can anticipate where the next play might go, you're a hundred miles ahead of the posse of freelancers dying to land an assignment from SI.

But a tack-sharp action shot won't be enough to satisfy Marvin. He has to come up with something at this Cotton Bowl as heart-touching as the picture he nailed at last year's, that classic shot of Ole Miss's Billy Kinnard coming off the field after beating TCU by one point and planting a kiss on Ole Miss cheerleader Kay Kinnard, who just happened to be his new bride. So, recollecting from last New Year's Day how mouthwatering the light was in that locker room, Marvin made it his first item of business when he saw Abe in Dallas to start schmoozing, start persuading Abe how discreet he'd be, how lickety-split he'd get in and get out, and how much his boss was counting on him . . . so could he *please* slip into the Frogs' locker room just before kickoff? Heck, Abe didn't need schmoozing. *Sure, Marvin! Why not drop by at halftime too?*

Guarantee you, Marvin can smell and taste his own pregame heebie-jeebies from that year he played end on the Brooklyn College football team at a preposterous 125 pounds, and from all those times just before he ran the 800 when he'd start hacking so much that he even tried sucking on a pebble, and he cut a deal with his gut not to bring up breakfast and lunch until he was just past the finish line, first more often than not.

Sure, he'll take snaps more famous than this. He'll bag that black-and-white shot of the World Series–winning homer soaring off Bill Mazeroski's bat as the scoreboard shows all the pertinent facts—3:36 p.m., ninth inning, score tied—of Game 7 between the Pittsburgh Pirates and the New York Yankees in 1960. He'll catch eyes all over the country with his picture of the newly widowed Jackie Kennedy clutching John-John's hand as they watch JFK's coffin go by. But 40-plus years after this New Year's Day in Dallas, long after his knees and hips have grown weary of all the kneeling and contorting and camera-bag banging, long after he's left sports photography to specialize in travel and city-skyline shots, and even after his pictures have been exhibited in all sorts of important places, he'll remember this picture almost as if he took it yesterday.

"They completely forgot about me," he'll say, sitting over the photo in his Manhattan apartment at age 71. "When photography works well, you can go inside the psyche of the people in the picture. You can see beyond the moment. I always loved this picture. I knew it was special. There hadn't been many photographs taken inside locker rooms, so I knew I was privileged. I couldn't have been standing more than 10 feet from Abe Martin. . . ."

". . . but we're not gonna shut down Jim Brown, boys. Not with one tackler. We're gonna have to swarm him. We'll slow him down. We'll go right at him when we've got the ball. He's not a great defensive player. We'll tire him out. We won't stop him. We'll outscore him. This game can put us right back where we belong, with the best teams in the country. Look inside yourselves and ask, Do I really want it? If you do, laddies, the goose hangs high. Now let's have the prayer."

Some of you might not quite grasp what's sitting and waiting for the Frogs in the room down the hall. Jim Brown stands 6'2" and weighs 225 pounds, which is at least 35 pounds more than the average halfback of his day, not to mention 22 pounds heavier than the average player on the biggest line in the country, Notre Dame's. He runs 100 yards in 10 seconds flat, high-jumps 6'3", hurls the discus 155 feet and once won six events for Syracuse in a track meet, which gave him the notion that it might be fun to enter the national decathlon championship, which he did on 10 days' practice and placed fifth. He scored 33 in a Syracuse basketball game and will be drafted by the NBA's Syracuse Nationals, not bad for a fellow who at the time was considered to have been the greatest lacrosse player in U.S. history. He's just finishing up a senior season in which he averaged 6.2 yards per carry, and he will average a record 5.2 yards per carry for the Cleveland Browns over the next nine years, leading the NFL in rushing in eight of those, before he'll hang it up, as MVP, at age 30. Forgive me if you knew all that, but some legends get so large, the particulars get lost.

Now, some of the Frogs are deeply worried about Brown. Others have been fooled by the three game films they've seen, because Brown looks slower on celluloid than he does when you're reaching for his heels. Still others think he's very good, but he can't possibly be better than John David Crow of Texas A&M.

Brown's sitting very still and silent right now. He's the sort of man who contains a lot more than he lets out, till he steps on the field, and maybe some of what he's holding in has to do with a question that's struck you already, looking around the TCU locker room: Where are all the black folks? There's not one playing football in the Southwest Conference, and there won't be one on scholarship till nine years down the road, after Chuck Curtis becomes an SMU assistant coach and recruits Jerry Levias. In fact, it was only two years before this that the first blacks played in TCU's stadium, when Penn State brought Lenny Moore and Rosey Grier to town and they had to sleep at a motel way out on Jacksboro Highway, because the team couldn't find a downtown Fort Worth hotel that would have them.

That wasn't going to happen to Brown. He decided before the Orangemen arrived in Dallas that he'd refuse to be separated from his teammates, but it hadn't come to that. Syracuse was staying in a hotel on the edge of Dallas that accepted the whole squad.

Sure, Brown's thoughts are fixed on football right now, 15 minutes before kickoff, but it would be a lie to say that another question isn't nibbling on his mind: What's going to happen when he's circled by nearly 70,000 white Texans, some of them wearing cleats? Abe hasn't said a thing to his boys about color. Before the game against Moore and Grier in '54, all he said was, "They're darn good football players, so it wouldn't make much sense to say something to get 'em mad."

Brown will never be the sort to live on the fumes of his past, or reminisce much. But even at 63, when he's running across America directing Amer-I-Can—an organization he founded to tackle gang problems and help prisoners get ready for life outside the walls—some of what coursed through him in that Cotton Bowl locker room will still be with him.

"I was concerned how their players would carry themselves, if there'd be any epithets," he'll say. "But I wasn't going to make that any kind of extra motive, or try to prove something. Racism is sickness, and I'm not gonna prove something to sickness. I was a performer with my own standards, and living up to them was all I worried about. For me, the time just before a game was always tense, like going to war without death. I always felt humbled. It's a very spiritual moment. I'd try to go into a pure state. No negative thoughts, even toward the other team. No rah-rah, because rah-rah's for show. Your butt's on the line, and you either stand up and deal with it, or . . . or you can't. You become a very difficult opponent for anyone or anything when you know that you can."

Let me tell you what happened that day, right after Marvin's last click. Chuck Curtis went wild. He called a run-pitch sprint-out series that no one expected from a dropback quarterback without much foot speed, and he threw two touchdown passes to stake the Frogs to a 14–0 lead.

Then it was Brown's turn. The tip that TCU coaches had passed on to the Frogs after studying film—that just before the snap Brown leaned in the direction he was about to go—was accurate, but it wasn't worth a Chinese nickel. As Brown carried a couple of more Frogs for rides, Abe spun toward his boys on the sideline and nearly swallowed his cigar, then howled, "Shistol pot! Can't anybody tackle him?"

Against Brown, everything the Frogs had learned about hitting a man in the thighs and wrapping him up went down the sewer—there was just too much power there. First tackler to reach him had to hit him high, delay him for a second, take some of the forward momentum out of those thighs, then wait for reinforcements to hit him low.

Brown bashed in from the two for Syracuse's first touchdown, kicked the extra point, then hurled a 20-yard pass that set up his own four-yard touchdown run and booted another point after to tie the ball game 14–14 just before intermission. Lonnie Leatherman, a backup end for the Frogs, would shake his head from here to the year 2000, yelping, "He ran through the whole stinkin' team! That man was bad to the bone! He was unbelievable! These are great football players, and they couldn't tackle him. Norman Hamilton was an All-America and couldn't tackle him."

A savage moment came early in the second half. Syracuse was on the TCU 40 and rolling—Brown had just made another first down on a fourth-down plunge—when Buddy Dike, with his battered kidney, threw caution to the wind. He hit Brown head-on, producing a sound Hamilton would never forget. "Like thunder," he'd recall. "Never heard a sound that loud from two men colliding. I thought, How can they ever get up?"

Dike's face mask snapped in two, the pigskin burst from Brown's grasp and TCU recovered it. Brown would not miss a play. The inspired Froggies again targeted Brown when he was on defense, flooding his side of the field with three receivers. Years later Leatherman would make no bones about it. "Brown was horrible on defense," he'd say. Joe Williams would be a trifle kinder: "Maybe their coaches didn't want to offend him by teaching him defense."

Curtis closed a drive by sweeping around the left end for a score, and Jim Swink found paydirt for the Frogs a few minutes later. Toad Pollard stepped on the field for the extra point. He was 3 for 3, and his side was up 27–14, but with nearly 12 minutes left and Brown yet to be corralled, the kicker's gut quivered with evil memories. To Jim Ozee, finally getting a few minutes at center, it seemed like eternity between his snap and the thud of Toad's toe against the ball. "What took you so long?" Ozee demanded seconds after the kick sailed true.

"I wanted to be sure," Toad said, breathing heavily—as if he knew that Brown would rip off a 46-yard return on the kickoff, then slam in from the one and bust open Toad's lip a few moments later. As if he knew that Syracuse would roar right down the field on its next possession, finally figuring a way to reach the end zone without Brown, on a touchdown pass with 1:16 left. As if he knew that Chico Mendoza, the lone Mexican-American on the Frogs' roster, would storm in from right end just after Syracuse's third touchdown and block Brown's point-after try, making the team that lost by one extra point in the Cotton Bowl in 1956 the winner by one extra point in 1957, by a score of 28–27. "All those white boys out there," Leatherman would point out, "and the Mexican and the black were the key players."

Brown would finish with 132 yards on 26 carries, three kickoff returns for 96 more yards, three extra points, the whole country's admiration . . . and no slurs. "They were nice human beings," he'd say of the Frogs. But Chuck-a-luck, who finished 12 of 15 through the air, would see Brown speak at the University of Texas-Arlington years later and leave sniffing that "he sounded like one of those Black Panthers."

Toad would remember "floating" at the postgame banquet, thinking he was saved from a lifetime of negative thoughts, but in his 60s that extra point he missed in the '56 Cotton Bowl would still occupy his mind more than the four he made in '57, and every kick he watched on TV would make his foot twitch up, as if the kick were his.

TCU? The Frogs wouldn't win another bowl game for 41 years. The rules changed on Abe: Free substitution and the end of the two-way player meant that a college needed at least 22 studs, and that a small school with a scrawny budget and even less national TV exposure had almost no prayer, no matter how sincere its players were 15 minutes before kickoff. When Abe quit nine years later, people said the game had passed him by.

Come 1999, that bare locker room would no longer be a locker room, that Southwest Conference would no longer exist, and that New Year's Day game would be known as the Southwestern Bell Cotton Bowl Classic, with a Web site.

One last thing. There's a saying Texans used to share about men in locker rooms awaiting battle, and pardon my French, but it goes like this: Brave men piss, cowards s————.

Which were you? Which was I? Guess I just can't walk out of this picture without asking questions like that. But I'll shut up now, in case you want to go back and catch Chuck-a-luck going watery-eyed as he leads the team prayer. Hurry, though. It's going hard on nine minutes to one.

VANITY FAIR

Madness Visible
and
The Forensics of War

These two in-depth reports of the war in Kosovo bring the reader to ground zero in an ugly war. For her eyewitness account, reporter Janine di Giovanni threw herself with great physical and emotional courage into the line of fire. She took repeated personal risks to bring the reader face to face with the suffering and despair of the brutalized victims. In the second article, Sebastian Junger skillfully reveals and details the forensic investigation that seeks evidence for the international community's attempt to bring the war criminals to justice. Both are compelling, memorable pieces of on-the-scene reporting.

Janine di Giovanni

Madness Visible

Mehije has the deadest eyes. She sits on a pile of old blankets in the corner of a converted factory and silently watches me cross the room. Except for her eyes her face is still. When I kneel next to her, she stares wordlessly, oblivious to the whimpering two-year-old at her feet—her daughter, Duka.

It is cold in the factory, but Mehije wears only a sweater, muddy bedroom slippers, and thin cotton socks, pink ones. She has a long messy plait running down her back. She does not return my tentative smile; instead, she reaches behind her back and hands me a package of loose rags tied with a blue ribbon. She motions for me to open it, and when I do, I see that the bundle of rags is alive, a tiny baby with gaping bird mouth. It makes no sound. It is Mehije's seventh child, a boy, born four days before in the woods while she was fleeing the Serbs.

Mehije registers my shock. Then she begins to talk about her flight from Kosovo. She is an ethnic Albanian from the village of Mojstir, and she has to think to calculate her age: 38. Married to Abdullah, a farmer. When she left Mojstir, it was burning. It is now a place that will cease to have any history, like the more than 800,000 people who have trudged over the mountain passes out of Kosovo, leaving behind a gutted country.

Before March 1998, when the war escalated in Kosovo, Mehije had a simple life that she did not question: pigs, cows, the children in school, Abdullah earning a meager living. But in the past few years, as Serb forces grew more prevalent in the area and Serb civilians more antagonistic, it became harder for Albanians to find employment, and there was an increase in tension. Throughout this last pregnancy, she had a nagging, ominous feeling.

"We felt something different, something strange in the air" is how her sister-in-law, Senia, who is sitting on a blanket next to Mehije, describes it.

Mehije does not understand military strategy, NATO maneuvers, political insurrection. She doesn't know that 4,000 people an hour are pouring over the Kosovan borders and will probably never return to their villages. She does not remember Yugoslav president and Serb leader Slobodan Milošević's rabid speech to the Serb minority in Kosovo on April 24, 1987. It was a speech that played to the Serbs' many resentments, recent as well as ancient. It was a speech that set in motion a hideous cycle of nationalism and ethnic hatred, first in Slovenia and Croatia, then Bosnia, and now spiraling wildly out of control in Kosovo.

She doesn't care about any of that. The only things Mehije ever knew were how to be a wife and a mother, how to bake bread, milk cows.

This is what happened: Sunday, March 28, was the fifth day of the NATO bombing, a campaign that does not make sense to her and her neighbors ("Our lives were easier before NATO got involved"). It was also Bajram, an important Muslim holiday, traditionally a day when children are scrubbed and dressed in their best clothes and families gather to eat special food, like roast lamb. Mehije was in her kitchen when the door burst open and her Serb neighbors—people she had known all of her life—pointed guns in her face and ordered her family out of their house. Her neighbors were not masked. She saw their faces, saw the anger and the determination.

"Take nothing. Just go quickly," they said, waving their guns. Mehije and Abdullah rounded up the children, put some bread in their pockets, and ran. "I had the birth pains when I was running," she tells me. But despite the warning of an imminent labor, "I ran anyway."

The family did not have a car, but found neighbors who were fleeing on a farm tractor. They stopped in a sheltered forest near Mojstir and tried to build temporary huts from branches. Other villagers—Mehije thinks around 200—were there, too, foraging in the snow for wood to make a fire, for small animals to eat, for water. Families were separated; there was the sound of wailing children. People kept asking: Have you seen my father? Have you seen my sister? Most of them were lacking papers: the Serbs had liberated them of their documents, making sure they would never return to Mojstir, in the same generous way that Serbs are charging refugees to cross the border out of Kosovo.

In the forest, Mehije's group heard reports of what was happening in their village. Their houses were on fire. Everything they owned had been either destroyed or loaded onto trucks and driven away.

Mehije stayed in the forest for three days. Her labor began. The temperature dropped to freezing. Then the same Serbs who had ordered them out of their village came back and ordered them to march up the mountain and over the border to Albania, a walk which would take three days. "Go back to your country!" they jeered. "Your village is burned! You have nothing left."

"I had never been to Albania before," Mehije says. "My family has always lived in Kosovo." But she did not argue. She gathered her six children and began to walk. She started to time her contractions, which were coming closer together.

The baby, whom she called Leotrim, came while they were wading through waist-deep snow. Mehije walked until she could not walk anymore and then she dropped to her knees. The men cleared a space for her in the snow, and she lay on twigs. Senia, who has an eighth-grade education and no nursing experience, acted as midwife. There was no water, no blankets, no food, no privacy. Mehije says the baby came quickly, within three hours. Senia cut the cord with a knife. Afterward, when her sister-in-law handed her the baby, Mehije remembers thinking that this last child came into a world of confusion, of terror, born under a strange, foreign sky. He will never know his home.

"He won't remember this," Mehije says now, holding Leotrim. She is still in shock: she has the look of a raw, bleeding animal that someone has kicked and beaten. She repeats herself, as if by saying it she can make it reality: "He won't remember any of this."

She says the baby has nothing, not even diapers. She says she has not seen Abdullah since the family arrived in Rožaj, a town on the Montenegrin-Kosovan border about 50 kilometers from her home. She is worried for his safety.

"We heard they were taking away men and boys," another one of the women sitting near her on a mattress says in a frightened voice. It is a chilling thought, because everyone in the room remembers what happened in Bosnia, at Srebrenica, when the supposed U.N. safe haven finally fell in July 1995: the men were rounded up and sent to the forest and never returned.

I stand and say I will go to the village to try to find Abdullah (who, it will turn out, is fine; they had been inadvertently separated in the chaos of the march) and to get some things for the baby at the apothecary. On the way out of the factory, I pass an old man with a bloody stump instead of an arm. He wears a beret and is sitting upright in a wheelbarrow, smoking. He is talking to himself, muttering the same thing over and over in Albanian. No one is listening to him.

This is what it is like: no matter how many times you listen and record someone's story, no matter how many refugees you see crossing over mountaintops wearing plastic bags on their heads to protect themselves from the freezing rain—you don't ever really get used to it. And yet, when there are so many, it is easy to dehumanize them. They have the same faces, the same stories; they come down the road with their lives in two carrier bags. And by the time they get herded into abandoned schools or warehouses, you forget that once they had lives and read books, that they have birthdays, wedding anniversaries, love affairs. You forget they had a favorite television show, a dog or a cat that they loved.

This is what ethnic cleansing means for them: they lose their history, their identities, their sense of belonging. Nothing feels safe anymore. Anything can happen.

**Travnik, Central Bosnia,
October 12, 1992**

A different conflict, the same war. The intensive-care unit of a makeshift hospital. The smell of blood and urine. A low, primal moaning, like that of an animal. I follow it to find a 12-year-old boy with his torso ripped open from chin to pubic line, writhing in agony on a bed. Shrapnel wounds in his intestines. A Muslim, he was trying to escape from Turbe, his burning village, when the Bosnian Serb army lobbed a shell into the fleeing column of people.

The boy, named Salko, got separated from his father in the confusion. Someone got him to the hospital, but he's been alone for nine days, and the exhausted doctor has only enough painkillers to give him an injection once a day. "You cannot imagine the pain he is feeling," the doctor says.

I sit by his bed. Salko has a long, thin face, gray eyes, lank blondish hair plastered to his face with sweat. His mouth is gaping with pain. It seems unlikely he will live.

"What do you expect?" says a passing nurse, not unkindly. "He barely has a stomach left."

T he day after the first NATO bombs fall, I catch a flight from London to Zagreb, the Croat capital. Despite the pilot's announcement that the plane has been diverted to Slovenia because the airspace over Croatia is closed, we do land in Zagreb—the first plane in two days. Outside the airport, there are joyous taxi drivers waiting.

"At last! Passengers!," Marko, my driver, says, rubbing his hands. Having lived through three wars in eight years, he knows that war always brings profit to the lucky ones. My destination is the border between Kosovo and Montenegro, a 10-or-so-hour drive through Croatia, Bosnia, and Montenegro. Marko says he could also drive me down the highway toward Belgrade and leave me at the Croat-Serb border if I want. "You can walk over the border to Serbia," he says. "Me, I'll never go there again."

The Croats are frightened. Not only have the air strikes ruined their chances for a decent tourist season, but they are terrified of being sucked into that black hole from which they recently emerged. They are only now, six years after their cease-fire with the Serbs was declared, starting to recover psychologically. The Croats were not blameless in their war—in 1995 they ethnically cleansed the Krajina region of an estimated 170,000 Serbs who had lived there for generations—but they have also suffered. The mental images from the Croat war are indelible: air raids in Zagreb; vicious battles in eastern Slavonia; 400 men taken from the village hospital in Vukovar, 260 of them executed and dumped in a mass grave.

Marko drives me as far as the Croat city of Dubrovnik. Residents of this medieval coastal town, which eight years ago withstood a nine-month siege and daily bombardment at the hands of its Montenegrin neighbors (who are now being bombed by

NATO), have more sanguinary feelings about the air strikes than do their countrymen in Zagreb.

"This bombardment comes as the justice of God," Mišo, a former Croat commander who defended the city, tells me. "It comes as a puncture in this awful balloon of evil." He is not a vindictive man, and says that the Croats "are not a bellicose people." But he cannot forget what happened here. Essentially, this is the story of the Balkans. This place is haunted by the dead. There is too much weight of history, too much destruction, too many grudges and blood feuds to forget.

I rise at five a.m. the next day and thumb a lift to Bosnia with a Danish U.N. worker going to Sarajevo via Republika Srpska (the Serb-run territory in Bosnia). Several hours into the journey, a radio report comes in: 20 men in Goden, a remote village in Kosovo, were lined up in front of the school and shot through the head. Clean, methodical killing like the other recent massacres in Kosovo: March 1998, 52 coffins lined up in Prekaz; and in Racak, January 1999, 40 more ethnic Albanians murdered.

We do not know it yet, but today another massacre is taking place in the village of Mala Krusa: around a hundred men executed by Serb forces. At great risk, a survivor, Milaim Bellanica, will record the aftermath on a family video camera. He will smuggle the tape, which depicts gruesome images, to the BBC. He will later say, "I have done this so that my son and my grandson, the next generation, will never forget what the Serbs have done to the Albanian people."

Though the NATO campaign is just beginning, already there are casualties. A Stealth plane is shot down somewhere near the road on which we are driving. In Belgrade they are jubilant with their victory: like winning the lottery. At the demonstrations, they carry placards which say, SORRY, WE DIDN'T KNOW IT WAS INVISIBLE.

The Dane and I stop to eat. A Serb farmer at a roadside stand is roasting a whole lamb gored through its midsection with an iron stick. He gives us plates of greasy hunks of meat. We eat with our hands, silently. An unsmiling youth brings bread, offers *loza,* a local brandy, preferred drink of the Serb forces. It is around 11 a.m. and the farmers gathered around another wooden table are deep into their *loza.* I remember the Serb gunners dug into trenches high above Sarajevo: they were always drunk by lunchtime. The safest time to get into the city was early morning because they were sleeping off their hangovers.

I turn down the brandy.

We enter Bosnia. The Dane says that Muslims from the Bosnian-Serb border are flooding into Sarajevo on buses, fleeing from the NATO bombing. "They are terrified that once again the Serbs will turn on them," he says. I think of the sick irony of the situation: people finding refuge in Sarajevo. During the siege, I remember families risking snipers and minefields to cross the airfield at night to escape from the place. The first thing you saw when you entered the city was graffiti on a burned-out building: WELCOME TO HELL.

Farther down the road, we pass signs with arrows pointing toward towns in eastern Bosnia. We pass through Olovo, once a front line, blackened, leveled, and we pass the roads leading in the direction of Goražde and Srebrenica. We begin to talk about the recent massacre. The Dane says quietly, "It is not a good thing if they are taking the men away."

In Srebrenica, they separated the men from the women. Despite the fact that then U.N. commander General Philippe Morillon swore "I will never leave you" and the place was called a U.N. safe haven, it fell in July 1995. Five thousand people are still not accounted for. Seven thousand Muslims were slaughtered. It is difficult to imagine 7,000 skulls, 7,000 sets of bones. Counting 10 dead bodies is horrific enough.

**Near Srebrenica,
April 17, 1993**

C hain-smoking, I am hunched over a ham radio, the only contact a group of fellow journalists and I have with Srebrenica. The Serb infantry has broken the Bosnian front lines southeast and northeast of the town. Fourteen international aid workers and 30,000 terrified civilians are trapped inside.

The voice, desperate and broken by static, comes over the radio describing the town: "like a scene from hell." There are dead in the streets. Hand-to-hand fighting. A U.N. command post was hit by a mortar.

"The Serbs are getting closer," says the voice. Every day for two weeks we have spoken to the voice. I feel as if I know him intimately. Once, he asked if we had cigarettes, and what kind. Now he is being surrounded on all sides by Serbs. Shortly, he will be killed, and we will sit by and listen, unable to do anything. His voice has taken on a new note: high-pitched panic.

"We beg you to do something, whatever you can. In the name of God, do something!" The room is silent. We are paralyzed by our helplessness. "Does the world know about us?" continues the voice. "Does Clinton? Does John Major?"

The lucky ones, the refugees from Srebrenica, the ones who got out, are wandering the streets of Tuzla like the walking dead. Amputees, rape victims, people slowly going mad. And 13-year-old Sead, blinded by shrapnel while playing football. He knows he should have stayed in the basement during the worst bombardment, but it was a beautiful day and he wanted to go outside.

"I wanted to play," he says to me. Then he turns awkwardly in the bed. He has not yet gotten used to this new gift from the Bosnian Serb army, his blindness. "I would give anything to know what happened to my eyes."

Rožaj,
March 30, 1999
(Day Seven of the NATO Bombing)

T he Kosovan city of Peć, a place of deep historic and mythic symbolism for the Serbs, is burning. It has been bombed by NATO, and simultaneously torched by the Serbs, who are making the ethnic Albanians pay for the bombing campaign by running them out of their surrounding villages. All around the city, the refugees are fleeing, mainly on foot. The weather has turned bitterly cold—below freezing in the mountains—and the refugees are not dressed for it. They are wearing bedroom slippers and handknit cardigans. Few have hats or gloves or proper winter gear. When they fled, they took only what they could hold in their two hands. I used to ask people what they took with them when they left. Wedding photographs? Baby pictures? Birth certificates? Most of them would look at me blankly: "We take nothing," they said. Meaning, they took nothing personal, just the closest thing at hand.

I am standing on a border mountain pass while people trudge by on their way out of Kosovo into Montenegro. A woman, Anna, waits for her brother at the crossing. "Where is he? Where is he?" she asks, wringing her bare hands, examining every face that goes by. She is crying; she says she has been standing at the crossing point for four hours and he has not come in with the column of people. "I must find him. My brother. They may have taken him. They were taking away some of the men, and he is young. Please tell me, where is he?"

We drive down the road to look for him. Hundreds of people pass, in groups of five and six. A woman walks by pushing a pram with a baby inside, surrounded by three small children clutching hands. A man rides a bicycle in the snow, falling over every few minutes; stoically, he keeps picking the bike up and continuing on.

Anna's brother appears. He is a teenager, pale-skinned, with dark hair. He is wearing a jean jacket and has a teary look. Anna leaps into his arms, hugging and kissing him. Then she begins to kiss and hug me.

Some people walk alone. "A lot of people are crossing, but a lot of people are dead!" a woman screams at me later. She is a teacher, from Peć, and she is hysterical, weeping:

"They are dead! Hospitals are burning! They are killing teachers, doctors, anything alive. They are animals. No—animals do not treat one another like this."

Others are silent. That horrible stillness in the snow. An old woman, heavyset, wearing a scarf, stares straight ahead in deep shock, plodding up and up the mountain toward Montenegro. My colleague, a British journalist, puts her in his car and we drive her to the top of the pass. She stays in the heated vehicle and does not say a word, for hours. A child with Down's syndrome stumbles through the snow, laughing maniacally. He falls face-first into the snow. His mother chases him, tears running down her cheeks. Another mother sits in the snow with her four children, huddled, shivering.

When I offer the old woman sitting in the car a piece of bread she looks at me but does not take it. Nor does she push it away. She seems dead already.

**Kula Pass, on the
Montenegrin-Kosovan Border,
March 31, 1999**

Sometimes there is an arrogance to this profession. When reporters become careless, we tend to think of ourselves as indestructible. Because we are outside the conflict, observing, it is easy to forget that we are not protected by some higher power.

Sometimes you get strange vibes and you have to trust your instincts. Sometimes, if you ignore these instincts, you get into trouble. Earlier this day, a photographer said that he had seen drunk Serb soldiers at the crossing point. Soldiers aren't supposed to be wandering over the border, inflaming an already tense situation. Montenegro has been in a state of jittery panic all week because Milošević replaced the local army commander. There have been rumors of an army-led coup against the pro-West government. (Montenegro is still part of the Serb-dominated Yugoslav federation even though there are strong leanings among many Montenegrins to pull away.)

Later in the day, while using my colleagues' satellite phone on top of the border mountain pass, I look up and see for myself four or five Serb soldiers: aggressive, unsmiling, wearing dark glasses on a cloudy, gray day. They should not be on this pass. It is a surreal, menacing sight. But I need to stay to continue reporting, and, while the other journalists leave the mountain, I sit in an armored car belonging to two French television journalists, trying to keep warm.

One hour later. This time, the Serb soldiers swarm through the snow very quickly. What I hear next chills me. It is a man screaming: "No!" When I look out the window, I see one of the French journalists, half lying in the snow. He has been pushed down. His arms are above his head, in an instinctive act of surrender. A Serb soldier has a kalashnikov cocked and aimed at his head.

There are about 10 of them, Serb soldiers who have come over the border from Kosovo. They drag the Frenchman out of the snow and begin hitting him, kicking him. I am too stunned to feel frightened. It is the first time in seven years covering the Balkan war that I have seen Serbs actually strike a journalist.

If they are beating him up, I think, this is not good. In my encounters with the Serb army I have seen anger, stupidity, arrogance, cruelty. But this is different. In Bosnia, I was once held for three hours, strip-searched, and liberated from the £3,000 they found stuffed down my trousers ("You can get it back after the war, in Belgrade").

"You can't do this," I had said when they sent me walking into the darkness without any transportation or cash.

"We can do anything we want," one of the commanders said, grinning. "We're winning the war."

But this time, this is something else: these men are completely out of control. They seem far more emotional and disturbed—this is personal. We are no longer journalists, observers. We are part of the NATO conspiracy.

"You bombed Belgrade! You bombed Peć!" they scream. One sees me and drags me out of the car. They demand our passports: two French, one British.

"Mirage! Mirage!" one screeches, a reference to the French fighter jets. "NATO! Clinton!"

I look down, thinking it wise not to make eye contact. One of the journalists tries to explain that we are not responsible for the actions of our governments. The Serbs spit on the ground and scream. There appears to be no officer in charge, which makes them more crazed. One, who speaks Italian with me, vacillates between reason ("We're going to take you to Priština and arrest you for being spies") and madness ("You're going to die like people in Belgrade have died").

They are claiming we have wandered into Kosovan territory. "We'll go now," I say weakly. "We'll go back to Montenegro." (Borders in this part of the world are entirely fluid; there are no signs saying, WELCOME TO KOSOVO. DRIVE SAFELY.)

"You're a NATO spy! Now you're going to know what it feels like to be bombed and burned," the Italian-speaker barks. He shouts orders at a very young soldier. This one has pale red hair, wears a camouflage cowboy hat, and has wild, unfocused eyes. He keeps pulling out his pistol and aiming it at the terrified refugees, who continue walking single file past us, eyes dropped, trying not to be drawn into the situation.

The young one turns to me. "You we arrest," he says, pointing to me and clasping my wrists together as if they were handcuffed. "Because you have Italian blood. But the French, we kill." When they search the car, they find a photograph of one of the French in Bosnia with the U.N. The photo was taken on a rainy day and he had borrowed a soldier's jacket to protect his camera.

"NATO spies! Spies!" the young soldier yells. He appears delighted that they have hard proof with which to abuse us.

Later, looking back, I will realize they don't have a plan, that they have no idea what to do with us. They take all our gear—cameras, sat phone, mobile phones, armored car, passports, other documents—and tell us to turn our backs to them and march down the mountain and into Montenegro. I don't want to turn my back. They fire over our heads. We run, jump into the back of a truck carrying refugees. A Serb-army jeep, coming up the mountain, blocks our truck. These soldiers tell us to get out; we are marched back up to where we started.

This time, they make us sit in the French journalists' car. We hear shots—not fired in the air. When I turn around, I see they have lined up refugees. They are stealing their cars and rifling through their bags. One of the French says to me, "Don't turn around." I see one Kosovar boy who earlier was ferrying refugees up and over the mountain in a flatbed truck. The soldiers are beating him and hitting him with their guns; he makes noises like a whimpering dog. He falls to the ground like an empty sack.

Another shot. Into something. I do not look back this time, out of cowardice and fear. The three of us sit stunned, waiting. Then the soldiers decide to take us to Priština, in Kosovo.

"Follow us," says the Italian-speaker. "Drive slowly. Stay behind us. Now you will see what it is like to get bombed. Our commander will decide what to do. Prison, for a long time." He clasps his wrists together to indicate chains, and laughs.

We drive through the snow, down the other side of the mountain, passing hundreds of refugees going the opposite way. The ride is silent. In my bag, I still have a mobile phone that does not work and my notebook, full of a week of documentation of refugees: phone numbers of their relatives, testimonies, first and last names. I have been searched by Serbs before. I know how they react when they see what is written about them. It is not good to have the notebook with me—neither for me nor for the people I have interviewed.

Very slowly, I rip up my notebook. My colleague throws it out the open door, very carefully, watching to make sure the soldiers ahead of us do not see. It lands in the snow in the middle of the road. It leaves a black mark in the whiteness.

We drive about 30 kilometers. Then, somewhere inside Kosovo, the soldiers get a radio call. We see the Italian-speaker answering. Then he stops the jeep, gets out, and lights a cigarette. He tells us to get out of our car. It will soon be evening and we are now in an isolated spot, away from refugees, away from any witnesses. We are on the side of a freezing mountain. No one with any power to do anything about it had seen us taken. If we disappear, no one will know. The thought of rape has not crossed my mind—I am more worried about getting shot in the back.

The soldier smokes his cigarette thoughtfully while we wait. Then, slowly, he walks to the rear of the jeep. He stands outside the door thinking, then hands back our gear. "Get out of here," he says, in good English. "There are Albanian terrorists [the Serbs' phrase for the Kosovo Liberation Army] everywhere. It's very dangerous. Go away. Never come back."

Then he does the oddest thing. He kisses me on both cheeks. He hugs the French, almost as though he is trying to demonstrate communion: that we are all in a place where we do not want to be. He crushes the cigarette under his heel, jumps in the jeep, and speeds off toward Peć.

We drive back into Montenegro. When we get to Rožaj, we hear that the Serbs on the Macedonian border—on the other side of Kosovo from Montenegro—had taken three American soldiers hostage around the same time as the other soldiers got us. A male refugee approaches me as I set up the sat phone in the back of the armored car in the pouring rain.

"It's you, thank God," he says, speaking perfect English, touching my shoulder gently. "We saw them march you off. We saw them take you at gunpoint. You were very lucky. God was with you."

His name is Mustafa, and he says he is a professor at the University of Priština. He speaks, in addition to English, perfect French, Italian, and Danish. He has been living with his family in Denmark, and came to visit his sister in Peć when the air strikes began.

As an intellectual who has frequently entertained Western journalists in his home, he says that he was targeted by the death squads, the Serb paramilitary. He says he was worried about Arkan—the indicted Serb war criminal (real name: Zeljko Ražnatović) who, along with his paramilitary squad, the notorious Tigers, has been accused of some of the worst atrocities during the Bosnian war. It is rumored that Arkan and his men have gone down to Kosovo to help their Serb brothers—a terrifying thought.

Mustafa asks me if I can help get him and his wife and four children, who are sheltered somewhere on the mountain, out of Montenegro as soon as possible.

"If Milošević marches into Montenegro, which everyone says he will do soon," Mustafa says in a soft voice, "I will be killed. All of our lives hang on very little here."

We sit and have a coffee in a noisy bar blaring hip-hop music. I cannot stop shaking, from cold and nerves. I say I will phone the Italian Consulate in the morning.

"God was with you today," Mustafa repeats, adding sugar to his Turkish coffee. His eyes have the look of someone haunted. Like all of the refugees on the border, he has seen too much in the past few weeks. "Usually the Serbs just shoot. They don't have a change of heart."

Mustafa will get out. He and his family will take the ferry from Montenegro to Italy and fly to Denmark. He is now safe, and will probably never return to Kosovo.

Raće, a Serb Stronghold in Montenegro, April 4, 1999 (Easter Sunday in the West)

uite simply, Serbia had already lost Kosovo—lost it, that is, in the most basic human and demographic terms," wrote the British historian Noel Malcolm last year before the Serb offensive began and before the NATO bombing. But he did not foresee, as NATO did not foresee, the diehard feelings of the Serb people, solidified during the bombing campaign, and how unwilling they are to give up their spiritual heartland, their Jerusalem.

Kosovo, to the Serbs, is more than a political stronghold: it is sacred. Here are some of their greatest monasteries and the remains of their most revered saints. It is also the place of their holy battlefield, Kosovo Polje, which they had lost before, in 1389, to the Turks. The place has taken on mythic proportions. During the Balkan war of 1913, which reclaimed Kosovo from the Turks, one Serb soldier wrote:

> The single sound of that word—Kosovo—caused an indescribable excitement. This one word pointed to the black past—five centuries. In it exists the whole of our sad past—the

tragedy of Prince Lazar [who lost the battle of Kosovo Polje] and the entire Serbian people. . . . Each of us created for himself a picture of Kosovo while we were still in the cradle. Our mothers lulled us to sleep with the songs of Kosovo.

Kosovo's fate was more recently sealed when Milošević gave his April 1987 speech: "Yugoslavia does not exist without Kosovo! Yugoslavia would disintegrate without Kosovo! Yugoslavia and Serbia are not going to give up Kosovo!" In 1989, he would revoke Kosovo's autonomy within the Yugoslav federation, fire Albanians from state-run institutions, and ban the teaching of the Albanian language and its literature.

In Raće, a remote, Serb-dominated village outside of Podgorica, the Montenegrin capital, they support the current push to drive every "Turk" (Albanian, Muslim, the same thing in their eyes) out of Kosovo. Here, there are no "servants of NATO" and no "traitors." This is a hard-core, barren place, a village carved out of a gray mountain. This is Slobodan Milošević country, full of simple people who might not have supported him before but will now go to their graves for a greater, united Serbia.

On the drive out, through the stony mountains, I see graffiti which chill me: ARKAN, the indicted war criminal. And the Cyrillic symbol for "Only unity can save the Serbs," which was often painted on burned-out houses in Bosnia and Kosovo.

In a small café I meet a farmer and his wife and three children. They sit under a portrait of Slobodan Milošević, the adults drinking beer. The children eat sweets and drink Cokes and laugh. The farmer, Rajko, is at first hostile, then buys me a coffee and tries to explain his position: his family has lived in these hills forever and ever. He considers himself a Serb, not a Montenegrin, and he will die fighting for Greater Serbia if the Montenegrin separatists follow the pattern of the other former Yugoslav republics and try to break away.

"Someone is going to stay in this country," he says. "And it will be a Serb. They can't shoot every single one of us." He says that he does not believe what is said to be happening in Kosovo to be true. There is no such thing as ethnic cleansing—people are fleeing the NATO bombs and the "Albanian terrorists." Kosovo belongs to Serbia, emotionally, historically, and politically.

I leave feeling more depressed than on any other day of the trip. Not only are these people living in denial, but it is clear that the Kosovo conflict is rapidly destabilizing the rest of the region. That night, in Podgorica, there is a demonstration in the town square by Milošević supporters. It is billed as a peace effort, but the square is full of people waving anti-NATO, anti-Clinton signs and wearing targets pinned to their chests. Journalists are advised not to go, as the anti-Western feeling has been building up. All day the city has been rife with tension.

I wander through the crowd, listening to the dreadful Yugoslav rock. An aging rocker screams, "Serbia! Serbia!" I listen and try to blend in and not look like a journalist. Momo, a Montenegrin friend of mine, leads me by the hand and tells me not to speak English.

I do what he says. But what I feel from that crowd, standing in the middle of it, is a naked antipathy toward Westerners that I have not felt before, a surging sense of anger, suspicion, hatred.

Podgorica,
April 7, 1999

I t is two days before Serb Good Friday, the day after the anniversary of the devastating German air attack on Belgrade in 1941 (when, ironically, Serbia was aligned with the Western powers). Milošević asks for a cease-fire to respect the upcoming Orthodox Easter. It is a joke: cease-fire in the Balkans means playing for more time.

I meet an 80-year-old man who cannot give his name, a general under Tito, who drove all night from Belgrade to Podgorica when he heard the rumors that a coup d'état was imminent here. "I am old, but I can offer some advice," he says earnestly. He tells me old war stories: In December 1941, when he was 21, he led a partisan battalion of 431 men in guerrilla warfare against the Germans and the Italians. During one battle, he remembers "fighting from early morning to early night." They ambushed Italian tanks. They fought hand to hand. In the morning, it was his job to count the casualties: 180 wounded, 82 dead. "And that was the saddest morning of my life."

But he believed in something, so he fought to the end of the war and was highly decorated. After the liberation of Belgrade, he became a general at 26, and later a respected diplomat.

"In those days, we lived so close to death that you became older and more clever with double speed," he tells me.

The next day, I find him drinking coffee in an outdoor café. NATO bombs have fallen on Montenegro, hitting Serb-army targets. Belgrade, where his family is, is in flames. The Pentagon has found evidence of mass graves in Kosovo. More refugees are pouring over the border, bearing more stories of atrocities. The war NATO thought would be over in a few days appears to be drifting into an abyss.

The general is distraught. His hand trembles as he holds the coffee cup. He has lived through the destruction of his country by German warplanes, then the renaissance of "brotherhood and unity" for all Yugoslavs under Tito. He watched the war in Slovenia, Croatia, Bosnia. Now, aged 80, he has come to offer his services to the Montenegrin separatists who may have to fight against Milošević. He is frightened at what he is witnessing.

"Everything is ruined," he is saying in a shaky voice. "Everything is ruined. There is no more fraternity and unity. The last 10 years, everything is ruined." He pauses and puts down his cup. "I lost so many friends during World War II, so many young people trying to create a new country. Now everything is falling down because of ideas. Who are these people? Are they insane? Why are they cleaning out Kosovo?"

**Somewhere Inside
Southwestern Kosovo,
May 10–12, 1999**

I have managed to cross the border into Kosovo with a special-forces K.L.A. unit. A major Serb offensive is under way to take back territory the K.L.A. won two weeks ago. It also happens to be the night of the heaviest NATO bombing in Kosovo since the campaign began over a month ago. I am lying in a muddy ditch with a helmet that has no strap, getting bombed by Serb planes trying to hit us—and by NATO planes trying to hit the nearby Serb ground forces. Shells and rockets fall intermittently.

I am with a young soldier, an Albanian born in Kosovo who has recently been living in the U.S. and Canada. Dardan is 25 years old, handsome, wearing a Polo Ralph Lauren hat under his helmet. He has also lived in London, where he was so good at mixing cocktails that he was voted the fifth-best bartender in Britain. He's proud of that fact, and proud that he paid for his own plane ticket from Vancouver to arrive here at this front line to fight with the K.L.A.

Dardan has never fired a gun before. Now he's got a Chinese-made kalashnikov to defend his country against the Serb offensive, which has been going on for four days. In the dark there is chaos: every time a plane roars through the sky and drops a bomb with a terrifying dense thud, we do not know where it is coming from.

"Who's bombing us? Who's bombing us?" one of the younger soldiers yells to an older soldier. No one knows, but someone says that four soldiers who died earlier, hit as they lay in their tents, were victims of NATO. There is confusion about how many people are dead, how many are wounded. This is what war is: confusion, uncertainty, not knowing which direction the shooting or the rocket fire is coming from.

For two nights, we have slept in ditches on muddy slopes covered in soldiers' excrement, surrounded by wounded soldiers whose flesh has been ripped away by hot pieces of shrapnel. I have always thought of myself as squeamish. But when you are under this kind of intense fire, some things become irrelevant. There are people around me dying on dirty stretchers, and they are young.

I once asked a Bosnian soldier how old he was. "Eighteen," he replied. Then he added, quickly, "Don't look at me like that. I know what you are thinking." What I was thinking was this: I don't know if this kid is ever going to reach his 19th birthday. And I hated Slobodan Milošević for making him fight this war when he should be at parties or sitting in a café looking at girls. One of his comrades showed me a helmet with a picture of a model from Victoria's Secret taped inside. "If I ever get out," he said, "my girlfriend is going to look like this."

Lying in the ditch, Dardan and I are talking to each other as if we were meeting for the first time at a cocktail party.

"I left Priština in 1992," he says. "My whole generation left. We didn't want to get drafted by the Serbs and fight against the Bosnians. But I came back to fight for my country. To fight for freedom. To be an Albanian inside Kosovo is no life at all. That's why we're here—liberation." His voice is drowned out: heavy machine-gun fire. The Serbs are attempting to encircle our camp. There are eight soldiers at the end of our ditch who are meant to guard us from an infantry assault.

"Split up! Split up! Fifty meters apart! Move down the canyon!" shouts one commander, who has taken control. Though my night vision is poor, I grab my pack, my helmet—which will do me little good if I get hit by a grenade—and run. I have no flak jacket; neither do the soldiers around me.

"Split up—if one of you gets hit, all of you won't die! I need all of you alive!" the commander barks. A young soldier is crying. Another soldier, his body and face torn up by shrapnel, is squatting in the mud motioning me to bring him water. He is weeping with fear and pain. He is shitting himself. I wipe his forehead, and then throw myself back on the ground as another rocket lands. I am facedown in the mud. Then I run down a ravine, stumbling on rocks until I find a tree. I sit against it, leaning uphill.

The battle continues as day breaks. During a lull in the fighting I wander over some hills and find the wreckage of a Serb plane that has (allegedly) been shot down by NATO. Near the river bordering our camp I find the tents of the four soldiers who were supposedly hit by friendly fire. It may also have been the Serbs, no one really knows. Three were young soldiers, one was an older man with a beard. I see one of the bodies being taken away, in a military jeep, to a morgue in a nearby town.

I see a cow with its hind legs blown off, covered in flies. Then a white horse, startled by the bombs, apparently dead of a heart attack, lying on the side of the hill. And everywhere I look are the craters of mortar fire and bombs. In the middle of it all is a small, white, idyllic farmhouse—untouched. Someone has left washing outside, hanging on the clothesline.

I make my way to the front. The soldiers here, dug into their trenches and foxholes, are tired but strong, and I feel oddly confident of their ability, even though we are pinned down by a 15-minute firefight. In an abandoned stable serving as a bunker, I stumble onto a unit of soldiers pumped up by a recent victory. They are high-fiving and hugging one another. I am told the K.L.A. has managed to take out two Serb tanks and kill 60 Serb soldiers. In a David-versus-Goliath war, that is a major victory.

That night, during another pause in the fighting, we eat bean soup and bread for dinner. The tents are eerily quiet. The mood is different than it was before last night's bombardment began, when the soldiers were singing K.L.A. songs. Tonight we sit up in our sleeping bags, tension growing. One of the commanders tells me to prepare for a horrible night.

Someone lays out the plan: when the bombing begins, we are to run out into a ditch because the Serbs will certainly be targeting our tents and can pick up body heat with infra-red lasers. We are to run in the darkness, one by one, and be prepared for aerial, artillery, and possibly even infantry attacks. "Be prepared for everything," one of the commanders tells me. My fear is an infantry attack: what will the Serbs do if they find me inside the camp?

As the night and the wait drag on, one senior commander, whom I know from the war in Bosnia, is sketching plans for an offensive. A soldier, a devout Muslim, is praying. Another, a Swede, a former U.N. soldier in Bosnia who has come to Kosovo as a K.L.A. volunteer, is cursing silently as he tries to fit his boots—which he will need instantly once the bombardment begins—inside his sleeping bag. One of the young soldiers is snoring gently. I can smell the breath of the man lying next to me. At around one a.m. I drift off, forgetting momentarily where I am.

We are all awakened at three by the whine and crash of a bomb dropped by a Serb plane. I too am sleeping with my boots on, and I fumble to sit upright and get out of my sleeping bag.

"Journalist! Where are you?" calls out the Swedish soldier. "Ten seconds and exit!"

"No lights! No matches!" someone screams.

I push the tent flap aside and plunge into darkness, sliding down a hill on my back, unable to get my footing.

From three to six a.m., lying in a muddy trench, I watch the sky lighten, the stars just marginally brighter than the illumination of the bombs. At dawn, some of the soldiers build a small fire. I drift in and out of a painful sleep on the muddy slope, covered by a blanket that one of the commanders has placed protectively over me. As if in a dream, I see an old village woman taking her sheep up to pasture in the middle of the bombardment. She is completely unfazed. I watch her with a mixture of horror and fascination.

Around seven a.m., I wake for good, thanks to the *thud* of a shell landing nearby. I see Dardan, the young bartender, looking out into the sky, which is bright blue flecked with pink and orange—a Turner painting. It is perfectly, painfully beautiful.

Dardan is smoking a cigarette. I can see only his silhouette. He looks like a soldier from World War II with his old helmet and his kalashnikov slung over his shoulder. He is staring at the sky in amazement, his mind far away from this place, this time, this war. He is shouting, to no one in particular, "Look! Look at that beautiful light! Look at that light!"

Then he sees that I am awake and he turns to me: "Janine! Look at that sky! We're still alive! Isn't it wonderful—we're still alive!"

**Kukës, Northern Albania,
May 14, 1999**

Yesterday I left the K.L.A. and crossed over into Albania. The heavy bombardment by Serb forces is continuing. I hear the K.L.A. is getting shelled by rockets, mortars, and tanks. I hear that there have been many K.L.A. casualties. I keep thinking of Dardan. I don't know whether he's dead or alive.

Eighty-four years ago, the American reporter John Reed, author of the famous account of the Russian Revolution, *Ten Days That Shook the World,* traveled throughout war-torn Eastern Europe. Reading his Balkan reports, one has an awful sense of history endlessly repeating itself; no one here has learned from past mistakes. What Reed wrote then could easily be lifted from any newspaper today: "In the Serbian schools the children are taught not only the geography of old Serbia, but of all the Serbian lands, *in the order of their redemption*—first Macedonia, then Dalmatia, Bosnia, Herzegovina, Croatia. . . . Now Kosovo is avenged and Macedonia delivered."

In the Balkans, one is always aware of that weight of history. "We are in a time vacuum here," the Sarajevo poet Mario Susko once told me. "We are trapped in a terrible cycle of everything happening again and again, and we cannot stop it."

Before crossing into Kosovo I had visited Cetinje, the capital of old Montenegro, where I found the onetime summer palace of the Petrović family, the last Montenegrin dynasty. Montenegro was recognized as a kingdom in 1878 at the Congress of Berlin. In 1918, in the aftermath of World War I—which had started with an assassination in 1914 in Sarajevo—the kingdom of Montenegro ceased to exist with the single stroke of a pen. It was annexed by Serbia, swallowed up into Yugoslavia. The Petrović dynasty, which had ruled for 222 years, crumpled. King Nikola fled to Italy and died in exile.

In his old summer palace, I felt a sense of tragedy and irrevocable sadness. A local historian let me in and opened up the shutters, flooding the dusty place with weak sunlight. I saw King Nikola's books, his Turkish weapons, a medal given to him by Queen Victoria. I saw ancient sepiaprint photographs, and his wife's silk-and-lace dresses, and the polished Chippendale dining-room table. I saw the ghostly piano imported from Leipzig. No one visits here anymore.

"We do not have a romantic history," said the man who gloomily guided me through the rooms. "We have a tragic one. We have no freedom to choose our own destiny."

"Destiny" is a word that is used often here. There is a sense that it is history that controls the Balkans and not the other way around. But the late British writer Rebecca West would have argued that point. After traveling throughout Yugoslavia on the eve of World War II, she concluded that what was done in Yugoslavia was always carried out with a fatal plan. "Why did the Yugoslavs choose to perish? It must be reiterated that it was their choice, made out of full knowledge," she wrote. "On none of them did their fate steal unawares."

When I look at a map of the old Yugoslavia now, what I see are not borders but people I knew and loved, or people I met for only a day or an hour. During the 1991–95 wars in the former Yugoslavia, more than 2 million people out of a prewar population of 24 million were displaced; in Kosovo now, another 800,000 and counting have fled. I think of their empty houses, of the things they left behind, or else of the people who are homeless, mutilated, dead. The dentist living underground in central Bosnia, to whom I once gave a packet of aspirin, causing her to burst into tears. A young mother walking up a mountain path in Kosovo, or the teenage champion swimmer who lost a breast during a mortar attack in Sarajevo.

Nedžarići, Serb-Held Sarajevo, December 17, 1992

This is my strongest and most terrible memory: A road gutted with shell holes. Temperature: 15 degrees below zero. A nursing home, ironically called the Center for the Protection of Old People and situated between two front lines. A Serb sniper situated in a house 25 meters away.

Ten old people dead in three days, frozen to death in their beds, and no one to remove the bodies. Most of the staff ran away when the heavy shelling began. The U.N. can't decamp because of the heavy fighting. A 78-year-old man went outside to chop firewood to try to keep the place warm and got shot between the eyes.

I step over broken glass, broken bricks, seared blankets. It is so cold my breath comes out in puffs. The windows are all shot out, replaced by U.N.-supplied plastic.

A long, frozen hallway. Corpses wrapped in dirty blankets. Empty rooms. I open one door and count six dead bodies, still in their beds, not yet wrapped and laid on the floor. Faces frozen in their last expression. They die at night, the coldest time, alone.

The farthest bed is occupied by a pile of rags. I bend over, and a tiny arm, no bigger than a child's, reaches up. A tiny hand grabs my arm. It is not a pile of clothes, but an ancient woman, still alive, with lavender-colored eyes and broken teeth. Her skin is translucent with the cold.

"Zima," she whispers. Her lips are split. She does not have enough calories in her system to focus, to concentrate on my face. "Zima." *Winter.*

Exhausted by her effort, she drops my arm. I try to talk to her. Speak to me, I say. Stay alive, at least until a doctor gets here. But I know, as she does, that there is no doctor coming.

The woman says she once played the violin. She doesn't remember if she is Muslim, Serb, or Croat. She is from Sarajevo, that's all. Then she pulls the covers over her head and retreats under the blankets. She becomes, once again, a pile of clothes.

Sebastian Junger

The Forensics of War

Homo homini lupus.
(Man is a wolf to man.)

Plautus, *Asinaria.*

No one knows who he was, but he almost got away. He broke and ran when the Serbs started shooting, and he made it to a thicket before the first bullet hit him in the left leg. It must have missed the bone, because he was able to keep going—along the edge of a hayfield and then into another swath of scrub oak and locust. There was a dry streambed in there, and he probably crouched in the shadows, listening to the bursts of machine-gun fire and trying to figure out a way to escape. The thicket stretched uphill, along the hayfield, to a stand of pine trees, and from there it was all woods and fields leading to the Albanian border. It didn't offer much of a chance, and he must have known that.

He tied a sweater around the wound in his thigh and waited. Maybe he was too badly hurt to keep moving, or maybe he didn't dare because the Serbs were already along the edge of the field. Either way, they eventually spotted him and shot him in the chest, and he fell backward into the streambed. His killers took his shoes, and—months later, after the war ended—a fellow Albanian took his belt buckle and brought it to the authorities in Gjakovë. It was the only distinctive thing on him, and there was a chance that someone might recognize it.

I saw the dead man in late June, two weeks after NATO had taken Kosovo from the Serbs. It was a hot day, and my photographer and I stood peering at his corpse, in the same mottled shade that the man had tried to hide in. His skull was broken open and his jawbone was a short distance away. The sweater was still tied around his leg. I had walked into the thicket braced for the worst, but he wasn't particularly hard to look at. He'd been killed two months earlier—on April 27, around midday—and he looked less like a person than a tipped-over hat rack draped in blue jeans and a cheap parka. The young man who had led us there leaned on a shepherd's crook and told us that the dead man was in his early 20s and had probably come from a nearby village. The Serbs had swept the valley from Junik to Gjakovë in retaliation for an attack by the Kosovo Liberation Army, which for two years has fought for independence for Kosovo. They'd taken the men from more than half a dozen little villages and gunned them down in a field outside of Meja. Then they came back in the middle of the night to bury them. They missed a few.

The shepherd identified himself as Bashkim; he was a handsome blond kid with a wispy goatee and a shy smile that never left his face. "They came at five a.m.—not shooting, just yelling," Bashkim said. "They made 200 people lie down against a compost heap, piled cornhusks on them, and then machine-gunned them. Then they set them on fire. . . . It was local militia from Gjakovë. They were wearing green camouflage and black ski masks. One of them was called Stari; all the women saw him. They recognized him from Gypsy Road, about five kilometers from here."

Meja was just a scattering of tile-roofed farmhouses along a dirt road in the middle of a broad agricultural valley. Wheat and hay fields gave way to brush-covered hills and then the Koritnik Mountains, which run along the Albanian border. Bashkim escaped the roundup of men in the valley because he was in an isolated house that the Serbs missed. While telling the story, he seemed undisturbed by the massacres, his own close call, or even the body at his feet. He just kept smiling and smoking the American cigarettes we offered him. After 20 minutes or so, he led us back into the hot sun of the hayfield and past the compost heap where the men had been shot. There was a human leg in the grass, and then another leg, and then more remains in a ditch. They were harder to identify. Stuck into the compost heap was an old umbrella. "Why is that there?" I asked.

"It was found near one of the bodies," Bashkim said. "Maybe someone will recognize it and know who he was."

The worst of the violence didn't come to southwestern Kosovo until the evening of March 24, when NATO jets streaked overhead on their way to bomb command-and-control targets in Serbia. Within hours, Serb special police, soldiers, and hastily deputized militia units were walking through the streets of nearby Gjakovë, pumping incendiary rounds—known locally as "butterflies"—into houses and storefronts in the Albanian part of town. When the buildings finished burning, the Serbs knocked the walls over with bulldozers and then used Gypsies to clear the rubble from the streets so that they were passable for tanks. Anyone who stood around and watched was shot.

There was little the K.L.A. could do but hide in the hills and wait for it to be over. In two years of fighting, the K.L.A. never won a battle or held a town for long, but it did know how to ambush. And in mid-April, just outside of Meja, it pulled off an ambush that would bring the full wrath of the Serbs down on the valley.

Their target was a Serb commander named Milotin Prasović, who was particularly loathed by the local Albanians. A week or so earlier, Prasović had driven through Meja warning the residents that he was going to return to collect all the weapons in town, and if there weren't any for him, he'd burn their houses down. True to his word, he came back in a brick-red Audi filled with police. They drove through town, shot into the air, turned around, and drove straight into a K.L.A. ambush. The first rocket-propelled grenade blew the right rear door off. That was followed by another round and sheets of automatic-weapon fire. Everyone in the car was killed except for Prasović, who managed to dive out of his seat and start shooting back from the edge of the road. It was over within seconds; the K.L.A. shot him down from their hiding place and then retreated into the hills above town.

The retaliation, when it came, was swift and implacable. Shortly before dawn on April 27, according to locals, a large contingent of Yugoslav army troops garrisoned in Junik started moving eastward through the valley, dragging men from their houses and pushing them into trucks. "Go to Albania!" they screamed at the women before driving on to the next town with their prisoners. By the time they got to Meja they had collected as many as 300 men. The regular army took up positions around the town while the militia and paramilitaries went through the houses grabbing the last few villagers and shoving them out into the road. The men were surrounded by fields most of them had worked in their whole lives, and they could look up and see mountains they'd admired since they were children. Around noon the first group was led to the compost heap, gunned down, and burned under piles of cornhusks. A few minutes later a group of about 70 were forced to lie down in three neat rows and were machine-gunned in the back. The rest—about 35 men—were taken to a farmhouse along the Gjakovë road, pushed into one of the rooms, and then shot through the windows at point-blank range. The militiamen who did this then stepped inside, finished them off with shots to the head, and burned the house down. They walked away singing.

By conservative estimates, the Serbs killed at least 10,000 people in Kosovo. There are so many bodies—both human and animal—lying around the countryside that much of the rural water supply is contaminated. There are parts of Kosovo where not one village has been spared, and there are villages where not one house has been left standing. In the Decani district, bodies have been dumped in the wells of 39 of 44 villages surveyed. When NATO tanks rumbled into Kosovo on June 12, they found a level of destruction that hadn't been seen in Europe since World War II.

The first big massacre occurred in March 1998, when Serb forces surrounded the village of Prekaz and wiped out 58 civilians, many of them women and children. The attack was in retaliation for a shoot-out between K.L.A. and Serb police a couple of weeks earlier, and it was the beginning of a horrible symbiosis between the two forces. Every time the K.L.A. carried out a guerrilla attack, Serb forces would destroy the nearest village and massacre as many of the inhabitants as they could. And every time the Serbs massacred people in a village, more grief-stricken survivors joined the K.L.A. "For every massacre Serbs commit, we get 20 more recruits," one K.L.A. commander told a journalist friend of mine a few weeks before the NATO bombings started.

Ethically speaking, there's an extremely thin line between ambushing Serb forces and deliberately provoking Serbs into massacring civilians, but the strategy worked. Around eight p.m. on March 24, the first NATO warplanes struck targets deep within Serbia. And two months later, on May 24—just as the first sketchy peace agreements were being explored with Belgrade—the Hague war-crimes tribunal indicted Slobodan Milošević and four other government and military leaders. The indictment was based on eyewitness accounts of massacres which took place between January and April of 1999 in the villages of Racak, Krushe e Mahde, Krushe e Vogel, Bellacerka, Izbica, and Padalishte; the indictment listed, by name, more than 340 ethnic Albanians who had been killed. Within days of NATO's arrival in Priština, war-crimes investigators donated by many NATO countries were sifting through the mass graves named in the indictments, gathering evidence.

.   .   .

The crimes that Milošević and his compatriots were charged with fall under the Geneva Conventions of 1949, which were a direct outgrowth of the post-World War II Nuremberg trials. When the Germans surrendered on May 7, 1945, the Allies were suddenly faced with an unprecedented problem: they had in their custody Nazi officials who had started a war in which nearly 50 million people had been killed. Many of the dead were exterminated in concentration camps, and the question was: What kind of justice should be brought to bear on the men who carried out such slaughter? The British initially suggested that the hundred or so main German culprits simply be taken out into the woods and shot (an idea embraced by Joseph Stalin, who jokingly—or maybe not—proposed upping the number to 50,000). Ultimately, though, due process prevailed. The accused would be given trials, which "they, in the days of their pomp and power, never gave to any man," as the chief American prosecutor, Robert Jackson, put it. The trial would be open and fair, conducted in both English and German, and the accused would be represented by lawyers who would call their own witnesses and cross-examine others.

As idealistic as it was, the idea had inherent flaws. First, it was, by definition, a victor's justice, and there was no suggestion that the victors would ever face the same scrutiny as the vanquished. The Soviets, for example, had invaded and occupied eastern Poland in 1939, in close cooperation with the Nazis; they massacred thousands of Polish officers and buried their bodies in the Katyn Forest. The Allies had firebombed Dresden, killing several hundred thousand civilians, and the Americans had firebombed Tokyo and then dropped nuclear bombs on Hiroshima and Nagasaki. These were all direct attacks on civilians—and therefore clear violations of international law—but they would never make it to the docket at Nuremberg.

·　　·　　·

Second, the Nazis were charged with, among other things, crimes against humanity, which includes crimes committed by a government against its own people. At the start of World War II the law didn't exist, and because the Holocaust was completely legal under German law, the perpetrators had technically never committed a crime. To charge them ex post facto was illegal and would never have stood up in a regular judicial proceeding.

These objections amounted to legal parlor games, however; the reality was that the Nuremberg trials were about as fair as things ever get in wartime. Out of the 22 Nazi leaders who were tried, 12 were sentenced to hang—including Reichsmarschall Hermann Göring, who swallowed a cyanide pill shortly before his execution; 7 were sentenced to long prison terms; and 3 were acquitted. Three years later, the legal principles used in the trials were codified as the four Geneva Conventions and the Genocide Convention. Along with the Additional Protocols of 1977, they form the basis today of international war-crimes trials. Because they are rooted in something called "customary international law"—which flows from norms evolved over centuries, rather than from treaties—the conventions are binding even on nations which have not signed them. A state, in other words, cannot exclude itself from the constraints of customary law any more than an individual can.

The indictments announced in The Hague on May 27 charged Yugoslav president Slobodan Milošević, Serb president Milan Milutinović, Deputy Prime Minister Nikola Sainović, Chief of Staff Dragoljub Ojdanić, and Serb minister of internal affairs Vlajko Stojilković with three counts each of crimes against humanity, and one count each of violation of the laws and customs of war. Copies of the arrest warrants were sent to all member states of the United Nations and the Yugoslav minister of justice; U.N. member states were asked to freeze the assets of the accused. The announcement of the indictments was delayed until representatives from international agencies could safely leave the former Yugoslavia, and eyewitnesses wouldn't be identified until the accused were arrested. They could then be properly sheltered from threat and intimidation.

Of the two charges, violations of the laws and customs of war is the older and more traditional. It attempts to reconcile human suffering with the need of an army to defeat its enemy. Although constraints on wartime behavior date back to ancient Hindu and Greek law, the first European wasn't tried in a civilian court until the late 15th century, when an Austrian nobleman named Peter von Hagenbach was sentenced to death for atrocities committed under his command. A hundred and fifty years later, a Dutch lawyer named Hugo Grotius wrote *The Law of War and Peace,* which is considered the foundation of modern humanitarian law. "Throughout the Christian world . . . I observed a lack of restraint in relation to war, such as even barbarous races would be ashamed of," Grotius wrote. "[A] remedy must be found . . . that men may not believe either that nothing is allowable, or that everything is."

Modern laws and customs of war are direct descendants of Grotius's work. In essence, these laws acknowledge that death and suffering are inevitable in armed conflict, but that deliberately inflicting unnecessary suffering is a criminal act for which individuals can be held accountable. If you shell a military base and happen to kill civilians, you have not committed a war crime; if you deliberately target cities and towns, you have. Killing prisoners, civilians, or hostages is a war crime, as is enslavement of civilians, deportation, plunder, wanton destruction, and "extensive destruction not justified by military necessity."

What is and isn't justified by military necessity is, naturally, open to interpretation. One of the key concepts, though, is the law of proportionality. A military attack that results in civilian casualties—"collateral damage"—is acceptable as long as the military benefits outweigh the price that is paid by humanity. A similar concept is applied to weapons. No matter how many people you kill, using a machine gun in battle is not a war crime because it does not cause unnecessary suffering; it simply performs its job horrifyingly well. Exploding bullets, on the other hand—which were banned in the St. Petersburg Declaration of 1868—mutilate and maim foot soldiers without conferring any additional advantage to the other side. A wounded soldier is usually put out of commission when he is hit. There is no reason to maximize his suffering by using an exploding bullet.

Despite the graceful logic of these principles, warfare remains a chaotic business which will always resist governments' efforts to legislate it. Still, it is all too clear that Serb forces in Kosovo violated just about every law in the book. Furthermore, the violations were carried out on such a massive scale that they also qualified as crimes against humanity—that is, they represented a widespread and systematic campaign against a particular population. Massacring noncombatants—as countless armies have done, including our own—is simply a war crime; trying to drive an entire group of people from your country is a crime against humanity. One could reasonably argue that the Turkish pogrom against the Armenians during World War I qualifies as a crime against humanity, as does the United States' ethnic cleansing of Native Americans.

The novel thing about the 1949 humanitarian law was that it protected the citizens of an offending state as well as those of foreign states, and it applied to peacetime as well as war. Until then, governments could do pretty much what they wanted with their own citizens; the most that another nation could do was express its "concern" over the situation. After 1949, in theory a government's conduct at home would be subject to the same standards as its conduct abroad, and human-rights abuses could no longer be dismissed as simply an "internal matter." National sovereignty, in other words, would never again protect a government from the bite of the law.

The Hague's press spokesman in Kosovo after NATO's takeover was a young Englishman named Jim Landale. Dressed in jeans and a fleece jacket, with a backpack over his shoulder, he looked more than anything like a college student striding around the streets of Priština. After returning from Meja, I found him in the new U.N. headquarters, a concrete office building behind the huge, ghastly Grand Hotel at the center of town. A nearby apartment block was smoking slowly from an arson fire, and a lot of young ethnic Albanians were hanging out in front of the hotel, looking for work with the foreign journalists. Landale and I crossed the street to one of the cafés that had just opened and ordered the last two beers that they had in stock.

The tribunal's full name is the International Criminal Tribunal for the Former Yugoslavia—or I.C.T.Y., as it's commonly known. It was created in May 1993 to prosecute Bosnian war crimes, and it was later joined by another tribunal for Rwanda. The I.C.T.Y. has successfully prosecuted several cases from the Bosnian war, mostly against Serbs, despite being hampered by evidence that was in some cases several years old. But it has never before investigated war crimes that were committed so recently, and they have never indicted a head of state during an ongoing armed conflict. Landale, between interruptions by cell phone, explained to me the I.C.T.Y. strategy in Kosovo.

"This is our biggest undertaking by far," he said. "We're still trying to assess and prioritize all the sites. The murder of civilians is a war crime . . . what we'd try to assess would be: How do the various factors relate to our investigations for indictments against certain individuals? . . . Most villages have some sort of crime scene—every one's got their massacre site just around the corner. To be realistic, we are not going to be able to visit every site in Kosovo."

The criteria for prioritizing sites are unflinchingly pragmatic. One would think that Meja—where several hundred men were machine-gunned in a field—would make a better investigation site than, say, a house where just one family was wiped out. Or that the murder of 20 women and children in a basement would be easier to prosecute than the summary execution of 20 K.L.A. soldiers after a battle. Not so; for the most part, sites are chosen simply for the quality of corroborating evidence that can be gathered. During the NATO bombing campaign, investigators in the refugee camps systematically recorded hundreds of eyewitness accounts of massacres; it was information from those interviews that led to the original indictment handed down in May. A small site with excellent eyewitness accounts, in the eyes of a war-crimes prosecutor, is far more valuable than a large site with none.

Similarly, a massacre in an area where a certain military or paramilitary group—such as Arkan's "Tigers," who allegedly committed numerous massacres around Gjakovë—was known to have been working is higher priority than a massacre site where the killers are unknown. And a site that presents any sort of access problem is quickly superseded by one that can be worked on immediately. Land mines are considered an access problem, as are remote areas and sites with too many bodies. The amount of labor required to dig up even one body is considerable, so a mass grave like the one in Meja requires backhoes and bulldozers. The first crime teams flown into Kosovo didn't think to bring any.

"One of our hopes is that the tribunal will work as a deterrent," said Landale when I asked him—given the chance that Milošević will never be brought to trial—what the point of all this is. "And it will also help to relieve a collective sense of guilt. Not all people on one side are guilty—just certain individuals. The investigations should make that clear."

There are more than a dozen crime teams in Kosovo, totaling some 300 people. Scotland Yard, the Royal Canadian Mounted Police, and the F.B.I. have all sent teams, as have police agencies from Germany, Denmark, France, Holland, and Switzerland. Their job is to photograph and diagram massacre sites named in the I.C.T.Y. indictments and to gather evidence such as shell casings, bullets, bloody clothing, and anything else that might identify the killers and the method of death. Then the teams attempt to identify human remains—at least to the extent of knowing the age and sex—and conduct autopsies to determine the cause of death. The large mass graves with hundreds of bodies will be investigated months later, after the delicate surface evidence has all been gathered. Buried corpses change very slowly. Most of the evidence they contain is still there a year later.

The F.B.I. team, consisting of 64 people and 107,000 pounds of equipment, arrived in Skopje on June 22 in an airforce C–5. The team was completely self-sufficient, and it included, on loan from the Armed Forces Institute of Pathology, a forensic anthropologist, two forensic pathologists, and a criminalist, as well as F.B.I. evidence-collection experts, two caseworkers from Physicians for Human Rights, a trauma surgeon, and heavily armed Hostage Response Team agents. From Skopje, the team continued by Marine helicopter and truck convoy to Gjakovë, where they set up their tents and field morgue under some shade trees inside the Italian-army field base. On the flight over, they got their first glimpse of Kosovo's devastation: entire villages burned to the ground and cows lying in fields, their hindquarters blown off by land mines. Early the next morning in Gjakovë, they got to work.

They had to go no farther than across the street to investigate one of their first crime scenes, a house where Serb special police had executed six men in the middle of the night. A seventh man was wounded but didn't die. He managed to crawl out of the house as it burned and—with the help of female relatives—eventually make it to Albania before dying from loss of blood.

The F.B.I. quickly moved through three more sites in Gjakovë, including one where Serbs had taken 25 men at gunpoint and mowed them down with machine-gun fire. There were no survivors, but there were eyewitnesses, and, again, their accounts were recorded by I.C.T.Y. investigators. The I.C.T.Y. was running into a problem, though: there were so many bodies in Kosovo that every time they investigated a site, locals would tell them about several more, and the list was growing almost exponentially. The F.B.I. team, which had originally been charged with investigating only two sites, worked so quickly that the I.C.T.Y. tacked seven more on. Most were in and around Gjakovë and two were outside Peja, in the northwestern corner of the province.

The more remote of the two sites near Peja was known as "the Well," outside a little village named Studenica. Around midday on April 12, Serb paramilitaries identifying themselves as Arkan's Tigers executed nine people at a farmhouse and then dumped the bodies down the well. They then smashed the stone-and-mortar wall surrounding it and dropped the rubble down the hole. Two months later, villagers returning to the area dug the well out and pulled up nine badly decomposed bodies. Eight of them were buried at some distance, but one—that of 86-year-old Sali Zeqiraj—was buried in the yard in front of the farm.

I drove up to Studenica early in the morning with the F.B.I. convoy. It was a beautiful spot, smack up against the Koritnik Mountains, with all of Kosovo spread out below us. Plumes of smoke rose over the valley from Serb houses that had been set on fire by the K.L.A. The field had not been de-mined, so the F.B.I.

investigators climbed carefully out of their army vehicles and approached the farmhouse along the tire ruts that had been left by previous cars. Roger Nisley, leader of the mission, went ahead to scout the house out and then gathered the investigators in front of the lead Humvee. "It looks like shots were fired through the window," he said. "So get a sketch of that. And we have a body here, apparently it's the grandfather, but we only have permission to dig up one body. There is a total of nine."

While evidence-collection people photographed the house and picked through it for shell casings and bullet holes, four diggers started opening up the grave. Family members stood in the field, anxiously stripping grass stems—just far enough away that they didn't have to see anything they didn't want to see. Only one of them—a young man named Xhevat Gashi, who lived in Germany and had come back only the day before—stood close by. The body came up swaddled in clear plastic sheeting, tied with rope at both ends. The investigators, dressed in white Tyvex jumpsuits with face masks that pinched their nostrils closed, untied the rope and carefully unwrapped the body. The dead man was dressed in pants and socks and a plaid shirt; the investigators cut the clothes off him and laid him out on a blue tarp. He'd been in water for two months, and his flesh had a doughy look, as if he were a mannequin made out of bread. It was very hard to make a connection between the body on the tarp and a human being. Out in the field, one of the family members started to cry. Xhevat, the grandson, shifted on his feet and kept watching.

The investigators quickly found something of interest. "We have an entrance gunshot wound in the back of the head," said Dr. Andrew Baker, one of the pathologists on loan from the Armed Forces Institute of Pathology. "You've got a sharp edge on the outside, blunt edge on the inside. I don't see an exit wound so far."

The fact that there was no exit wound was important because it meant that the bullet—a crucial piece of evidence—might still be in the skull. Baker made an incision in the back of the scalp and pulled the skin forward until he had peeled the face down like a thick rubber mask. Then he opened the skull and probed inside the cavity. It took 15 minutes to search the skull and the countless folds of the brain; Baker found neither the bullet nor an exit wound. He pulled the face back up, reassembled the head, and rewrapped the dead man in plastic. Then the four diggers lowered him back into the grave.

One of the advantages to investigating a shooting murder (as opposed to a knifing or a bludgeoning) is that ballistics is a precise science and bullets act in fairly predictable ways. By reconstructing the path of a bullet—through a room or through a body—it is possible to know a lot about where it was fired from. For example, a round from an AK–47 assault rifle leaves the muzzle of the gun at 2,300 feet per second, twice the speed of sound. When it hits a person, the density of the tissue forces the round to yaw to one side until it is traveling sideways, or even backward. Shock waves ripple through the tissue and create a cavity that can be as much as 11 times the size of the bullet. The cavity lasts only a few thousandths of a second, but the shock waves that created it can shred organs that the bullet never even touches. In head wounds, the temporary cavity is particularly devastating because the skull—being rigid—can respond to the sudden deformation only by bursting. If the gun barrel is actually touching the victim, rapidly expanding gases inside the barrel get trapped in the wound and blow blood and tissue back out. It is safe to assume that some of the killers in Studenica walked away literally covered in the people they killed.

Even if the bodies are not recovered, though, a very good idea of what went on at the moment of death can be had by something called "bloodstain pattern analysis." Drops of blood splash differently depending on the angle at which they strike a hard surface, and arcsine equations can be used to reconstruct the path that the blood took through the air. If there are more than two bloodstains, something like triangulation can be used to figure out—down to an area about the size of a grapefruit—where in space they all originated. "That's useful in saying, 'Well, the person was standing up when they were shot,'" says Grant Graham, a criminalist with the Armed Forces Institute of Pathology. "'The person was on their knees. The person was lying down.' . . . There are all different types of bloodstain patterns—swipes, wipes, drips, arterial spurts, gushes—and you can reconstruct what happens in the crime scene as things move along. . . . It's a moving, flowing event."

Unfortunately, many of the dead in Kosovo were burned beyond recognition. The report for 157 Millosh Gillic Street states that F.B.I. investigators went to a burned-out residence and found "the skeletal remains of an indeterminate number of victims." But even a charred pile of bones can contain enough evidence to identify the dead and the method of death.

"The human skeleton is a dynamic part of the body," says Dr. Bill Rodriguez, the forensic anthropologist attached to the F.B.I. team. "It is constantly altered by activity. In a runner, changes occur in the bones of the leg; in a dockworker, changes occur in the upper torso. Bones are just like fingerprints . . . their structures are so unique that you can make a positive identification."

To identify the remains, the investigators need something to compare them with. Determining that you have a dead male in his mid–30s who probably did a lot of heavy lifting doesn't do much good unless you also have descriptions of missing people to pick from. X-rays provide the most accurate matches, as do dental work and injuries, but absent those kinds of records, forensic anthropologists can still provide a huge amount of information about who was killed and how. There is only one right femur in a body, for example; the number of right femurs in a pile of bones tells you how many people there were. Not only that, but bones differ enough between sexes, races, and age groups that it is often possible to define quite narrowly who these people must have been.

In 1948, an anthropologist working for the army's Office of the Quartermaster General—using war dead from Guadalcanal, Iwo Jima, and other Pacific battlegrounds—improved upon an already strong statistical connection between body height and femur length. If you multiply the length of the femur by 2.38 and then add 61.41 centimeters, you get the height of a person to within a fraction of a centimeter. Further military studies found that the shafts of the long bones of the body—known as the diaphyses—gradually form solid bonds with the caps of the bones throughout a person's teens. Different bones solidify at different times, providing a good indication of the dead person's age. Hundreds of dead American soldiers were identified using medical records and such statistical techniques; the same techniques can be applied to determine whether the dead in Kosovo's mass graves match accounts given by people who witnessed the killings.

"From a war-crimes standpoint, we document the number of individuals, determine the sex ratio, and then determine the ratio of adults to children," says Rodriguez. "From there, we can move on to identifying the dead individually. We can also find evidence of blunt-force trauma, stab wounds, gunshot wounds, malnutrition, and torture. . . . We deal with death on a daily basis. We're scientists of death."

The F.B.I. convoy rolled out of Studenica in midafternoon. The family had reconvened in front of the house and was going through a pile of clothes that had been pulled up from the well along with the bodies. There were ski parkas, blankets, sweaters, a fake-fur coat. One man spotted the fake fur, knelt on it, and started sobbing. Xhevat, the grandson who had just returned from Germany, stood around a little uncomfortably, unsure what to do.

"Tell me about him," I said to Xhevat, pointing to the grave where the old man was now reburied.

"He was a farmer—he saw World War I and World War II," Xhevat said. "He was a soldier for the Germans in World War II. He always lived right here; he never considered leaving—everybody fled, but he didn't. 'You are on my land. . . . No one will come and throw us out of here,' he would say."

"How long are you staying?" I asked him.

"Oh," Xhevat said, glancing at the rotting clothes in his front yard. "I go back to Germany on Friday."

In February 1994, German police took into custody a Bosnian Serb named Dusko Tadić, who had been hiding in his brother's apartment in Munich. Tadić, had been recognized by Bosnian Muslims who had survived the infamous Serb death camp of Omarska, near the city of Prijedor. Tadić, wasn't officially in the Bosnian Serb army—he was a local café owner and karate teacher—but he would show up in the evenings to personally direct the torture of chosen prisoners. An I.C.T.Y. indictment one year later accused him of rape, torture, 13 murders, and—in his most infamous act—forcing a prisoner to bite the testicle off another, who subsequently died. Two years later, after a trial that lasted from May to November 1996, he was convicted of violating the laws and customs of war and of crimes against humanity and was sentenced to 20 years in prison.

The Tadić, case was the first successful prosecution of a war crime by the I.C.T.Y. It has indicted 90 people for crimes committed in the former Yugoslavia, and has an unknown number of secret indictments. Thirty of the accused are now in custody, including 10 Bosnian Croats who surrendered in 1997 and three

Bosnian Serbs who surrendered in 1998. One was killed resisting arrest. On July 25, 1995, South African judge Richard Goldstone, acting as the tribunal's chief prosecutor, indicted Bosnian Serb president Radovan Karadžić and his chief of staff, General Ratko Mladić, with genocide, war crimes, and crimes against humanity. Four years later, neither one has been caught; Mladić is said to spend his days on a Bosnian Serb military base, tending beehives and a herd of goats. Each goat has been named after a Western leader or U.N. commander.

Considering the time and effort that it takes to indict someone for war crimes, the question of whether the investigations serve a purpose—in the absence of arrests—is a hard one to avoid. Judge Goldstone, who now heads an independent commission on NATO's use of force in Kosovo, is adamant that they do. "To turn people for the rest of their lives into international pariahs is not something that any rational person would like," he says. "Karadžić was no longer able to continue in office and had to disappear from the international scene. . . . The quality of their life is diminished considerably. . . . One is looking over one's shoulder every day of one's life."

Slobodan Milošević, as president of Yugoslavia, is not looking over his shoulder in quite the same way, but his is a precarious existence nonetheless. There is widespread discontent in the army, the country's infrastructure and economy are in ruins, and Montenegro wants to abolish the Yugoslav Federation. Because of the international arrest warrants, Milošević cannot flee to another country, and the United States is withholding economic aid to Serbia until he has been removed from power. "It is in the interest of the peoples of Serbia that [he] be transferred to The Hague," maintains David Scheffer, United States ambassador-at-large for war-crimes issues. "It will remain a very difficult proposition to bring Serbia into the international community and into, frankly, the New Europe if Serbia remains a de facto sanctuary for indicted war criminals. . . . We think the odds are with us."

.   .   .

Because of the turmoil in Yugoslavia, there is a good chance that Milošević will one day stand trial. (Indeed, he has reportedly started making inquiries about hiring an English lawyer.) He has already been charged with crimes against humanity and violations of the laws and customs of war, and may be charged with genocide as well, the most serious breach of humanitarian law. To convict him, the I.C.T.Y. would have to show that he intended to destroy, "in whole or in part," the Albanian population of Kosovo. The fact that his forces generally spared women and children does not disqualify him from charges of genocide; theoretically, even one murder could be considered genocide if there was intent to harm the rest of the group. By that standard, the policies of the Milošević government easily qualify.

The atrocities in Kosovo are so well documented that Milošević will probably not bother to challenge them in court; instead, he may try to claim that he was unaware they were happening. He may already have had an eye toward that kind of defense when he encouraged paramilitary and militia forces to carry out many of the actual massacres in Kosovo. NATO has been eavesdropping on Serbian forces in the field since the beginning of the air war, though, and that will make an ignorance defense difficult. "To prove chain of command we are relying to a great extent on intelligence agencies in the Western countries," says Landale, spokesman for the I.C.T.Y. "They are obliged to give it to us. We will try to show knowledge of crimes and failure to prevent them or to punish them."

When one hears accounts of the massacres in Kosovo, one is struck by both their terrible efficiency and their even more terrible savagery. Many of those responsible were hastily deputized militiamen who—judging by the sheer creativity they showed in killing people—must have been quite intoxicated by their sudden power. They shot people one by one and they mowed them down in groups; they burned them alive and they cut their throats; they tortured them and they just walked up and shot them in the back of the head. They briefly wielded absolute power in their brutal little lives and must have never stopped to think that they might one day be held accountable for it.

ESQUIRE

And the Leni Riefenstahl Award for Rabid Nationalism Goes to ...

The Last Great Movie of the Century

Tom Carson, who covers the whole range of media that come to us, in one form or another, via screens, is a critic with confidence, intelligence, and scope. He can stop a trend or spot a trend. In his column on Saving Private Ryan, *he stands against the crowd of admirers—just as he can be ahead of the crowd by identifying important movies such as* Being John Malkovich *long before the rest of the world caught up with it. All in all, Carson has what a great critic must have—a steady eye and the courage of his convictions.*

Tom Carson

And the Leni Riefenstahl Award for Rabid Nationalism Goes to . . .

A reconsideration of *Saving Private Ryan*

L ast summer, Steven Spielberg's *Saving Private Ryan* surfed on the sort of hype that transcends its own nature—hype with a halo. *Newsweek*'s cover story led with the haggard recollections of real-life Normandy vets, practically obliging moviegoers to thread their popcorn into a rosary. *The New Yorker* lauded *Ryan*'s lack of ideological agendas, an astonishing claim to make about a movie that begins and ends with a luminous Stars and Stripes filling the screen. *Vanity Fair*'s James Wolcott not only hailed Spielberg for "getting it right"— one of the hoopla's mantras—but preemptively bashed any "media-savvy smart-asses" cynical enough to be unmoved. (Talk about the pot painting itself red, white, and blue, if I may speak for the kettles.) On a PR tour undertaken, so he said, only to warn under-fifteens off his movie's graphic carnage, the director piously deprecated its box-office potential, which in $400-mil-and-counting hindsight makes him look like a man wetting his finger to test the breeze while standing inside a wind machine.

And poor Bob Dole, out of luck as usual. If the damn thing had come out two years earlier, he might be president today. A state-of-the-art Spielberg thrill ride disguised as a patriotic hymnal—and vice versa, which was its double-whammy genius—*Ryan* was the pinnacle of our new idolatry of World War II and the generation that fought it, a cultural tic I'd attribute partly to those fin-de-millennium blues and partly to the boomers' predictably startled recognition that their parents are about to die. In a fallacy that, since *Schindler's List,* Spielberg has all but patented, to dislike his movie was to proclaim your snickering contempt for the hell that Dad (or Granddad) went through.

The choir's silliest sing-along was the chant, led by the director, that every previous war flick had been a jingoistic cheese-fest starring John Wayne. But Wayne actually made only a handful of uniformed shoot-'em-ups—westerns were his métier—and the most famous, *Sands of Iwo Jima,* is one of the few movies in which he dies, on a sacrificial note that's not much different from *Ryan's* blubbery finale (except for being less overwrought). It's also an anomaly, since, after V-J Day, few of Hollywood's plenitude of serious-minded war films in the forties and fifties played up battlefield heroics. Flagrant cartoons like 1967's *The Dirty Dozen* don't feature action any more rabble-rousing than Spielberg's pull-out-the-stops last battle, and even movies made during the war didn't go further in portraying the enemy as subhuman. However puerile they could be, one appeal of yesteryear's World War II films is that they were made by and for people who remembered the real thing, lending a been-there-done-that equanimity to their jauntiness that I far prefer to *Ryan's* fetishistic hysteria. Spielberg's stunning combat scenes were praised for their greater realism by critics chary of admitting that lustrous technology and filmmaking flair also make them more sensational—a turn-on.

If sentimental oomph is the yardstick, nobody can say Spielberg doesn't deliver the goods. Working your adrenal glands and tear ducts simultaneously, he manages something impressive enough to deserve being called dangerous: He makes nostalgia exciting. But in light of the platoon of Oscars that *Ryan*'s likely to take marching home this month—which its technical wizards and splendid cast deserve—last summer's binge could use a bucket of cold water, and this media-savvy smart-ass had his doubts from the get-go. It's absurd for a movie so romantically, primitively rah-rah to be acclaimed for setting the record straight; *Ryan* would hardly be the ultimate World War II film as ultimate Spielberg lollapalooza if it didn't incorporate every cliché of the genre in a way that looks new mostly because it's out to flatten you.

Ryan bets the farm on its opening Omaha Beach sequence— instantly famous as the most harrowing portrait of battle in movie history. No question it's intense—hectic but amazingly detailed; the turmoil and clatter never let up. Yet there's often an appalling disjunction between the chaotic slaughter being re-created and the ostentation of the virtuoso filmmaking on display, bragging up distractingly showy effects (the blood flowering from the men shot underwater) when it isn't indulging in pat ironies (the soldier who catches a bullet in the head while marveling at his narrow escape).

More to the point, the intro fudges the average soldier's experience on Omaha in one crucial aspect, which you could figure a glorifier like Stephen Ambrose wouldn't call Spielberg on even if America's favorite D-day wannabe hadn't been on the *Ryan* payroll the whole time *Newsweek* et al. were trotting him out to vouch for its accuracy. Back in bland old 1962, even a spectacular as bowdlerized as *The Longest Day* affectingly showed what *Ryan* does not—that the miserable men on the beach stayed huddled there, panicked into paralysis as the casualties mounted, for several hours. Depicting the same event on a budget most high school pageants would scoff at, for-real invasion vet Samuel Fuller's *The Big Red One* featured a haunting image: the recurring shot of a dead soldier's wristwatch lapped by surf, the water turning redder—the part Spielberg filches—as the morning crawls by. *Ryan*'s beach attackers face a much costlier (in both senses) inferno, which does look more believable. But they also recover to storm the German pillboxes in twenty-five minutes of what's presented to us as real time, lionizing exactly the sort of dauntless heroics the movie was praised for downplaying. Spielberg has gotten huge credit for showing us combat's terrors, but except for Tom Hanks's brief, mute aria of dazed shock, he doesn't show us any of his good guys acting terrified—which means they're superhuman.

On top of that, the celebrated opening is actually superfluous to the story. But it's a brilliant piece of showmanship, since the big number Spielberg pulls off up front half cows and half wows the audience into accepting that the whole movie has been made in the same somber, gritty spirit. It hasn't, of course; commercially speaking, he's not that big a fool. Once Hanks's Captain Miller and his men set off on their rescue mission, trudging from encounter (the reprise of *Full Metal Jacket*'s sniper sequence) to encounter (Ted Danson as the world's oldest paratroop officer) across what no longer looks much like Normandy, the movie comfortably dilates into the longest, most overblown episode of the old TV series *Combat* ever filmed. Measured against the complexity and tension of comparable parts of *The Wild Bunch*—a movie Spielberg's far more indebted to than his interviews suggest but whose opening massacre, unlike this one's, is integral—*Ryan*'s let's-argue-about-the-mission-when-we're-not-killing-Nazis scenes are psychologically and thematically vapid.

For all their sententious airs of high purpose, Spielberg's shaggy-dogface stories just mark time until the slam-bang finale—which the director, ever the movie buff, mounts as a set-piece imitation of the climax of *Rio Bravo*, right down to the mortar rounds being lobbed by hand, just like the sticks of dynamite hurled in the Howard Hawks film. However impressively staged, the last half hour is comicbook stuff on a grand scale, crammed with visual stunting more reminiscent of the Spielberg who directed *Jaws* and *Raiders of the Lost Ark* than the one who did *Schindler's List*—the panzer bursting into view as menacingly as Bruce the shark, the gag of Miller seeming to have blown it up with a pistol shot until the fighter plane that did the job zooms by. In the guise of apotheosizing the GIs' valor, this *Sgt. Fury* extravaganza insults the opening's jittery verisimilitude. One enthusiastic write-up deemed *Ryan*'s big finish "almost unbearably thrilling," which it is. But given the movie's pretensions, didn't it cross anyone's mind that maybe it shouldn't be?

One reason the onscreen debates about the mission's value go in such circles is that the down-to-earth answer to the movie's big question—is one man's life worth risking eight?—is so screamingly obvious: No. It's a weird reversal of the usual proportions of the selfless-gallantry genre, in which one man dies to save many. As a parable of this nation's World War II sacrifices, the story would be truer to what the GIs deserve being honored for if Ryan were a European. Then again, *Saving Monsieur Renault* might not have gripped the modern Stateside audience: Who cares about some damn snail eater? Instead, in a way that's both solipsistic and tautological, saving the world gets redefined as saving ourselves—which must mean we are the world. It isn't lack of patriotism that makes me despise the simplemindedness of the coda's blessing on America—the wife's affirmative answer when the aged Ryan asks, "Have I led a good life?" which symbolically validates our history in the fifty far-from-irreproachable years since World War II. Since the guileless farm boy that Matt Damon plays so marvelously (especially in his big monologue) is also a Jesus figure, the movie amounts to an extrapolation of what must be the ultimate American fantasy—one in which our guns and courage prevent the crucifixion, letting Jesus move to the suburbs and, in old age, take the kids on sentimental journeys back to Golgotha.

But that's only because the saintly Miller has died for him, with an exalted grandeur—far in excess of any earlier World War II film's—that left me more appalled than inspired. To call this an antiwar movie is lunacy; if I were seventeen, I'd have left the theater with a woody to enlist. *Ryan*'s ending elevates a gallant death into the noblest of romantic destinies while transforming the grim necessity of defeating the Axis from a past test of national resolve—which indeed we did meet—into a mystical summons to future greatness: "Earn it." (Question: Even if Americans had just sat on their duffs and played pinochle after 1945, would that mean the GIs died in vain? Of course not.) Hanks has often recounted how his character evolved from the original script's bellicose Medal of Honor winner into the average guy he plays. But the movie's most treacherously brilliant piece of double-dealing is that Miller's actions weren't revised to match; it's precisely because his martyrdom is presented as a triumph of humdrum, ordinary decency—qualities the herrenvolk myth claimed, too—that the hero's Wagnerian finale should leave us queasy. The actor's wonderful performance has moments of great beauty—Miller's bemused reaction to the German loudspeakers blaring, "The Statue of Liberty is kaput," his long scene with Damon. But it's an incoherent part; there's no reason why someone like Miller would keep his past a mystery, except as a gimmick to set up the big speech about fighting to get home that's more shameless than anything in *Bataan.*

The speeches that Spielberg got congratulated for leaving out are the wheezers about fighting to save democracy. But I'd have welcomed some reminder that the United States is one. *Ryan* is actually more reverential of authority, and less tolerant of dissent, than the average Wayne (or war) film—discomfitingly so, since its *dulce et decorum est* therapy for our soft epoch is explicitly divorced from merely utilitarian justifications. The only lesson that Spielberg's robust, good-hearted GIs learn on their way to Valhalla is that they're better off obeying even orders they can't rationalize. For all its pretenses of regret, the movie depicts Americans as a great warrior race—often in distastefully supremacist terms, with the paratroopers who save Miller's men in one shootout looming up like olive-drab Terminators; it's as if the only thing wrong with SS men was which side they were on. In a bygone movie era, Barry Pepper's divinely inspired, Scripture-quoting sharpshooter would have been played as a psycho—for satiric purposes in the sixties, and just for yuks after that. Spielberg turns him back into Sergeant York, and his feats make the real one's look like tiddlywinks. Meanwhile, the enemy is shown as lice to be exterminated—people who don't deserve ordinary decency, because they'll only use it against you—and noncombatants are painted as insignificant, if not unworthy. Honestly, I can't see much that Hitler would have wanted changed in *Saving Private Ryan*, except the color of the uniforms.

The giveaway is the Jeremy Davies character—the lily-livered egghead attached to the squad (note that this weak sister isn't even allowed to belong to it), who's treated pretty much the way a Jew would be in a Nazi film. Naturally, he isn't one; instead, Davies's Corporal Upham is an Anglo-Saxon—suspect because he's educated enough to speak foreign languages—whose ultimate baseness is his failure to rescue the strapping, all-American Jewish GI played by Adam Goldberg. But the stereotyping is no less vicious for being reversed. In symbolic terms, it's also tripe; whatever their sins, liberal U.S. intellectuals were hardly spineless about opposing Nazism. In a movie otherwise in control of its own flamboyance, the delirium of this rabid, baiting caricature of the thinker as traitor and coward is a jaw dropper. As soon as he's introduced, Upham grabs a tattletale German helmet instead of a good American one, then gets hit with a scrawny-dick joke—Hanks holding up the stub of pencil that defines him. At a crucial point, he's also used as Spielberg's indictment of his own kind, peering at action he can't participate in and doesn't understand through a rifle scope that subs for a director's viewfinder. When the other men want to shoot a German prisoner, it's Upham who insists that they play by the rules; then the perfidious kraut turns up at the climax, making Upham metaphorically responsible for Miller's death.

There's an obvious paradox here, because when he isn't behind a camera, Spielberg, like Hanks, is among Hollywood's best-known liberals. Yet he's made one of the most mindlessly adulatory war movies of all time—one that treats combat as horrific, but only on the way to making it sublime, and calls the result the ultimate tribute to our national character while egging us on to live up to it. (How? This movie makes fighting Nazism look like an opportunity younger generations have been cheated of.) While I don't think he's a hypocrite, that's mainly because hypocrisy requires some forethought; for all his gifts, Spielberg is less reflective than almost any movie director of his caliber. Now that he's decided to be mature, he's making the witlessly earnest mistake of equating artistic seriousness with momentous topics—the Holocaust, slavery, and now the "good war." But all he can think of to say about them is to state the obvious smashingly—working us over with his full panoply of techniques for inducing excitement and going for primordial effects while remaining oblivious to their implications.

If anything, *Saving Private Ryan* proves just how unreal World War II has become to Americans. There's no way a movie like this could have been made about an event that still felt like part of our national experience. Maybe every last piece of equipment is accurate, but the meanings and behavior are so magnified they're sci-fi; the director is so intent on having us worship these men that he never lets us identify with them. Just like plenty of people who've gushed about *Ryan*, I had a father, too. Mine spent D-day on a destroyer escort off the sector of Omaha that's depicted in the film. So I'm all for tributes, but the fact that we can think a Steven Spielberg blockbuster is an adequate one doesn't mean we've learned how to honor our past. It just means we're movie-mad.

Tom Carson

The Last Great Movie of the Century

Yeah, yeah, the year's not over, but nothing's likely to eclipse the transcendent weirdness of *Being John Malkovich*

You may have gotten fed up with Spike Jonze without even knowing his name. He's the director whose maddeningly clever video for Weezer's just-plain-maddening ditty "Buddy Holly" plunked the band down in Arnold's diner from *Happy Days,* suturing those inane but catchy *oo-wee-oo*s to the audience's cortex every time MTV aired it. His most famous musical clients are the Beastie Boys, who specialize in testing how humane snottiness can be. However, Jonze is also responsible for one of the most haunting videos ever made. Set to Wax's petulant "California," it's a single, slow-motion tracking shot of a man in flames running down an L.A. street while passersby—oblivious or just unimpressed?—go about their business. At the end, the camera pans to the kind of SoCal gamine who's never bothered to sort out the difference between despair and boredom. Losing interest in the human torch, she gives the camera a bleak look as the bus that it turns out we're riding moves on.

Then again, *haunting* doesn't necessarily count for much on MTV, where significance is commonly affected, and/or appreciated, primarily as decor. Either more wised-up than its elders or unaware of any distinction, this culture's youth demographic no longer considers ulterior motives a fatal artistic flaw. But to purists, rock videos are still meretricious by definition—just like their evil twin, commercials, including Jonze's own notorious "Doctors" ad for Levi's, with the bleeps of an emergency-room EKG cuing a sing-along of Soft Cell's "Tainted Love." Even in Hollywood, land of glass houses, calling a movie MTV-influenced is always pejorative, connoting opportunism and shallow flair as well as manipulativeness more kinetic than an earlier generation's hacks can compete with. Much as they'd love to.

Yet that's not remotely the style of Jonze's big-screen debut, *Being John Malkovich,* a one-of-a-kind masterpiece whose curious title turns out to be a perfectly accurate plot summary and whose only explosions go off in your mind. This revelatory dark comedy about celebrity as a conduit for other people's fantasies owes rock video mainly for the unfazed nonchalance with which Jonze turns a century's worth of avant-garde kitsch into a new kind of witty, psychologically acute pop naturalism. Like Godard's *Breathless,* which copped to the truth that the movie-fed flimsiness of modern life was what made it exciting, *Being John Malkovich* is the kind of breakthrough that leaves every other movie around looking clueless; it's about all the things that they don't know they're saying.

Forty years ago, Godard changed the way we look at the world by finding elemental beauty in the crummy B movies about hoods and molls that Hollywood used to grind out. Jonze and his scriptwriter, Charlie Kaufman, perform a similar alchemy on the even more feckless genre they probably cut their own movie-going teeth on. The Reagan era lapped up farces that turned out-of-body experiences into a chance to test-drive an alternate life. Today's cyberspectacles provide the same wish fulfillment by telling us that we live in a manufactured illusion, to please-don't-throw-me-in-the-briar-patch effect; that *The Matrix* ends with the heroes joyfully testing themselves in cyberspace, rather than escaping it immediately, is a dead giveaway.

Being John Malkovich at once spoofs these scenarios and gets to the bottom of their appeal. It's no wonder that even the movie's press handout begs off from explaining its brilliantly goofy central conceit, since Jonze and Kaufman's version of *Back to the Future*'s magic DeLorean and *The Matrix*'s computer grid is the brain of the title character, who appears as himself. Like Alice tumbling down the rabbit hole, John Cusack's Craig Schwartz fetches up inside the actor's head one day. After a few eerie but pleasurable moments as Malkovich, he's spat back out again—into a ditch alongside the New Jersey Turnpike, something Alice certainly never had to contend with. What does Craig do? This being America, he starts selling tickets. Soon, Malkovich's consciousness has been turned into a themepark ride by a mob of strangers willing to fork over $200 a pop to spend a Warholian fifteen minutes inhabiting it.

One of the movie's best jokes is that Malkovich, of course, isn't even all that famous; he's not the sort of star people fixate on. Nor does anyone here, except insofar as slipping into his skin lets them pursue yearnings (and derangements) that they'd have anyway. They aren't even fans of his. He's the vehicle, rather than the object, of their desires—their passport to another realm, where most of them just enjoy themselves for a while before returning.

Early on, you may be bothered by the way the movie seems to be exploiting weirdness for weirdness' sake, from the claustrophobic grotesquerie of Craig and his wife's home life to the bizarreness of his work surroundings. But Jonze isn't just playing film-school games; he's setting up a contrast with the placid blandness of Malkovich's environment. In fact, at least until the actor catches on that he's no longer got his life to himself, the snippets of it that the kibitzers share are perfectly humdrum, and he's got rather less personality than those who want to swap it for theirs. Yet no one's disappointed. In the movie's scheme of things, stardom is what lets you be ordinary; it's everyone else's world that is freakish and appalling.

Or so they perceive it—and, as a metaphor for why people who need *People* aren't the luckiest people in the world, the implications of this are obvious. Jonze and Kaufman don't waste time castigating the audience for living vicariously or the culture for erecting false gods, and they don't peddle any of the claptrap we're used to from movies that berate us for responding to media stimuli—except the indignant one at hand, naturally—as if that's a sickness unrelated to "normal" life. Instead, melding satire and empathy, the filmmakers take it for granted that the chimera of celebrity is a convenience devised to serve human needs, which tend to be complicated and various. It's also a modern version of Aladdin's lamp, whose uses depend on who rubs it.

Cusack's character isn't the nebbish who usually wins the lottery in Hollywood fairy tales. He's a caustic take on that beloved romantic figure, the artist as victim, a puppeteer enraged that people don't appreciate his brilliance. We're predisposed to sympathize with him, but he's actually self-pitying and creepy—a frustrated man who retreats into his marionette workshop to avoid the menagerie of animals that his wife, Lotte (Cameron Diaz, almost unrecognizably frumpy and woebegone), brings home from the pet shop where she works. She's intimidated by his genius act but also knows they're broke, which is why Craig puts his dexterity to practical use by taking a clerking job at the company presided over by a mysterious, feyly chatty dotard named Dr. Lester (Orson Bean).

Despite an arrogance that Cusack eventually makes downright

chilling, Craig is also suggestible—in a somewhat masochistic way. He decides he's in love with his tart-tongued new coworker Maxine (Catherine Keener) *because* she's contemptuous of him. She rejects his advances yet recognizes that he's lucked into a gold mine. Lotte, having been let on to what her husband and his new business partner are up to, grows addicted to the experience. That's partly because, like Craig, she's infatuated with Maxine—who, on her end, feels attracted to Lotte only when Lotte is Malkovich. The role confusions triggered by a romantic triangle that actually has four participants take a turn toward dementia when a newly cocky (so to speak) Lotte, spouting self-actualization clichés, starts pondering transsexual surgery and snapping at Craig to suck her dick.

The ultimate comment on the audience's relationship to fame, *Being John Malkovich* effortlessly links the thirst for recognition to everything from the uses of art to male egotism at war with female fulfillment. On one level, the intricate interplay among Kaufman's quartet of archetypes adds up to a study of erotic projection and emotional S&M that puts the solemn puerilities of *Eyes Wide Shut* to shame. On another, the movie is a fabulous twist on Nabokov's *Pale Fire,* with Cusack as the increasingly malignant Kinbote to Malkovich's unwitting John Shade. Because it never stops being cheeky and ridiculous, it's also audaciously, jaw-droppingly funny—a bedroom farce whose slamming doors are the invaded actor's eyes.

Far from being wild, though, the tone is beautifully controlled, integrating surreal slapstick with what let's call meta-plausibility to overwhelming effect. At one point, Malkovich insists on taking the same trip into his own mind that everyone else has made and sees a nightmare of performer's narcissism—a party whose only guests are versions of himself, endlessly repeating his name. (He comes out bug-eyed, babbling to Craig about the horror of it all.) Later, there's a mind-boggling chase sequence that sends two characters racing pell-mell through room after room of the actor's subconscious, from traumatic childhood to finky sexual fetish-ism. But you're so caught up in the movie's world that you don't even register how tricky these scenes are; in context, they make perfect sense. Despite finding room for diversions that range from Charlie Sheen's droll cameo as the movie's reality principle to a simian burlesque of *Lord Jim* to the climactic explanation's proof that Kaufman has never forgiven Ron Howard for *Cocoon*, Jonze stays unruffled, as if he's directing a chamber drama—which, in a way, he is.

The movie's richness almost defies summary, and I haven't even begun to give away its surprises. But it's chockablock with the sort of moments that can stay in people's memories for years, like the piteously funny one when Malkovich cries, "I'm free!" as one hobgoblin leaves his skull—seconds before the next shift takes over. The ending, which is spookily perfect, is also frightening enough to remind you that Hitler started as an artist, too.

THE NEW YORKER

The Man in the Mirror

Waugh in Pieces

In his film and literary criticism, Anthony Lane outdoes himself with nimble thinking, beautifully crafted sentences, and strikingly unexpected views on artistic work both popular and highbrow. This work consistently combines a mastery of subject and elegance of style with humor and a sharp eye for ordinary detail. In these two pieces on André Gide and Evelyn Waugh, Lane achieves what all good criticism should: providing not simply an assessment of the material at hand but a new way of reading and seeing it.

Anthony Lane

The Man
in the Mirror

The enduring confessions and unmatched hedonism of André Gide.

In June, 1940, André Gide—novelist, diarist, sometime Communist, and a hub of French literary life for half a century—found himself in Vichy. It was a loaded place to be, and there were many things to keep a Frenchman awake at such a time, but for Gide the cause was specific:

> Through the open window of my room giving onto the end of the park, I heard, three times, a heart-rending cry: "Pierre! Pierre!" and almost went down to find the poor demented man who was uttering that call, desperately, in the night. And for a long time I could not go to sleep, ceaselessly imagining that distress.

Such are the helpless sympathies of the creative mind: the sound of a single voice suggests a story, or an auspicious predicament, and the writer is instantly condemned to a desire to know more. For Gide—not just a fervent homosexual but an avid connoisseur of longing in other men—the possibility that Pierre was not only lost but lusted after, like the faithless lover in a medieval lyric, provided the evening with further bewitchment. All of which must have made it something of a letdown when, the next morning, Gide learned that what he had listened to was the local night watchman, who had seen a lit window and was warning the occupant of the room to observe the wartime blackout: "*Lumière! Lumière!*"

You can't help admiring Gide for his honesty here; some writers, with a cautious eye cocked at posterity, might have kept Pierre and killed the light. But this incident arises in Gide's journals, which, more than any of his other works, are the test site for his politely explosive belief that, whatever else happens, we should aim for sincerity. As convictions go, this is seldom practicable and sometimes close to indefensible, especially when, as in Gide's case, other people get caught in the blast. But it feels alarmingly apposite to our own era, when a few insincere words to the press corps are almost enough to unseat a President, and Alan Sheridan can be proud of himself for producing "André Gide: A Life in the Present" (Harvard; $35) with such an elegant sense of timing.

He is not alone in his endeavors. The French critic Claude Martin recently brought out "André Gide, or the Vocation of Happiness" (Fayard), which has yet to be translated into English. Like Sheridan's book, it runs to well over six hundred pages, but it covers only half of the story; a second volume will appear later. Given that Martin founded the Association of the Friends of André Gide, in 1968, and that he has hitherto written or edited *twenty-two* books by or about Gide, I can understand that he has a fair amount to say. Then, there is Jonathan Fryer's "André & Oscar: The Literary Friendship of André Gide and Oscar Wilde" (St. Martin's; $24.95), and, on a less gossipy level, Naomi Segal's "André Gide: Pederasty and Pedagogy" (Oxford; $65). I make a point of trying to read one completely unreadable book every year, and Segal's study looked promising; sadly, it's brilliant stuff, expertly tracking the contrary motions of outpouring and restraint in Gide's unpolluted prose. But the larger question remains: Why the refreshed interest in Gide himself?

The last—and, for most of us, the only—time we were likely to have encountered the man was in high school, where novellas such as "Strait Is the Gate" and "The Pastoral Symphony" were used to prod us along the pathways of French style. Both are models of lucidity and stateliness, so much so that, as Sheridan tells us, one London publisher turned down "Strait Is the Gate" in the early nineteen-twenties "on the charming grounds that the French of the original was not difficult enough to justify a translation."

There may have been other grounds, more treacherous underfoot. Gide is actually quite hard to translate; beyond the curt simplicity of his sentences, which makes him a more formidable recorder of physical action than his reputation gives him credit for, there is what he called the gait of thought. The pacing of this passage from "The Vatican Cellars" cannot be faulted, but where, exactly, is the author directing its steps?

> They had no sooner settled in Rome than they arranged their private lives independently of each other—he on his side, she on hers; Veronica in the care of the household and in the pursuit of her devotions, Anthime in his scientific researches. In this way they lived beside each other, close to each other and just able to bear the contact by turning their backs to one another. Thanks to this there reigned a kind of harmony between them; a sort of semi-felicity settled down upon them; the virtue of each found its modest exercise in putting up with the faults of the other.

There is a punctilious courtesy in such prose that could stiffen into staidness, were it not for the sense that underneath the good stylistic manners, as under the life of Anthime and Veronica, lurk all kinds of animosity; to the seasoned ironist, indeed, propriety is the only possible outlet for the perverse. The young man who, in the same novel, passes his penknife over a flame, jabs it into his thigh, grimaces "in spite of himself," and then sprinkles drops of peppermint water on the wound, all in an effort to cool a fit of anger, is like a model of the novelist's method, and well-bred English readers of the nineteen-twenties could be forgiven for suspecting that there was something not quite nice about the unflappable M. Gide.

In the English-speaking world, in fact, the vogue for Gide started late and faded fast, without quite reaching the fist-clenching mania that attended Camus and "The Stranger." Nevertheless, there was a time when to be seen with a copy of "The Immoralist"—Gide's sparse yet luxuriant tale of a man who, in the philosophical interests of liberty, tries to pig out on life—was de rigueur for young males of errant libido and unsound mind, otherwise known as students. It was not until 1926 that Gide dignified one of his works, "The Counterfeiters," with the rank of "novel"; the rest of his output was a melee of travel writings, poems, plays, polemics, lectures, essays, neoclassical dialogues, studies in criminology, apologias both political and sexual, librettos, autobiographies in numerous guises, and what he liked to call *récits* and *soties*—respectively, simple first-person narratives and light-fingered literary games. Plowing through the Gidean landscape is a lengthy business, though seldom an arduous one, and it is more in awe than in ridicule that one pauses for breath to reflect that most of his working life was spent writing about André Gide, or, on more generous days, engaging in a heartfelt struggle not to write about André Gide.

He was born in 1869 and died in 1951. The dates alone hint at his extraordinary span: here was a man who befriended Wilde,

visited the ailing Verlaine, and attended the legendary *mardis*—
the tobacco-filled Tuesday discussions at the home of Stéphane
Mallarmé—but who also lived long enough to observe the crushing of the Nazis, to fall in and out of favor with Soviet Commu-
nism, to niggle over the newly fashionable Sartre ("I'm willing to
be an Existentialist, provided I'm not aware of the fact"), and, at
the age of seventy-eight, to get terribly excited by the Kinsey
Report. In 1908, he helped found the *Nouvelle Revue Française,*
which, first as a journal and later in its links to the publishing
house of Gallimard, became one of the more efficient power-
houses of French culture. It is hard to recall an equivalent figure in
the English-speaking world; Edmund Wilson had some of Gide's
persistence in a multitude of literary forms, and each man showed
a laudable determination to muscle his way through disapproval
in the pursuit of what he held to be right, even if, in repeated
instances, he turned out to be wrong for the right reasons. (Wilson, who once called Gide "the fairies' Dostoevsky," would not
have welcomed the comparison.) But Gide had a head start on
Wilson, by more than a quarter of a century, and even his briefest
encounters suggest someone wandering between two worlds—a
vigorous hedonist cloaked in the guise of an Edwardian man of
letters. He could be found in Cannes in 1912 with the unlikely duo
of Arnold Bennett and Pierre Bonnard, and during a trip to Calvi
in 1930 he divided his time between open-air debauchery with
naked Corsicans and Thomas Hardy's "The Woodlanders."

Gide himself insisted that there was a dash of doubleness in his
nature from the start. "You know how complicated I am," he wrote
to a friend in 1902, "born of a crossing of races, situated at the
crossroads of religions, sensing within me all the yearnings of
Normans for the South, of Southerners for the North." In fact, as
Sheridan points out, Gide was a foursquare Northern Protestant,
and you had to go back a few generations on his mother's side to
stumble across any bona-fide Catholics. Nevertheless, he repre-

sents an intriguing case history in French Protestantism, with its stern sense of persecution; James Baldwin, in a shrewd essay on Gide, remarked that the Protestant faith "invested all of his work with the air of an endless winter." On Gide's first day of school, as he recounts in "If It Die," his wonderful memoirs, he was asked "Are you a Cat or a Prot?" by the other boys in the yard. His own reading of this incident was that "all Frenchmen, of whatever age or class of society, have an innate need to take sides," a need that seems to have driven him not into sedition so much as toward a chronic—and, in France, far more dangerous—ability to approach any given issue from every direction.

The Protestant attitude to mortal cravings makes for an interesting feast. In Gide's case, it came ungarnished with guilt; in his more youthful projects, there is a blatant attempt to squeeze faith and sensuality onto the same plate. Given that his adoring parents had read him both the "Arabian Nights" and the Book of Job, what else could one expect? His 1897 publication "Fruits of the Earth," a deliquescent prose poem that just about rouses itself to tell a story, became a bible to restless young pleasure-seekers, although thirty years later he strove to defend it as more than a glorification of desire. Citing "the doctrine of the Evangelist," Gide wrote of "finding in the forgetfulness of self the most perfect realization of self" and of a "limitless allowance of happiness." Whether St. John would have countenanced Gide's idea of an allowance is open to question. The writer himself remained unabashed by the attention he paid to his own body; "If It Die" contains a famous passage in which the young André is expelled from school for three months for "enjoying alternately my pleasure and my chocolates" beneath a classroom desk. His parents send him to the family doctor, who points to a row of Tuareg spearheads on the wall behind him and declares that such weapons are commonly used to operate on boys who persist in self-abuse. The lofty Gide is unimpressed: "This threat was really too thin for me to take it seriously."

It is this two-tone constitution—the hot blood in his veins and the icy ink in his pen—that makes Gide's egotism, which should be unbearable, close to captivating. No other writer could have so mournfully, almost liturgically, expressed "a regret not for having sinned, but for not having sinned more, for having let some opportunity for sinning slip by unused." Experience, he claimed, "is usually nothing but exhaustion, a repudiation of the best that one once had." His autobiography draws readers through a roster of enthusiasms, inquiring coolly, "In the name of what God or what ideal do you forbid me to live according to my nature?" There are many honorable answers to that question, but Gide, by the time he was twenty, was in any case living according to his Nietzsche: he had infiltrated literary Paris, and in 1891 he published "The Notebooks of André Walter," forging a fictional hedonist who bore a marked resemblance to Gide himself. The book drips with symbolist languor and with dreams of "the softness of brown skins." The impressive thing is that instead of merely playing with this idea—under the desk, as it were—the adult Gide decided to quit town and hunt the real thing. He sailed for Africa.

From here on, Alan Sheridan's book grows crammed to the point of confusion. It is not really his fault: Gide was such a mover, travelling tirelessly between Africa and Europe, between France and her eastern neighbors, and between Paris and the family home at Cuverville, in Normandy, that there were times when I wondered whether Sheridan should have dumped the whole idea of a biography and simply provided a highly detailed map. You would need crisscrossing lines for routes, green spots for oases of creative tranquillity, and clusters of little red flashes for sites of carnal interest. In Tunisia, for example, at the end of 1893, Gide lost his virginity to a boy in Sousse and then, in the New Year, lost it again with a female prostitute in Biskra.

This sounds like a busy schedule, and Gide was true to his inconstancy; he would never relinquish his sweet tooth for young Arabs, or for teen-agers of any race, but, on the other hand, he would marry his cousin Madeleine in October, 1895, and remain unhappily married until her death, in 1938. It was not even a question of keeping the two halves of his existence apart; on their honeymoon, in Africa, Gide left Madeleine and sought out willing companions from his earlier trip, and in 1898, in Rome, he would photograph young men on the Spanish Steps and invite them back to his apartment while his wife was out. Theirs was, as Sheridan says, a *mariage blanc,* forever unconsummated, and it was no coincidence that Gide's beloved mother—he was, of course, an only child—had died a little over two weeks before he announced his engagement. A few months later, he wrote in his journal, "How often, when Madeleine is in the next room, I *forget* that she is not my mother!"

There was a moment when this wretched alliance reached critical mass: after more than twenty years of marriage, Madeleine told her husband that she had burned every one of his letters to her. It was her sole surge of insurrection; for the rest of her stay on earth, she was as quiet as a nun. Gide's reaction, predictably, was to call this lost correspondence—only a small portion of his twenty-five thousand letters—"the treasure of my life, the best of me," and to compare its destruction to the death of a child. He does not appear to have asked himself what deeds of his—or want of them—may have forced her to such a flamboyant gesture. Sheridan quotes Gide's idealistic claim that only a gay man "can give a creature that total love, divested of all physical desire" and that "I thought I had built the very temple of love." As Sheridan sharply adds, "This is not an intelligent man of 1998 speaking, but it doesn't sound like an intelligent man of 1919 either." In the one area where he had most need of it, Gide's dazzling willingness to see the other person's point of view deserted him. Only after

Madeleine's death did it hit home; Gide was hollowed out with grief and remorse, and it served him right. There are limits to happiness, after all, and they transform his biography from an adventure, and a notable success story, into a cautionary tale.

A purist would argue that we must sift out the chaff, and that Gide's disloyalty does not corrupt his achievements on the page. The trouble is that, more than any other writer of his time, he kneaded his life and art together into an indistinguishable mass. This is partly an issue of his many romans à clef; it takes a minimum of biographical skill to turn the *clef* and discover the figures locked inside the novel—to see in the devout and spinsterly Alissa of "Strait Is the Gate," say, not just a portrait of Madeleine Gide but a more subtly horrified pondering of what she might yet become. Beyond such identifications—always, by their nature, unsatisfying—there is a sense that Gide was conducting his life as if it were itself an art form. His embattled quest for spiritual peace, his tendency to plan a new trip as if it were the next chapter, his rhythmical frequenting of high literary society and low-rent hustlers on the streets: all these lent shape to his experience, and they give Sheridan's account of it a more juicy, Balzacian feel than the thin and bitter taste that sometimes stains the fictions of Gide himself. Even his longest and most intricate novels, "The Vatican Cellars" and "The Counterfeiters," are inclined to sound shrill these days, with their shrewish lampoons of Catholic piety and their disappointingly bloodless stabs at the fantastical. "The Vatican Cellars" is best remembered for an incident in Book Five when one character pushes a total stranger out of a railroad compartment: the infamous *acte gratuit,* mean and motiveless. You can construe the scene as a contribution to the history of Surrealism, as a deliberate affront to the laws of civilization, or as a pastiche of the thriller; at a distance, however, it feels more like the mischievous dream of an author whose writing desk, in his Normandy house, looked not outward into the countryside but directly into a mirror. As the murderer muses just before the deed, "It's not events that I'm curious about, but myself."

The same loyalty—to self rather than to others—was the mark of Gide's love life. His sexual capacities, fully and soberly explored in Naomi Segal's book, suggest that if the writing had failed him (which it rarely did) he could always have found employment in Hollywood, or in the old industries of Forty-second Street. His close friend Roger Martin du Gard wrote in 1921, after a technical discussion:

> Gide needs to empty himself out completely of sperm, and he reaches this state only after coming five, six, or even eight times in succession. I don't need to mention that there was no trace of bragging in his account. . . . First he comes twice, more or less at the same time, "like a singer," he said, "who takes a second breath. . . . The second orgasm," he went on, "seems to climb on the shoulders of the first." . . . The third one happens soon after. He can rarely come more than three times with the same person. When circumstances permit, he then finds himself a second person and comes the fourth and often fifth time. After that he is in a very special state.

I bet he is. Martin du Gard adds that the final flourish, No. 7 or 8, tends to take place at home, alone. The remarkable thing is that Gide found time to do anything else. A typical diary entry for 1922 lists three hours of piano practice, an hour of Shakespeare, an hour of Sainte-Beuve's criticism, two hours of correspondence, six hours of novel writing, and thirty minutes or more of exercise, so how he ever slotted in a couple of sexual partners I have no idea. No wonder Madeleine couldn't control him; she would have needed one of those Texans who fly in to cap oil rigs. Fortunately, she never learned of a day in 1922 when Gide, more or less as a favor, had sex with a friend named Elisabeth Van Rysselberghe; at his first attempt, he fathered a child—Catherine, who at the age of thirteen was told of her father's identity, and to whom he maintained a touching devotion.

This capacity to surprise never failed: Gide accepted the Nobel Prize in Literature in 1947, but he spurned the invitation to join the Académie Française, which, considering his eminence, was like a bishop refusing to go to church. Most impressive of all is the sheer stamina of the man—his mental powers competing with his physical ardor in a race to disprove the theory of human decline. Two impassioned nights in Tunis, for instance, with a fifteen-year-old known simply as "F." were treasured for their "joyful lyricism" and "amused frenzy"; the boy "seemed to care so little about my age that I came to forget it myself." Gide was seventy-two. Shortly afterward, plainly rejuvenated, he returned to the task of translating "Hamlet" into French.

The most unexciting but telling fact about Gide, apart from his devoutly regular reading of the Bible, is that he inherited a private income—not vast but big enough to cushion the blows. As often happens with the conscientiously wealthy, he was generous to others but increasingly parsimonious with himself; leaving a hotel, he tried to run back to his room to find and finish a half-smoked cigarette. He never had to work for a living; his most sustained bout of enterprise came during the First World War, when he devoted sixteen months to helping Belgian refugees. We should not begrudge him his leisure, but neither can we help wondering how he would have conducted his life without a safety net. The young Gide believed in *dénuement,* in stripping life down to its spiritual and sensory essentials (with a prose style to match). As Sheridan points out, there was "something ludicrous" about a man's "sitting in the luxury of the Hôtel Kühn at Saint-Moritz, on the first stage of a honeymoon that was to last seven months, preaching the virtues of *dénuement.*"

Sheridan is never fooled by his subject, and often takes him to task. In the nineteen-thirties, for instance, Gide abandoned his evenhanded political skepticism and, in common with many Frenchmen of the age, stared longingly and uncomprehendingly at the Soviet Union, with its "unlimited promise of the future." To his credit, though, Gide did what other fellow-travellers never bothered to attempt: he went to the promised land and reported back. At first, the Russians lionized him; he stood next to Stalin and Molotov in Red Square. But Gide, who began by crediting a parade of Soviet youth with "perfect taste," quickly saw behind the show-pieces, and on his return he wrote "Back from the U.S.S.R." Reading it today (and it's available only in French), you will find it mild and compromised. But to French Communists, who brought to their totalitarian faith the kind of exclusive rigor that was formerly the preserve of French Catholicism, it was blasphemy. Gide's collected works were banned in the Soviet Union, and one year after his death they were placed by the Vatican on the *Index librorum prohibitorum*. This is a fine double whammy: any author who is deemed wrong by so many people must be doing something right.

What Gide did right was perhaps not as simple as the version that he offered to the world on receiving the Nobel Prize. "If I have represented anything," he wrote, "it is, I believe, the spirit of free inquiry, independence, insubordination even." He was a rebel with innumerable causes, it is true, but his protests, like his more unseemly political affiliations, have faded from our hearing, leaving behind a calmer but still frighteningly acute tutorial in self-inspection. What prevents many of Gide's novels from taking on a life of their own is his desire to hire characters for the purpose of investigating his own life instead. One of the heroes of "The Counterfeiters," Edouard, writes in his journal:

If I were not there to make them acquainted, my morning's self would not recognize my evening's. Nothing could be more dif-

ferent from me than myself. . . . My heart beats only out of sympathy; I live only through others—by procuration, so to speak,
and by espousals; and I never feel myself living so intensely as
when I escape from myself to become no matter who.

This was published in 1926, when all but one volume of
"Remembrance of Things Past" had already appeared, and it reads
like a dark, metaphysical riff on the more benign Proustian discovery that social life disperses the self among other people—that
it is only through the courtesy of friends and gossips that we
somehow exist at all. Sheridan's biography certainly leaves you
with just such a queasy sensation; the Gide who demonically har-
ried his young prey is himself out of reach—one friend called him
"ungraspable." If you think the pursuit worthwhile, you must sup-
plement the new biography with the journals—the core of his creative burrowings, I think, and not just an addendum to the formal
works. In French, they are best followed, or picked over, in the
two-volume Pléiade edition; my copy of the first volume, according to a stamp on the title page, was withdrawn from the library of
the Facultés Catholiques in Lyons—a proscription that Gide, who
lost one friend after another to the lure of Rome, might well have
relished. In English, there is a four-volume translation of the journals by Justin O'Brien, which is now out of print, as is a one-vol-
ume rescension published by Penguin. Surely someone could
hitch a ride on the Sheridan biography and release the unabridged
journals again for American readers. Who can afford to miss this
entry, from October, 1940?

> Art inhabits temperate regions. And doubtless the greatest
> harm this war is doing to culture is to create a profusion of
> extreme passions which, by a sort of inflation, brings about a
> devaluation of all moderate sentiments. The dying anguish of
> Roland or the distress of a Lear stripped of power moves us by
> its exceptional quality but loses its special eloquence when

reproduced simultaneously in several thousand copies. Isolated, it is a summit of suffering; in a collection, it becomes a
plateau. . . . The artist does not know which way to turn, intellectually or emotionally. Solicited on all sides and unable to
answer all appeals, he gives up, at a loss. He has no recourse but
to seek refuge in himself or to find refuge in God. That is why
war provides religion with easy conquests.

The logic—the brute truth—of such a passage feels hard and
steely, and yet there is tenderness in its plea for moderation.
Against all expectations, Gide can be as companionable as Mon-
taigne; indeed, the two men could be read as bookends to the bold,
compendious tradition of French self-interest that takes in such
contrary spirits as Rousseau and the Baudelaire of "My Heart Laid
Bare"—an interest so clear-eyed, so supple in the honor it does to
the vagaries of mental mood, that by the end it hardly feels like
vanity at all. Reading Gide at his best is like watching the skies—
fogged by sadness, sharp as ice, or foully clouding over with doubt.
"I love life passionately," he wrote, "but I don't trust it." His daily
commentaries on both World Wars—on the weak victory in the
first (Gide had foreseen a "long, dark tunnel, full of blood"), which
led to French capitulation in the second—work as a discomforting
analysis of a people and also as a downcast reflection upon his own
infirmities. We like to think that diaries are written in the wings—
in the half-dark, away from the action and the spotlight. Since his
death, however, Gide's journals have moved to center stage:

I am not writing these Memoirs to defend myself. I am not
called on to defend myself, since I am not accused. I am writing
them before being accused. I am writing them in order to be
accused.

This magnificent masochism is a ringing rebuff to our current
mania—barely more than a tic—for the confessional mode. We

are besieged by personal revelation on every side, and at first blush Gide looks like a useful antecedent. In fact, he set a standard of honesty—on the page, at least—that shames the new bunch of plaintiffs. He does not settle scores or start rumors; he refuses to cry vengeance or claim compensation. "It was in the very excess of their modesty," he wrote of Baudelaire and Dostoevsky, "that their pride sated itself." Strange to say, Gide, after a lifetime of looking the mirror, was not in it for himself.

Anthony Lane

Waugh in Pieces

Cruelty and compassion mingle in the short stories of a master.

In July, 1956, Evelyn Waugh gave a dinner party for his daughter Teresa. In anticipation of the event, he wrote to a friend, Brian Franks, with a description of the menu, closing with the words "Non Vintage champagne for all but me." Rarely has an edict been issued with such a firm smack of the lips, yet nothing could be sadder. At Oxford in the nineteen-twenties, Waugh had chosen his friends on the basis of their ability to handle, or entertainingly mishandle, the effects of alcohol; "an excess of wine nauseated him and this made an insurmountable barrier between us," he wrote of one college acquaintance. Now, thirty years later, he would sit in solitude, grasping his glass, bullishly proud that there was nobody present who deserved to share a drop. The hint is clear enough: Waugh, and Waugh alone, was of vintage stuff.

The years since Waugh's death, in 1966—and, in particular, the past decade—have been marked by studious attempts to savor his achievements. We have had biographies in two volumes from Martin Stannard and in one volume from Selina Hastings; more recent, and more slender still, is David Wykes's "Evelyn Waugh: A Literary Life," which bravely introduces us to the new adjective

"Wavian"—helpful to scholars, perhaps, but unlikely to gain a wider currency. Best of all, we have a fresh gathering of primary material: "The Complete Stories of Evelyn Waugh" (Little, Brown; $29.95). The title is clear, although in the Waugh canon a short story is not easily defined. The unfinished yet gracefully rounded tale "Work Suspended," for instance, which consumes eighty-four pages of the present book, feels almost a match for "The Loved One," "Helena," and "The Ordeal of Gilbert Pinfold"—the brisk, peppery, death-haunted trio of novellas that Waugh produced in his riper years, and which are available only in individual volumes. He himself was a chronic bibliophile and a connoisseur of typography, who was admired in his youth for his capacity to illustrate rather than compose a text, and his fussing is contagious; as a rule, I am quite happy to read any cruddy old softback with splinters of wood pulp poking out of the pages, yet I treat my early edition of "Vile Bodies," with its vibrantly woodblocked title page, like a frail and endangered pet. The craving for Waugh can come upon one without warning, especially when the tide of public folly or private slush rises to flood level, but I resent having to slake my need with an emergency Penguin. The new batch of short fiction is a necessary purchase, and you should be able to claim it against tax as an aid to professional sanity, but the I.R.S. might frown at the luridly whimsical dust jacket offered by Little, Brown. The hushed grays of the English edition, published by Everyman, would stand you in better stead.

The choice, nevertheless, is instructive. Is Waugh in hock to the riots that he records, or does he purvey a more Apollonian calm? Is "Vile Bodies," his Anglo-Saxon chronicle of the nineteen-twenties, the last word in madcap, or does it represent the lethally coherent findings of an onlooker? Max Beerbohm once labelled himself a "Tory Anarchist," and the tag hangs well on Waugh, too; his nostalgia for abandoned glories (largely of his own devising) was matched only by his relish for current catastrophe. It is never enough, whatever the temptation, to mock the age in which you live; the mockery must continue to peal, like an echoing bell, long after the objects of your scorn have been decently laid to rest. Take the cruise liner; now little more than a floating mall for the retired and the tan-crazy, it was once a decorous addition to the Grand Tour, tricked out with just enough raffishness and cultural ambition to lure the satirically minded. Waugh got a whole book, "Labels," out of a Mediterranean cruise that he took in 1929, and, four years on, he distilled the swaying, semi-nauseated atmosphere of those days into six pages:

> so we had champagne for dinner and were jolly and they threw paper streamers and I threw mine before it was unrolled and hit Miss P. on the nose. Ha ha. So feeling matey I said to the steward isnt this fun and he said yes for them who hasnt got to clear it up goodness how Sad.

If you had to pick a single Waugh word—the syllable that registers his demeanor as reliably as the "Sir" of Dr. Johnson—it would be "so." Designed to establish a causal connection, it may equally gesture toward a run of events so fluid that cause and effect can be found giggling under the table. The hurler of paper streamers is a case in point; beneath the chirpiness, her emotional logic is on its last legs. The passage comes from "Cruise: Letters from a Young Lady of Leisure," and it skewers a small world as cleanly as anything in "Gentlemen Prefer Blondes"; you could argue that comic ventriloquists such as Waugh and Anita Loos are among the most zestful descendants of Joyce—at least, of the Joyce who spoke in the tongue of Molly Bloom. Waugh detested "Ulysses"; I once heard him, during a television interview, decry it as "gibberish" with a hard "g"; but, as many of the stories make clear, the caddish young novelist was not averse to pilfering any modernist techniques that could be of service. The cinematic clamor of competing voices in "Vile Bodies" bears traces of the pub talk in "The Waste Land"; you can still hear it in "Excursion in Reality," written in 1932, with its clicking exchange of dry-hearted lovers:

> "I say, was I beastly tonight?"
> "Lousy."
> "Well, I thought you were lousy too."
> "Never mind. See you sometime."
> "Aren't you afraid to go on talking?"
> "Can't, I'm afraid. I've got to do some work."
> "Simon, what can you mean?"

Note the absence of guidelines: no "he said," or "she replied." Note, moreover, how little you need them; never in a Waugh conversation do you have to backtrack and work out who is speaking. (Try this some day in the privacy of your own writing, and see how hard it is.) The tones are tethered tightly to character, yet at the same time they seem to float upward like a plainsong of fatigue.

The miracle of Evelyn Waugh is that withering cannot age him. The "Complete Stories" comprises nearly six hundred pages of weariness, withdrawal, disappointment, tweediness, harrumphing snobbery, and flashes of red-faced rage; by rights, the book should grind you down in gloom, instead of which you emerge braced and bolstered, as if by a cold shower and a cocktail. There are thirty-eight tales in all, composed over fifty-two years. Some will be familiar, having been corralled in "Work Suspended and Other Stories"; others, including a trove of juvenilia, were never easy to unearth, and it is gratifying to find them so readily to hand. The earliest effort, written in 1910 and new to me, is "The Curse of the Horse Race." It is thrilling stuff:

> On they went aintil they were face to face with each other. the peliesman lept from his horse only to be stabed to the hart by

Rupert then Tom jumped down and got Rupert a smart blow on the cheak.

Not bad for a seven-year-old. Such boyish taste for Victorian melodrama was hardly uncommon; one surprising revelation of "The Complete Stories of Evelyn Waugh" is that the adult story-teller never shook it out of his system. We are so accustomed to the legend of Waugh the patient craftsman—or, less happily, to the honeyed ruminations in which "Brideshead Revisited" gets stuck—that we tend to neglect his talent for whipping a tale along. There may be no unsung masterpieces in this latest volume, but nor is there the slightest temptation to skip, and some of Waugh's openings leave you ravenous for further particulars: "The marriage of Tom Watch and Angela Trench-Troubridge was, perhaps, as unimportant an event as has occurred within living memory." Or, "John Verney married Elizabeth in 1938, but it was not until the winter of 1945 that he came to hate her steadily and fiercely."

Marital friction, or the farce of wedded lethargy, was one of Waugh's enduring obsessions; he himself married a woman named Evelyn Gardner in 1928. They were known as He-Evelyn and She-Evelyn: the perfect couple, at least until the following year, when she fell in love with another man. Waugh filed a petition for divorce in September, 1929, and it is a commonplace of Waugh criticism to point out that his fiction was henceforth stained by the rich mortification of the cuckold. Tom Watch and Angela Trench-Troubridge can't even make it through their honeymoon without adultery rearing its tousled head. Tom alights from their train ride to the country, gets left behind, meets an old school friend whose name he can't remember, drinks, hunts, and gets lost; Angela arrives too late to find him there, but thrives anyway. ("*Quite all right,*" she cables. "*Your friend divine. Why not join us here.*") Nothing is stated, but we learn in passing that the young bride is thinking of taking a cottage out of town.

This sly history of betrayal, "Love in the Slump," was created in 1932, three years after Waugh's own downfall. The whole thing clips along with the curtness of a telegram; under the pressure of his own fury, the young writer had discovered a species of suffering that he could be funny about. Turn to the back of the book, however, and the chronology of humiliation hits a bump. There you will find a ragbag of fiction from Waugh's time at Oxford, including a cod-historical romance called "Antony, Who Sought Things That Were Lost." I naturally warmed to the title, but the story doesn't really come alive until the death rattle of the last page. Count Antony is imprisoned with his betrothed, the Lady Elizabeth: "And they made a bed of straw on the step and thus among the foul and creeping things was their marriage made." The Lady soon tires of her paramour and looks for a replacement. The only candidate is the pockmarked jailer; she makes love to him in full view of the agued Antony, who then rises up in silence and throttles her. Five years after the creation of this cheerful scene, Waugh entered the holy estate of matrimony.

One should not read too much into the excesses of youth; it does seem, though, that Waugh the undergraduate was preparing himself, consciously or otherwise, for a lifelong scrutiny of bad faith. The whole point of excess was that it should be reported; if you indulged in it personally, good for you, but your pleasure still awaited the cool stroke of a pen and the careful coloring of exaggeration. The joys of "Decline and Fall," as of the early stories and the barbarous deadpan of the letters, are those of drunkenness recollected in sobriety; even the perpetration of serious crimes seems to be leavened, if not pardoned, by the punctiliousness of the prose. In the 1923 story "Edward of Unique Achievement," an undergraduate murders his tutor for no better reason than that he dislikes him. The slaughter is blamed on a fellow-student, Lord Poxe, who is censured by the Warden with the words "It was a foolish act, Lord Poxe, an act of wanton foolishness, but I do not wish to be hard on you. . . . Lady Emily Crane, your great aunt, you will remember, married a Mr Arthur Thorn, my grandfather. I feel that the College owes it to your position to treat this matter as discreetly as possible." Poxe is fined thirteen shillings.

All of Waugh is there in bud: the rude names, the wrongful accusation, the clashing rocks of good behavior and evil deeds, and the lunatic conviction that human worth can be measured by genealogy. (There are moments in "Brideshead" when Waugh, devoutly in love with the fine old Catholic name of Marchmain, veers ominously close to the Warden.) Like Lord Poxe, the author himself never killed anyone, although he once made a hapless attempt on his own life, swimming out to sea from the Welsh coast; as he recalls in his autobiography, he met a shoal of jellyfish and turned back. (It's a fine joke against himself; only the thoroughly spineless would be deterred by invertebrates.) "All fates are 'worse than death,'" he noted in his diary in 1963, and he delighted in submitting his characters to unlikely varieties of doom and dénouement. "The Balance" (1926) imagines its hero downing a blue bottle of poison; the aging Irish hostess of "Bella Fleace Gave a Party" (1932) expires a day after her extravagant but unattended ball, the invitations to which she forgot to put in the mail; the heroine of "On Guard" (1934) is guaranteed a dismal spinsterhood when her jealous poodle, Hector, in a bid to repel all suitors, bites off her ravishing nose.

Then there is McMaster, otherwise known as "The Man Who Liked Dickens." The story was written in 1933, but it had taken root the year before, when Waugh, who spent much of the nineteen-thirties in a punishing series of explorations, stumbled across a desolate Brazilian ranch and discovered Mr. Christie. With his loosely extended family, curious theories on the doctrine of the Trinity, and a winning way with rum and lime, Christie was a gift; he stewed in Waugh's mind and emerged as McMaster, who dopes an English visitor, Paul Henty, with strong brews and never lets him go. In reality, Waugh set out freely after a night in

Christie's company; but reality was always too meagre for the writer's liking, and he made it the business of his fiction to think along paths not taken—to wonder just how infernally, with a little help from mischance and a touch of sunstruck malice, life might have turned out. And so "The Man Who Liked Dickens" underwent a final fermentation, and became the penultimate chapter of "A Handful of Dust," with Henty becoming Tony Last— another dreamy cuckold on the run—and McMaster retransfigured into the morbidly named Mr. Todd, requesting one more recitation of "Little Dorrit" from his helpless guest.

It is as plausible a portrait of damnation as you could wish for; even now, however, we have not reached the end of the affair. "The Complete Stories of Evelyn Waugh" has an eight-page offering, "By Special Request," that was used as a quiet climax to the serialized version of "A Handful of Dust." This time, there is no Brazil; no Christie, no McMaster, no Todd; merely the glum prospect of Tony returning to his errant wife, and the resumption of their stony existence. "All the old faces," she remarks as they sit down in a new restaurant, amid the tribal savagery of a London lunch. The story ends with Tony taking over the apartment that his wife had found so useful for infidelity. Again, we are left to fill in the details, but it is a good bet that the cycle of deceit will lurch into motion all over again. To the comfortless, Waugh offers little more than a choice of living death: malarial mire or furnished flat? A delicious story of 1932, "Incident in Azania," makes the parallel explicit, and sniggers at the blessings of civilization:

> Far away in the interior, in the sunless secret places, where a twisted stem across the jungle track, a rag fluttering to the bough of a tree, a fowl headless and full spread by an old stump marked the taboo where no man might cross, the Sakuya women chanted their primeval litany of initiation; here on the hillside the no less terrible ceremony was held over Mrs Lepperidge's tea table.

.   .   .

This balanced disdain must be kept in mind as we enter the treacherous terrain that is ruled by Waugh the snob. A skim through his journals will provide ample proof that he was a racist, anti-Semitic, misogynist reactionary; but that is the trouble with skimming. The deeper you plunge into him, the more you realize that no one was spared the knife. His novels rejoice in the fact that the sinned against are as open to the attentions of satire as the sinning. Having joined the Catholic Church in 1930, Waugh saw no reason to be softer on the shortcomings of others than he was on his own. The trouble with liberalism, for example—and one can hardly begin to imagine the fun that Waugh would have had with the political dispensations of today—was that it provided unfair exemptions to original sin. If he laughed at the mimicry of European customs which he saw at the coronation of Haile Selassie, and which found full expression in "Black Mischief," how much harder he laughed at the inability of Europeans to unbend in the presence of the alien. Waugh is fond of Mr. Youkoumian, the Armenian fixer who pops up in "Incident in Azania" and, later, in the pages of "Black Mischief," but his real venom is reserved for the English community: "It did them good to find a foreigner who so completely fulfilled their ideal of all that a foreigner should be."

As the years progressed, Waugh himself swelled into the sort of Englishman who fulfilled a foreigner's ideal of all that an Englishman, if left rank and unweeded, might become. It was a sight guaranteed (and probably designed) to perplex the nineteen-fifties: pink and apoplectic, armed with cigar and ear trumpet, Waugh laid into the decline of modern manners with ill-mannered contempt. No one who claimed to prefer his books to his children ("A child is easily replaced") can have been *that* easy to love, and his journal adds to the insult, describing his own brood—he had six children by his second wife, Laura—as "feckless, destructive, frivolous, sensual, humorless." All in all, the privilege of reading Waugh is rivalled only by the relief of never having had to

encounter such a rare, irascible beast in person; the privilege is all
the more acute because, with age, his fiction starts to shimmer
with self-consciousness—a quickened Falstaffian shame, far
beyond the reach of your average club bore—about the mon-
strous figure that he knows he must cut. That is why this volume
contains no senilia. "Basil Seal Rides Again," written three years
before Waugh's death, is crisp with mischief and suffused with
wintry regret:

> His voice was not the same instrument as of old. He had first
> assumed it as a conscious imposture; it had become habitual to
> him; the antiquated, worldly-wise moralities which, using that
> voice, he had found himself obliged to utter, had become his
> settled opinions.

Reading this, you ask yourself what manner of fear and uncertainty could lead someone—especially so lithe a social animal as
the young Waugh—to wall himself in against the assaults, real and
imaginary, of a hostile world. Waugh's biographer Martin Stannard passes a particularly harsh sentence: "His art was a theatre of
cruelty; his temperament instinctively uncharitable." That sounds
decisive, but it drags Waugh toward the arena of Artaud and
Genet, where he most definitely does not belong. For one thing,
his unkindness is made compelling by the pitch and frequency of
his jokes—seldom registered by Stannard, whose industry is
untroubled by humor. Dip at random into the letters, some of
which are right up there with the great wit-shows of Horace Wal-
pole and Sydney Smith, and you will immediately stumble upon
plain events blooming into the surreal. When Lady Mary Lygon
was elected to the London Library in 1946 (not a major achievement), Waugh wrote to congratulate her:

> I hope you will always remember to behave yourself with suit-
> able decorum in those grave precincts. Always go to the closet

appointed for the purpose if you wish to make water. Far too many female members have lately taken to squatting behind the Genealogy section. Never write 'balls' with an indelible pencil on the margins of the books provided. Do not solicit the female librarians to acts of unnatural vice.

Is this "instinctively uncharitable"? I think I smell the milk of human kindness: faintly curdled, perhaps, but brimming with licentious glee. During the Second World War, the novelist was described by his commanding officer as "so unpopular as to be unemployable," yet he was also a byword for physical courage, and, in the years that followed, his cruelty began to be infiltrated, if not by charity, at least by a nagging sense of those occasions which would be improved by goodness and mercy. The "Sword of Honour" trilogy, published between 1952 and 1961, is a masterpiece of ruefulness; who but Waugh could have woven the surrender of spiritual hope into the winning of a global fight? The stories from that era are suffused with a similar disillusion; "Scott-King's Modern Europe," about an English schoolmaster adrift in a sunny totalitarian state, is written with the peculiar shade of purple that Waugh could summon at moments of high irony—Latinate, unglutinous, and so steeped in the mock-heroic that susceptible readers may be moved by its dust-covered grandeur. "No voluptuary surfeited by conquest, no colossus of the drama bruised and rent by doting adolescents, not Alexander, nor Talleyrand, was more blasé than Scott-King." More mouse than man, Scott-King joins the caged, uncomplaining collection of Waugh protagonists: Paul Pennyfeather, in "Decline and Fall"; Adam Symes, in "Vile Bodies"; William Boot, in "Scoop"; Guy Crouchback, in "Sword of Honour"—mock heroes by any standard, each of them a blend of prig and punching bag. The "Complete Stories" has a roster of new recruits: the narrator of "Work Suspended," for instance, a writer of detective fiction who tucks himself away in a Moroccan hotel, and Major Gordon, the stolid Scot at the center of "Compassion."

This last tale is reason enough to buy "The Complete Stories of Evelyn Waugh." Unlike "Work Suspended," "Scott-King's Modern Europe," and ten others, it was tricky to find before the book came out. You could read it, more or less, in "Unconditional Surrender," the last third of "Sword of Honour," where it is split and scattered among other strands of plot; here it comes in concentrated form, tense with moral stupefaction. Major Gordon, like Waugh himself, is sent to wartime Yugoslavia—Northern Croatia, to be exact, where Tito's partisans are filling the vacuum left by departing Nazis. Gordon, like everyone else, is fouled up in the political tangle, but there is one issue he needs to straighten out: a band of Jewish refugees, desperate to find a home. Nobody wants them, not least Gordon; his first instinct is to wash his hands of them, with "their remnants of bourgeois civility." Slowly, against all odds, this unimaginative man takes up their case, and then their cause; by the end, they are all that matters to him in a dishonored conflict. "He had seen something entirely new, which needed new eyes to see clearly: humanity in the depths, misery of quite another order from anything he had guessed before." Even then, by one of those stabs of lousy luck which Waugh likes to inflict, the Major lets his charges down. He achieves almost nothing, and you could say the same of Waugh; how can all the casual anti-Semitism, the slangy thirties use of lower-case "jew" that darkens his letters and journals, possibly be redeemed by this one tale? I can only point to the drama of Gordon's conscience; if he had been tolerant to begin with, the story would be an easy read, but there is something overwhelming in the erosion of prejudice and the dawn of unlikely love:

> Major Gordon did not forget the Jews. Their plight oppressed him on his daily walks in the gardens, where the leaves were now falling fast and burning smokily in the misty air. . . . By such strange entrances does compassion sometimes slip, disguised, into the human heart.

I would not be so precipitate as to claim the discovery of a new and unsuspected creature: a nice Evelyn Waugh. For every Major Gordon, there are a dozen bigots and yellowbellies rustling in the background, and, without them, we would miss the extensive and brightly feathered range of mortal sinners that readers have always sought in Waugh's menagerie. If he had entertained a profound respect for the Welsh, we would have no "Decline and Fall"; without his unsqueamish autopsy of California culture, "The Loved One" could not exist. Waugh was well aware of the price that had to be paid by anatomists such as himself:

> Humility is not a virtue propitious to the artist. It is often pride, emulation, avarice, malice—all the odious qualities—which drive a man to complete, elaborate, refine, destroy, renew his work until he has made something that gratifies his pride and envy and greed. And in so doing he enriches the world more than the generous and good, though he may lose his own soul in the process. That is the paradox of artistic achievement.

With the publication of the "Complete Stories," the paradox of Evelyn Waugh is given another twist. That he enriched us with the unalloyed gleam of his prose—far purer than any of his leaden imitators can manage—is now beyond debate. He could certainly be odious, even to those who found him amiable; many friends were shocked by the lashes that he meted out in the diaries. But who can tell whether a soul was lost? In his short novel "Helena," underrated by all but the writer himself, the heroine offers a tremulous prayer to the Magi: "How odd you looked on the road, attended by what outlandish liveries, laden with such preposterous gifts! . . . For His sake who did not always neglect your curious gifts, pray always for all the learned, the oblique, the delicate." Those who know only the Waugh of popular myth—the hard, the unhappy, the truculent—should prepare to be shocked by his delicacy. It may at times be the delicacy of the dagger, but, for all his preposterous opinions, there is not a thud of clumsiness in his work, and the figures who wander through it, grievously tricked or drunkenly dim, will continue to console us with their company. He recognized that the struggle between low brutish beings and what he called "an almost fatal hunger for permanence" was both too solemn and too hilarious ever to be resolved. Waugh himself died on Easter Sunday, 1966, after Mass, in the lavatory; he could not have dreamed of a more fitting passage to the life to come.

THE HUMAN RIGHTS
QUARTERLY

The Rape of Dinah

To read this compelling first-hand account of a human rights catastrophe is to encounter an unforgettable example of advocacy reporting. Civil war in Liberia was ranked by Doctors without Borders as one of the most underreported stories of the twentieth century. This penetrating analysis chronicles the staggering magnitude of the carnage, as well as the shocking disinterest of the international community—including journalists—in a war deemed too high-risk and too geopolitically insignificant to be reported outside Africa.

Kenneth L. Cain

The Rape of Dinah

Human Rights, Civil War in Liberia, and Evil Triumphant

Now Dinah, daughter to Jacob, went out to visit the daughters of the land. Shechem son of Hamor the Hivite, chief of the land, saw her, and took her and lay with her by force. Jacob heard that Shechem had defiled his daughter Dinah. Hamor came to Jacob and his sons, saying, "my son Shechem longs for your daughter. Please give her to him in marriage" and offered Jacob landrights in return. Shechem also spoke to Jacob and the sons, "Do me this favor, and I will pay whatever you tell me ... only give me this maiden for a wife." Jacob's sons were indignant and very angry, because he had committed an outrage in Israel by lying with Jacob's daughter by force—a thing not to be done. The men thus answered with guile, instructing Hamor and Shechem that the sons of Hivites must be circumcised, only on this condition would they agree. The words pleased Hamor and Shechem who convinced the men of their town that in order to usher in an era of profitable relations with their neighbor Jacob, all men of the town must be circumcised.

On the third day, when the Hivites were in pain, Simeon and Levi, two brothers of Dinah,

> *took each his sword, came upon the city unmolested, and slew all the males. They put Hamor and his son Shechem to the sword, took Dinah out of Shechem's house and went away. The other sons of*

Jacob came upon the slain and plundered town, because their sister had been defiled. They seized their flocks and herds and asses, all that was inside the town and outside, all their wealth, all their children, and their wives, all that was in houses, they took as captives and booty. Jacob said to Simeon and Levi, "you have brought trouble on me, making me odious among the inhabitants of the land, the Canaanites and the Perizzites; my men are few in number, so that if they unite against me and attack me, I and my house will be destroyed." But they answered, "Should our sister be treated like a whore?"[1]

The Rape of Dinah
Genesis, Chapter 34

The looters, the plunderers, the obsessively ambitious must not be allowed to block the cravings of the vast majority. What wickedness.[2]

William Twaddell
US Ambassador to Liberia

They are writing "Angels of Death." Look, I am no Angel of Death and I am going to prove it in this town. I am very serious, me, Charles Ghankay Taylor, I will prove that I am no Lord of War and I am no Angel of Death. If you don't respect this presidency, you'll respect it or I am going to lock horns with some people here one on one. They think ECOMOG here to support their nonsense and their talks. ECOMOG will not stop me. It's almost reaching now that we will make sure that different processes; due processes of law maybe, and in some cases, the laws of the jungle to bring things under control in this town. You know Charles Taylor, we will straighten things out.[3]

Charles Taylor
5 November 1995

What the journalists have failed to point out is that this time, unlike previous fighting in Monrovia, the civilians have not really suffered. . . . In the past, fighters would rip out people's intestines and use them to string up road-blocks, or cut off people's heads. This time there has been none of that.[4]

**National Patriotic Front of Liberia
(NPFL) Spokesman J.T. Richardson
amidst carnage in Monrovia
April, 1996**

Right temporarily denied is stronger than evil triumphant.[5]

Dr. Martin Luther King

I. Introduction

L iberia is important in its own right—human beings live and die there. In the immortal words of Primo Levi, as he struggled to make some moral sense out of Auschwitz, "We are in fact convinced that no human experience is without meaning or unworthy of analysis, and that fundamental values, even if they are not positive, can be deduced from this particular world which we are describing."[6] Liberia, however, has no strategic importance. It enjoys no diplomatic or political cache in international circles. Despite the ineffably violent character of the war that took place there between 1990 and 1997, no single ethnicity was targeted to a sufficient extent to warrant the special opprobrium of "genocide." The international community has thus responded to human rights in Liberia with unqualified neglect.

The 200,000 casualties of the Liberian civil war (approximately the same number as died in the war in the Former Yugoslavia)[7] provide a depressingly eloquent testimonial of the extent to which affirmations of a universal commitment to human rights, emanating from the United Nations and the orthodox human rights community, are demonstrably vacuous. The fact is that from the perspective of any constituent element of the international human rights apparatus—UN investigations, international tribunals, truth commissions, diplomatic opprobrium, vigorous condemnation and advocacy from the international human rights movement—it is as if tens of thousands of ethnic cleansing, execution, rape, and torture cases never happened. Even a wholly rhetorical denunciation of named perpetrators has been beyond the will of the international community. Evil Triumphant.

When Charles Taylor's National Patriotic Front of Liberia (NPFL) attacked a government outpost on Christmas Eve 1989, Liberia was the first sovereign entity to degenerate into a newly conceived category: the failed state. The origin of Liberia's degradation into that ignominious class lies in the pathological legacy of slavery. The pernicious effects of the West African slave trade had landed with force on the Grain Coast, Liberia's precursor, by the mid-seventeenth century. The abrupt repatriation and colonial settlement of freed American slaves two centuries later, in an area already populated by indigenous Africans, closed an ugly circle. Upon independence in 1847, this oligarchy of freed-slave, 'Americo-Liberian' settlers systematically and thoroughly deprived the indigenous majority of equal access to land, education, justice, wealth, and political power, and violently repressed the inevitable series of revolts.

A more proximate line of responsibility for state failure begins in 1980 with Samuel Doe, a twenty-eight year old, semi-literate Sergeant-Major. Doe's violent coup against the Americo-Liberian elite, and subsequent use of his ethnic Krahn brethren as a palace guard and brutal security apparatus, begot more violence, coup attempts, ethnically based reprisals, and vengeful counter-attacks, ultimately rendering sufficient chaos to induce Taylor to attack.

With alarming alacrity, Taylor's bid precipitated a descent into a seven-year civil war characterized by total state collapse and a relentless campaign of sadistic, wanton violence unimaginable to those unfamiliar with the details of man's capacity to visit the abyss. By August 1990, President Doe had been tortured, mutilated, and killed, and the NPFL had propagated a splinter faction, the INPFL,[8] soon to be joined by several other new factions and the rump government army, the AFL.[9] Amidst the carnage, a West African Peacekeeping Force, ECOMOG,[10] was quickly assembled, sponsored primarily by Nigeria. ECOMOG exacerbated the conflict by arming and supporting Liberian splinter factions and effectively occupying the country for seven years.

All state authority ceased to function outside of Monrovia. Lightly armed, drugged, marauding teenage "rebels" devastated Liberia on behalf of their adult patrons. Out of a prewar population of approximately 2.5 million, the factions are responsible for 200,000 casualties (the vast majority civilians), creating 750,000 international refugees and more than 1.2 million internally displaced (IDPs),[11] and a mind-boggling number of cases of execution, torture, rape, and cannibalism. The math speaks for itself: casualties plus refugees plus IDPs equals 85 percent of the population.

Direct responsibility for this human rights catastrophe lies with the faction leaders: George Boley of the LPC,[12] Alhaji Kromah of ULIMO-K,[13] Roosevelt Johnson of ULIMO-J,[14] Prince Yordie Johnson of the INPFL, Charles Taylor of the NPFL, and their senior lieutenants. These individuals recruited, supplied, trained, and led their rebel forces into the operations that resulted in a litany of abuse. In the words of the US Department of State, not generally thought to overstate such matters:

The factions committed summary executions, torture, individual and gang rapes, mutilations, and cannibalism. They burned people alive; looted and burned cities and villages; used excessive force; engaged in arbitrary detentions and impressment, particularly of children under the age of eighteen; severely restricted freedom of assembly, association, and movement; and employed forced labor.[15]

While addressing the conduct of all factions, this analysis emphasizes the culpability of Charles Taylor and the NPFL. Taylor warrants heightened scrutiny for the following reasons, *inter alia:* the NPFL initiated armed conflict; inaugurated the use of grade school-age children as scouts, spies, and cannon fodder; explicitly employed terror tactics, ethnic cleansing, and political assassinations; was numerically the largest faction by threefold; consistently controlled the most territory, including intermittent control of all areas of Liberia outside Monrovia; deployed sophisticated arms; and exhibited something approximating a chain-of-command. Taylor has latterly mutated into an elected president and currently enjoys status as the Head of State of a recognized government. Predictably, his new government immediately kidnaped, tortured, assassinated, and mutilated a leading opposition figure and his family, appointed an infamously murderous former rebel commander as Police Chief, and closed independent radio stations and newspapers. Evil Triumphant.

Scholarly analysis and media reporting of the conflict in Liberia has been limited and sporadic. Other than journal articles emphasizing West African politics and the formation of ECOMOG, superficial press stories, and descriptive reports from international human rights advocacy groups, there has been no attempt to systematically analyze the role that human rights has played in the conduct of the war, the intervention by ECOMOG, the UN's monitoring mandate, and the US response.[16] The goal of this article is to undertake that missing analysis in detail.

II. Ethnic Killing

P resident Doe's elevation of the Krahn ethnic group as a privileged elite in the government and among his various security services incensed leaders of the two largest Liberian ethnic groups, the Gio and Mano. In 1985, a popular Gio General in the AFL, Thomas Quiwonkpa, attempted a coup. Doe survived the coup; AFL soldiers captured Quiwonkpa, tortured and mutilated him, and ate his body parts.[17] Government forces then went on a rampage in Quiwonkpa's, and the Gio's, stronghold of Nimba County, killing as many as 3000 civilians.[18] When Taylor's raiding party attacked in 1989, they were soon joined by hundreds, then thousands, of Gio and Mano from Nimba County, explicitly seeking revenge on the Krahn, as well as the Mandingo, whom the NPFL regarded as having been overly intimate with the Doe regime. They soon wrought that revenge.

In a passage that could read from a report about ethnic cleansing in Bosnia, *mutatis mutandis,* the State Department reported in 1990 that

> rebel [NPFL] forces routinely singled out members of the Krahn and Mandingo ethnic groups for killing. . . . The NPFL ordered residents to evacuate areas under its control and forced them through checkpoints where anyone suspected of being Krahn or Mandingo or a former government employee was identified and killed. At one such checkpoint dubbed "no return," the NPFL was reliably reported to have killed more than 2,000 people. . . . At food distribution points and medical clinics, the NPFL required that registrants identify themselves by tribal affiliation. Krahns and Mandingos were subsequently sorted out and killed.[19]

These attacks intensified as the NPFL approached Monrovia and Grand Gedeh County, a Krahn stronghold, where, in the words of the State Department, the NPFL was "hunting down and killing Krahns."[20] In a confidential statement to UN investigators, an eyewitness from this period provided the following account of NPFL actions as it approached Monrovia:

> [When the NPFL arrived] they told the residents they were there to free the people. After a few days, however, they began taking people from their homes, stripping them naked and carrying them down to the water. They moved from house to house, looking for Krahns, Mandingos and Government officials. [Once], an NPFL vehicle arrived, NPFL soldiers opened the trunk and pulled a man out. The man began to beg, "don't kill me, I'm not a Krahn man." The soldiers pushed him into a ditch and shot him. Later, a dumptruck arrived from Monrovia loaded with men, women and children. . . . [T]he truck dumped people in the water, [rebels were] shooting them as they fell in the water.[21]

As the war continued into 1991, Krahn defense groups formed, further fueling ethnic attacks by the NPFL. A former NPFL rebel bluntly described Taylor's tactic to Africa Watch: "When we entered towns, we asked the townspeople for Mandingo, Krahn and remaining forces. We killed the ones we found. In July, we attacked [a small village], and killed about 175 people—women, children and soldiers."[22] In general, ethnic differences among Liberians are not readily observable, and language became the basis for the Liberian version of "selections."[23]

Taylor and the NPFL have been particularly explicit about their lethal hostility toward the Mandingo, who, as Muslim traders with origins in Guinea, are a notably vulnerable minority. In private discussions, NPFL officials are often quick to inform foreigners that the Mandingos, most of whom have lived in Liberia for generations, "are not really Liberian" and would be wise to "return" to

Guinea. In early 1990, Doe had lost control of much of rural Liberia, but maintained control in Monrovia. In May of 1990, Doe's supporters in Monrovia executed eighteen Gio and Mano. Taylor was widely quoted as having responded to this attack with a definitive expression of the logic of ethnic slaughter: "If you're a Mandingo, it doesn't matter who you are or what you've done. That's it. It's tit for tat."[24] Soon after making the statement, the NPFL captured the trading port of Buchanan and executed large numbers of civilians, including many Mandingos.[25]

There is a heuristic challenge to delineating an appropriate point of departure for an analysis of ethnic killing in Liberia. North American and European slave traders were guilty, paradigmatically so, of a most cruel form of ethnically motivated crime, as were their African collaborators. Later, the freed American slaves thoroughly colonized the indigenous residents of Liberia, and systematically discriminated against them in all aspects of life, based on their tribal identity *per se*. Doe's coup was an attempt to undo this *de facto* apartheid, but his regime quickly degenerated into a brutal new Krahn oligarchy—which in turn provoked the Gio and Mano, whose ire was exploited by an opportunistic and ambitious Charles Taylor, who then proceeded to lead a lethal campaign of ethnic cleansing. Taylor and the NPFL are most recently and obviously culpable, but the precedent for their actions is tragically long and deep.

Thoughtful human rights lawyers, schooled *ab initio* on the premise of individual criminal accountability, are nevertheless forced by these facts to confront the implications of traditional patterns of attribution of responsibility. Recognition of this theme is immaterial as to criminal culpability. Cultural differences regarding the potency and potential ramifications of ethno-tribal group identity, however, cannot be wished away, and are ignored at the peril of the putative analyst. For example, the Justice and Peace Commission of the National Catholic Secretariat of

Liberia, the country's oldest and most respected human rights group, addressed the topic with dexterity, and is worth quoting at length:

> Life in the interior proceeds according to the traditional pattern notable for its indulgence in superstition. The illiterate and superstitious mind is most amenable to poor reasoning. Simple and clear-cut solutions are applied to complex problems. Many innocent people lost their lives in the war, for example, simply because they were members of Doe or Quiwonkpa's tribes, although they had never served in the government. Had our people been educated and the quality of their lives improved, this war might not have taken the destructive course on which it has embarked.
>
> The practice of collective responsibility for crime which characterizes the traditional culture is another factor that made the war most reckless and extensive. The individual alone is not responsible for his crime but also members of his family, his tribe, and his associates. Consequently, not only Doe but also all Krahn people, members of his government, his family and friends were held responsible for his crimes against the nation. By the same token the people of Nimba [C]ounty were considered as enemies of Doe merely because Quiwonkpa originated from that County. Thus they were massacred for the attempted coups led by Quiwonkpa.[26]

III. Political Assassination

thnicity is but one among many potentially mortal attributes in Liberia; opposition—or even proximity—to Taylor can be lethal. On 28 November 1997, four months after Charles Taylor's inauguration as

President, a prominent opposition politician from Taylor's home base in Nimba County, Samuel Dokie, left his home for a family wedding in Nimba, accompanied by his wife, a niece, a cousin, the wedding gown, and gifts. When he reached Iron Gate, a notorious NPFL check point at the entrance of Taylor's former headquarters in Gbarnga, Dokie and his wedding entourage were arrested, first by the Gbarnga District Police Chief, then by agents of the government's Special Security Service. The wedding entourage disappeared for five days. Taylor, his Police Chief, and the Justice Minister consistently claimed that they were not aware of any arrest and only belatedly made any pretense to investigate. On 2 December, the Justice Minister, Peter Jallah, proclaimed with a straight face:

> It is [only] through the alarm raised through the press by the [Dokie] family that the Government got to know what is happening. . . . At the moment President Dr. Charles G. Taylor is seriously concerned. . . . [T]he Government is concerned and will leave no stone unturned to find out as to what really happened. There are laws and order. Our people must and will live a peaceful life. We do not want such to be repeated after this one.[27]

On 3 December, all four decomposing bodies were found; Dokie had been tortured, mutilated, beheaded, burned, and his eyes had been gouged out—his wife, niece, and nephew had also been tortured and burned before being executed.[28]

Dokie had been a central figure in the NPFL until his defection in 1994, at which point Taylor publicly threatened to "deal with" Mr. Dokie and his defecting faction, who would not be safe from Taylor's wrath "even in the womb."[29] Jaded Taylor observers cringed when he reasserted his government's commitment to human rights after the bodies were found, pledging to conduct a full investigation and hold responsible parties accountable. Ultimately, four junior security operatives were detained, "tried" by a government-controlled tribunal, and quickly acquitted and released. Despite lamentations and plaints for justice by human rights groups, Taylor has exercised prosecutorial discretion and chosen not to arrest himself.

The Dokie assassination is the most recent manifestation of a familiar pattern of conduct throughout the war. Taylor is an Americo-Liberian but claims Gola ancestry (his wife is Gola) and a base in Nimba County. He has systematically killed senior leaders from Nimba, thereby eliminating any competition from aspirants for power with a more legitimate claim to the Gola constituency, including the actual winner of the disputed 1985 elections, Jackson Doe. A senior NPFL dissident has, in fact, asserted publicly that the orders for the assassination of several of these Nimba leaders came directly from Taylor, affirming a commonly held suspicion.[30]

In one revealing incident in April 1996, an outspoken critic of the NPFL was detained by Taylor's rebels and forced to view the decapitated corpses of known Taylor critics as a warning.[31] In August 1992, after what the NPFL claimed was an aborted coup attempt, Taylor executed approximately fifty NPFL fighters, and in September of the same year, several more senior commanders were executed for "desertion."[32] In December 1993, Taylor admitted to ordering executions of senior commanders after the NPFL lost its Gbarnga headquarters to a rival faction (ULIMO).[33] Though the facts of these and numerous other executions of NPFL insiders are confirmed and corroborated, the motives are more ambiguous: elimination of rival bases of power, physical demonstrations of authority, and brutally *ad hoc* methods of internal discipline all blur in the absence of any form of procedural accountability or transparency within the NPFL.

Nationality provides an additional class of victims. In 1990, when ECOMOG first intervened in the war in order to prevent the

NPFL from occupying its final unrealized objective, Monrovia, Taylor announced on NPFL radio that the NPFL would kill one ECOMOG national in response to every Liberian killed by ECO-MOG.[34] Thousands of Nigerians, Ghanaians, Guineans, Gambians, and Sierra Leoneans were rounded up and held at detention camps in the interior of the country and at the Nigerian embassy itself. Hundreds were executed.[35]

The NPFL fought bitterly with ECOMOG in 1990 based in part on Taylor's accusation that ECOMOG was a Nigerian-led, Anglophone occupation force, not an impartial peacekeeper. ECOWAS[36] then imposed upon Francophone Senegal to contribute troops in order to mollify Taylor's purported objection. In April 1992, the NPFL demonstrated the disingenuousness of its rhetoric by ambushing Senegalese forces during a cease-fire period, capturing, torturing, and executing six Senegalese peacekeepers.[37]

Even American nuns were not exempt. On 15 October 1992, the NPFL commenced "Operation Octopus," its second attempt to capture Monrovia. NPFL forces went on a series of authorized rampages as they progressed toward Monrovia. On the first day of the attack, two sisters from the Convent of the Adorers of the Blood of Christ were ambushed by NPFL forces as they drove along the highway, their vehicle commandeered, and their bodies deposited onto the road. A week later, an NPFL squad led by "Commander Devil" appeared at the convent, demanded the keys to the convent's vehicle, and proceeded to execute the three remaining nuns.[38]

IV. Rake

ystematic rape as a means of instilling terror in civilian populations has received considerable scholarly and journalistic attention in the context of UN war crimes prosecutions in the Former Yugoslavia and

Rwanda. Aside from one-sentence references in press stories and human rights reports, the prevalence of excruciatingly violent rape cases in the Liberian conflict has received no attention.

The findings of one of the few studies available on the subject provide a clue to the scope of rape cases. In 1994, the World Health Organization (WHO) office in Monrovia interviewed 450 women from fifteen displaced persons shelters in Monrovia. Thirty-three percent of the respondents reported that they had been raped. Eighty-four percent of this group had been raped during periods of active fighting. In more than 50 percent of the cases, more than one attacker was involved, with weapons being used in 86 percent of the cases. In approximately 50 percent of the cases, family members were present during the attacks. Eighty percent claimed that they experience sexual problems as a result and feel hatred and resentment toward men in general.[39]

While the pool of subjects in a displaced camp is theoretically an unrepresentative sample, 1.2 million Liberians were internally displaced during the war. Thus, discounting for roughly 100,000 infants and young girls, 500,000 Liberian women and older girls[40] would generally correspond to WHO's sample pool. While the methodology of WHO's finding that one-third of displaced women had been raped may not have been rigorously scientific, it is generally recognized that rape cases are significantly underreported by victims, particularly in a traditional society such as Liberia's. If thirty-three percent of displaced women is accepted, *arguendo,* as a rough guide, then one-third of 500,000 displaced women and children, or 168,000 victims, were raped during the war. While this number may defy comprehension (and belief), additional evidence exists. According to Amnesty International, for example, in 1995, UNICEF registered 652 rape cases within *less than six* months in just one town, Buchanan.[41]

Between March and August 1994, a small number of fighters were demobilized in an energetic—if brief—UN effort to disarm the factions. During this interlude in fighting, the United Nations was able to interview 3449 fighters in an official demobilization questionnaire, using trained Liberian staff as interviewers. Again, the sample pool is inherently distorted in that the 3449 fighters who volunteered to demobilize—and were permitted by their commanders to do so—out of a pool of approximately 35,000 fighters,[42] by definition have differentiated themselves from the typical fighter. Also, the professionalism and competence of the UNOMIL[43] demobilization team was a continuous source of acute embarrassment for the United Nations; the scientific rigor with which their investigation was conducted can safely be assumed to be limited, and, in the author's opinion, anything produced by the demobilization team is suspect. Nevertheless, the team published a summary of findings from the demobilization interview process in a restricted circulation UN document, and the evidence therein is one of the few quasi-scientific sources available.

The demobilization team found that eleven percent of the 3449 fighters interviewed admitted to raping with violence more than ten times.[44] Starting with a benchmark of 35,000 as the estimated number of fighters, these findings imply that, by 1994, 3850 fighters had committed more than ten rapes each, or an unknown amount greater than 38,500 rapes. Fully recognizing the limitations of the data, namely, the high likelihood that fighters would underreport to UN officials the number of times they had raped, the fact that the sample was taken four years into a seven-year war, and that the class of fighters that had voluntarily disarmed would differ substantially from the fighters that remained in the field, UNOMIL's findings nevertheless confirm the essence of the WHO study's findings. An extraordinarily high number—tens upon tens upon tens of thousands—of Liberian women were raped by rebel forces over a seven-year period.

Anecdotal evidence received by the author was similarly abject and confirmed the WHO's finding that many rapes occurred in the view of family members, multiplying the trauma and humiliation. In a victim statement presented to the author, one woman from an LPC-dominated area in the Southeast offered the following account:

> I was forcibly taken into the bush with my three children and husband by the LPC fighters under the accusation of [trying to kill] "General War Boss" and "General Kill the Bitch." We have always been accused and tortured by these rebels because many of us are Bassa by tribe. My husband was tied to a thorny tree; black driver ants were put all over his body while I was raped as a pregnant woman in front of my three children by four LPC fighters. Later, an order was given that my husband should be beheaded in front of my children and me. My husband cried for mercy, but the LPC did not listen and cut his esophagus and my husband finally died.[45]

A second victim reported, "I came to Buchanan because I am tired of being raped by LPC soldiers. I was forcibly taken [from my home] and raped by six LPC fighters. . . . [L]ater . . . the rebels entered our town and raped all the women."[46] A third victim reported:

> The LPC fighters entered my village in the bush and [tortured my neighbor] and many others. . . . There were about eighteen armed men. I was raped along with my two younger sisters in the village by ten LPC armed men. After the acts of raping, our wearings and property were looted.[47]

The WHO report included the following testimonial:

> I was nine months pregnant. When the fighters came, they grabbed me and my husband and tied us up. The head of my

husband was cut off in front of me. I was then raped by about fifteen young men. I delivered my baby a day after. Now my womb cannot stay in place.[48]

In an official report to UN Headquarters in Monrovia and New York after a helicopter mission across rebel lines in 1996, the author presented the following findings:

In conducting human rights investigations in five United Nations Peacekeeping missions, the UNOMIL Human Rights Officer has never encountered such an explicit consensus of reports, among a cross-section of witnesses and sources, about the scale and scope of rape cases. All contacts at each site reported that if women leave the ECOMOG controlled towns they are subject to rape by ULIMO-K forces. (Unfortunately it is often the women who are expected to move in the bush to collect food and firewood, etc.) One credible witness in Sinje reported that rape in the bush and along the highway outside of ECOMOG positions "is a daily occurrence." Even ECOMOG enlisted men, who are generally not particularly vocal about such issues, expressed outrage over the scope of rape cases. The ECOMOG platoon commander in Bo reported an incident in which an ECOMOG vehicle, carrying four Liberian women, attempted to travel from Bo to Kle and was stopped by ULIMO-K at Gbah; the women were forced out of the vehicle, the ECOMOG soldiers were told to continue to Monrovia, and when the ECOMOG vehicle returned to Gbah, the four women had all been raped by ULIMO-K fighters at the checkpoint.[49]

The factions were indistinguishable in their conduct as to rape. All factions perpetrated the crimes detailed above. No Liberians have been investigated or prosecuted for rape cases during the war. The leaders of the factions have made no statement formally addressing the use of rape as a tactic of terror. No international organization (including the United Nations) has made any substantial effort to investigate or publicize the phenomenon. It is as if tens upon tens of thousands of sadistic rape cases never occurred.[50]

V. The Small Boys Unit (SBU)

Relief and human rights officials become inured to the nightmare scenarios they inhabit in Bosnia, Rwanda, Somalia, Chechnya, and elsewhere. One specifically Liberian image, however, stuns even the most hardened observer: a combat-deployed rebel carrying an AK–47 almost as big as his eight-year-old body. When Taylor attacked, and gained ground and support in Nimba in 1989 and 1990, he immediately developed a useful and innovative tactic that eventually came to symbolize the depravity of the war for many observers: the NPFL's Small Boys Unit. Taylor consciously recruited young boys to form special units of intensely loyal rebels, unburdened by the independence of thought or moral restraint of adulthood—a prepubescent Liberian rebel version of the cult of personality.[51] The small boys, who uniformly refer to Taylor as "our father," participated in all aspects of rebel conduct, including serving in front line combat operations, atrocities against civilian populations, and even rape. UNOMIL's Chief Operating Officer told Africa Watch, "It's a children's war. Kids get promoted in rank for committing an atrocity; they can cut off someone's head without thinking."[52]

The boys were recruited among vulnerable populations, and originally included many orphans from President Doe's counter-insurgency campaign against the Gio and Mano civilians in Nimba. As the war dragged on, many children were forcibly recruited; others joined simply to gain access to looted food, or as a means of protecting their families by being on the inside of a potentially lethal threat. The children were given alcohol (cane juice) and drugs, including marijuana and amphetamines, especially before combat. In 1992, for example, a nine-year-old from the SBU surrendered to ECOMOG and reported to the Justice and Peace Commission that he had been given hallucinogenic drugs by the NPFL.[53]

During intense fighting for control of Monrovia in 1996, Howard French of the New York Times reported a chilling example of the manner in which children are deployed by all factions:

> Whenever the gun battles for control of [Monrovia] grow particularly fierce, the leaders of Liberia's warring militias, like commanders anywhere, decide that the fighting is just too intense to risk the lives of their most experienced men.
>
> The leaders do not pull back and regroup, however. Instead, the battle . . . becomes a bloody all-kid affair. . . .
>
> In one of many such firefights . . . , the adults took cover in the ruins of buildings or behind wrecked vehicles, sniping with their automatic rifles at anything that moved.
>
> Meanwhile, boys, some no older than seven or eight, were sent out to dash through the streets, making obscene gestures and dancing, with the express purpose of drawing enemy fire.[54]

ECOMOG soldiers were horrified in 1992 when they realized that the front lines of the NPFL assault against ECOMOG's positions on the perimeter of Monrovia were comprised of small children. ECOMOG soldiers reported that they were initially reluctant to return fire, but ultimately did. The children were NPFL cannon fodder.[55]

Approximately ten percent of the fighters were below fifteen years old, and many more are between fifteen and eighteen.[56] Thus, out of approximately 35,000 fighters, as many as 3500 were children. Protocol II to the Geneva Conventions prohibits the use of children under fifteen in any armed force, including non-governmental forces, and forbids their participation in hostilities.[57] All the factions to the conflict (with the exception of the AFL) were in continuous and clear violation of the Geneva Conventions, and they admit it.[58] The NPFL's ubiquitous spokesman, John T. Richardson, told Human Rights Watch:

> We did it also to protect the kids—to make sure they eat, wash and read. These kids wouldn't go to church or wash if they were left alone . . . [they] are assigned way away from combat. Only some are armed. . . . Of course, responsible people in the field recognize that mistakes have been made. Everybody has fought—planes haven't discriminated where they bombed. . . . Lots of kids and women and older people have been killed in this war.[59]

The armed children were at their most haunting at rebel checkpoints, a pervasive spectacle as they harassed passengers at key checkpoints on national highways throughout the war. The pathos and violence in the glazed visage of an orphaned rebel child, incapable of fully controlling his loaded automatic weapon let alone comprehending the drama in which he had been assigned a leading role, leaves an indelible impression on the traveler whose fate at the checkpoint rests on a child's capricious whim—and bequeaths a searing legacy to the fate of the nation.

VI. Torture

Systematic use of torture by all rebel factions to instill terror among opposing factions and civilian populations has been inherent to the conflict throughout. Each year, the US State Department's human rights report as well as reports by Amnesty International and Africa Watch document a relentless pattern of torture. The uniquely sordid, degenerate nature of these crimes is as unpleasant to recount as it is to read. It is, nevertheless, important to establish with some precision the full variety and nature of rebel conduct in order to undertake an informed analysis of the international response.

Rebels have taken a particularly keen interest, for example, in pregnant women and babies. UNOMIL's Chief of Security reported in a confidential memo to Monrovia headquarters in 1995 that

> [t]here are numerous reports of fighters moving among the displaced of various areas looking for pregnant women. When they find one they gamble on the sex of the unborn baby. They then cut the mother's womb open and pull out the baby to see who won the bet. The mother and baby are then thrown to the side of the road, as the fighters go looking for their next victim.[60]

In a separate case in which he interviewed civilian survivors of a rebel attack, the Chief of Security encountered "[a] 16–18 year old girl who was pregnant—fighters [had] jumped up and down on her stomach causing a miscarriage, she was then severely beaten."[61]

In 1994 a Liberian trauma counselor recounted a similar vignette to *Africa Report Newsmagazine:*

> A pregnant woman [was] walking toward Monrovia with her mother, father, husband, and pregnant sister. The group was ambushed by armed rebels, who publicly beheaded her husband, and then her father and mother, before subjecting her to multiple rapes. . . . The woman was forced to watch as her pregnant sister was raped, her stomach ripped open and her unborn

baby thrown into a pit latrine. She was spared, made it to Monrovia, but for months refused to utter a word. She refused to eat, went to the toilet where she sat and lost the will to live.[62]

A witness to an NPFL attack told Africa Watch in 1991, "[A] woman I knew . . . ran when the rebels came, and the rebels took her baby. They called to her in the bush and told her to come and get her baby. They shot her as she was coming, then used a cutlass [machete] and cut the baby in half."[63]

Sexual torture is also as common as it is inexplicable. In 1995, the State Department reported that "NPFL fighters in Rivercess [County] routinely tortured women by placing hot metal between their legs and forcing men to rape women. . . . Displaced persons reported that the LPC frequently burned women between their breasts . . . [and] burned men on their genitals. . . ."[64] The Justice and Peace Commission reported, "Another outrageous revelation made [to our investigators by witnesses] was that of forceful interfamily sex. That is, the father will be forced to have sex with the daughter, the mother with the son, the sister with the uncle, and so on."[65]

In a landmark 1980 case arising out of government-sponsored acts of torture in Paraguay, *Filartiga v. Peña-Irala,*[66] the US Court of Appeals for the Second Circuit held that, based on universal principles of international law prohibiting torture, those responsible for acts of torture in a foreign country are not immune from civil liability under an action brought in US courts. Judge Kaufman assigned the torturer a moniker appropriate to the Liberian case: "[T]he torturer has become like the pirate and the slave trader before him *hostis humani generis,* an enemy of all mankind."[67] The Liberian version of Judge Kaufman's *hostis humani generis* has been neither tried nor investigated—and currently governs.

VII. Cannibalism

The human rights record of the Liberian conflict reached the point of degradation whereby Liberia's most respected human rights organization found itself offering the following remarkable insight:

Cannibalism is another phenomenon attached to the bandits. The displaced . . . attested to seeing a bandit cut off a women's breast, roasting and eating it, while leaving her to die of blood-loss.. . . *Cannibalism adds a whole new dimension to human rights abuses. The right to life is based on a persecutor's appetite, and there is fear of persecution based on one's fitness for consumption.*[68]

In 1994, a UNOMIL team distributed questionnaires to 3449 demobilized fighters[69] and reported finding that "more than 3 percent (of the sample) agreed that they ate human parts at least once during the war."[70] While recognizing that the scientific rigor of the investigation is suspect, that the probability of underreporting cannibalism to UN officials is high, and that the small survey of demobilized fighters is not representative of the fighters remaining in the field, a finding of three percent of an estimated 35,000 fighters implies that 1000 fighters may have engaged in cannibalism during the war. In 1994, the US State Department referred to estimates by human rights groups that three to six percent of fighters have participated in cannibalism.[71] Even if these numbers are taken as merely an impressionistic indication of incidents of cannibalism, it is sufficient to establish an inconceivably brutal pattern.

Anecdotal evidence abounds. In a witness statement presented to the author, one victim described the following incident:

I was living in my village as a Town Chief and as a slave. I was a slave because my liberties were all ceased under the barrel of the NPFL's guns. You can see my back; I was badly beaten by the NPFL's rebels. . . . I was [once forced by the rebels] to carry 9 gallons of palm oil to the market to sell. While traveling, I heard the NPFL rebels saying to a man, "we want to buildar your engine." Immediately, I saw the NPFL fighters killed the man and removed his heart, kidneys, and livers for cooking and eating.[72]

(The translator provided the following notation on the witness statement: "'Buildar' means to cook for eating and 'Engine' is the inside organs of the human.")

The UNOMIL Chief of Security conducted a series of interviews with survivors of a massacre at Yorse Town, near Buchanan, in April 1995, in which sixty-two civilians had been hacked to death by NPFL rebels. According to the ensuing report, one witness, who had been struck by a machete and survived by lying in a pile of dead bodies until the fighters retreated, "said he saw the fighters kill a young girl, then butcher her and eat some of her body parts."[73] In its 1995 human rights report, the US State Department concluded that "[t]here were credible reports that [fighters from all active factions] committed acts of cannibalism. In some instances, the fighters ate specific organs in the belief that it would make them stronger."[74]

Reports of human sacrifice were not unheard of in Liberia before the war, including the convictions of senior governing officials of Maryland County for ritual murder in 1979.[75] These cases would often arise out of rituals performed in secret "Poro" societies of cult initiates—a rare but nevertheless recognized phenomenon in much of West Africa (as well as Haiti). A leading scholar on Liberia, Stephen Ellis, has associated Charles Taylor with such a cult:

In some cases, the appalling atrocities committed by fighters, particularly the practice of cannibalism, contain direct references to the symbolic language of Poro or similar cultic rituals. Charles Taylor himself has been reported, probably accurately according to some who know him well, to have drunk the blood of sacrificial victims. A former associate has stated that Taylor and his closest aides form an elite society known as the Top Twenty, which practises a cult of cannibalism.[76]

Anthropological analysis of the role that sadism and violence have played in the Liberian conflict is worthy of pursuit. The salient point here, however, is that the practice of cannibalism perpetrated by rebel fighters has been documented and corroborated, and was sufficiently pervasive to instill horror among vulnerable civilian populations.

VIII. Looting

Another variable that has helped to confer *sui generis* status on the Liberian war among scholars and human rights practitioners is the scope, intensity, and centrality to the conflict itself of looting. Looting took two forms. First, rebel fighters were unpaid and functioned in an extremely loose deployment, discipline, and chain-of-command regime. Operational units (roughly corresponding to a large platoon) were led by a group of adolescents who arrogated the rank of "General" and commanded what amounted to a criminal gang of younger members. Other than periodic clashes of some intensity (perhaps two or three times a year on average), these units seldom engaged opposing factions in pitched battles. Rather, they were armed by the senior, 'adult' leadership and ordered to occupy and hold small amounts of territory. They then proceeded to move from village to village, looting all available goods. Typical operations proceeded first with a scouting mission (conducted by less conspicuous child soldiers) to identify any goods of value and their ownership in a given village. The unit then 'attacked,' generally in a state of alcohol- or drug-induced intoxication, firing their weapons randomly, rounding up village elders, demanding that all valuable goods, including cash and food, be produced, and in the process, executing anyone who offered resistance and raping vulnerable women.[77]

Looted goods included harvested produce, bags of rice, cooking supplies, corrugated tin roofs, clothing, generators, medical and school supplies—anything at all of potential value. For example, the author conducted an official UNOMIL investigation in 1995 of the "Tappitta Massacre." Tension between two NPFL units as to looting rights to the town's sole power saw resulted in a lethal intrafactional firefight, execution of town leaders and civilians, and systematic looting of Tappitta. The looting included, inexplicably, medicines and laboratory equipment from the local hospital, which were of no conceivable value outside a functioning medical facility and had no apparent fungibility. Rebels simply looted whatever was available as a matter of course.

Membership in the faction conferred looting privileges for the area under occupation. Indeed, the promise of looting privileges was fundamental to the recruitment of young rebels, and was used by the leadership to motivate the young fighters. In testimony before the US House Subcommittee on Africa, Deputy Assistant Secretary of State for African Affairs Robinson made explicit reference to this theme in describing Taylor's tactics before attacking Monrovia in 1992: "In the weeks preceding the ... attack, Taylor imported tons of new weapons, then motivated his young fighters to storm the city with promises of unlimited looting if they took Monrovia."[78] As a result of these tactics, all items of any value throughout the countryside, and ultimately in Monrovia as well, have been thoroughly plundered.

In a report filed amidst the fighting and looting that destroyed Monrovia in April of 1996, the Washington Post captured the tragi-comic nature of Charles Taylor's attempt to adopt the mantle of responsible leadership while simultaneously partaking in bold-faced plunder.[79] Taylor met with rival faction leader Alhaji Kromah and reporters, purportedly to criticize the wholesale looting of Monrovia and to warn rebels of his commitment to an imposition of discipline, manifested by what he claimed was a new "shoot-on-sight" regime against looters. The problem, of course, was that Taylor and his men initiated the fighting and partook rabidly in the plunder. According to the Washington Post,

> [i]n Taylor's motorcade of bodyguards [that brought him to the news conference], whose arms run the gamut from assault rifles to four-barreled antiaircraft guns, one vehicle bore the insignia of Doctors Without Borders. The French medical organization, along with other major United Nations and nongovernmental aid agencies, ceased operations here after their offices and depots were looted. Another vehicle was so laden with booty that a heavy package wrapped in blue plastic fell off the open tailgate at a checkpoint—nearly setting off a gun battle among acquisitive young guards there.[80]

The second form of looting paid for the "tons of new weapons" referred to in Assistant Secretary Robinson's testimony. Faction leaders systematically looted the natural resources of areas under their control, sold them to unscrupulous international commercial interests, and made personal fortunes, thereby funding arms purchases, luxurious motorcade escorts, and rebel operations generally. The resources affected included virgin tropical timber forests—the yield of which fetched enormous profit on the European market; alluvial diamond mines—control over which provoked some of the most intense fighting of the war; and gold, rubber, and iron ore—the production of which was effected by recourse to forced labor.[81]

The State Department estimates that, between 1990 and 1994, Liberia's diamond exports totaled $300 million annually, timber $53 million annually, rubber $27 million annually, iron ore $43 million annually, and gold $1 million annually. In the absence of a governing authority, these revenues fell exclusively into the hands of the rebel faction in control of commodity-producing areas, with an estimated $75 million annually accruing to Taylor himself.[82] Acting US Assistant Secretary of State for African Affairs Twaddell offered the following characterization of this theme in congressional testimony in 1996: "All this leads up to a grim picture: warlords wantonly exploiting their countries' resources to keep themselves and their rag-tag forces in weapons with virtual international impunity, and in some cases, complicity."[83]

In *The Transformation of War*, a 1993 book regarded by many senior Pentagon officials as prophetic, Israeli military historian Martin van Creveld predicted that "[o]nce the legal monopoly of armed force, long claimed by the state, is wrested out of its hands, existing distinctions between war and crime will break down. . . ."[84] Van Creveld's prediction is precisely what befell Liberia after Taylor attacked in 1989. Military operations and criminal motivations have been so hopelessly intermingled as to become indistinguishable. The leading scholar on the subject of the role of unregulated and illegal commercial interests in fueling war in Liberia and Sierra Leone, William Reno, speaks for a consensus of observers in concluding that "[t]he war has been as much a battle over commerce inside and beyond Liberia's borders as it has been a battle for territory or control of the government."[85]

This nightmare prompted Thomas Friedman to characterize Liberia as "an African 'Clockwork Orange.'"[86] The pursuit of looted material—both at the operational, platoon level and at the leadership echelon—inspired the factions to systematically disassemble the infrastructure of the state, the *body politique*, and in the process, the physical corpus of the citizenry.

IX. Synopsis of Additional Cases

The preceding list enumerates specific categories of atrocities. The categories correspond loosely to classes of war crimes, grave breaches of humanitarian law, and crimes against humanity as defined in the Geneva Conventions and their additional protocols, (including intrastate conflict) further developed at Nuremberg and Tokyo, and more recently at the UN International Criminal Tribunals for the Former Yugoslavia and Rwanda. The list identifies representative examples of conduct in violation of international humanitarian law; it is not intended to be comprehensive, and does not imply that grave breaches were limited to those enumerated. Additional cases of attacks on civilian populations and violations of the laws of war abound.

Opposing factions targeted civilians with much greater frequency and ferocity than they did each other. In the words of the State Department, "[t]he leaders of the warring factions condoned, and in some cases seemingly encouraged, the murderous savagery that affected civilian populations more than the combatants."[87] For example, ECOMOG intercepted the radio transmission of an order from the NPFL leadership to commence a "reign of terror," targeting civilian populations—soon to be followed by a series of civilian massacres.[88] The NPFL referred to these tactics as "Surgical Guerilla Military Operations."[89] In 1992, as NPFL forces approached Monrovia, hundreds of civilians were executed as they fled NPFL forces and attempted to reach safety behind ECOMOG lines. One witness reported to UNOMIL investigators that NPFL rebels stated to her that orders to execute fleeing civilians came from Taylor himself.[90] During the attack on Monrovia in 1992, the NPFL fired artillery and various ordnance indiscriminately at civilian population centers, causing significant casualties.[91] In 1994, NPFL headquarters were attacked by a coalition of rebel forces and ultimately fell. Taylor and his forces retreated while perpetrating another round of executions, including binding twenty men, women, and children with rope and throwing them into a river.[92] Simultaneously, NPFL forces detained forty-three UNOMIL Military Observers and disrobed and beat them. According to the UN Secretary General's report covering the incident, the NPFL used UN personnel as a human shield to deter attacks from rival factions.[93]

It is important to reiterate that all factions were guilty of grave breaches. Indeed, two massacres that received substantial international attention, the St. Peter's Lutheran Church massacre of 600 displaced civilians in 1990 and the Harbel massacre of 600 civilians in 1993,[94] were both attributed to the AFL.[95] While the preceding survey of ethnically motivated killing, political assassinations, rape, impressment of child soldiers, torture, cannibalism, and looting has focused on the NPFL, the INPFL, AFL,[96] ULIMO-J, ULIMO-K, and LPC are all responsible for analogous abuses, and have been documented, with plentiful corroboration, as such. Tragically, there is no challenge to making the case against the Liberian factions as to war crimes; the challenge at bar is to make some sense out of the international response.

X. The Response of the International Community: the United States, the United Nations, and ECOMOG

A. The International Criminal Tribunals' Enumeration of War Crimes: Prosecutorial Discretion?

The Statute of the International Tribunal for the Prosecution of Persons Responsible for Serious Violations of International Humanitarian Law Committed in the Territory of the Former

Yugoslavia Since 1991[97] (subsequently adopted in large part by the International Criminal Tribunal for Rwanda in Arusha[98]) maintains jurisdiction over the following crimes, *inter alia:* Article 2 of the Statute, *Grave Breaches of the Geneva Conventions of 1949:* willful killing, torture or inhumane treatment, willfully causing great suffering or serious injury to body or health, extensive destruction of property not justified by military necessity and carried out unlawfully or wantonly, taking civilians as hostages;[99] Article 3, *Violations of the Laws or Customs of War:* attack, or bombardment by whatever means, of undefended towns, villages, dwellings, or buildings, plunder of public or private property;[100] Article 5, *Crimes Against Humanity:* murder, extermination, enslavement, torture, rape, persecutions on political, racial, and religious grounds.[101] (Article 4 of the Statute refers to the crime of genocide, which is not applicable to the Liberian case.[102])

As to individual criminal responsibility, the statute holds that

(1) A person who planned, instigated, ordered, committed or otherwise aided and abetted in the planning, preparation or execution of a crime referred to in articles 2 to 5 of the present Statute, shall be individually responsible for the crime. (2) The official position of any accused person, whether Head of State or Government or as a responsible Government official, shall not relieve such person of criminal responsibility nor mitigate punishment. (3) The fact that any of the acts referred to in articles 2 to 5 of the present Statute was committed by a subordinate does not relieve his superior of criminal responsibility if he knew or had reason to know that the subordinate was about to commit such acts or had done so and the superior failed to take the necessary and reasonable measures to prevent such acts or to punish the perpetrators thereof.[103]

The crimes of the Liberian case, as enumerated above, are the same crimes (with the exception of genocide) as those enumerated in the enabling statutes of the International Criminal Tribunals for Yugoslavia and for Rwanda. The point here is not to advocate that the international community ought to prosecute the leaders of the Liberian factions for war crimes (although the specter of such prosecutions would indeed be edifying). The point is, rather, to illustrate that the very conduct that, in the Bosnian and Rwandan cases, has elicited a sufficient political, diplomatic, and legal response to establish the first war crimes tribunals since Nuremberg, has been ignored *in toto* by the international community in Liberia.

It is important to note, before providing some detail as to the scope of that neglect, that both ECOWAS and the United Nations have, in their official utterances, recognized and affirmed the international legal implications of the Liberian factions' conduct in war. For example, the final communiqué of the first session of the ECOWAS Standing Mediation Committee in Banjul, 7 August 1990, read:

> The failure of the warring parties to cease hostilities has led to the massive destruction of property and the massacre by all the parties of thousands of innocent civilians including foreign nationals, women and children, some of whom had sought sanctuary in churches, hospitals, diplomatic missions and under Red Cross protection, contrary to all recognized standards of civilized behaviors.[104]

On 7 November 1992, an ECOWAS communiqué included the following language: "Heads of State and Government in the face of mounting evidence of atrocities, warned all warring factions against the commission of war crimes and crimes against humanity in Liberia."[105] Again in 1996, six years into the war, ECOWAS' rhetoric was fulsome in invoking international law by threatening sanctions for parties not in compliance with the final peace plan of 1996. ECOWAS warned that measures to be applied (hypothetically) against any defaulting party would include "[i]nvoking of the Organization of African Unity 1996 Summit resolution calling for the establishment of a war crimes tribunal to try all human rights offences against Liberians."[106]

Similarly, a team headed by the Kenyan Attorney General, Amos Waco, dispatched by the UN Secretary General to investigate the massacre at Harbel in 1992, concluded the following: "All parties to the conflict are considered to have been responsible for a pattern of gross human rights violations, including gruesome killings and mutilations, abductions, torture, cruel and inhumane treatment, arbitrary detention and other flagrant violations of humanitarian law governing the treatment of civilians in internal conflicts."[107] Indeed, in establishing the investigation, the UN Security Council requested that the Secretary General conduct a "thorough and full investigation of the massacre, including any allegations as to the perpetrators, whoever they might be."[108] The UN Security Council "warn[ed] that those found responsible for such serious violations of international humanitarian law will be held accountable for such crimes."[109]

The US government, for its part, provided a detailed enumeration of violations of international humanitarian law in its annual State Department human rights reports, but was circumspect as to invoking international law *per se* as to war crimes or crimes against humanity. One exception to this demure approach was a State Department official who slipped, in an interview with Africa Watch in 1993, and compared the fighting in 1992 to that of 1990: "It was not the same *concerted effort at ethnic cleansing*. . . . Murder was incidental to robbing."[110] Nevertheless, as quoted above, the legal implications of the State Department's official characterization of the conduct of the war are clear:

> The factions committed summary executions, torture, individual and gang rapes, mutilations, and cannibalism. They burned people alive; looted and burned cities and villages; used exces-

sive force; [and] engaged in arbitrary detentions and impressment, particularly of children under the age of 18. . . . [111]

In spite of the clarity of the facts, the recently promulgated law
at the Hague and Arusha, and the official iterations of recognition
of the gravity of the Liberian case, no action has been taken in any
meaningful manner by the international community as to prosecution, investigation, establishment of a truth commission (or
advocacy thereof), or even a frank and public attribution of criminal responsibility to any entity or attribution of individual
responsibility of any kind to any known perpetrator. From the
perspective of the international community, it is as if crimes
against humanity, grave breaches of humanitarian law, and war
crimes never happened in Liberia.

Indeed, three years into the war, the sum total of action taken
by the international community specifically addressing the
human rights catastrophe it had described in such explicit terms
was the UN Security Council's 1993 issuance of the following
mandate—the sixth of eight discrete, mandated tasks—for
UNOMIL: "To report on any major violations of international
humanitarian law to the Secretary-General."[112] No one was assigned to the job in UNOMIL, however, and the United Nations
did not address human rights issues in any manner[113] until 1995,
five years into the war, when the Secretary General was moved to
"act": "Given the frequency of reported human rights violations in
Liberia, I have decided to appoint a legal/human rights officer
to UNOMIL. This officer will, among other things, work with
UNOMIL military staff, ECOMOG, the Liberian National Transitional Government and local community groups to investigate
these reports."[114] Thus, five years after the war had started and two
years after first mandating a human rights reporting function
within UNOMIL, the United Nations finally deployed one human
rights officer.

The author commenced activities as that human rights officer in Monrovia in September 1995. Immediately upon arrival, the author was summoned to meet with UNOMIL's diplomatic and military leadership to discuss modalities for implementing the mandate. The UNOMIL leadership directed that the human rights reporting mandate be interpreted as applying to events from the arrival of the human rights officer forward; i.e., by explicit directive, the human rights record of the Liberian factions from 1990 through November 1995 was to remain officially and formally ignored by the United Nations. The Special Representative of the Secretary General (SRSG), Anthony Nyakyi of Tanzania, and his senior staff justified this directive by invoking the ubiquitous UN rationale for inaction, "the issue is very sensitive," and asserted with palpable disingenuousness that raising human rights questions carries the potential of "derailing the peace process."[115] On this spurious basis, the UNOMIL human rights officer was explicitly instructed by the SRSG to refrain from investigating, reporting, or even raising the subject of historical abuses in public or official fora.[116]

This directive was only the first in a series of successful efforts by UNOMIL senior staff to narrowly define the human rights mandate itself and to limit and impede implementation of what remained. For example, the SRSG required that any investigation into activities of the Liberian factions be authorized by the relevant faction leader. The first major case upon the author's arrival was the Tappitta massacre in December 1995, in which two factions of the NPFL ransacked the village of Tappitta. By arrangement between Taylor and the SRSG, the author and the entire UN investigative team were chaperoned by an infamously violent NPFL commander, Isaac Mussa.[117] Mussa assigned an armed NPFL "security escort" to the investigators and thereby successfully prevented any substantive independent investigation, rendering confidential witness interviews, in particular, impossible.

Additional cases were not investigated for weeks after violent incidents became known publicly, while the SRSG waited passively for the relevant faction leader to acquiesce to an investigation in his territory. Moreover, the United Nations had required itself, via Security Council mandate, to rely exclusively upon ECOMOG for armed security escort. Thus, even after faction leaders agreed to an investigation, ECOMOG officials prevented deployment by delaying or, indeed, refusing escort assistance—because of their own illicit alliances with various factions, both military and economic.

It was, nevertheless, still possible to gather detailed information about human rights abuses without conducting a rigorous, independent investigation—and even a delayed, guided tour of a massacre site, choreographed by the representatives of the perpetrators, revealed valuable information. When UN security restrictions on movement could be avoided and ECOMOG escorts bypassed, the UN reporting mechanism did begin to function and a number of quasi-investigative information-gathering exercises were indeed conducted. UNOMIL leadership insisted, however, that the resulting human rights reports (highly edited and sanitized) be sent directly to UN headquarters in New York and directed that the information not be disseminated in Liberia. Unable to function under these conditions, the author attempted to win authorization for a more robust action by presenting the following argument to UN Headquarters in New York:

> The current mandate calls upon UNOMIL to report to the Secretary General on violations of Human Rights. The problem with this aspect of the mandate is that once the reports are forwarded to New York Headquarters, the relevant parties on the ground, including the Factions, the LNTG (Liberian National Transition Government), UN agencies, international NGOs, Liberian local NGOs and Liberian citizens are not informed of the findings. Therefore, while UNOMIL's mandate is fulfilled

on a daily basis, in terms of reporting human rights issues to UN-NY, relevant parties in Liberia are left with the impression that the activity is confidential and ultimately is not relevant to the situation on the ground—i.e., UNOMIL's human rights information is immediately "exported" to New York, notwithstanding all the concerned parties in Monrovia. The Liberian human rights groups and civic bodies themselves are frustrated that the destination of the product of UNOMIL's human rights investigating function is New York and not Monrovia. It is therefore hereby recommended that a mechanism be created whereby a summary of status reports be published regularly by UNOMIL and distributed widely, such that UNOMIL's human rights mandate is rendered relevant to the parties on the ground.[118]

UN New York responded thus:

In regard to the idea of regularly publishing a summary of UNOMIL's human rights activities, while this would have certain benefits, *care should be taken to ensure that it does not have a negative impact on the peace process.* As an alternative means of publicizing UNOMIL's work on human rights, you may wish to consider the idea of holding regular meetings on the human rights situation with members of the international community to brief them of your activities and share the information you have been able to gather on human rights violations.[119]

Monrovia-based leadership, of course, interpreted this directive to mean that no human rights information was to be disseminated in any formal manner at all among the relevant actors in Liberia. Unable to function, the author resigned.[120]

Eventually, an expanded team of three human rights officers was deployed to Monrovia to monitor the crucial pre-electoral period in 1996–97. The team conducted extensive investigations of torture and execution cases, including use of sophisticated forensic evidence and comprehensive interrogations of witnesses and victims. UNOMIL leadership, however, never permitted the findings of these investigations to be made public, nor any action taken based on the findings and recommendations therein. For example, the twenty-first Progress Report of the Secretary General of January 1997 reported that UNOMIL was conducting seven ongoing human rights investigations.[121] The results of these investigations were never made public, and they resulted in no action.[122] As far as all of the relevant parties are concerned, and as a matter of public record, it is as if these investigations had never taken place.

International NGOs on the ground in Liberia, and Liberian civil society itself, were outraged that the UN human rights mechanism was calibrated toward New York—from whence emerged silence and inaction—and was irrelevant as to the actual conditions in Liberia. Ambassador Albright was aware of the United Nations' failure and, in her visit to UNOMIL and her press statements, made several references to the US government's interest in vigorous implementation of the UN human rights mandate. In the US Representative's statement of 25 January 1996 to the Security Council, Ambassador Albright said:

> When I was in Monrovia, I stressed to UNOMIL officers that in addition to monitoring the disengagement and disarmament of the combatants and assisting in their demobilization, we expect UNOMIL to follow through urgently on its other responsibilities, including investigating and reporting to the secretary-general on human rights abuses, any major violations of humanitarian law. . . . We have noted with some concern the criticism from the NGO community that UNOMIL is failing to meet these responsibilities.[123]

UNOMIL indeed failed to meet these responsibilities because

its leadership feared that any meaningful human rights *démarche* with the Liberian authorities would compromise its ability to mediate and negotiate among the protagonists. The problem with this logic is that, by 1996, six years of diplomatic and military efforts to end the conflict had failed, casualties were approaching 200,000, thousands had been tortured, the majority of Liberian civilians had been rendered refugees or displaced, and tens of thousands of women had been raped. The value of continued diplomatic relevance as a tradeoff for a frank human rights posture was demonstrably bankrupt. Further, because the United Nations had never confronted the faction leaders with a meaningful human rights critique, there was no basis upon which to conclude that a substantive human rights *démarche* would indeed preclude continued diplomatic negotiations—unproductive as they were. The United Nations simply had never attempted a robust human rights posture. Former Liberian President Amos Sawyer articulated this theme to Africa Watch in 1994: "The question of casting blame for anything—including human rights violations—is the last thing the U.N. wants to get involved in. It stands in the way of access. The U.N. is being unwittingly manipulated by the so-called parties, because it wants to maintain its relevance to those parties."[124]

B. The United States

While the United States, to its credit, publicly chided the United Nations for its failure to meaningfully address human rights, Ambassador Albright similarly refused to offer any substantive expression of a US determination to hold Liberian leaders responsible for their conduct, even if only as a rhetorical matter. For example, in a speech to the UN Security Council, Ambassador Albright congratulated herself for the following flaccid approach:

I delivered a blunt message to the Liberian leadership in Monrovia: the era of the child soldier in Liberia must come to an end—immediately. It is an outrage by any standard of civilization that children under the age of 15 and numbering between 4,000 and 6,000 are toting automatic weapons, slaughtering innocent civilians, and ignoring the rule of law. They have no identity other than through the weapons they carry. We believe UNICEF can play a key role in rehabilitating these abused children. . . . [125]

After criticizing the United Nations' human rights passivity and introducing the subject of a profound human rights disaster in Liberia—the use of child soldiers—Ambassador Albright then failed to articulate any explicit human rights critique of her own. She proffered no conclusions as to responsibility for the recruitment, armament, and command of the child soldiers to which she referred with such umbrage. Instead of denouncing this blatant violation of international law by naming the responsible parties, Charles Taylor, George Boley, Alhaji Kromah, and Roosevelt Johnson, Ambassador Albright chose instead, at the climax of her remarks, to offer a weak plea for rehabilitation assistance from a UN agency. If it is an outrage for child soldiers to be carrying guns, who recruited, armed, and commanded them? The United States justifiably criticized the feeble UN approach to human rights but simultaneously failed to undertake its own leadership responsibility—at the very least, to clearly delineate responsibility and to condemn perpetrators by name. At what cost would making an official US condemnation a part of the public record come?

The US approach was consistently passive, even in its rhetoric, throughout the war. US officials frequently expressed general outrage at the carnage, but never explicitly characterized the human rights situation as amounting to war crimes or crimes against humanity. No individual responsibility for the conduct of the war was ever attributed to any individual leader or malfeasant actor.

C. The Africa Watch Approach

The problem of empty human rights rhetoric is not limited to the United Nations and the US government. The orthodox human rights groups, led by Amnesty International and Africa Watch, did an admirable job of documenting human rights violations in Liberia throughout the war; indeed, this article relies heavily on that documentation. These organizations failed entirely, however, to offer any realistic, pragmatic, meaningful program, plan, or strategy to actually address human rights abuses on the ground. Neither did the human rights groups undertake any vigorous or effective advocacy for an international response, including the most realistic option—formation of an internationally sponsored truth commission.

Instead, these organizations tended to advocate that abstract, ideal standards be met and to articulate aspirational human rights goals that had no hope of actually being implemented in the real world. The moral authority of the message was thereby neutered, and relevant parties could easily and blithely ignore the toothless critique *in toto,* without repercussion. The result is that the work product of the international human rights groups ultimately amounts to human rights cheerleading, in which righteous ideals are articulated, but no pragmatic program for action proffered, nor any results-oriented advocacy effected. In the process, it is difficult to ascertain precisely how victims of human rights abuses are actually served by fanciful references to the international covenants[126] and whimsical human rights cheerleading.

A good example of the theme—all too familiar and a source of enormous frustration for human rights officers who are actually operating at the field level—comes from an Africa Watch recommendation in 1997, advocating domestic legal accountability for human rights crimes in Liberia:

Accountability for Human Rights Abuses: Having come out of a situation of brutal conflict in which civilians were overwhelmingly targeted by all factions, there is a need for the government to take steps to hold those responsible for committing gross abuses of human rights accountable for their crimes. Reconciliation and rebuilding efforts will continue to be haunted by the fact that there has been no punishment for those who have committed some of the most unimaginable atrocities. Unfortunately, international efforts to negotiate peace in Liberia dispensed with accountability in an effort to find a political solution.... Human Rights Watch/Africa believes that those who commit gross abuses of human rights should be held accountable for their crimes. It is the responsibility of governments to seek accountability regardless of whether the perpetrators of such abuses are officials of the government itself.[127]

In a 1993 publication advocating the same approach, Africa Watch added the following caveat:

Africa Watch recognizes the difficulty that some governments may face in holding members of their own armed forces accountable for human rights abuses, but we do not believe that these difficulties justify disregard for the principle of accountability. Despite these obstacles, the alternative is far worse. *It is important to note that our position calling for investigation, prosecution and punishment of those responsible for gross abuses is premised on a reconstituted court system that would conform to internationally recognized principles of due process of law.*[128]

These recommendations were wholly ignored by all relevant actors because they are devoid of meaning for two reasons. First, the Taylor Government, to which the 1997 recommendations are addressed, is constituted by the leadership of Taylor's NPFL, the party most substantially implicated in war crimes, as personified most emphatically by Taylor himself. Thus, the probability that Taylor would recognize the persuasive logic of Africa Watch's argument, hold himself accountable for his crimes, and turn himself in to the Monrovia Central Prison and the Jurisdiction of the Liberian National Police is rather low, at least on this earth in this lifetime. Indeed, the idea of Taylor or any of his Ministers turning themselves in to the custody of the Chief of Police, Joseph Tate, Taylor's cousin and one of the most notoriously abusive NPFL operatives throughout the war, is actually quite comical.

Secondly, Africa Watch notes that its advocacy of domestic criminal proceedings against these war criminals is dependent on a reconstituted court system that would conform to the standards of due process. It would be interesting to know precisely to which reconstituted system Africa Watch refers. The Liberian criminal justice system before the war—under a recognized, peacetime, civilian government—failed miserably to meet international standards of due process and was justifiably documented as such by the US State Department and Africa Watch itself.[129] It is therefore hopelessly unrealistic, *a fortiori,* to imagine that trials could conceivably meet such standards when the government has collapsed, courts have ceased to function, and discipline is consigned to marauding rebel faction commanders, many still in their teens and most under the influence of an ugly cocktail of narcotics, cane juice, and voodoo.

Rather than squandering the potentially constructive effect of the moral authority of human rights advocacy on an inane and utterly unrealistic, legalistic proposal, Africa Watch would have done better to simply state that based on the facts and the law, Charles Taylor, Alhaji Kromah, George Boley, Roosevelt Johnson, and their senior commanders are responsible for war crimes, and all international contact with these figures should be constrained by, and calibrated to, an appropriate level of opprobrium. Or, even better, Africa Watch could have deployed its considerable personnel resources, fundraising capacity, and press relations apparatus to provide, for example, direct counseling, material support, advocacy, and protective services *in Liberia* for rape victims, displaced persons, and traumatized child soldiers.

In a land of dismembered, decaying, cannibalized bodies, Africa Watch's wholly unreal legal advocacy is meaningless and irrelevant. If the goal is to take, and be perceived as taking, a highly righteous public position on another peoples' tragedy, Africa Watch perhaps succeeds here; if the goal is to participate meaningfully in addressing the human rights catastrophe of actual human beings in Liberia, human rights cheerleading is an egregious dereliction of duty.

In sum, while State Department human rights reports and periodic reports from Africa Watch and Amnesty International have documented abuses, neither the United Nations, nor United States, nor the international human rights groups have actually addressed the violations, violators, or victims in any pragmatic, substantial, or effective manner. In direct contrast to the Bosnian and Rwandan cases, no entity has made the fundamental first step of effective human rights work, matching the abuse with the name of the abuser. Though international law has been violated blatantly and evoked rhetorically, no entity has attached an individual's name to a crime. It is fair to conclude that there has been no human rights response from the international community to the war in Liberia. Evil Triumphant.

D. Enter Nigeria

It is a sad commentary on the salience of human rights in the Liberian context that the only entity to take any significant action based on even a spurious human rights rationale was the Nigerian-led West African peacekeeping force, ECOMOG. ECOMOG explicitly justified its armed intervention based on the scope of violence suffered by Liberian civilians. In practice, however—not surprisingly, given the abusive nature of the sponsoring Nigerian regime—the seven-year ECOMOG intervention actually prolonged the war, exacerbated the carnage, and manifested myriad indicia of absence of good-faith humanitarian bona fides: ECOMOG used rival Liberian factions as surrogates, with murderous consequences; violated the laws of war; participated in the transshipment of narcotics; engaged in corruption so endemic and systematic as to impugn the motives for intervention; and avoided accountability and transparency.

In 1992, for example, Nigerian Air Force Alpha jets conducted an indiscriminate aerial bombing campaign in NPFL territory, targeting civilian entities protected under intentional law, such as medical facilities, humanitarian supply warehouses, and civilians themselves.[130] ECOMOG soldiers also tortured and executed civilians. According to the State Department's human rights report for 1997 alone,

> there were a number of incidents in which individual ECOMOG soldiers killed civilians. . . . In May during a cordon-and-search operation for illegal weapons . . . ECOMOG soldiers tortured and murdered two men. In June ECOMOG soldiers also beat to death a man . . . while interrogating him. . . . During several cordon-and-search operations in which ECOMOG arrested, interrogated, and shot several former combatants, ECOMOG left the victims, who in some cases suffered life-threatening injuries, untreated. . . . [131]

Nigerian officers used Liberia, particularly the Freeport in Monrovia, as a transshipment point in the global Nigerian narcotics trafficking enterprise. In addition, ECOMOG soldiers not only availed themselves of prostitutes, but did so abusively and coercively, including girls as young as eight years old.[132]

However, the most egregious human rights issue was ECO-

MOG's use of proxy factions as peacekeeping surrogates. As enumerated in detail above, the Liberian factions perpetrated atrocities of the most grave order on Liberian civilians. At various points in the war, ECOMOG sponsored, supported, and armed these factions. Indeed, the brutal course of the war can be traced via ECOMOG's shifting alliances among the various Liberian factions, some of whom ECOMOG actually helped create. Initially, ECOMOG's natural allies were Doe's AFL and the NPFL's first rival, the INPFL. Under a series of early peace agreements, AFL forces were officially confined to barracks in Monrovia, and the INPFL had proven to be dangerously untrustworthy. ECOMOG therefore facilitated the emergence of two new factions, the United Liberation Movement of Liberia (ULIMO) and the Liberian Peace Council (LPC). ULIMO pressured the NPFL from the Northwest, and the LPC engaged from the Southeast. ULIMO eventually split into ethnically based rival factions (ULIMO-J and ULIMO-K), again with ECOMOG encouragement, and the civil war stalemated. ECOMOG was thus fully implicated as all factions perpetrated ethnic massacres, political assassinations, torture, rape, cannibalism, and systematic looting.

E. The United Nations Sees No Evil

No entity exists in West Africa with sufficient authority to constrain Nigerian conduct. Into this vacuum the United Nations might have stepped constructively and effectively. Indeed, ECOMOG was operating in Liberia under a UN imprimatur. The UN Security Council never formally authorized the ECOMOG intervention under the regional enforcement provisions of Chapter VIII of the UN Charter. Yet, when the Security Council authorized the deployment of UNOMIL to monitor the peace process in coordination with ECOMOG, the Security Council did note "that this would be the first peace-keeping mission undertaken by the United Nations in cooperation with a peace-keeping mission already set up by another organization, in this case ECOWAS."[133] And in 1993, the Secretary General noted that Liberia was "an example of systematic ... cooperation between the United Nations and [a] regional [entity], as envisaged in Chapter VIII of the Charter."[134]

Nevertheless, the ECOMOG intervention was characterized by the total absence of human rights accountability and transparency internally, exacerbated by derelict monitoring from the United Nations. One telling example, among many, of the manner in which ECOMOG handled any effort to hold it accountable— and UN impotence in response—arose out of widespread accusations in 1996 of executions during ECOMOG cordon-and-search operations to locate and disarm rebel forces. UN human rights investigators succeeded in locating the grave of one execution victim and assembled comprehensive evidence of the culpability of ECOMOG soldiers. The UN investigators filed their report with the United Nations' envoy to Liberia. The Special Representative of the Secretary General, Anthony Nyakyi, though generally disinclined to confront ECOMOG in any manner, was forced by the detailed nature of the evidence to submit the report to ECOMOG leadership, with an emphatically gentle and diplomatic request for a response. The response came immediately: ECOMOG guards protecting the UN headquarters (under Security Council mandate to offer such protection) were withdrawn. The ECOMOG Force Commander, General Victor Malu, then informed Ambassador Nyakyi that, because the United Nations had concluded that ECOMOG soldiers were human rights violators, the guards would stand down until the United Nations offered them a comprehensive human rights training course. Only upon completion of such a (nonexistent) course would the United Nations benefit from ECOMOG protection. The SRSG hastily met with Malu, and apologized for any misunderstanding; the guards returned, and the investigation was dropped.[135]

Another manifestation of its willful avoidance of accountability was ECOMOG's steadfast refusal, throughout its seven-year presence, to enter into a Status of Forces Agreement (SOFA), despite having explicitly committed to do so in a series of duly signed peace agreements.[136] The SOFA is a basic contractual document defining the power, authority, and limitations of an intervening military force in relation to the sovereign powers of the host nation. It is entered into, as a matter of course, at the earliest feasible stage of any UN intervention. Without a SOFA, and in the absence of strong sovereign institutions, the authority of an intervening force is, hypothetically, limitless and begins to resemble the status of an occupying force. ECOMOG exploited this authority and regularly apprehended and detained, often *incommunicado,* a broad spectrum of Liberians, including suspected rebel fighters, politicians, journalists, and attractive women who were unfortunate enough to stand accused of curfew violations.

In one well-publicized case, ECOMOG apprehended an NPFL associated politician, Peter Jallah, and detained him for eighteen months without charge.[137] The Center for Law and Human Rights Education petitioned the Liberian Supreme Court for release of the detainee under a writ of *habeas corpus.* The Supreme Court held that, in the absence of a SOFA conferring such authority, ECOMOG "as a peacekeeping force has no legal right to arrest and detain any citizen. . . . [Such arrest is] unconstitutional and therefore illegal."[138] While Jallah was eventually released as a result of this ruling, ECOMOG continued to apprehend and detain hundreds of Liberians without charge or due process, demonstrating ECOMOG's refusal to recognize any authority superior to its own, including remnant vestiges of Liberian sovereignty such as the Supreme Court.[139]

At the policy level, the United Nations never confronted ECOMOG on any of these important points. By failing to address abuses, monitor effectively, or constrain ECOMOG legally, the

UN Secretariat in New York squandered the authority it might have constructively wielded to constrain ECOMOG and bring it into conformity with international standards. For example, the Security Council could have offered to authorize a formal, Chapter VIII intervention, on the condition that ECOMOG meet minimum UN standard operating procedures, such as signing a SOFA, issuing a specific mandate distinguishing between peacekeeping and peace enforcement authority, promulgating rules of engagement, and deploying a civilian apparatus to address political and legal issues in Liberia—each of which is a *sine qua non* for UN peacekeeping missions. By implying support, but demanding nothing in return and maintaining sufficient ambiguity for ECOWAS to exploit, the Security Council adopted the least effective and weakest bargaining position conceivable. Nigeria and ECOWAS could thus claim full UN authority, but avoided any imposition of discipline and legality. In sum, the United Nations conferred legitimate peacekeeping status on a precedent-setting regional intervention without demanding that any conditions be met to qualify for such status.

Operating on the same negotiating principle of preemptive capitulation, once the UNOMIL observer mission itself was in place in Liberia in 1994, UNOMIL failed to use its monitoring authority on the ground to any constructive effect. At the request of the Security Council in periodically reviewing its operations, the Secretary General has published twenty-three "progress reports" on Liberia. These reports are drafted by the mission in the field and edited at UN Headquarters in New York for the signature of the Secretary General and are the principal vehicle for expression of UN policy for active peacekeeping operations. The contents of these reports are read closely by relevant parties for indications of policy nuance, and the wording of the reports is thus subject to substantial debate among various UN officials competing for policy influence. In none of the twenty-three progress reports did the UN explicitly criticize ECOMOG conduct, despite full knowledge of ECOMOG culpability for executions, indiscriminate bombing, support for rival Liberian factions, and systematic corruption. Indeed, in the context of UNOMIL's reluctance to investigate meaningfully and report on numerous cases of ECOMOG executions, Africa Watch made the following remarkable charge: "The failure of UNOMIL to investigate these incidents and to release these reports raises questions as to whether the U.N. has played a part in covering up human rights violations committed by ECOMOG soldiers."[140]

Among the United Nations' most oft-cited achievements is sponsorship of an ever-expanding series of international instruments purporting to create a panoply of specific, legally binding human rights protections and guarantees. Where the rubber meets the road, however, the United Nations is as reluctant to confront human rights abuses as is the average government. The United Nations' willingness to capitulate to ECOMOG's ardor for full operational control and unchallenged authority in the field ultimately created a scenario whereby the United Nations itself could credibly be accused by a recognized US human rights organization of actually covering up human rights violations. The United Nations' legacy in Liberia must include this dereliction of duty. (It is worth noting that despite the gravity of Africa Watch's accusation that the United Nations participated in covering up evidence of ECOMOG human rights abuses, publication of the accusation had no observable effect on any relevant actor—the accusation did not even elicit a denial.)

The fainthearted character of the United Nations' supervisory and monitoring role over ECOMOG is apparent in the following passage from an internal report submitted to headquarters by a UN advance team mandated to evaluate the situation on the ground in 1993, in preparation for deployment of the UN observer mission in 1994:

ECOMOG's perception of its impartiality: ECOMOG is extremely sensitive to any suggestion that they are not impartial, and anything but a professional military, peacekeeping motivation drives their actions. These sensitivities are very close to the surface and, while we must continue to publicly stress the role of UNOMIL to be one of verifying complete neutrality, *any suggestion that ECOMOG is anything but a professional peacekeeping force should be publicly avoided.*[141]

As this passage demonstrates, the United Nations' policy of demurring from any public critique of ECOMOG was not analyzed, it was simply asserted: public criticism of ECOMOG should be avoided. Ambassador Anthony Nyakyi, the United Nations' envoy to Liberia from 1994 to 1996, for example, responded to any negative information about ECOMOG conduct with a rote recitation that the United Nations was ECOMOG's partner and any confrontation would "derail the peace process." This was followed by the UN diplomat's ubiquitous rhetorical substitute for analysis: "the issue is very sensitive." The precise manner in which a public critique of ECOMOG would derail the peace process was never made clear. Indeed, the Ambassador seemed to interpret his role primarily as a spokesman for and defender of ECOMOG's position. ECOMOG's myriad operational dysfunctions were therefore never addressed by the United Nations—and thus were never solved.

In one comic scene at a tense staff meeting, days before heavy fighting erupted in Monrovia in 1996 (which ultimately killed as many as 3000 civilians),[142] the Ambassador scolded his staff for emphasizing a report that ECOMOG had permitted Taylor's NPFL cadres to enter Monrovia heavily armed and that the ECOMOG had established arms caches throughout the city. The Ambassador instructed his staff not to discuss intelligence that ECOMOG had permitted these arms caches to develop because "such talk is not helpful to the peace process."[143] One exasperated junior staff member queried, "Yes Sir, but what about the arms caches themselves? Are they helpful to the peace process?"[144]

This passivity rendered no service to the peace process, to the Liberian people, or, ultimately, to ECOMOG itself. In any large, bureaucratic organization, there is a range in the degree of professionalism. A constructive critique from an entity with the moral authority (or at least neutral objectivity) of the United Nations could have strengthened the hand of reformers and professionals within ECOMOG. Passivity and silence in the face of gross and obvious malfeasance, however, only served to embolden corrupt and undisciplined elements. If ECOMOG could quite literally get away with murder under the noses of UN officials, why should a potential reformer within ECOMOG risk his career to attempt to restrain misconduct? If the United Nations was silent amidst obvious malfeasance, why should an unscrupulous officer resist the temptation to loot? The only entity with the capacity to restrain ECOMOG in Liberia was the United Nations; its failure to do so facilitated ECOMOG's corruption and abusive conduct.

This pattern is, of course, not unique to Liberia. The cowardice of UN officials in grasping the destructive and debilitating consequences of the organization's passive capitulation to evil, under the cover of a misguided rendition of "diplomacy," is directly responsible for the United Nations' precipitous loss of credibility on the ground from Cambodia to Rwanda to Bosnia and beyond.

XI. Conclusion: Whither Universalism?

Human rights advocates and UN officials offered themselves fulsome praise and congratulations at the World Conference on Human Rights in 1993 for including in the final Vienna Declaration the assertion that "[t]he universal nature of these [human] rights and freedoms is beyond question."[145] Specific controversy at the conference over "universalism" arose out of an important but abstruse debate between the human rights community and leaders of a few authoritarian Asian states who argue that collectivist "Asian values" somehow supercede the specific tenets of the human rights doctrine.[146]

The principle at stake, however, is profound. One overly fecund laboratory for inquiry into the international community's sincerity in undertaking to act upon the principle of the universality of human rights is the oldest republic on the African continent. Liberia has no strategic importance. It enjoys no diplomatic or political cachet in international circles. Liberia's immediate environs are bereft of the intercontinental air facilities, luxury hotels, and exotic "rest and recreation" destinations that tend to attract journalists and itinerant young human rights activists. Liberia and its human rights catastrophe have, therefore, been ignored by the media, scholars, the human rights community, the United States, and the United Nations.

Between 1990 and 1997, approximately 200,000 Liberian citizens were killed in war; between 1992 and 1995, approximately 200,000 citizens of the Former Yugoslavia were killed in war.[147] Both wars included brutal campaigns of ethnic cleansing, executions, torture, rape, and destruction of civilian targets. War crimes in the Balkans prompted the United Nations to form the first war crimes tribunal since Nuremberg and to deploy batteries of human rights monitors, forensic pathologists, lawyers, and criminal investigators. War crimes in Liberia prompted the United Nations to take no action whatsoever—even a wholly rhetorical condemnation of the perpetrators was beyond the United Nations' will. Same moment in history, same number of casualties, same war crimes. Whither universalism?

ENDNOTES

Human Rights Quarterly 21 (1999) 265–307 © 1999 by The Johns Hopkins University Press
Kenneth L. Cain has served as a human rights officer on UN peacekeeping operations in Somalia, Rwanda, Haiti, and Liberia, and as a monitor for the International Human Rights Law Group in Cambodia. He holds a J.D. from Harvard Law School. The author wrote this article while serving as an International Affairs Fellow in residence at the Council on Foreign Relations in New York, and would like to thank the Council for its research support.

1. *Genesis* 34:1–31 (excerpted).
2. Jeffrey Goldberg, *Without Purpose in a Country Without Identity*, N.Y. Times, 22 Jan. 1995, § 6, at 37.
3. Charles Taylor, Address at Monrovia, Liberia (5 Nov. 1995) (transcript on file with author).
4. Howard W. French, *Ledger for Liberia's War: Profit(eering) and Loss*, N.Y. Times, 30 Apr. 1996, at A8.
5. The author was introduced to this quotation posted on the office wall of Liberia's leading Human Rights advocate, Samuel Koffi Woods of the Justice and Peace Commission, October 1995.
6. Primo Levi, If This is a Man: Remembering Auschwitz 65 (1986).
7. Estimation of casualties is an enormously unscientific enterprise. The US Department of State estimates 200,000 casualties for Liberia, *see* U.S. Dep't of State, *Liberia*, in Country Reports on Human Rights Practices for 1997, at 181 (1998) [hereinafter 1997 Report on Liberia], and as many as 263,000 in the former Yugoslavia, *see* U.S. Dep't of State, *Bosnia and Herzegovina*, in Country Reports on Human Rights Practices for 1995, at 791 (1996). Most American media sources use an esti-

mate of 200,000 casualties for the former Yugoslavia, but the International Committee for the Red Cross, among others, has challenged this figure and estimates a much lower casualty figure. *See* Peter Cary, *Bosnia by the Numbers,* U.S. News & World Rep., 10 Apr. 1995, at 53. Nevertheless, the analysis here takes as its point of departure the international response to the two analogous wars, and thus, analogous casualty estimates, regardless of the scientific accuracy, are comparable as to the impact the estimates have or have not had on the international community.

8. Independent National Patriotic Front of Liberia.

9. Armed Forces of Liberia.

10. Economic Community of West African States Cease-Fire Monitoring Group.

11. *See* U.S. Dep't of State, *Liberia, in* Country Reports on Human Rights Practices for 1996, at 147, 149 (1997) [hereinafter 1996 Report on Liberia].

12. Liberia Peace Council.

13. United Liberation Movement for Democracy in Liberia-Kromah.

14. United Liberation Movement for Democracy in Liberia-Johnson.

15. 1996 Report on Liberia, *supra* note 11, at 149.

16. The one exception to this lack of analysis is the courageous work of Samuel Koffi Woods and the Justice and Peace Commission, which has published a long and substantial series of human rights analyses. Unfortunately, however, it is difficult for most scholars to access this body of work outside of Liberia.

17. *See* The Justice and Peace Commission of The National Catholic Secretariat of Liberia, The Liberian Crisis 14 (1994) [hereinafter The Liberian Crisis].

18. *See* Herbert Howe, *Lessons of Liberia, ECOMOG and Regional Peacekeeping,* 21 Int'l Security, Winter 1996–97, at 145, 148.

19. U.S. Dep't of State, *Liberia, in* Country Reports on Human Rights Practices for 1990, at 192, 196 (1991) [hereinafter 1990 Report on Liberia].

20. 1990 Report on Liberia, *supra* note 19, at 196.

21. Confidential witness statement presented to the author, April 1996, Monrovia, Liberia (document on file with author).

22. *Liberia: The Cycle of Abuse: Human Rights Violations Since the November Cease-Fire,* Hum. Rts. Watch/Afr., October 1991, at 6 [hereinafter *The Cycle of Abuse*].

23. *See* U.S. Dep't of State, *Liberia, in* Country Reports on Human Rights Practices for 1992, at 135, 142 (1993) [hereinafter 1992 Report on Liberia].

24. William O'Neill, *Liberia: An Avoidable Tragedy,* 92 Current Hist. 213, 215 (1993).

25. *See id.* at 215–16.

26. The Liberian Crisis, *supra* note 17, at 17–18.

27. Throble K. Suah, *Dokie's Whereabouts Still Unknown,* Inquirer (Monrovia), 3 Dec. 1997, at 1.

28. *See Cold Bloody Murder,* Nat'l Chron. (Monrovia), 6 Dec. 1997, at 1.

29. Howard W. French, *Liberia Waits: Which Charles Taylor Won?,* N.Y. Times, 17 Jan. 1998, at A3.

30. *See* Amnesty International, Liberia: A New Peace Agreement—An Opportunity to Introduce Human Rights Protection 17 (1995) (A.I. Index AFR 34/01/95).

31. *See* 1996 Report on Liberia, *supra* note 11, at 149.

32. 1992 Report on Liberia, *supra* note 23, at 136.

33. *See* U.S. Dep't of State, *Liberia, in* Country Reports on Human Rights Practices for 1994, at 132, 134 (1995) [hereinafter 1994 Report on Liberia].

34. *See* 1990 Report on Liberia, *supra* note 19, at 196. An "ECOMOG national" is a national of a country that contributed troops to ECO-MOG.

35. *See The Cycle of Abuse, supra* note 22, at 13.

36. Economic Community of West African States, ECOMOG's diplomatic sponsor and parent organization.

37. It is interesting to note that one year hence, on the other side of the continent, Mohamed Farah Aideed of Somalia became the subject of an approximation of an international arrest warrant, as mandated by the UN Security Council, and a concerted US-led manhunt on the basis of similar conduct—ambushing and killing twenty-four Pakistani Peacekeepers: prosecutorial discretion. *See* U.S. Dep't of State, *Somalia, in* Country Reports on Human Rights Practices for 1993, at 258, 259 (1994).

38. *See* The Liberian Crisis, *supra* note 17, at 47.

39. *See Rape—A Silent Scourge of the Liberian Conflict,* World Health Org. Newsl. (WHO Office, Monrovia, Liberia), Apr.–June 1995, at 1, 4 (on file with author) [hereinafter WHO Newsl.].

40. Liberian rapists did not distinguish between women and girls.
41. Amnesty International, *supra* note 30, at 8–9.
42. Estimates of the number of fighters have fluctuated wildly depending on the interests of the putative analyst. For example, when the United Nations was attempting to raise money, fighter estimates were high, as many as 53,537, *see* UNOMIL Demobilization Unit, Liberia Disarmament/Demobilization Plan (Dec. 1995) (restricted circulation document on file with author) [hereinafter UNOMIL Demobilization Plan], but then celebrated as a success was the 1996 demobilization of approximately 21,000 fighters. *See* 1997 Report on Liberia, *supra* note 7, at 182. No one assumes that all of the fighters were demobilized in 1996, and throughout the war a realistic figure seemed to be 40,000. The author uses the figure 35,000 as a conservative, compromise estimate.
43. United Nations Observer Mission in Liberia.
44. *See* UNOMIL Demobilization Plan, *supra* note 42, at 48, 52. The authors of the relevant section on rape noted that "[t]he analysis provided here is based on information attained from combatants during the general demobilization of 1994." *Id.*
45. Confidential witness statement provided to the author, Monrovia, Liberia, Nov. 1995 (on file with author).
46. Confidential witness statement provided to the author, Monrovia, Liberia, Nov. 1995 (on file with author).
47. Confidential witness statement provided to the author, Monrovia, Liberia, Nov. 1995 (on file with author).
48. WHO Newsl., *supra* note 39, at 1.
49. Author's Memorandum to Ambassador Anthony Nykayi, UNOMIL Special Representative to the Secretary General, *Mission Report: Bo, Tienni, Sinje and Dia* 3 (1 Mar. 1996) (on file with author).
50. One newspaper account of the torture and execution of opposition politician Samuel Dokie, *see supra* Part III, included the following account of the treatment of Dokie's wife and niece by their executioners before they died: "Mr. and Mrs. Dokie were reportedly taken to Kokoya road where Mrs. Dokie was violently raped by four men before her womb came out and [was] killed in the fore view of her husband. Dokie was later beheaded and body burnt while his car was set ablaze. Serena Dokie and Emmanuel Voker were according to reports taken to Geneive Town where Serena was also reported raped before flogging

them to death." *Cold Bloody Murder,* Nat'l Chron. (Monrovia), 6 Dec. 1997, at 1.

51. *See* Stephen Ellis, *Liberia 1989–1994: A Study of Ethnic and Spiritual Violence,* 94 Afr. Aff. 165 (1995).

52. Human Rights Watch, Easy Prey: Child Soldiers in Liberia 32 (1994) [hereinafter Easy Prey].

53. *See* The Liberian Crisis, *supra* note 17, at 69.

54. Howard W. French, *When the Gun Play Kills the Kids' Play,* N.Y. Times, 12 May 1996, §4, at 3.

55. *See* Easy Prey, *supra* note 52, at 24.

56. *See id.* at 2–3.

57. Protocol II Additional to the Geneva Convention of 12 Aug. 1949, and Relating to the Protection of Victims of Non-International Armed Conflicts, *adopted* 8 June 1977, U.N. Doc. A/32/144, art. 4, ' 3(c), 1125 U.N.T.S. 513 (*entered into force* 7 Dec. 1978), *reprinted in* 16 I.L.M. 1442 (1977).

58. The NPFL's abuses were uniquely egregious, however, in inaugurating the use of small children upon commencement of hostilities, in institutionalizing their use within the Small Boys Units, and in the national scope of NPFL operations throughout the war.

59. Easy Prey, *supra* note 52, at 21–22.

60. Confidential Report of the UNOMIL Chief of Security to UNOMIL Headquarters, Monrovia, Liberia 12 (24 May 1995) (on file with author) [hereinafter UNOMIL Confidential Report]; *see also* Amnesty International, *supra* note 30, at 11.

61. UNOMIL Confidential Report, *supra* note 60, at 11.

62. Peter Da Costa, *Counselling Victims of the Civil War,* Afr. Rep. Newsmagazine, Mar.–Apr. 1994, at 30, 31.

63. *The Cycle of Abuse, supra* note 22, at 5.

64. U.S. Dep't of State, *Liberia, in* Country Reports on Human Rights Practices for 1995, at 140, 144 (1996) [hereinafter 1995 Report on Liberia].

65. The Justice and Peace Commission of the National Catholic Secretariat of Liberia, Report on Fact-Finding Mission to Gbarnga 3 (14–17 July 1994) [hereinafter Gbarnga Report].

66. 630 F.2d 876 (2d Cir. 1980).

67. *Id.* at 890.

68. Gbarnga Report, *supra* note 65, at 4 (emphasis added).

69. *See supra* Part IV.

70. UNOMIL Demobilization Plan, *supra* note 42, at 52.

71. *See* 1994 Report on Liberia, *supra* note 33, at 137.

72. Confidential witness statement provided to the author, Monrovia, Liberia, Nov. 1995 (on file with author).

73. UNOMIL Confidential Report, *supra* note 60, at 11.

74. 1995 Report on Liberia, *supra* note 64, at 144.

75. *See* Ellis, *supra* note 51, at 190.

76. *Id.* at 192 (footnote omitted).

77. *See* Amnesty International, *supra* note 30, at 14.

78. Deputy Assistant Secretary of State for African Affairs Robinson, Address to the House Committee for African Affairs (19 November 1992), *in* The Liberian Crisis, *supra* note 17, at 170, 172 [hereinafter Robinson Address].

79. This is a recurring Taylor motif: to orchestrate chaos then to present himself as the only leader capable of imposing order.

80. Jonathan C. Randal, *Militia Chiefs in Liberia Assail Looting; Aid Donors Demand End to Lawlessness,* Wash. Post, 16 Apr. 1996, at A10.

81. Indeed, Liberians consistently referred to incidents of forced labor, particularly in relation to palm oil production, performed by civilians under threat of violence from rebel fighters. The State Department specifically cited NPFL leadership with responsibility for operating involuntary labor camps in Grand Gedeh County. 1992 Report on Liberia, *supra* note 23, at 139. One victim submitted the following testimonial statement: "The NPFL commanded me to provide them with palm oil and meat for eating. Due to my failure to provide these, I was badly beaten and wounded. We have always been forced to wash the NPFL clothes, clean their yards, and carried loads on our heads at six or seven hours distance walk." Confidential witness statement provided to the author, Monrovia, Liberia, Nov. 1995 (on file with author).

82. *See* Testimony by William H. Twaddell, Acting Assistant Secretary of State for African Affairs: Hearing on Liberia Before the House International Relations Committee, 26 June 1996, *available in* Charles W. Corey, *US Faces Dilemma in Liberia,* USIA File ID 96062702.AAF, 27 June 1996, <gopher://gopher.state.gov:70/00ftp%3ADOSFan%3AGopher%3A04%20Geographic%20Bureaus%3A03%20Africa%3A01%20Releases%20-%20Statements%3A960626%20Twaddell%20-%20Liberia> [hereinafter Twaddell Testimony].

83. *Id.*

84. Martin van Creveld, The Transformation of War 204 (1991).

85. William Reno, *The Business of War in Liberia, in* Current Hist. 211 (1996).

86. Thomas L. Friedman, *Heart of Darkness,* N.Y. Times, 21 Jan. 1996, § 4, at 15.

87. 1994 Report on Liberia, *supra* note 33, at 133–34.

88. *See* U.S. Dep't of State, *Liberia, in* Country Reports on Human Rights Practices for 1993, at 148, 152 (1994) [hereinafter 1993 Report on Liberia].

89. *See* The Liberian Crisis, *supra* note 17, at 72.

90. Confidential witness statement provided to the author, Monrovia, Liberia, Apr. 1996 (on file with author).

91. *See* Robinson Address, *supra* note 78, at 172. According to Amnesty International, "thousands" were killed by the shelling. Amnesty International, *supra* note 30, at 16.

92. *See* Amnesty International, *supra* note 30, at 17.

93. *See id.*

94. The Harbel Massacre also spurred a formal UN investigation. United Nations Panel of Inquiry, Report: The Carter Camp Massacre, Results of an Investigation into the Massacre near Harbel, Liberia on the night of June 5/6, 1993 (1993) (restricted circulation document on file with author) [hereinafter Harbel Report]. An Executive Summary of this report is available in Regional Peace-Keeping and International Enforcement: The Liberian Crisis 382 (Marc Weller ed., 1994).

95. *See* 1990 Report on Liberia, *supra* note 19, at 192; Harbel Report, *supra* note 94, ¶ 71–72.

96. The AFL did not recruit child soldiers.

97. *Report of the Secretary-General Pursuant to Paragraph 2 of Security Council Resolution 808 (1993),* U.N. SCOR, Annex, U.N. Doc. S/25704 (1993), *reprinted in* 32 I.L.M. 1163, 1192 (1993).

98. *See generally* Payam Akhavan, *The International Criminal Tribunal for Rwanda: The Politics and Pragmatics of Punishment,* 90 Am. J. Int'l L. 501 (1996).

99. *Report of the Secretary-General Pursuant to Paragraph 2 of Security Council Resolution 808 (1993), supra* note 97, at art. 2.

100. *Id.* art. 3.

101. *Id.* art. 5.

102. *Id.* art. 4.

103. *Id.* art. 7.

104. *The Final Communiqué of the First Session of the Economic Community of West African States Standing Mediation Committee* (7 August 1990), *in* The Liberian Crisis, *supra* note 17, at 83, 84.

105. *Communiqué on ECOWAS Summit in Abuja, Nigeria* (7 November 1992), *in* The Liberian Crisis, *supra* note 17, at 151, 154.

106. *Letter Dated 21 August 1996 from the Charge d'affaires a.i. of the Permanent Mission of Nigeria to the United Nations Addressed to the President of the Security Council*, U.N. SCOR, Annex, at 5, U.N. Doc. S/1996/679 (1996). No action was ever taken on this threat.

107. Harbel Report, *supra* note 94, at 3, ' 9.

108. *Id.* '' 71–72.

109. *Id.*

110. *Liberia: Waging War to Keep the Peace: The ECOMOG Intervention and Human Rights,* Human Rts. Watch/Afr., June 1993, at 12 (emphasis added) [hereinafter *Waging War to Keep the Peace*].

111. 1996 Report on Liberia, *supra* note 11, at 149.

112. S.C. Res. 866, U.N. SCOR, 3281st mtg., ' 3(f), U.N. Doc. S/RES/866 (1993) [hereinafter Res. 866].

113. This is with the one exception of the Harbel massacre investigation and report. However, no follow-up action was taken based on the Harbel Report, and none of its recommendations for a robust investigative mechanism was implemented.

114. *Tenth Progress Report of the Secretary-General on the United Nations Observer Mission in Liberia,* U.N. SCOR, ' 12, U.N. Doc. S/1995/279 (1995).

115. From the author's notes taken at the Special Representative of the Secretary General to UNOMIL's staff briefings, 1996, Monrovia.

116. From internal policy discussions with senior UNOMIL staff upon the arrival of the author in Monrovia for duties in UNOMIL, Sept. 1995, Monrovia, Liberia.

117. Mussa was otherwise known as the "Butcher of Buchanan" because of the brutality of his actions as an NPFL commander in operations in and around Buchanan.

118. Kenneth Cain, *UNOMIL and Human Rights Overview,* code cable to UN Headquarters New York, 20 Jan. 1996, Monrovia, Liberia (on file with author).

119. Outgoing code cable from UN Headquarters New York to Ambassador

A. Nyakyi, SRSG of UNOMIL, 13 Feb. 1996, (on file with author) (emphasis added).

120. *See* 1996 Report on Liberia, *supra* note 11, at 154. The State Department's report for 1996 reads: "Although [UNOMIL] has responsibility for monitoring human rights, for most of the year no one carried out this function. No UNOMIL reports on human rights were made public. The trained human rights observer assigned to UNOMIL in October 1995 resigned in November 1995 [sic], claiming lack of support for his work by the [SRSG]." *Id.* The author's resignation actually took place in April 1996, not November 1995.

121. *Twenty-First Progress Report of the Secretary-General on the United Nations Observer Mission in Liberia,* U.N. SCOR, " 25–30, U.N. Doc. S/1997/90 (1997), *cited in Liberia Emerging from the Destruction: Human Rights Challenges Facing the New Liberian Government,* 9 Hum. Rts. Watch/Afr., Nov. 1997, at 31 [hereinafter *Emerging from the Destruction*].

122. *See id.*

123. Statement of Madeleine Albright, US Ambassador to the United Nations, before the Security Council, 25 Jan. 1996, *available in* <Gopher://198.80.36.82.70/or677894–689046range/archives/1996/pdq> [hereinafter Albright Statement].

124. *Liberia: Human Rights Abuses by the Liberian Peace Council and the Need for International Oversight,* Hum. Rts. Watch/Afr., 17 May 1994, at 8.

125. Albright Statement, *supra* note 123.

126. International Covenant on Civil and Political Rights, *adopted* 16 Dec. 1966, G.A. Res. 2200 (XXI), U.N. GAOR, 21st Sess., Supp. No. 16, U.N. Doc. A/6316 (1966), 999 U.N.T.S. 171 (*entered into force* 23 Mar. 1976); International Covenant on Economic, Social and Cultural Rights, *adopted* 16 Dec. 1966, G.A. Res. 2200 (XXI), U.N. GAOR, 21st Sess., Supp. No. 16, U.N. Doc. A/6316 (1966), 993 U.N.T.S. 3 (*entered into force* 3 Jan. 1976).

127. *Emerging from the Destruction, supra* note 122, at 27.

128. *Waging War to Keep the Peace, supra* note 110, at 32 (emphasis added).

129. *See, e.g., Liberia: News from Liberia: Nine Years of Doe's Rule,* Afr. Watch, Oct. 1989, at 2–3, 5.

130. *See* 1993 Report on Liberia, *supra* note 88, at 152; *see also Waging War to Keep the Peace, supra* note 110, at 15–19.

131. 1997 Report on Liberia, *supra* note 7, at 184–85.

132. *See* 1994 Report on Liberia, *supra* note 33, at 138.

133. Res. 866, *supra* note 112.

134. *Further Report of the Secretary-General on Liberia*, U.N. SCOR, ' 17, U.N. Doc. S/26200 (1993).

135. This material was reported to the author in an interview on 15 Dec. 1997 in New York by a former UNOMIL human rights officer who participated in the investigation and read General Malu's letter to the SRSG. While serving as a UNOMIL human rights official in Liberia, the author participated in similar failed attempts to investigate ECOMOG malfeasance. These attempts were generally aborted at the authorization level by senior UN staff in Monrovia, and when they did succeed in reaching ECOMOG, were disposed of with alacrity by senior ECO-MOG commanders, in the absence of support for the investigation from UN headquarters, Monrovia.

136. *See, e.g., Letter Dated 14 October 1994 from the Permanent Representative of Ghana to the United Nations, Addressed to the President of the Security Council* (transmitting the text of the Akosombo agreement), U.N. SCOR, Annex, Part I, sec. C, art. 4, Count 6, U.N. Doc. S/1994/1174 (1994) (stating that "the Liberian National Transitional Government shall enter into a status-of-forces agreement with ECOWAS within 30 days from signing this Agreement").

137. *See* 1994 Report on Liberia, *supra* note 33, at 135.

138. Bai M. Gbalal, *Status of Forces Agreement: What and Why Is It?* New Democrat Newswkly. (Monrovia), 28 Sept.–3 Oct. 1995, at 6–7.

139. Demonstrating the complexities of the loss of sovereign authority, several Liberian civic organizations actually opposed ECOMOG entry into a status of forces agreement because they believed any diminution of authority as to ECOMOG, however illegitimate that authority might have been, would accrue to the leadership of the warring factions— among whom Charles Taylor in particular maintained a venomous hatred for "Monrovia-based politicians," his potential competitors for power, and consistently threatened to "deal with" them. From the perspective of the Monrovia-based civil society, it is better that ECO-MOG's authority not be defined and, thereby, not be limited, thus enabling ECOMOG to provide protection and cover against the unrestrained and abusive tendencies of the warring factions. *See* Disarmament Watch (Center for Democratic Empowerment), 22 Feb. 1996. The irony of civilian politicians relying on the ill-defined authority of

a military intervention force sent by neighboring dictatorial military regimes to protect their right of expression and association as politicians was lost on no one.

140. *Emerging from the Destruction, supra* note 122, at 32.

141. *Report on Technical Mission to Liberia,* UN restricted circulation internal memorandum, 20 Aug. 1993 (on file with author) (emphasis added).

142. *See* 1996 Report on Liberia, *supra* note 11, at 147.

143. From the author's notes taken at the Special Representative of the Secretary General to UNOMIL's morning senior staff briefing, 21 Feb. 1996, Monrovia.

144. *Id.*

145. Vienna Declaration and Programme of Action, U.N. GAOR, World Conf. on Hum. Rts., 48th Sess., 22d plen. mtg., part 1, 1, U.N. Doc. A/CONF.157/24 (1993), *reprinted in* 32 I.L.M. 1661, 1664 (1993).

146. For a discussion of Asian values and human rights, see generally Jonathan Wright, '*Asian Values' Dead, Amnesty International Says,* Seattle Times, at Nation & World, 17 June 1998, *available in* <http://www.seattletimes.com/news/nation-world/html98/altasia_061798.html> (visited 22 Feb. 1999); William Theodore De Bary, Asian Values and Human Rights: A Confucian Communitarian Perspective (1998); Lee Chang-sup, *Indonesian Turmoil Symbolizes Fallacy of 'Asian Values': President Kim,* Korea Times, 23 May 1998.

147. *See supra* note 7 on casualty figures.

Permissions

2000 ASME Board Of Directors

National Magazine Award Winners

General Excellence

1973   Business Week
1981   ARTnews
       Audubon
       Business Week
       Glamour
1982   Camera Arts
       Newsweek
       Rocky Mountain Magazine
       Science81
1983   Harper's Magazine
       Life
       Louisiana Life
       Science82
1984   The American Lawyer
       House & Garden
       National Geographic
       Outside
1985   American Health
       American Heritage
       Manhattan, inc.
       Time
1986   Discover
       Money
       New England Monthly
       3–2–1- Contact
1987   Common Cause
       Elle
       New England Monthly
       People Weekly
1988   Fortune
       Hippocrates
       Parents
       The Sciences
1989   American Heritage
       Sports Illustrated
       The Sciences
       Vanity Fair
1990   Metropolitan Home
       7 Days
       Sports Illustrated
       Texas Monthly
1991   Condé Nast Traveler
       Glamour
       Interview
       The New Republic

1992   Mirabella
       National Geographic
       The New Republic
       Texas Monthly
1993   American Photo
       The Atlantic Monthly
       Lingua Franca
       Newsweek
1994   Business Week
       Health
       Print
       Wired
1995   Entertainment Weekly
       I.D. Magazine
       Men's Journal
       The New Yorker
1996   Business Week
       Civilization
       Outside
       The Sciences
1997   I.D. Magazine
       Outside
       Vanity Fair
       Wired
1998   DoubleTake
       Outside
       Preservation
       Rolling Stone
1999   Condé Nast Traveler
       Fast Company
       I.D. Magazine
       Vanity Fair
2000   National Geographic
       Nest
       The New Yorker
       Saveur

Personal Service

1986   Farm Journal
1987   Consumer Reports
1988   Money
1989   Good Housekeeping
1990   Consumer Reports
1991   New York
1992   Creative Classroom

1993	Good Housekeeping
1994	Fortune
1995	SmartMoney
1996	SmartMoney
1997	Glamour
1998	Men's Journal
1999	Good Housekeeping
2000	PC Computing

Special Interests

1986	Popular Mechanics
1987	Sports Afield
1988	Condé Nast Traveler
1989	Condé Nast Traveler
1990	Art & Antiques
1991	New York
1992	Sports Afield
1993	Philadelphia
1994	Outside
1995	GQ
1996	Saveur
1997	Smithsonian
1998	Entertainment Weekly
1999	PC Computing
2000	I.D. Magazine

Reporting

1970	The New Yorker
1971	The Atlantic Monthly
1972	The Atlantic Monthly
1973	New York
1974	The New Yorker
1975	The New Yorker
1976	Audubon
1977	Audubon
1978	The New Yorker
1979	Texas Monthly
1980	Mother Jones
1981	National Journal
1982	The Washingtonian
1983	Institutional Investor
1984	Vanity Fair
1985	Texas Monthly
1986	Rolling Stone
1987	Life
1988	The Washingtonian and Baltimore Magazine

1989	The New Yorker
1990	The New Yorker
1991	The New Yorker
1992	The New Republic
1993	IEEE Spectrum
1994	The New Yorker
1995	The Atlantic Monthly
1996	The New Yorker
1997	Outside
1998	Rolling Stone
1999	Newsweek
2000	Vanity Fair

Feature Writing

1988	The Atlantic
1989	Esquire
1990	The Washingtonian
1991	U.S. News & World Report
1992	Sports Illustrated
1993	The New Yorker
1994	Harper's Magazine
1995	GQ
1996	GQ
1997	Sports Illustrated
1998	Harper's Magazine
1999	The American Scholar
2000	Sports Illustrated

Public Interest

1970	Life
1971	The Nation
1972	Philadelphia
1974	Scientific American
1975	Consumer Reports
1976	Business Week
1977	Philadelphia
1978	Mother Jones
1979	New West
1980	Texas Monthly
1981	Reader's Digest
1982	The Atlantic
1983	Foreign Affairs
1984	The New Yorker
1985	The Washingtonian
1986	Science85
1987	Money
1988	The Atlantic

1989	California
1990	Southern Exposure
1991	Family Circle
1992	Glamour
1993	The Family Therapy Networker
1994	Philadelphia
1995	The New Republic
1996	Texas Monthly
1997	Fortune
1998	The Atlantic Monthly
1999	Time
2000	The New Yorker

Design

1980	Geo
1981	Attenzione
1982	Nautical Quarterly
1983	New York
1984	House & Garden
1985	Forbes
1986	Time
1987	Elle
1988	Life
1989	Rolling Stone
1990	Esquire
1991	Condé Nast Traveler
1992	Vanity Fair
1993	Harper's Bazaar
1994	Allure
1995	Martha Stewart Living
1996	Wired
1997	I.D.
1998	Entertainment Weekly
1999	ESPN The Magazine
2000	Fast Company

Photography

1985	Life
1986	Vogue
1987	National Geographic
1988	Rolling Stone
1989	National Geographic
1990	Texas Monthly
1991	National Geographic
1992	National Geographic
1993	Harper's Bazaar
1994	Martha Stewart Living

1995	Rolling Stone
1996	Saveur
1997	National Geographic
1998	W
1999	Martha Stewart Living
2000	Vanity Fair

Fiction

1978	The New Yorker
1979	The Atlantic Monthly
1980	Antaeus
1981	The North American Review
1982	The New Yorker
1983	The North American Review
1984	Seventeen
1985	Playboy
1986	The Georgia Review
1987	Esquire
1988	The Atlantic
1989	The New Yorker
1990	The New Yorker
1991	Esquire
1992	Story
1993	The New Yorker
1994	Harper's Magazine
1995	Story
1996	Harper's Magazine
1997	The New Yorker
1998	The New Yorker
1999	Harper's Magazine
2000	The New Yorker

Profiles

| 2000 | Sports Illustrated |

Essays

| 2000 | The Sciences |

Reviews and Criticism

| 2000 | Esquire |

Essays & Criticism

1978	Esquire
1979	Life
1980	Natural History
1981	Time
1982	The Atlantic
1983	The American Lawyer
1984	The New Republic
1985	Boston Magazine
1986	The Sciences
1987	Outside
1988	Harper's Magazine
1989	Harper's Magazine
1990	Vanity Fair
1991	The Sciences
1992	The Nation
1993	The American Lawyer
1994	Harper's Magazine
1995	Harper's Magazine
1996	The New Yorker
1997	The New Yorker
1998	The New Yorker
1999	The Atlantic Monthly

Single-Topic Issue

1979	Progressive Architecture
1980	Scientific American
1981	Business Week
1982	Newsweek
1983	IEEE Spectrum
1984	Esquire
1985	American Heritage
1986	IEEE Spectrum
1987	Bulletin of the Atomic Scientists
1988	Life
1989	Hippocrates
1990	National Geographic
1991	The American Lawyer
1992	Business Week
1993	Newsweek
1994	Health
1995	Discover
1996	Bon Appétit
1997	Scientific American
1998	The Sciences
1999	The Oxford American

General Excellence In New Media

1997	Money
1998	The Sporting News Online
1999	Cigar Aficionado
2000	Business Week Online

Single Award

1966	Look
1967	Life
1968	Newsweek
1969	American Machinist

Specialized Journalism

1970	Philadelphia
1971	Rolling Stone
1972	Architectural Record
1973	Psychology Today
1974	Texas Monthly
1975	Medical Economics
1976	United Mine Workers Journal
1977	Architectural Record
1978	Scientific American
1979	National Journal
1980	IEEE Spectrum

Visual Excellence

1970	Look
1971	Vogue
1972	Esquire
1973	Horizon
1974	Newsweek
1975	Country Journal
	National Lampoon
1976	Horticulture
1977	Rolling Stone
1978	Architectural Digest
1979	Audubon

Fiction & Belles Lettres

1970	Redbook
1971	Esquire
1972	Mademoiselle

1973	The Atlantic Monthly
1974	The New Yorker
1975	Redbook
1976	Essence
1977	Mother Jones

Service To The Individual

1974	Sports Illustrated
1975	Esquire
1976	Modern Medicine
1977	Harper's Magazine

1978	Newsweek
1979	The American Journal of Nursing
1980	Saturday Review
1982	Philadelphia
1983	Sunset
1984	New York
1985	The Washingtonian

Special Award

| 1976 | Time |
| 1989 | Robert E. Kenyon, Jr. |

PUBLICAFFAIRS is a new nonfiction publishing house and a tribute to the standards, values, and flair of three persons who have served as mentors to countless reporters, writers, editors, and book people of all kinds, including me.

I. F. STONE, proprietor of *I. F. Stone's Weekly*, combined a commitment to the First Amendment with entrepreneurial zeal and reporting skill and became one of the great independent journalists in American history. At the age of eighty, Izzy published *The Trial of Socrates*, which was a national bestseller. He wrote the book after he taught himself ancient Greek.

BENJAMIN C. BRADLEE was for nearly thirty years the charismatic editorial leader of *The Washington Post*. It was Ben who gave the *Post* the range and courage to pursue such historic issues as Watergate. He supported his reporters with a tenacity that made them fearless, and it is no accident that so many became authors of influential, best-selling books.

ROBERT L. BERNSTEIN, the chief executive of Random House for more than a quarter century, guided one of the nation's premier publishing houses. Bob was personally responsible for many books of political dissent and argument that challenged tyranny around the globe. He is also the founder and was the longtime chair of Human Rights Watch, one of the most respected human rights organizations in the world.

.   .   .

For fifty years, the banner of Public Affairs Press was carried by its owner Morris B. Schnapper, who published Gandhi, Nasser, Toynbee, Truman, and about 1,500 other authors. In 1983 Schnapper was described by *The Washington Post* as "a redoubtable gadfly." His legacy will endure in the books to come.

Peter Osnos, *Publisher*